Library of
Davidson College

SUCCESS WITH YOUR
INVESTMENTS

By John W. Hazard

SUCCESS WITH YOUR INVESTMENTS
CHOOSING TOMORROW'S GROWTH STOCKS TODAY
THE INVESTMENT BUSINESS (with Milton Christie)
THE KIPLINGER BOOK ON INVESTING FOR THE YEARS AHEAD
(with Lew G. Coit)
SUCCESS WITH YOUR MONEY

John W. Hazard

SUCCESS WITH YOUR INVESTMENTS

A Complete Guide to Strategies in the Seventies

Doubleday & Company, Inc.
Garden City, New York
1973

ISBN: 0-385-03824-0
Library of Congress Catalog Card Number 72-88708
Copyright © 1973 by John W. Hazard
All Rights Reserved
PRINTED IN THE UNITED STATES OF AMERICA
FIRST EDITION

For Helen

and our investment in the future:

ANNE
JOHN
AMANDA
THOMAS
CHARLOTTE
CHARLES

ACKNOWLEDGMENT

I am indebted to the publisher of *Changing Times,* Austin H. Kiplinger, and to the editor, Robert W. Harvey, for permission to make use of certain material previously appearing in *Changing Times.*

I express my appreciation to Marjorie E. White, assistant managing editor of *Changing Times,* for editing the manuscript, and to Frandy Turgeon who checked it for accuracy. If errors there are, they probably are due to the changes that may have taken place in the economy and securities markets since the book went to press, for we are in one of the fastest changing periods of our history.

JOHN W. HAZARD

CONTENTS

1 A Better Life but a Continuing Struggle to Achieve It   1
Government controls over the economy / Population / Environment / Consumerism / Rise in importance of services / The securities markets / Social changes

2 The Seventies—A Prosperous Decade   9
Is another depression likely? / What about the "baby bust"? / Real income is rising

3 An Ever-expanding America   16
Pollution control / Health / Communications / Microelectronics / Agriculture / Oceanography / Transportation / Power / Recycling

4 Inflation   26
Cost-push inflation / New methods of control / Consumer psychology / Defenses against inflation

5 The Search for Equities   33
Where to put assets / Precious metal / Real estate / Common stocks

6 Common Stocks—Most Suitable Equities   42
How to develop selectivity / Performance investing / Determining guidelines / Cyclical stocks / The ins and outs of the growth stock theory

7 Competing Against the Insiders   51
Inside information / The regulations: what and why / Stock watches and other protections

Contents

8 Industries That Can Cope in the Seventies 61
Quality of life / Family formation / Energy / Business growth and development / Inflation / Government Controls / Company size / Social responsibility

9 Choosing Stocks 71
Earnings growth / Return on invested capital / Growth of sales / Operating profit / Current assets versus current liabilities / Equity-to-debt ratio / Spending on research and development / Freedom from competition / Low labor costs / Price flexibility / Over-all quality

10 Examples of Industries and Companies 76
200 outstanding investments in the areas of Autos, Building and Homes, Business Services, Chemicals, Consumer Products, Drugs, Electrical Equipment, Electronics, Environment, Financial, Glass, Health Care, Insurance, Laborsaving Machinery, Metals and Mining, Office Machines and Equipment, Oils, Recreation, Research, Utilities

11 Where to Get Help and Information 123
Stock guides and reports / Using your broker / Advisory services / The big financial services / Trust departments of banks / Investment counselors / Investment counseling services / Investment trusts

12 Picking a Brokerage House and a Broker 133
Choosing a broker / You may have problems / How to deal with your broker / Commission rates

13 How to Be a Stockholder 145
Leave it in street name? / Single or joint ownership? / What records? Where? / Can you borrow? How much? / Those financial reports / Tax tips

14 Dollar Cost Averaging 161
*How averaging works / A plan of your
own / Formal plans / Investment clubs*

15 Mutual Funds and Closed-end Investment Trusts 174
*Various types available / Objectives /
Price quotations and management fees /
The Pros and Cons / Making a choice /
Examples of investment companies*

16 Mutual Funds—What's Going On? 200
*Money-making functions / Protecting the
shareholder / "Give-ups" / Legal and
performance problems*

17 New Issues—Should You Buy Them? 207
*The need for capital / Underwriting / How
the SEC protects investors / Should you
buy new issues? / SBIC's*

18 Speculating 225
*Short selling / Commodity futures trading /
Buying stocks on margin / Puts and calls /
Charts and graphs*

19 Safety and Income 249
*Bonds / Income / Withdrawal plans /
Annuities*

20 Trust Funds 282
*Definitions / Fees / Basic types of trust /
What a trust can do / Ways to use a trust /
A couple of alternatives / Common trust
funds*

21 The Stock Market—Old Style 292
*The specialist / Odd lots / Over-the-counter
stocks / The exchanges / Over-the-counter
markets*

22 The Stock Market—New Style 308
*Paperwork crisis / Financial crisis /
Remedies / The Martin Report / The over-
the-counter market / The role of the
individual investor*

Contents

23 Real Estate—Going It Alone   321
Raw land / Rental property / Second mortgages / Precautions

24 Real Estate—Real-life Examples   331
A young man starting out / A neighborhood syndicate / A neighborhood real estate company / Advice from an established investor

25 Real Estate Investment Trusts and Syndicates   340
Equity trusts / Mortgage trusts / A trust for you? / Real estate investment companies / Real estate syndicates

26 Real Estate—Home or Farm   351
The neighborhood / The house itself / What should you pay? / Shopping for terms / Hankering to buy a farm? / Advice / Farm management / Financing / Farm valuation

27 Insurance—A Prerequisite to Investing   364
Life insurance / Health insurance / Liability insurance

28 Money Management   386
Business methods for the family / How to get the funds you need / Programs to help you save / Rainy-day money—where to invest it

INDEX   410

1

A BETTER LIFE BUT A CONTINUING STRUGGLE TO ACHIEVE IT

"Quality of life" is becoming the phrase that expresses a new goal for Americans. The basic securities of job, food and housing have been achieved for most of us. Now we look toward more leisuretime activities, better health care, college education for our children, cleaning up the environment and an early and richly rewarding retirement. At the same time we want the ever-widening variety of goods and services that our ingenious and efficient engineers, inventors and businessmen offer us. These once were considered luxuries, but now they seem almost a requirement of our everyday lives. In fact, even though we have achieved a financial security that our grandparents would have envied, we want so much more that we find ourselves pinched financially, not because we are hungry or ill clothed, but simply because our reach exceeds our grasp.

In short, even though Americans have achieved the highest material standard of living in the history of the world, most of us still have to save, even scrimp, and keep our savings invested prudently if we are to achieve the quality of life that is so important to us today. And in many ways, good money management is harder today than it was, say ten or fifteen years ago. In the decade of the 1950's and in the early 60's inflation was not the problem that it is now. And the stock market was in a long upward trend. The investor who purchased any good-quality growth stock was almost bound to make out well over the long pull. This is no longer true. The United States is going through rapid and far-reaching economic and social changes that require new approaches to savings and investing. In particular, it is becoming a great deal more difficult to select profitable investments. Consider briefly what some of these changes are.

Government controls over the economy Inflation seems to have become a way of life in America, and classical methods of control no longer seem to work. New and experimental ones are being tried, some involving restrictions on the activities of business. The inflation dilemma came into sharp focus at the start of this decade when the country found itself in a mild recession with unemployment at a relatively high level, while at the same time prices were rising faster than the public would tolerate. Furthermore, the Vietnam war was being wound down rapidly, and defense spending had stabilized so that the country was in more of a peacetime than a wartime economy. Historically, these conditions—slow business, relatively high unemployment and a peacetime economy—do not cause prices to rise. But they were rising at around 6% a year, in spite of the fact that the administration and the Federal Reserve Board were using the classical inflation remedies: restriction of credit, higher interest rates and attempts at reducing, or at least stabilizing, federal expenditures.

The result of all this was dismaying. People complained about the seemingly perpetual rise in prices, but they also complained about the effects of the classical remedies. Tight credit and high interest rates were anathema. Unemployment at 6% was politically intolerable. And, in fact, the Full Employment Act of 1946 required the government to take action to keep unemployment at a minimum. Politically powerful groups demanded programs calling for government expenditures far in excess of what acceptable taxation rates could bring in. It became apparent that no administration in Washington, Republican or Democratic, could long stay in power using classical methods of inflation control. Hence the Nixon Administration concluded in 1971 that other methods of price and wage control were called for.

Direct controls over prices and wages, and indirect controls over dividends, interest rates and profit margins were imposed. This unprecedented peacetime action has raised the serious question in the minds of many analysts as to whether the great and growing corporations, whose common stocks have been such a popular medium of investment, will eventually be turned into the equivalent of regulated public utilities with strictly limited growth potential. At the very least, even if the economy returns to the relative freedom it enjoyed prior to 1971, the threat of controls will hang over it like a sword of Damocles, and this threat is bound to influence decisions on prices, wages and investments.

During periods of fast-rising prices and costs, most businesses find that costs rise faster, which puts them in a profit squeeze. Labor leaders and many politicians insist that when controls are contemplated or applied, they bear down harder on prices than on wages. Demands are even heard that direct controls be extended to profits, even though in recent years profits have lagged behind other statistical measures of the economy. In these difficult circumstances, some industries and companies will be hard hit while others will manage to prosper and grow despite governmental restrictions. For the investor to select the most promising companies becomes more difficult than ever.

Population The birth rate has turned down, the rate of population growth has begun to decline and there is talk of "zero population growth" by the end of the century. Thus, the mix of goods and services turned out by industry will have to be adjusted to changes in the country's age distribution.

Environment The movement to clean up the environment is bound to affect a number of industries, such as autos, coal, oils, utilities and chemicals.

Consumerism Consumers, led by vociferous advocates, are

holding business more closely responsible for the quality and safety of the products it markets. Traditionally, shrewd investors have bought into companies that made profits in any legal way, regardless of the quality of the products or services produced. It was not thought to be smart to buy into a company just because you liked or had confidence in what it made. In the future it would seem that the powerful consumer movement will penalize companies that produce inferior or unsafe products, or those not accompanied by ironclad guarantees and warranties. Shrewd and aggressive company management can no longer be the sole criterion of the potential of a company's stock.

Rise in importance of services As the basic ingredient of the economy changed years ago from farming to manufacturing, now it is changing from manufacturing to service. Efficient factories can easily turn out the products we need. Also, America has given its secrets of mass-production methods to the rest of the Western world, and countries such as Japan, West Germany and others now can beat us at our own game. We import great amounts of foreign goods, but services are essentially domestic operations. The speed-up in our daily lives causes us to use more services—we pay to have things done for us that once we were forced to do for ourselves. This also applies to businesses, which more and more are farming out such jobs as building cleaning, maintenance and security, tax and statistical work, and personnel recruiting.

The securities markets Rising costs and failure to modernize business methods are changing the securities industry to an extent not seen since the days of the New Deal. A wave of financial failures, or near failures, has caused many old-line brokerage houses to go out of business or to be merged with stronger competitors. Stock exchanges and the vast over-the-counter market are being tied together in one great network. Transmission of orders and even market making in securities are being done less and less by humans and more and more by electronics. The securities markets cater more to institutions and less to individual investors.

Social changes As a cacophonous background to all this, society is in a ferment, moral customs that have prevailed for generations are openly flouted, the crime rate is high and young people, who are coming of voting age in tremendous numbers, are highly critical of what they call the establishment. None of this, of course, gives investors a high sense of confidence in the future.

All these political, social and economic crosscurrents certainly will bring some permanent changes. But if you can rise above the confusion and obtain a clear, mountain-top look at the landscape, you can see that certain strong trends in the economy are persisting. The two most important from the investor's point of view are a continuation of growth and prosperity, and a continuation of inflation.

It may be hard, in view of the problems enumerated above, to see continued growth and prosperity. In fact, it is only too easy to be pessimistic. But remember that even though Americans are noted for their optimism, they have consistently underrated their own future. Benjamin Franklin thought it would take hundreds of years to settle the American continent. Thomas Jefferson figured on 25 generations for the occupation of the Louisiana Purchase. Predictions of employment, national income and the gross national product by even the most respected economists have tended to fall far short of actual accomplishments. Goals have often been reached five or even ten years ahead of long-term predictions.

In recent years particularly, Americans have been especially prone to self-criticism and have acquired a kind of mass guilt complex in many social areas. The day-to-day hand-wringing of the commentators tends to blind us to what we have accomplished. Statistics show that this country continues to pass mileposts that do demonstrate a continuing growth and prosperity. The basic figures prove that the economy is moving ahead, despite short-term fluctuations, at about the historical rate. No serious proof has yet been given that over the long run this trend will not continue. On the contrary, econometric models of the economy indicate that by 1980 we may look back on the present decade with as much pride and satisfaction as we view the 50's and 60's. And if, indeed, this period will be comparable to the recent past in terms of over-all growth and prosperity, then the outlook is more favorable than appears on the surface.

A quick look backward will show that economically, at least, we have been in a tremendous forward surge.

Hugh Johnson, publisher of *Johnson's Investment Company Charts,* has succinctly summarized the period of the 1960's in the following terms:

• Population grew from 182.2 to 206.5 million, an increase of 13.3%.

• The gross national product (the end value of all goods and services produced) grew from $503.7 billion to $976.8 billion, an increase of 93.9%.

• National income grew from $415.5 billion to $801 billion, an increase of 93.2%.

• Personal income grew from $401 billion to $801 billion, an increase of 99.8%.

• Corporate earnings grew from $26.7 billion to $44.4 billion, an increase of 66.3%.

• Corporate dividends grew from $13.4 billion to $25.2 billion, an increase of 88.1%.

A person 62 years old in 1971, he predicted, would see the economy double again. A person 42 years old would see it quadruple. A person 24 years old would see it increase eightfold.

The last census showed that most people, despite concerns about unemployment and inflation, were better off than they were a decade earlier and enjoyed comforts unprecedented in history. The following figures give a picture, in material terms, of conditions in 1970.

• About 30% owned two or more cars compared with 16.4% in 1960.

• Over one out of three homes had color TV, compared with about one out of 15 homes only six years previously.

• About one-fourth of all families owned dishwashers, a fourfold increase from 1960.

• Over a third of U.S. households had air-conditioning, triple the number a decade earlier.

• Two or more TV sets were found in 30 out of every 100 homes compared with 17 in 1960.

• Clothes dryers were owned by over two out of every five families compared with one out of six families ten years earlier.

Ownership of refrigerators, washing machines and freezers has increased, and there has been a boom in purchases of small appliances, some of which—electric carving knives, hair dryers, electric toothbrushes, hot combs—were hardly known ten or twelve years ago. The average family in 1970 had five radios.

Looking a generation back, the 1950 median family income was $3,300—half of U.S. families got more than that, half got less. When the 1970 census was taken, median income per family averaged $8,870. Even if this figure is deflated to correct for the decline in the real value of the dollar, the 1970 median family income in terms of actual purchasing power was $6,100, which means that the average family was twice as well off in 1970 as it had been 20 years earlier.

Will this trend continue despite current problems? The best statisticians and economists say it will. The Wharton School of Business of the University of Pennsylvania has operated a computerized model of the economy for several years. In it are detailed data on all major U.S. industries. The professors who constructed the model have made these assumptions: that there will be no major wars in the decade of the 70's; that the federal government will turn more of its attention to reconstructing cities, combating pollution and revitalizing our social and economic environment.

Even with those rather heavy burdens on the public sector of the economy, the model shows that by 1980 the gross national product (GNP) will be double the level of 1971. Unemployment will stabilize at around 4.5%. Personal disposable income will almost double. Total profits will rise. The hours we work will decline. And, believe it or not, federal, state and local budgets will eventually come close to being balanced. Prices, however, will continue to creep up at a rate estimated at 2.5% to 3% a year.

It is this strong, continuing inflationary force that must be taken into account by investors along with the underlying strength of the economy. Inflation means that money put aside for future goals, the goals that will give us this improved quality of life that we so much desire today, must be invested where it will grow much faster than the price level is rising. Savings accounts, bonds and other fixed-dollar investments are not the answer. Only equities, such as common stocks and real estate, offer safety from the continued erosion of the dollar. How to find and invest in promising equities in today's changing economic and social conditions will be the investor's biggest single problem in the years ahead, and the major theme of this book.

2

THE SEVENTIES—
A PROSPEROUS DECADE

The decade of the 70's is likely to be a period comparable in measure, although not in kind, to the 60's. This hopeful outlook is based on the following assumptions:

• That GNP will double in the 70's as it did in the 60's.

• That government and industry will keep price rises from running wild even though wages and other income keep going up —government to do its part by judicious manipulation of the money supply and by use of only moderate controls over wages and prices; industry to do its part by constantly improving methods of production through increased automation and efficiency so that goods and services become more abundantly available; workers and their unions to increase productivity, or output per man-hour, about as fast as prices are permitted to rise.

• That expenditures on research by government and industry, though perhaps somewhat reduced by curtailment of military projects, will continue to be large enough to produce many new products and methods that will enrich our society.

• That the buffers and cushions built into the economy over the past 40 years will make a depression all but impossible.

• That even though the birth rate is declining, this will affect only the number of children of primary school age during the decade of the 70's. The 25- to 34-year-old group is, of course, already born. And it is this group that is starting new households and buying homes, cars, appliances and all the other appurtenances desired by today's prosperous and demanding families. This group, also, probably will conform to the age-old laws of nature and have children and thus start another baby boom similar to the one that started after World War II. The number of women in childbearing ages—15 to 44—will be greater between now and 1985 than in the 1960's by 30%. Even though women plan on fewer children, there are just so many women that they will provide a definite stimulus to the economy in the latter years of the decade.

• That cleaning up the environment can be done by American industry, under the supervision of various levels of government, with one hand tied behind its back. And it will make a profit on it.

• That the social unrest and frustration of minority groups and young people will gradually iron themselves out. This has already happened to some extent.

Consider first two troublesome questions.

Is another depression likely? There *could* be another one, that's true. But here are some of the arguments that make it seem highly unlikely. Today the federal government has assumed responsibility for keeping employment high and business good. To do the job, it has established various snubbers, cushions and stabilizers that were not available in the 1930's. Income taxes are vastly higher. When business begins to slide off, a hefty tax cut can put billions of dollars back into the spending stream. Furthermore, the government can borrow tremendous amounts and pump billions into various public programs. Bank deposits and savings accounts are now insured, generally up to $20,000 per account. Farm prices are supported when they decline below certain levels. Home mortgages are amortized monthly, instead of falling due every three to five years as used to be the case. Many mortgages are guaranteed or insured. In contrast to the old days, millions of people now have a floor under their incomes. The older ones draw monthly checks from social security and pension plans. The sick are helped financially by Medicare. Unemployment compensation stands ready to take up slack when unemployment grows.

All in all, it would appear that though we may still have recessions, we probably never again will have a real blockbuster of a depression. And the recessions we have had since World War II have been relatively mild. History indicates that the stock market can ride out such recessions very well.

What about the "baby bust"? The 1970 census revealed the greatest decline in the nation's under-five population during the 120 years for which statistics have been kept. According to the Washington Center for Metropolitan Studies, children under five years of age decreased during the 1960's from over 20 million to about 17 million, a decline of 15.5%. The largest previous recorded loss in this age group occurred during the severe depression of the 30's when the preschool population dropped by 8%. Apart from this decrease, and a much smaller drop of 1% during the 20's, every decade from 1850 showed an actual increase among children of preschool age.

This startling change in the birth rate presents the possibility that zero population growth may be achieved by the year 2000. Yet the consequences for the 70's are not all that bad. Of course, manufacturers and distributors of diapers, for example, are not doing as well right now as they did when the post World War II infants were in their cribs. The toy industry has already begun to suffer from a declining market. Actual surpluses of classroom space began to show up as early as 1971. Eventually, if the trend continues, such youth-oriented industries as clothing, records and motorcycles will feel the effect of the decline in teen-agers. Looking even further ahead, new family formation will decline and those businesses that provide new houses and appliances will be affected. But note that this will not happen until the decade of the 1980's. In the meantime a new baby crop will be started. Even though the birth rate is down four million, more babies will be born in the 1970's than in the 1960's.

During the rest of this decade the economy will still feel the effects of the tremendous crop of war babies born when the servicemen came home after World War II. These babies made a recognizable hump in the population curve, and this hump is continuing to move up through the various age brackets. In 1956, at the end of the first ten years after the war, these youngsters ranged in age from 0 to 10 years. In 1960 the bulk of them were 4 to 14. In 1970 they were 14 to 24. In 1980 they will be 24 to 34. Thus in this decade, 1970 to 1980, the war babies will be young adults, in the ages noted for good income, low saving and high consumption of basic goods and services involved in setting up households.

But what of the long-term future, the zero population growth and all that? Even though businessmen traditionally count on an ever-increasing number of spending Americans to provide an ever-expanding market for their wares, this may not be all bad for business, either. Tempo, General Electric's center for advanced studies at Santa Barbara, Calif., operates a demographic-economic computer model to picture the effect of future population changes on the economy. Dr. Stephen Enke, of Tempo, has made some observations based on output of this model. A decline in fertility rates, he points out, results in a less youthful age distribution and a higher ratio of work-age adults to total population. Hence, there tends to be more output per head of population. This, in turn, permits increased savings and investments, more capital per worker and increased productivity.

Says Dr. Enke, "All the computer runs of economic-demographic models that have ever been made under the supervision of the author indicate that a reduction of fertility results in little difference in GNP as compared with the difference in population. Were the nation to move toward ZPG [zero population growth], there would be fewer persons employed than there would otherwise be by 2000, but there would be more capital investment employed with them. Moreover, the comparatively unchanged GNP is shared among fewer people, so output and income per person are higher."

Families would spend more, according to Dr. Enke, for cars and appliances, entertainment and travel, and the many other things that take proportionately more of the disposable incomes of better-off people. Thus, industries would be affected differently.

The Seventies—A Prosperous Decade

Fewer diapers would be sold, but most business managements can shift into other lines of production, given time. Possibilities for the diaper industry are such things as wash towels, sheets and bedspreads.

"Profits and losses," he points out, "ordinarily result not from changes in population growth but from decisions on new product lines and locations, mergers and replacement of executives, and by the actions of government. If some corporations were to experience falling profits within the next 70 years, while the U.S. is attaining ZPG, a slowing population would provide no excuse.

"Even if ZPG were 'bad' for business, which is untrue, the end of population growth under realistic assumptions about fertility declines is at least 75 years away."

Even the future value of land should not be adversely affected by ZPG, according to Dr. Enke. "It is true," he says, "that, if one can imagine a 'typical' acre of land, it should be worth less after 50 years with lowered fertility than with unchanged fertility. Computer runs indicate that the present discounted value of the difference in value is under one percent. Moreover, with lower fertility, there will presumably be fewer owners of land. Eventually each acre may command a lower rent than otherwise, but each land owner may own more acres."

Now consider more favorable aspects.

Real income is rising Not only will there be more young families in the 70's, but their "real" income is increasing. Let us agree that in some cases wages or income has fallen behind the rise in the cost of living. Obviously, there are hardship cases. But overall, the statistics prove that on the average the annual spendable income for families in the United States—*after* taxes have been paid and *after* a deduction has been made for the rise in living costs—has been rising, and it continued to rise even during the high inflation years of 1970 and 1971. The U. S. Department of Commerce compiles these statistics meticulously, and they show that from 1962 to 1972 the "per capita disposable income in constant prices," which means the real purchasing power after taxes, rose nearly 35%.

Perhaps this is hard to believe when you review your own personal finances. But it is easy to overlook several factors that go into the computation. Most important is that our standard of living—what we demand of our income—is rising. All the time we want better things, better and safer autos, more electric appliances, color television instead of black and white, more opportunity to send kids to college, longer and better vacations, boats, skis, campers, station wagons. We are a fast-earning and fast-spending people. Whereas once we were content to wear old and worn-out dress clothes around the house, now we must have sports clothes for leisure wear. We are constantly upgrading, so we sometimes tend to think we are worse off than we really are.

Another factor: We are saving more and therefore increasing our net worth. Back in 1962, as a nation, we were saving 5.6% of our real, disposable income. In 1971 we were saving over 8% and not much less in 1972.

Looking at it another way, families have been moving upward into higher income groups—and by higher income is meant "real" income in "constant" dollars. The following table tells the story.

TABLE 1

Family Income in Constant Dollars

	1960	1965	1970
Under $5,000	29.7%	24.1%	19.3%
$5,000 to $9,999	41.4%	36.9%	31.7%
$10,000 to $14,999	19.3%	24.3%	26.8%
Over $15,000	9.5%	14.6%	22.3%

We are better educated. Education goes hand in hand with prosperity. Consider now only Americans over the age of 25. Twenty years ago only 33.4% had completed high school; today 55.2% have. Twenty years ago 6% had completed four years of college; today 11% have.

The trend is toward "more" of everything And this trend will continue as far ahead as anyone can see. There will be more young families starting out, more families in the middle- and upper-income levels. They will be buying more goods of all kinds, more medicines, more houses; taking more vacations and trips abroad; traveling faster; communicating more rapidly. There will be more education and more brain power, multiplied by computers, to apply to the problems of the day and the future. There will be change, innovation, new methods of achieving goals, new ways of behavior.

3

AN EVER-EXPANDING AMERICA

One of the greatest prime movers of the economy is research and development, known in industry as R&D. Consider that only a few years ago there were no lasers, cordless electric tools, color TV, silicon solar cells, hydrofoil boats, communication satellites or electrostatic printing. Go back a few years further and there were no polyester, nylon or acrylic fibers, synthetic rubber, titanium, television, transistors, computers, antibiotics, jet planes, radioactive isotopes, instant photography or atomic energy.

Recently, industry has paused to catch its breath. Inflation shrinks the research dollar just as it does yours. But progress goes on. Industry, government and the universities together spend over $28 billion a year hunting for new products, new materials, new methods and just doing pure research for the sake of knowledge. As an example of a pure research project, scientists have smashed basic particles of the atom in a step that may lead to understanding what holds the universe together. Although no usable application of such a project is apparent, similar pure research in the past has often led to breakthroughs resulting in useful materials, products and methods.

Look at the chart on page 24 to see how expenditures on research have gone ever higher. In the 1950's, when aerospace research was in its prime, expenditures doubled every five years. By itself, aerospace has lost a bit of its glamour, but more dollars will go into preservation of the environment and the quest for a better life for all.

Here are some of the areas where tremendous changes are being seen, and will continue to be seen over the coming years. So remarkably wide and complex is this technological explosion that it is only possible to mention brief and random samples.

Pollution control Decades of callous neglect have left us with a huge backlog of water, air and solid-waste pollution problems. The targets for cleanup are known. More than 1,500 communities still dump untreated sewage into our streams. The U. S. Public Health Service estimates that we foul the air every year with 190 million tons of filth, equivalent to about a ton for every American citizen. All told, we create over 3.5 billion tons of solid wastes a year, and the mountain of refuse is growing twice as fast as the population.

Halting the deterioration of our environment is a high-priority item and likely to move higher. Getting breathable air and drinkable water will demand enormous expenditures by the federal, state and local governments. Close to $5 billion a year now goes into handling and disposing of household, commercial, municipal and industrial wastes. But it will take another $835 million over five years simply to keep abreast. To improve sewage systems, the experts predict we will need a four-year program costing $10 billion—and that will pay only for equipment, not operating expenses. The bill for cleaning up our air will be equally big, estimated to reach $2.8 billion in four years merely to control sulphur oxides and soot and solids from industrial fuel-burning facilities.

More and more companies are responding to the lure of pollution-control products: garbage collecting and processing equipment; incinerators; cooling towers; valves and pumps; air-cleaning devices, such as mechanical collectors, electrostatic precipitators; fabric filters and wet scrubbers and monitoring and control gadgets for measuring contamination.

That's just the beginning. If we are going to "recycle" solid wastes back into the production pipeline as raw materials, we'll need a whole host of new products. Packaging materials that can be more easily reused, industrial methods that can make use of more scrap and machines for sorting trash for reuse are examples. Scientists will have to come up with new fuels, control devices and drastic improvement of the internal combustion engine to make a dent in emissions from autos, a major contributor to air pollution.

Health Perhaps no other front is forging ahead as fast as American medicine. "Multiphasic health testing" bringing to bear an amazing array of medical gadgets is making preventive medicine a reality. A blood chemical analyzer, capable of testing 14 blood samples simultaneously and teletyping results in minutes, has already proved itself in major hospitals. Electronic data processing machines tied to computers can retrieve patients' records in seconds or transmit them across the country. Within a decade biomedics of this sort may be a $2.5 billion-a-year business.

Right now, automatic heart and lung machines and kidney dialyzers keep patients alive while they await treatment and while artificial hearts and kidneys are being developed. Control of mental conditions such as depression, schizophrenia and paranoia may be possible with implantable brain stimulators.

Heart trouble is the number-one killer of Americans. Those who survive the first attack are susceptible to a second, which often comes in hours or days. Medical engineers now have developed measuring devices that can be attached to the patient's body to give an early warning of recurring trouble. Twenty hospital patients at a time can be kept under observation by closed-circuit TV. If a warning signal is flashed, a nurse or doctor can respond with appropriate treatment.

Heart block is a common ailment that occurs when the electrical signals to the heart are disrupted by disease or injury. Electronic pacemakers can send electric shock signals into the heart to keep it beating evenly. The usual pacemaker is a battery-operated rig and must be replaced periodically. It also may compete dangerously with the patient's natural beat. Engineers have worked out one improvement called a "demand pacer," which functions only when the heartbeat actually stops. In addition to reducing the danger, the device can double battery life. Other experiments look toward a nuclear-powered pacemaker, which would operate for ten years without replacement, an implantable defibrillator that can correct wildly fluttering hearts, and an artificial booster pump to supplement the natural pumping action of failing hearts.

Ultrasonic or high-frequency sound waves sent into the human body can detect ills that x-rays do not always show. Just as sonar beamed through water can pick up the "echo" from a submerged object, ultrasonics can spot abnormalities in the body, such as gallstones, or slivers of glass, metal or wood beneath the surface of the skin or in the eye. Ultrasound can tell whether a woman has a multiple pregnancy, what the position of the fetus is and whether Caesarean surgery is required.

A simple way of diagnosing heart disease early by direct viewing of the arteries is a prime research dream. At present, the method means threading catheters into the arteries and an injection of x-ray dye to show up the narrowing. The method involves discomfort and sometimes pain, not to mention the risk of infection and bleeding. Medical researchers have developed an improvement called phonoangiography that enables doctors to listen for abnormal sounds without puncturing the patient. The sound of blood rushing through an artery that is unduly narrowed is picked up by a sensitive microphone, recorded and analyzed.

In one medical center, sound is being used to suppress pain when ordinary pain killers are undesirable for one reason or another. Patients wear earphones and turn up the sound correspondingly on a tape recorder-amplifier hookup to blot out the pain of surgery. In another, a tiny color camera beams live pictures from inside the body to a network of closed-circuit television monitors, enabling medical students and doctors to watch delicate brain surgery.

Communications Experiments look toward a phone setup in which you speak the number you want instead of dialing it. More significant by far is the infinitely small size and incredible speed at which communication systems absorb, store and send information over wires. Under development by Bell are magnetic bubbles just .0003 of an inch in diameter that are capable of doing the memorizing, switching and logic operations of computers. Magnetic bubbles would reduce present room-size computer memories to the size of a loaf of bread. They would handle extraordinarily complex information tens and hundreds of times faster than the human brain.

The laser—an intensified beam of light—may make it possible to increase by thousands of times the capacity for carrying telephone calls and TV signals. One new device enables technicians to impress one billion pieces of information onto a laser beam.

In the home, computers could print electronic newspapers tailored to special business or family interests, do shopping chores and even prepare income tax returns.

Overhead, earth satellites are doing remarkable workaday jobs. Nearly 900 man-made satellites awhirl in the heavens bounce TV pictures and messages between continents, gather weather information, and ferret out troop and submarine movements, rocket launchings and the like. This is just the beginning.

Imagine a light-amplifying device so sensitive that, when attached to a one-inch telescope, it can spot from Los Angeles a 50-watt bulb burning in Washington, D.C. Or a heat detector capable of feeling the "warmth" of an ice cube a mile away. These and other equally remarkable gadgets are being put to work in space on a host of jobs never dreamed of by Buck Rogers.

In agriculture, high-flying satellites using optical and infrared sensors will be able to sort out and count various types of crops so that accurate global forecasts can be made. In forestry, remote sensing instruments will spot the difference between hardwood trees, softwoods and mixed stands of both, enabling foresters to survey vast and remote timberlands almost at a glance. In map making, satellites could reduce from three years to three weeks the time it takes conventional photo-taking aircraft to do the job. Mineralogists also may learn from satellites likely places to look for metal and other minerals hidden deep in the ground. And satellites may lead archeologists to long-buried cities.

Microelectronics Integrated circuits, with refinement after refinement, still offer the most exciting possibilities. The IC, like the transistor, begins with pure silicon, one of the commonest elements found in nature. Silicon crystals are grown in the laboratory, sliced into thin wafers, and placed in a quartz "boat." This, in turn, is thrust into a furnace where temperatures of several thousand degrees fuse chemicals called dopants into the silicon, making an electrical conductor of it. The wafers are next marked with intricate "masks" or cutout patterns on the surface. Tiny areas of the silicon are "doped" here and there, creating regions of positive and negative charges. What emerges is a tiny chip (each wafer yields hundreds of chips) bearing a microscopic network of circuits that performs all the functions of an assembly of transistors, capacitors and resistors.

It was once routine to put the equivalent of 50 devices on a chip. Now the package called LSI—large-scale integration—can hold 5,000 to 8,000. In addition to performing the intricate switching operations that permit computers to solve problems, IC's are expected to do almost every job now done electromechanically. Household appliances and switches will be controlled by a panel that will fit into a pocket. TV sets with flat screens will hang on the wall. Computers will be everywhere, as common and as easy to use as telephones. Lawyers will be able to gain immediate access to prior cases and decisions. Doctors will feed symptoms into a machine, and then await the computer's advice on the diagnosis.

Agriculture New kinds of cheap foods are under development. Soybeans, pound for pound the cheapest source of edible protein, can be transformed into frozen food that tastes like fried chicken. So-called synthetic food is not the only innovation. Researchers are coming up with mammoth dates twice the size of ordinary ones. Pecan trees are being trained to produce larger nuts in half the usual span of ten years. Peanuts with half the calories are already available. Under development are dried strawberries, raspberries, apples and peaches you can reconstitute for use in pies. A new kind of white cream cheese and butter substitute is low in calories and helpful to the environment because it makes use of recycled whey, a by-product of cheese making.

Today the emphasis is on new and more powerful machinery. Tractors of over 50 horsepower now outsell smaller machines and permit faster plowing and harvesting, reduce vulnerability to adverse weather, and lengthen the growing season. Versatile new machines can pick the most delicate crops. One shakes fruit trees in such a way that only the ripe fruit falls into nets. In forests, experimental machines are snipping large-diameter pine trees and stacking them for pickup while other machines chew up the residue from the logging operation.

Oceanography Many of the ocean's vast resources are being tapped. Substances now recovered from the ocean include salt, tin, magnesium, barite, diamonds and bromine, but the biggest boom may be in the off-shore exploration of oil. U.S. production alone runs over one and a quarter million barrels a day. More rigs are being planned for many parts of the world, from Africa to Argentina and from Australia to Alaska, with industry planning to invest as much as $25 million in the 70's. Already being explored are ways to "pasture" fish by placing them in fertile parts of oceans and lakes, and then rounding them up for market in nets. In one trial, 10,000 pounds were caught with artificial electric light to attract them. A number of U.S. firms culture catfish and oysters and others are experimenting with shrimp and lobster and developing ways to wring protein from the sea to feed the world's hungry peoples.

From 50 fathoms deep, remote sensing devices hitched to a submersible machine send TV pictures and other data on fish schooling and spawning back to a mother ship.

Controlling ocean pollution will have a higher priority than ever. In the works is a plan to construct a test harbor where oil spill cleanup equipment can be tested under the most realistic conditions. The U. S. Coast Guard is also spending money with industry for the development of a model system that would be dropped from the air to contain oil spills.

The sea and air work together to create our climate. One of the most exciting prospects is for improved weather forecasting with knowledge obtained from the ocean. Directed by the new National Oceanic and Atmospheric Administration (NOAA), specialized marine centers will provide almost immediate warning of hurricane or other climatic hazards at sea.

Transportation More and more cities are building rapid-transit systems. Amtrak, the new rail passenger corporation, will modernize. Sometime in the 1980's tracked air-cushion vehicles will rush passengers from place to place, and by 2,000, high-speed trains, perhaps running in tunnels, may be commonplace. Present roads will be upgraded to link more medium-sized cities to the Interstate Highway System, due to be completed in the last half of the 70's. In the works are plans to limit some freeways to buses or cars with three to four passengers. Federal aid may be available for purchasing better buses.

Auto companies are working feverishly on improved internal combustion engines and emission-control devices in time to meet new government-pollution control standards. Though the gas engine will survive, vehicles run by electricity or natural gas will become practical alternatives for limited city driving.

Electronics will be used to ease traffic congestion and speed the flow of traffic. Along a stretch of one route near Boston, motorists are finding it easier to get into freeway traffic from entrance ramps. As cars move over sensors in the road, a computer figures how many cars are on the ramp and whether there are slots for them in the moving lane of traffic. The idea of the system is to have the motorist reach the freeway just in time to slide into the gap alloted to him. If no slot is available, cars are stopped for a few seconds at one of several traffic lights while the computer hunts for an opening. If no spaces show up, a sign advises the motorist to proceed with caution on his own.

Power Nuclear-powered generating plants will account for almost half of the U.S. electric power by 1985. Development of a fast-breeder reactor that makes fuel faster than it uses it will accelerate the conversion from fume-producing coal power. Liquid natural gas from abroad and gasification of coal will add to the fuel supply. The U.S. has vast recoverable reserves of coal, but better ways to control its choking sulphur dioxide emissions must be developed. Experiments look toward converting coal to petroleumlike liquid and obtaining oil from shale rock and harnessing energy from the sun. The heat the earth produces in abundance will be tapped as a source of energy.

Recycling Under development are all kinds of machines for taking waste and converting it to useful materials. As one example, the town of Franklin, Ohio, has a machine that weeds out cans, bottles and paper trash from garbage. The device makes use of air jets that separate waste by its weight. What is not salvaged is burned in a system that gives back usable heat and steam to the city. Other cities are testing and using way-out systems to recycle or neutralize the chemical effluvia of modern living, and companies are working on others. General Electric

CHART 1 MONEY INVESTED IN SCIENTIFIC RESEARCH AND DEVELOPMENT BY GOVERNMENT, BUSINESS AND UNIVERSITIES

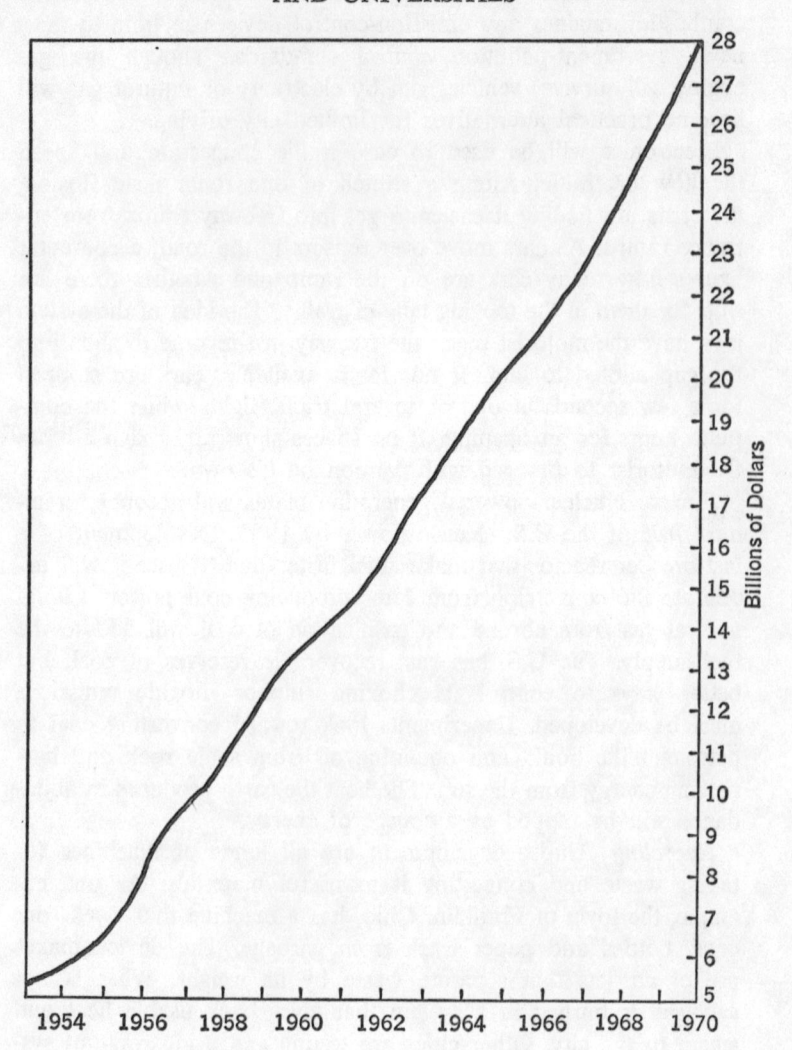

has a solid-waste disposal system that achieves virtually 100% combustion and reduces waste to sterile ash.

It is obvious that there is a vast amount of work for Americans to do—for scientists, engineers, public servants and businessmen to do, not to mention the role of citizens themselves in their private capacities. America has a restless energy that demands action and improvement. Americans are the great innovators of the free world. The recent problems involving the economy and the birth rate seem insignificant when you consider the challenge of vast problems and opportunities.

Huge amounts of capital will be required. Government will provide much. Investors will be expected to provide much more. You can have a part in all this by owning shares in progressive and aggressive companies led by innovative and competent managers. Investing in such companies can be rewarding. The danger of allowing your saved-up dollars to be eroded by inflation makes such investments almost a necessity. But selecting investments that will grow and offset inflation remains the most formidable task that faces the investor today.

4

INFLATION

Of all the problems that beset individuals, families, governments and even groups of nations, inflation is one of the most baffling and hardest to cope with. In these times it seems to defy the old laws. Historically, inflation has been spawned by wars and postwar shortages. Once the war period was over, it subsided by itself. Prices used to fall after a certain interval. In peacetime, in the old days, prices tended to be quite stable or actually decline in a gradual way. And in recessions prices tended to fall rather sharply. But all this is no longer true. Prices do not fall after wars, do not stabilize during peacetime and do not fall during recessions.

Inflation may be strictly defined as a state in which the supply of money and credit grows faster than the goods and services available. This has been called "demand pull" inflation; in other words, there are more dollars chasing a relatively smaller amount of goods and services, and the excessive demand pulls prices upward. Prices, however, can also be pushed up from below by an abnormally rapid rise in the cost of production. While this is not inflation in the classical sense, it is often referred to as "cost-push" inflation. Let us assume that production costs, including wages, are rising but that the output of goods and services is rising at an equal rate. Theoretically, prices charged for these goods and services should not have to be raised. But when the underlying production costs, including wages, increase faster than the increase in the output of goods or services, then the producer will have to raise his prices to cover his increased costs.

Under ideal conditions there is no cost-push inflation. Wages can be raised and prices held steady or even reduced. This occurs when productivity, or output per man-hour, increases. Say that a factory acquires new machinery that enables it to turn out 10% more units, using the same work force. Theoretically, the increased production will bring in 10% more income even at the same prices. However, some of this increased income will have to go to pay for the new machines. And in most cases, some will be available to raise wages. If the new machines are particularly more efficient than the old, there will be enough income to pay for the machines, increase wages and even reduce prices. In this, the best of all worlds, the increase in productivity is shared by industry (orders for the company that produced the new machines), by stockholders or bondholders who provided the capital to buy the machines (in the form of dividends or interest), by labor (in the form of increased wages) and by consumers (in the form of lower, or at least the same, prices).

One of the controversial questions today involves the measuring of productivity. In recent years, in certain industries, it is generally admitted that wages have gone up faster than productivity, which means that profits have been cut into and prices forced up.

Going back to the classical form of inflation, an abnormal increase in the supply of money and credit in relation to goods and services available, the situation theoretically can be controlled simply by slowing down the rise in the amount of money and credit being created. Traditionally, this is done by use of fiscal and monetary restraints. In times of high prosperity, when people have money to spend, when businessmen see a growing demand and tend to expand their factories and build up their inventories, the government curtails its spending and balances its budget, and the Federal Reserve Board tightens credit and lets interest rates rise. All this is supposed to dampen demand and cut the inflationary rise in prices.

These classical remedies no longer seem to work. Administrations in Washington, whether Republican or Democratic, have found that dampening inflation by the old methods means political catastrophe. High interest rates, tight credit and reduced government outlays are unpopular. For one thing, these remedies tend to cause a rise in unemployment. They also restrict the amount of money available for a host of government programs demanded by various groups and therefore popular with politicians. It would seem that no political party can stay in power after a period of using the simon-pure methods of inflation control.

This truism was amply proved during the landmark year of 1971. The previous year, 1970, was one of mild recession. Unemployment had risen to around 6%—not historically high, but nevertheless, politically unacceptable. Interest rates were historically high—high-grade corporate bonds were yielding over 8%. Even so, prices were rising at a rate of between 5% and 6%. The Vietnam war was being wound down rapidly, but inflation showed no visible signs of receding. The traditional monetary and fiscal restraints were being applied but seemed to have little effect. In fact, if anything, they aroused general dissatisfaction among labor, business, Congress and consumers. In August 1971 President Nixon and his powerful Secretary of the Treasury, John Connally, admitting the inadequacy of the old remedies, abruptly froze wages and prices, cut the dollar loose from gold and took other unprecedented steps that set the government on a totally new and radical course of controlling the economy.

Yet these direct limitations on the rise in prices and wages do little more than control the symptoms of inflation. They do not strike at the roots of the problem. There is much argument about what these root causes are, but little doubt that they still exist. Certainly a basic cause can be described as the country's feverish demand for more, more, more. One big demand is for more spending by the government to clean up the environment. Another is for more national spending on health care. Those representing a large segment of the population on welfare demand that the poor be given a minimum income at government expense. Older people, who suffer the most from inflation since their incomes tend to be fixed while the cost of living rises, demand larger social security and medical payments. The military insists on the need for continuing large expenditures on ever-more sophisticated and expensive weapons systems. Workers want their wages to rise, in many cases faster than their output of goods and services warrant. Corporations want their output and profits to grow at an ever-increasing rate. In fact, year to year growth has become the criterion by which a business is judged.

Perhaps the single most potent inflationary force stems from the Full Employment Act of 1946, which holds the government responsible for seeing that a job is available for every person who wants to work. This full employment, to which the government is now committed, automatically produces a fantastic array of goods and services. These, in turn, must be marketed, even though more may be turned out than consumers can easily absorb. To push these goods and services out into consumption, we have developed the most effective advertising media the world has ever known. We have created a mass psychology that says, in effect, that to be a good American you must have new cars, new color television sets, sports clothes, the most modern appliances and a host of gadgets that are invented and advertised with bewildering speed. If consumers cannot afford to pay cash for this ever-increasing flow of materials and services, they are expected to avail themselves of the easiest credit known to man. Almost anyone, through credit cards, charge accounts, consumer loans and easy-to-get mortgages, can, and is urged to, participate in the consumption race.

To fit into the glamorous picture of what he should have, or what the Joneses have, and to keep up the payments on what he has bought on credit, the consumer frequently is forced to moonlight, or the wife in the family goes to work. This, of course, increases the amount of goods and services produced, and speeds up the vicious spiral of production and consumption.

Where it will all end is hard to say. But one thing is almost certain. Until there is a radical shift in national attitude, the hectic pace of rising production and consumption will continue. And the underlying pressures will cause prices to rise, whether more slowly than in the past, under the heavy restraining hand of government, or more rapidly as in the 1970–71 period, it is impossible to predict with any certainty.

No matter how inflation is defined or where the blame is put, it produces certain definite results, almost all of them bad. Inequities are inevitable, since some groups, especially those well organized and with political clout, can keep their incomes rising as fast as or even faster than prices. Other groups, notably retired people living on fixed pensions, suffer terribly.

The insidiously harmful effects are apparent when you consider what is happening to your savings, the money you have stored up in one form or another for future use. Dollars saved for such emergencies as sickness or loss of job, for the college education of younger children, for protection of loved ones in the form of life insurance reserves, or for retirement in the form of pensions —these dollars are eaten away year by year as the cost of what they were intended to pay for rises.

It is in the best tradition of good money management to save. Savings are expected to earn interest or dividends. If you put money in a savings and loan association or in a savings account in a bank, you are lending your money for others to use. You expect to receive a return on it. The interest that the money earns usually is reinvested and makes the savings grow. But during inflationary periods, the price level often rises at a rate that nullifies the yield on savings. If prices go up 5% annually and your money is yielding 5%, you might as well have it stuffed in a mattress. You are receiving no return at all. In some recent years, the situation has been much worse. Savings have yielded 4½%, for example, while prices have risen at a rate of over 5%. This means, of course, that savings not only have earned nothing, but have shown a minus return. The dollars themselves, even including interest earned, have dwindled in purchasing power by ½% to 1% a year. A banker explains that the "pure risk" rate of interest for highest grade bonds is 3.5%, but the bonds must yield 7.5% to anticipate long-range price increases at about 4% a year.

It was not always thus. Although few can remember a year when the cost of living hasn't risen, there have been periods not too long ago when consumer prices actually declined. For example, during the three-year period from September 1937 to September 1940, the cost of living fell by 4%.

Imagine, if you will, the kind of life this made possible. You could keep your capital safe and growing in value merely by putting it in a savings account. While the cost of living, on the average, was declining by 4%, savings were yielding around 2%, with no particular risk. Income taxes, believe it or not, presented no problem. On an income of $6,000, which was quite adequate in those days, taxes amounted to about $140 a year. It is true that unemployment, even in the late 30's, was exceptionally high by today's standards—around 17%. The workweek was long— six days, or five and a half. Consumer credit, as we know it now, was unavailable to most. Yet a declining price level, resulting from an abundance of goods and services, took away much of the sting.

In recent years, by contrast, the rise in prices has approached or even exceeded what savings could earn almost as a matter of course. In other words, the purchasing power of money set aside in savings accounts or bonds for some future use either has grown only slightly in value or has actually declined. People who have worked hard all their lives have found their retirement income actually diminishing. Families who have saved to send sons and daughters to college have found education costs going up 6% to 8% a year, while their savings have grown at only 4½% or 5%. Families happily seeing their annual income rising have discovered that even though more dollars were coming in, the increasing demands on this income have put them in a frantic race to stay even with the board.

Obviously, if the dollar is declining in value year after year, dollars themselves are not the best things to invest in. Investing in dollars is just another way of describing the traditional saving process whereby you lend dollars to someone else for which he pays you a return known as interest. At some future time, you will receive the same number of dollars back.

Putting money into an equity, on the other hand, is quite a different arrangement. The word "equity" means the net value of a property owned, such as a piece of real estate or a common stock. Unlike money owed you, such as money in savings accounts, bonds or mortgages, you cannot demand to be paid back the exact number of dollars you invested in the first place. When you own a piece of real estate, a common stock, a coin collection or a piece of art work, you can get out of it only what others are willing to pay. Equities tend to have rather widely fluctuating values, with varying yields or returns, while debts tend to be relatively fixed in value, with fixed returns. Equities that may be expected to grow in value more rapidly than the cost of living obviously are a sensible place to have savings during inflationary periods. Yet because their value is not fixed, but can range up and down in response to all kinds of forces—supply and demand, changing tastes on the part of the public, the ability of business management—equities carry a lot of risk. The goal is to be able to pick those that have the surest potential increase in value and that, at the same time, can be converted back into dollars easily when the need for them arises.

The search for this kind of equity, as a defense against inflation, makes sense. The philosophy of this book is that most families should—and indeed must—strive to put some assets where they will grow much faster than the rate at which the purchasing power of money is declining. Most families, once they have life insurance, some kind of health insurance and an emergency backlog of old-fashioned savings, probably should have 75% of their assets in equities. But *what* equities? How and where can these havens be found where hard-earned dollars will grow at, say, 9% to 14% without too much risk of capital loss?

5

THE SEARCH FOR EQUITIES

The risk that comes with investing in equities scares many people away. Oddly enough, it scares many away just when equities would seem the best investment; that is, when consumer prices are rising fastest and savings are losing purchasing power. In the years closely following the end of World War II, when prices were rising faster than they ever had before, when the cost of living rose almost 15% in one year, most people wanted no part of equities but preferred savings bonds and bank deposits, which were then paying less than 3%. Several thousand families were interviewed under the auspices of the Federal Reserve Board in 1948 and asked their opinion on this situation: "Suppose a man decides not to spend all his money. He can either put it in a bank or he can invest it. What do you think would be the wisest thing for him to do with the money nowadays—put it in the bank, buy savings bonds with it, invest it in real estate or buy common stock with it? Why do you make that choice?"

The score was as follows—
For:

Savings bonds	60%	"Safe, not a gamble."
Bank deposits	32%	"Safe, not a gamble."
Real estate	9%	
Common stock	5%	

Against:

Common stock	62%	"Not familiar with, not safe, a gamble."
Real estate	58%	"Price too high."
Bank deposits	23%	"Interest rate too low."
Savings bonds	9%	

Even among men and women with incomes of $7,500 or better (high in those days), two-thirds said they wanted their investments to have a fixed value. In retrospect, those answers were foolish. Stocks and real estate, in terms of later values, were dirt-cheap. The Dow Jones Industrial Average, for example, was selling at somewhere around nine times one year's earnings, a bargain price that has not been equaled since 1951. Although numerical measurement is more difficult for real estate, it undoubtedly was equally cheap.

In subsequent years people began to discover the value of equities in a fast-growing and inflation-ridden economy. The pendulum swung sharply in the early 1960's. And the financial community, like other parts of the free-enterprise system, was eager to meet popular demand. It began to make equities available in many forms: new issues of common stocks, many in new and unseasoned companies; mutual funds, many thrown together to offer a participation in a group of mediocre securities; small real estate lots in the vast scrublands of Florida and Arizona; uncirculated rolls of nickels, dimes and quarters; ownership of Scotch whisky warehouse receipts and the like. As it became clear that inflation would continue and grow more severe, wealthier and more sophisticated investors turned to antiques, paintings, collections of gold coins—anything that might be expected to offer an ever-growing scarcity value, anything that promised a better haven for assets than the ever-eroding dollar.

Where to put assets Today, the problem of where to put assets remains the same. A certain proportion of family assets should be kept in an emergency fund, and this part of a prudent financial program is easy to handle. Bank and savings and loan accounts are mostly guaranteed up to $20,000. Interest yields are fairly stable and predictable. But when it comes to equities, the field is wide open. Psychology plays a part and the investor too often becomes emotionally involved. Gold and silver, or gold and silver mining stocks, have a deep-seated ancient appeal. Real estate, especially in remote tropical climes, always carries a romantic tinge. Shares in intriguing ventures involving space-age products, perhaps not yet fully developed and proved, or fanciful schemes for making money through franchising or providing new and far-out services are all too likely to evoke a greedy response in the mind of the eager investor.

The field of equity investing extends around the world and into every nook and cranny of business enterprise, minerals, farm commodities, hobbies, real estate ventures and the arts—all the places where rapid changes in value are expected or projected. Thus, the continuing inflation and erosion of the dollar throws the investor into a position where he, or she, must make a choice among a tremendously wide and confusing range of possibilities. Consider a few of them.

Precious metal Gold and silver, whose buying power traditionally goes up when that of paper currency goes down, would seem to be a logical place to put assets during a period of inflation. Yet in actual practice, particularly in modern times when so many nations are phasing precious metals out of their coinage, the supposed protection offered by gold and silver has been largely illusory. Gold, though still the ultimate store of value in the minds of peoples around the world, is becoming more and more an industrial commodity and less and less a treasure of stability or even predictability.

American citizens have been forbidden to own most forms of gold since 1934, yet ownership of antique gold coins of the vintage of 1934 and earlier is permissible, as is ownership of the common stocks of gold mining companies. Both types of investment are ultimately tied to the price of gold, which for some years now has been allowed to float free in world and domestic markets. In 1971, President Nixon cut America's official tie to gold, which

CHART 2
PRICE OF STOCK OF HOMESTAKE MINING COMPANY

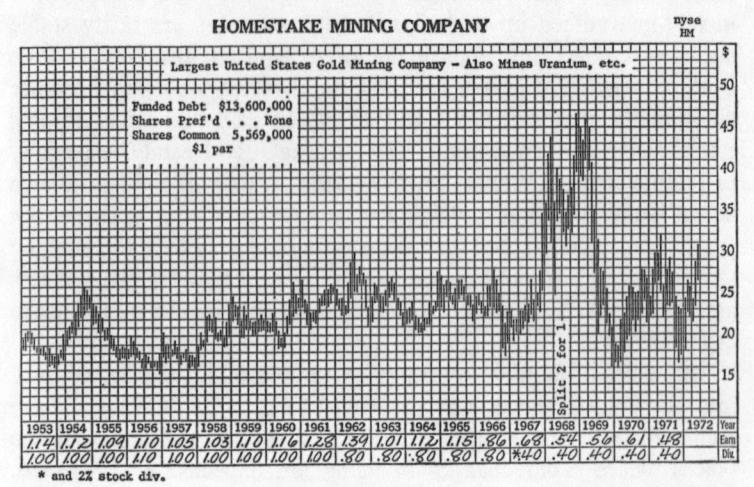

Chart: Homestake Mining Company stock price, 1953–1972, showing Earnings and Dividends per year.

CHART COURTESY OF M. C. HORSEY & CO., INC.,
SALISBURY, MARYLAND. 21801.

for some 37 years had stood at $35 per ounce. Then in 1972 the official price was raised to $38. Chart 2 shows the seemingly irrational movement of the price of a leading domestic gold stock, Homestake Mining Company, during the period when the United States was going through a severe inflationary period.

To satisfy the demand for a stake in gold that presumably will hold its value as the purchasing power of the dollar declines, dealers and coin exchangers have offered various ways to own antique gold coins in bulk. But here again, superimposed on the problem of predicting the value of gold, is the fact that such dealers ask a substantial premium over the intrinsic gold value of the coins. This premium can be as much as 50%. In addition, the spread between the buy price and the sell price can range from 5% to as high as 40%. It is somewhat disconcerting to be asked to buy a commodity for, say, $17 and realize that if you turned around and sold it, you would receive only $11.50.

Silver, silver coins, silver mining stocks and silver futures, have had as erratic and unpredictable values as gold. The nations of

CHART 3 PRICE OF STOCK OF HECLA MINING COMPANY

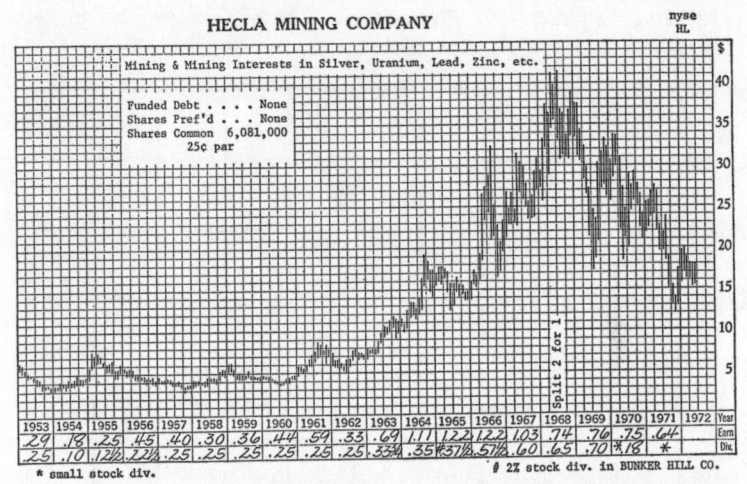

CHART COURTESY OF M. C. HORSEY & CO., INC.,
SALISBURY, MARYLAND. 21801.

the world, more and more, are abandoning silver in their coins. Desperate efforts are being made by photographic companies to develop a substitute for silver in the developing of films. And the world supply and demand picture in silver is vastly confusing, depending to some extent on the degree of hoarding in such large areas of the world as India. Chart 3 shows the price pattern of a leading domestic silver stock, Hecla Mining Company, during the same period of fast-rising consumer prices.

Probably the best investment involving gold and silver is a collection of fine coins carefully selected with the advice of an expert, and patiently and safely held. Chart 4 shows the appreciation in value of a little composite coin collection consisting of a 1932 $20 gold piece, an 1802 silver dollar, a 1921 half-dollar, a 1918 nickel and an 1865 two-cent piece. These particular coins were selected in 1968 by Stack's, 123 W. 57th Street, New York, N.Y. 10019.

Paintings, antiques and similar art objects present greater problems. Judgment of value is more difficult. Storage is a real problem. And such objects are difficult to exchange for cash.

CHART 4 VALUE OF A SMALL COIN COLLECTION

1932 $20 gold piece; 1802 silver dollar; 1921 half-dollar; 1918 nickel; 1865 two-cent piece. Figures courtesy of Stack's, New York, N.Y.

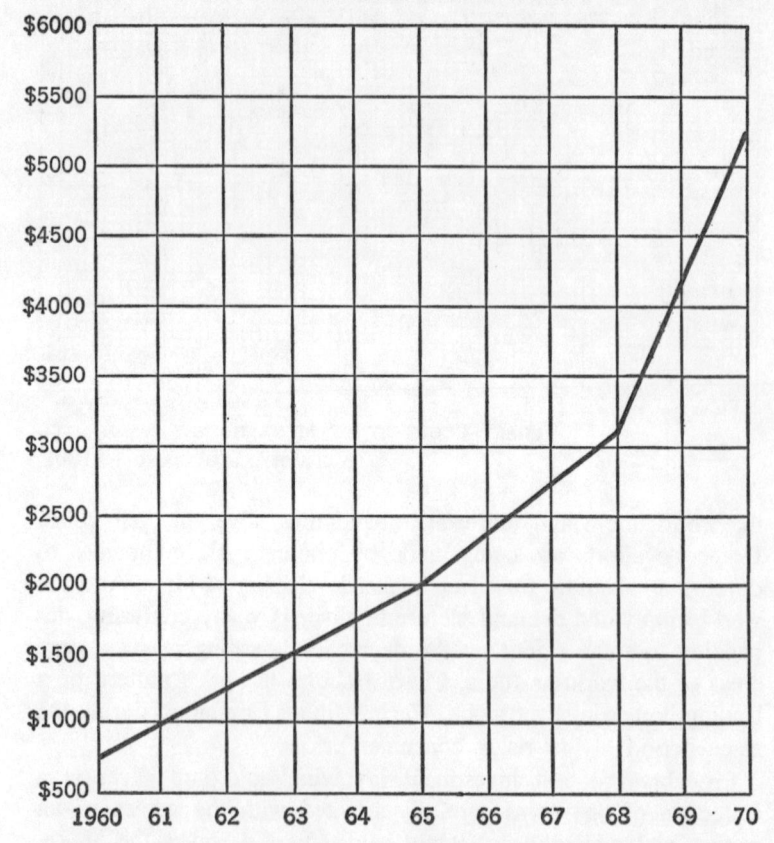

Real estate Land has one of the greatest potential scarcity values of any equity if—and this is a big "if"—it is carefully selected so that someone definitely will want it at ever-increasing prices. Too many people have bought lots in vast platted areas of scrubland in Florida, Arizona and New Mexico only to find some years later that there is no demand for their lots except at 40% off the original cost. In some developments the selling agents offer lots for, say, $10,000 apiece while a real estate office across the road is offering resales of similar lots at $6,000 without takers.

Nevertheless, carefully selected real estate, for example recreation land or vacation homes, offers one of the soundest equities available today. A broad measure of land values shows a rising trend. Look at Chart 5, which shows the average value of five

CHART 5 AVERAGE VALUE OF FIVE
ACRES OF FARMLAND

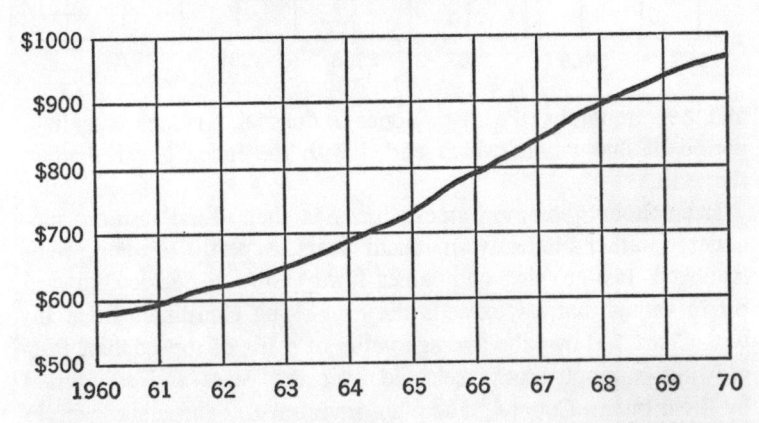

acres of farmland, as computed by the U. S. Department of Agriculture. Carefully chosen land in the path of development and waterfront and mountain property should do much better. Even a house, preferably the one owned and lived in by the individual, if well located and maintained, is usually a fine investment.

Common stocks The stocks of well-managed, growing companies are probably the most satisfactory inflation hedge available to the ordinary investor. Such stocks are easily and cheaply acquired, can be safely stored at no expense and can be converted into cash at a moment's notice. It is true that the run-of-the-mill stocks can fail the owner, especially over the short haul. Even the Dow Jones Industrial Average, if you had been able to buy a pro-rata stake in it, would not have served you well during a recent five-year period of fast-rising consumer prices—1965 to 1970. Chart 6 shows that when the cost of living was rising 4%, 5%

CHART 6 DOW JONES INDUSTRIAL AVERAGE

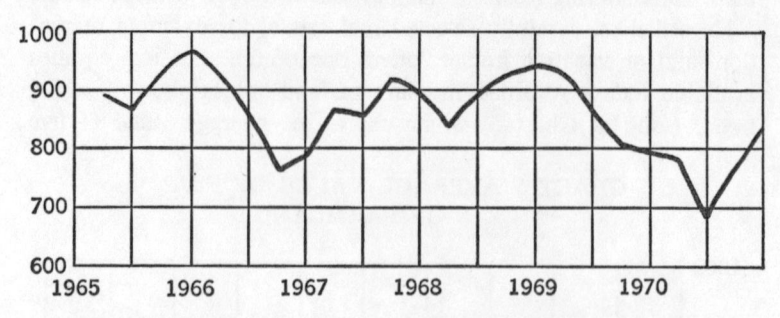

and 6% annually, the Dow Jones Industrial Average was in a period of fluctuation, which ended with the index lower than at the start.

Even though common stocks have, in their usual fashion, meandered rather aimlessly in recent years, expertly selected, well-managed, fast-growing companies have shown a decided upward tilt in values that far exceeds the ever-rising Consumer Price Index. Chart 7 shows the average value of a list of top-quality, fast-growing common stocks selected over the years and supervised by Investment Counsel, Inc., an investment counseling firm in Grosse Point, Mich.

Ideally, an equity investment should have these characteristics:
• It should have prospects for a continuing rise in value.
• It should be easily acquired without excessive commission costs.
• Information should be readily available on which to make a judgment of value.
• Safe storage should be easy and inexpensive.
• It should be quickly and easily convertible back into cash.

The type of equity that best fits this description is the common stock of good-quality companies whose sales and earnings are growing faster than the economy as a whole. Perhaps the second likeliest candidate is real estate. Though it is less liquid and more expensive to hold, these disadvantages are offset by its usually solid value and potential scarcity. Besides, an interest in real es-

CHART 7 RESULTS OF INVESTING IN GROWTH STOCKS SELECTED BY INVESTMENT COUNSEL, INC., OF GROSSE POINT, MICH.

FAST-GROWTH LEADERS
Index of Performance Compared With General List of Market Leaders

Results 34-1/4 Years Later, of each $100 Invested in 1938

INVESTMENT COUNSEL'S FAST-GROWTH LEADERS

DOW JONES INDUSTRIALS

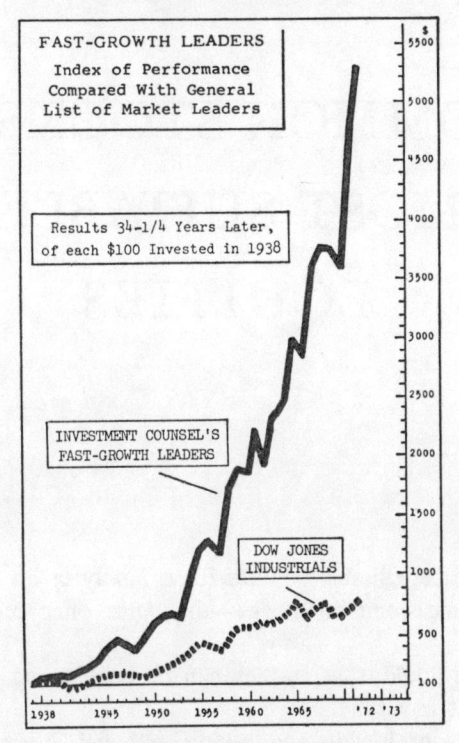

CHART USED BY PERMISSION OF INVESTMENT COUNSEL, INC.

tate can be acquired through participation in syndicates, real estate trusts or real estate investment companies.

Coin collection, while having some of the characteristics of an ideal equity investment, calls for special expertise that is outside the scope of this book.

For the ordinary investor, then, the equities to be recommended in succeeding chapters will consist of common stocks of good growth companies and real estate or a combination of both.

6

COMMON STOCKS— MOST SUITABLE EQUITIES

Of the two most suitable equities for a family or an individual—real estate and common stocks—the latter offer certain unique advantages.

- They are liquid; that is, they can be bought and sold quickly and easily at any time.
- The costs of buying and selling, although higher than they have been in the past, are still reasonable compared with other investments, such as real estate.
- Storage is easy and usually free.
- During ownership, dividends only are taxed. Taxes must be paid each year on real estate, but securities are taxed only when they are sold at a profit. And in this case the capital gains tax is less than taxes on income.
- Stocks offer diversity since they may be purchased in small amounts and a given sum of money can be spread over several securities.

• More information on companies and their stocks is available than on any other form of investment. A vast number of facts and statistics is contained in manuals that can be inspected in brokerage houses and libraries. Additional material can be read in relatively inexpensive financial publications.

• A great amount of advice also is available in market services and books. Though much of this is worthless, much also is sound and useful.

In fact, one of the biggest problems in investing in common stocks is that there are so many to choose from and such a bewildering amount of information about them. "Selectivity" is the key word here. Picking just the right stock or stocks from the tens of thousands that are traded every day worries and baffles traders and professional money managers as well as small individual investors.

To the trader and the speculator, the right stock is one that he thinks is due for a big rise. Maybe he has heard rumors of an impending merger, a stock split or an intriguing new product. His hope is to buy the stock before the good news gets around, then ride it up and sell out near the top when the uninformed public is just buying in.

A more sophisticated method of trying to get in at the bottom and out at the top is used by some professional money managers and publishers of advisory services. Elaborate charts are kept of hundreds of stocks showing price movment, volume of trading and other technical information. Or these statistics are fed into a computer. The chart or the computer is supposed to give an early warning signal when a stock is about to begin a significant rise or decline. As an oversimplified example, if the volume of trading in a certain stock began to pick up and its price also began to rise, it might mean that institutions, such as mutual funds, were beginning to acquire it in large amounts. This, of course, would be a buy signal for the chartist or user of the computer.

In the past few years professional money managers have become obsessed with what they call "performance." Translated into simple language, "performance" means making relatively quick and large capital gains. This, in turn, means buying a stock, getting a fast upward price move, and then selling it. It differs markedly from the old-fashioned method of careful investing used by most bank trust departments, mutual funds and other institutions back in the 50's and early 60's. In those days the accepted method was to buy quality companies, hopefully those promising a long-term upward movement in earnings and price, and then to hold them indefinitely.

Performance investing requires quick decisions and nimbleness in getting in and out of the market. This is because members of the performance cult tend to surge in the same direction. There are style changes in investing just as in clothes. At one point the utilities and oils will be in disfavor while the "in" stocks may be motel and restaurant franchise chains. As one group becomes unpopular and another group popular, the most aggressive institutional investors try to be the first to recognize a new shift and beat the crowd.

None of this is suitable for the individual investor. The day-to-day tips and rumors in the financial community are unreliable, and the short-term movements of individual stocks and the market as a whole are unpredictable even by the so-called experts. The professional money managers are hard put to outguess each other on the upcoming fads and changes in popularity among individual stocks or groups of stocks. For the small or medium-size investor to try to compete in the performance game is unprofitable and can be disastrous.

The best method for the individual is to block out a set of investment guidelines for himself, then stick to them through thick and thin. These guidelines should cover the following points: the basis on which buy and sell decisions will be made; the timing of buy and sell decisions; the method of selecting industries and companies.

There can be many reasons why an investor buys or sells any given stock. The most common probably is that his broker or a market advisory service has recommended it. Supposedly someone has done basic research on the company's position and its prospects. Wherever possible, however, it is best for the individual investor to do the basic research himself, or at least to check up on the research done by others.

There are three main reasons why a stock would appear to be a good buy: (1) Its earnings have been in a long-term upward trend. (2) It is a cyclical stock, and business as a whole is at the beginning of an up cycle. (3) It is a turnaround situation; that is, the company has been doing poorly but new elements have come into the picture that make a change in direction likely.

Taking these in reverse order, the prospect of a turnaround is a perfectly legitimate reason for buying a stock. Very often an old company that has plugged along for years without much imagination or oomph acquires new, young and aggressive management. Or a company that has one or more unprofitable divisions or products eliminates them and begins to concentrate on those that are profitable. Or a company that has been producing a line for which the demand is leveling off or declining acquires new product lines that have much more promise.

Professional or institutional investors are always on the lookout for turnaround situations. The individual investor can spot them if he is an assiduous reader of the financial news and, perhaps, subscribes to a really good advisory service. However, finding turnaround situations certainly shouldn't make up the whole of an investor's philosophy. There just aren't that many situations available and they *are* hard to find.

Buying cyclical stocks at the beginning of an up cycle in business and selling them at the top of the cycle sounds fine. In actual practice, it is one of the most difficult ways to make money. For one thing, the stock market simply does not conform to the business cycle. Many economists believe that the market anticipates changes in general business trends by about six months. In other words, the market usually starts down before a recession and starts up again before it's over. But the market goes down sharply at other times for no apparent reasons. A Wall Street wag has stated facetiously that the market has anticipated eight out of the last five recessions. And it might be noted that the 1968–70 bear market was the steepest in over 30 years, presumably anticipating the 1970 recession, which turned out to be the mildest since the end of World War II.

Another problem hard to cope with is that each business cycle is different. Every industry is subject to forces that are unique to the particular period in history: imports from abroad, changes in the age mix of the population, changing styles in consumer demand and so on. The industries that benefited from the last up cycle may not, for various reasons, benefit from the next one.

Probably the most suitable reason for making a buy decision, at least on the part of the nonprofessional investor, is that a company's earnings have been in a long-term upward trend. Admittedly, this means that the investor is basing his decision on what has happened in the past rather than on a prediction of what will happen in the future. However, companies tend to obey Newton's first law, which says that a body in motion remains in motion with a constant velocity unless an external force acts on it. Translated into terms of investing, this means that if a company's earnings have been growing at, say, 10% or 12% a year, they will continue to do so unless some unfavorable factor develops.

There are other arguments for this growth stock theory. Fast-growing companies usually are plowing back a large part of their earnings into research and into development of new products and new markets. This means that the dividend payout is small, but this is not a disadvantage. Most investors, notably those who have not yet reached retirement age, do not need, and should not want, dividend income. Dividends are taxable, and what's left after taxes can be frittered away. Earnings put to work by the company, on the other hand, are being reinvested by the best brains in American industry. The stockholder pays no taxes on such earnings, even though he owns a pro-rata share of them. He will be taxed on his profits when he sells his stock, but at that time only a capital gains tax will be due, which will be lower than his top income tax rate.

If the investor buys a company with steadily rising earnings and if they continue to rise, he can afford to sit back and forget the vagaries of the marketplace. Even if the investment turns out extremely well and he has a large paper profit, he should resist the temptation to nail it down by selling. If he lets his investment ride, it probably will continue to grow in value at least as fast as anything else he might buy. Second, if he sells his stock when he finds he has a paper profit, he incurs a capital gain and must pay the gains tax, not to mention the sales commission. Only a part of his profit then is left to reinvest. In addition, he suffers all the original headaches of making another good selection.

If at some point, however, the earnings cease to grow or begin to decline, the investor is faced with one of his toughest decisions. Has the trend of earnings actually been reversed? Or is the situa-

Common Stocks—Most Suitable Equities 47

tion only temporary, with the basic long-term trend still upward? Obviously, once he buys his stock, he must keep track of every company development. And once he is thoroughly convinced that things have turned sour, he should dump the stock at once and resist the temptation to hold for some temporary rise. It may never come.

When to buy? There are two sensible ways to buy at a reasonable price. One is to buy when the stock is relatively low. The other is to buy periodically regardless of price and thus average out.

Many people think that a stock selling at 10 is cheaper and more likely to show a big percentage increase than a stock selling at 100. This is foolish if you think about it. If two companies, A and B, had identical assets, liabilities and earnings and so on, but A had ten times as much stock outstanding as B, then the stock of A might well sell at 10 while the stock of B would sell at 100. Yet their value and prospects would be identical.

Another mistake that is easy to make is to assume that because a stock is selling for a lot less than it was six months ago, a year ago or five years ago, it must necessarily be cheap. Actually, if a company has serious problems, if its earnings are going downhill, if it is losing out to competitors, its stock will be going down. Just because it is less than it was does not by any means indicate that it is a bargain. On the contrary, a stock may well be a better buy if it is higher than it has been in the past. All other things being equal, the stock of a prosperous, growing company will be rising year to year.

Perhaps the best way to judge the price of a stock is to compare it with the company's earnings. This relationship is known as the price-to-earnings ratio. It is often referred to in Wall Street jargon as the stock's "multiple" or its P/E. Thus, a company that earned $2 a share last year and is selling for $30 a share has a P/E of 15. A more meaningful ratio might be comparison between its price and the best estimate of the current year's earnings. Thus, if the company is expected to earn $2.30 this year, its P/E based on current earnings would be 30÷2.30, or 13. Some analysts even try to calculate the P/E based on next year's estimated earnings.

Some groups of stocks traditionally have higher average P/E's than others. Thus the glamour growth stocks, such as computer and office machine companies, may have P/E's of 30 to 40 while the international oils have average P/E's of 10 to 12. Investors are willing to pay higher P/E's for fast-growing companies than for stable or slow-growing companies. The logic behind this is obvious. Take two companies, A, whose earnings are relatively flat, and B, whose earnings have been doubling every five years. The investor might be willing to pay 30 times earnings for company B, since in five years today's price will be only 15 times earnings, and he will have purchased a fast-growing company at a relatively low P/E. Company A, however, with its relatively flat earnings, might command a P/E of only 10.

Stock prices never stand still. They continually rise and fall, impelled by a variety of forces. The prospects for future earnings is one. If a company's earnings have been rising steadily at 10% a year, you might expect that its price also would rise by the same percentage. But obviously this does not happen. One of the biggest overriding forces on the market is investor psychology. Thus, the company whose earnings are rising steadily at 10% a year might sell at 25 times earnings at one period during a given year and only 15 times earnings at another period in the same year, even though the company's prospects would have shown no apparent change. A number of reasons could be cited to account for this apparent discrepancy. Institutional investors move into some groups and out of others as styles change. Investors go from optimism to pessimism for no apparent reason.

As inexplicable as it may seem, the stock of almost every company shows a rather wide P/E range each year. Thus, the P/E range of a growth stock might be from 20 to 30, on the average, year after year. A slower-growing company might show a P/E range of 10 to 20. Obviously, then, at some time during every year there will be an opportunity to purchase any stock at a relatively bargain price; in other words, at a P/E that is close to the historic low end of the range.

The annual P/E range of all listed stocks for ten or more years back is given in Standard & Poor's Listed Stock Reports. A crude but effective way to pick a target purchase price for any stock is to average the P/E lows for the past five years. At some time during every year the P/E for most companies will come close to this average low point. The exception might be in the case of so-called emerging growth companies. If a small or medium-size company is showing signs of a fast growth in earnings, it may attract the attention of investors as a potential high-quality growth company. In this case its P/E highs and lows may be moving into a higher range. Thus, each year's P/E low may be a bit higher than the previous year's, and it may never be possible to purchase it at the five-year average low. In such cases, it may be prudent to take as the target purchase price the median of the lows and highs of the past five years.

One of the biggest mistakes the investor can make is to be swayed by the crowd and buy only when everyone else is optimistic. This will almost guarantee that he will get in at the wrong time. Later, when gloom pervades Wall Street, he will be tempted to sell out at the low point in the range. There is a lot to be said for going contrary to the crowd—but it takes courage. Remember, though, that the big institutional investors are on a performance kick. They are continually shifting out of one industry or group into another. Since they all talk to each other and watch each other's activities closely, they tend to surge back and forth and give volatility to the market. One big institution alone can send the price of a stock tumbling if it decides to sell out and put the money somewhere else. Thus, even the unsophisticated individual investor will have many opportunities to purchase good stocks at bargain prices if he will keep his head and watch the P/E ratios.

All this calls for a good bit of study and work. An alternative is to buy periodically regardless of the level of the market. A favorite way is to decide on a certain sum of money to be invested every month, every quarter, every six months or once a year. This sum, then, is completely invested in shares of a selected stock. Known as "dollar cost averaging" or "dollar averaging," the method offers certain advantages. The given sum will buy more shares when the market is low and fewer when it is high. This results in a relatively low cost in the long run, provided the program is kept up faithfully. As a matter of fact, a program of dollar cost averaging kept up over a period of years will give an average *cost* that is lower than the stock's average *price*. In other words, if you invest a fixed sum each time, you will make out better than if you buy a fixed number of shares. A full discussion of how dollar cost averaging works is given in Chapter 21.

Can the small or medium investor compete with the professionals? Yes, if he will adopt a sensible philosophy and stick to it. One that has worked out well is made up of three basic points.

• Do not try to buy low and sell high or trade in and out of the market. Rather, stick to companies that have shown a record of earnings growth for at least five years. Earnings should have doubled over that period.

• Try to buy at a low P/E; that is, in the lower part of the range over the past five years. In the case of smaller, emerging companies, try for the median of the five-year high-low range. Alternatively, stick to dollar cost averaging.

• Once you have your stock, hang onto it as long as it continues to perform. Don't be tempted to nail down a big capital gain. But do keep the closest tab on company doings. And be ready to dump the stock if you are convinced that it has turned sour.

7

COMPETING AGAINST THE INSIDERS

As you can see, selecting good stocks and knowing how long to hold them is not easy. Some analysts and brokers believe that the little guy can never compete successfully against insiders and traders, and that he should simply stay out of the market. There is enough basis for this to warrant discussion.

Insiders and traders do receive early information on new products, changes in earnings and dividends, stock splits and prospective mergers. A company's board of directors obviously are the first to know about corporate decisions because they are the ones who make them. However, insiders are not supposed to use unpublished information to make money in a company's stock. There's a federal law against it. The New York and other stock exchanges also have rules forbidding it. When decisions are made that will affect the price of a company's stock, there must be an immediate announcement. The first place this news will appear probably will be over the Dow Jones broad ticker or the Reuter-Ultronic ticker. These tickers run all day reporting in good plain English financial events within a few minutes after their occurrence. Unless you happen to be watching the ticker in a brokerage office, or unless you have a large enough account to warrant a broker's phoning you at once, you will not get the news until you read the newspaper the next day. You won't even get it then, in fact, unless you read a paper that has complete financial coverage. You may get the news, by implication, only when you find that the price of the stock has taken a sudden rise or fall.

Admittedly, then, if you are an ordinary investor who must work at a job all day or raise a family, you'll probably be the last to hear the hot news about your stocks or ones that you might be planning to buy. It sounds bad, but it isn't fatal. Obviously, you can't make short-term gains in competition with professionals who get the news either in advance or within seconds after its announcement. But then you don't have to be a trader out for a short-term profit. You can, and probably should, be using the fundamental approach instead. Buy good-quality companies whose earnings are growing, and make your purchases either periodically or when prices seem reasonable in relation to earnings. Then if you hold for the long pull, you'll probably do as well as most traders and perhaps even better. As you will see later on, the development of a new product or a change in the dividend usually produces only a transient change in the price of a company's stock. The underlying forces and trends are what make the big profits (or losses).

Even though you are a long-pull investor, you certainly want to know as much as possible about the stocks you own or might want to buy at some future time. Congress has passed a law to help you get vital information as quickly as possible and to prevent insiders, who inevitably have the information first, from using it in a way that hurts your investments. The basic law is the Securities Exchange Act of 1934, Rule 10b-5. This rule forbids any person to deceive another person in connection with the purchase or sale of a security. It defines deception as either making an untrue statement of fact or omitting to state a material fact. This is a pretty broad stricture, and the SEC and the courts have interpreted it to mean that a person with inside knowledge of a company's affairs can't use this knowledge to buy or sell stock in that company, since the person on the other end of the deal would be deceived. By further extension, the law has been interpreted to mean that if *any* person has inside information that could affect the price of the stock, he may not trade upon it unless he first makes a public announcement of the information.

To see how this works, consider a few actual cases from the records. Several years ago the SEC brought action against the country's largest brokerage firm, Merrill Lynch, Pierce, Fenner & Smith and a group of institutional investors. The background, according to the SEC's official account, was this. From April through June 1966 Merrill Lynch was acting as prospective managing underwriter in the expected sale to the public of $75 million of Douglas Aircraft convertible debentures. In order to prepare a registration statement to file with the SEC, Merrill Lynch had to delve deeply into company operations.

On June 7 Douglas had released a report reflecting earnings for the five months ended April 30 of 85 cents per share. About two weeks later Merrill Lynch, by reason of its position as prospective underwriter, learned that Douglas' six months' earnings would be sharply lower than those for the five-month period, and in fact, that Douglas expected little or no profit for the 1966 fiscal year.

From June 20 to June 23, according to the SEC, Merrill Lynch passed this word on to certain large customers, including the Madison Fund; the investment advisers to the Dreyfus Fund, Fundamental Investors and Diversified Growth Stock Fund; along with quite a few hedge funds (speculative funds usually operated on behalf of a group of wealthy partners and not available to the public). Investors sold 190,000 shares of Douglas and made profits, in some cases by selling short, of $4.5 million. The price of the stock ranged from 83 to 88 on Friday, June 17, and was down to a range of 74 to 77 a week later. In the meantime, of course, Merrill Lynch customer's men were accepting buy orders for Douglas from ordinary investors without disclosing (and perhaps without even knowing) the bad news about Douglas' earnings. This bad earnings report was issued Friday, June 24; on Monday the stock was down to a range of 69 to 74.

The SEC took action in another famous insider trading case involving the great mineral discovery of Texas Gulf Co. In the fall of 1963 the company was seeking to diversify its operations into metal mining and was making aerial geophysical surveys in eastern Canada. After discovering anomalies—i.e., extraordinary variations in the conductivity of rocks—the company geologists began to drill a test hole on the Kidd 55 segment of land near Timmins, Ont. The test showed such an extraordinarily rich content of copper, zinc and silver that it was recommended that the tract be bought at once. Until this could be done, the test hole was hidden and every effort was made to keep the discovery secret.

On March 31, 1964, when the company figured it had the land sewed up, it resumed drilling. In the meantime, some of the company geologists, their wives and friends had been buying Texas Gulf stock in substantial quantities at prices ranging from 6 to 9 (adjusted for 3 for 1 split in 1968). In some cases they bought "calls," or options to purchase for, say, 90 days at a fixed price.

Early in April rumors of a major ore strike were circulating throughout Canada, and on the morning of Saturday, April 11, New York papers carried articles that the company had made a rich ore discovery. The next day Texas Gulf issued a press release playing down the magnitude of the strike and saying, in part, "These reports exaggerate the scale of operations, and mention plans and statistics of size and grade of ore that are without factual basis and have evidently originated by speculation of people not connected with TG." At this time the stock was selling for around 10 to 11. At 10 A.M. on April 16 a company official finally read to newspapermen a statement announcing a strike of at least 25 million tons of ore. The news appeared over Merrill Lynch's private wire at 10:29 A.M. and over the Dow Jones broad tape at 10:54. By May 15 the stock was selling at 19.

The SEC charged that certain geologists and officers of the company had used inside information to make money in the company's stock and also had tipped off others. These latter buyers, known as "tippees," also were charged with using inside information. The company itself was charged with issuing a misleading press release prior to the announcement of the true dimensions of the strike.

Here is another case. Early in November 1959 Roy. T. Hurley, then president and chairman of the board of Curtiss-Wright Corp., invited 2,000 members of the press, the military and financial

Competing Against the Insiders 55

and business communities to a public unveiling of a new type of internal combustion engine being developed by the company. This was the Wankel engine that now is in actual use in some types of autos. On the day following the news conference Curtiss-Wright stock was one of the most active issues on the New York Stock Exchange and was up over three points, closing at 35¼. One day later, on November 25, when the company's annual meeting was scheduled to take place, the stock was up to 40¾.

On the morning of this day Curtiss-Wright directors met to consider, among other things, the declaration of a quarterly dividend. One of the directors was J. Cheever Cowdin, a salesman or customer's man of the brokerage firm of Cady, Roberts & Co. (Representatives of brokerage firms frequently serve as corporate directors, a practice that some people question.) Although the company had paid a quarterly dividend (not earned) of 62½ cents per share for each of the three preceding quarters, the board cut the dividend for the fourth quarter to 37½ cents.

At 11 A.M. the board authorized transmission of this information by telegram to the New York Stock Exchange, and the corporate secretary of Curtiss-Wright immediately left the meeting room to arrange it. Because of a typing problem, however, there was a short delay in the transmission of the telegram—it was not delivered to the exchange until 12:29 P.M. And, although it was customary for the company to advise the Dow Jones News Ticker Service immediately of any dividend action, through some inadvertence this was not done until 11:45 A.M. The announcement did not appear on the Dow Jones broad ticker until 11:48 A.M.

Meantime, shortly after the directors voted to cut the dividend, the meeting recessed, and Mr. Cowdin phoned his brokerage office and left a message for one of the partners, Robert M. Gintel, saying that the dividend had been cut. Mr. Gintel received this message before the news of the dividend cut had been published. He immediately entered sell orders to clean out all Curtiss-Wright stock from the discretionary accounts of 11 of his customers, including the account of his wife. In his haste, Gintel didn't even take time to figure up how many shares were in each account. He simply entered a sell order for 2000 shares and an order to sell short an additional 5000 shares to make sure that all Curtiss-

Wright stock in the accounts would be sold. When he ended up with a net short, or oversold, position, he simply allocated the short sales to the account of his wife and one other customer.

These orders were executed at 11:15 A.M. and 11:18 A.M. respectively. When the dividend announcement appeared on the Dow Jones broad tape at 11:48 A.M., the exchange was compelled to suspend trading in the stock because of the large influx of sell orders. When trading resumed at 1:59 P.M., the price was down to 36½ and it closed at 34⅞.

The SEC did not hold Mr. Cowdin at fault, since when he phoned his office, he assumed the news of the dividend cut had already been publicized. He was interested primarily in determining the market reaction. The SEC did, however, suspend Gintel from the New York Stock Exchange for 20 days, and the exchange itself fined him $3000.

Traditionally, the New York Stock Exchange has insisted that companies whose stock is traded on the exchange provide their stockholders and the public with all pertinent information on company matters. In the words of an exchange vice-president, "The exchange believes that prompt disclosure of important corporate news is especially essential in today's fast-moving markets. Thus, we require that annual and quarterly earnings, stock splits, dividend actions, mergers or acquisitions, and key management changes be released to the press as soon as circumstances permit. Normally subject to the same immediate release policy are major product developments, discoveries, contract awards and plans for expansion.

"There are, of course," this official continues, "situations where the proper course of action may not be entirely obvious. Confidential merger discussions, for example, are especially ticklish to handle. While no announcement need be made until a decision is reached, strict internal security is vital to prevent leaks. And if the stock should suddenly become involved in unusual market activity, the company should be ready to issue a clarifying statement.

"When a company has news that should be made available, we ask that it be given 'immediate' release rather than being issued on a 'hold for release' basis. We suggest in our Company Manual that if a dividend is passed or increased, someone should leave the directors' meeting and by the fastest means of communication, usually the telephone, advise Dow Jones and the other news services before the meeting has adjourned. This precludes the possibility of leaks."

In order to detect evidence of such leaks of inside information, the stock exchange maintains a stock-watch program. A computer is used to spot abnormal volume and price changes in any of the 1,700 issues listed on the exchange. When the computer red-flags an unusual situation, an exchange official phones the company and tries to discover the cause. If advisable, the exchange will suspend trading in the stock, ask the company what is going on and, if there is something significant, request that a public statement be issued.

Here are two examples, provided by the NYSE, of what the stock-watch program turns up.

The board of directors of a certain company in a certain large city met at 11 A.M. and voted to double the usual quarterly dividend of 50 cents. This news seemed so important that the board decided to delay announcement until 4 P.M., by which time the markets would have closed. Early in the afternoon, however, the stock became very active; orders totaling 6,000 shares came in from the city in which the company was located. The price rose 2½ points. The stock exchange, alerted by stock watch, investigated and found that no officer or director of the company had bought a single share. What had happened, it turned out, was this: The stenographer who regularly typed press releases had been at lunch when the directors' meeting adjourned, so a new and inexperienced girl had typed the statement that was to be held for release to the press at 4 P.M. This girl went to lunch with her boy friend and told him that the company's dividend was going from 50 cents to $1. He went back to work and told his boss, who decided to buy some stock and passed the word on to other friends, from whom it spread like wildfire.

In the other case, rumors one day swept the floor of the exchange saying that Company A was planning to make a tender offer of $18 a share for stock in Company B. Since Company B's stock was selling for only $14 a share, there was a potential profit of $4 a share if the rumors were true. The stock exchange called the chairman of the board of Company A, who admitted that a meeting between the two parties was even then taking place. As a result the exchange stopped all trading in the shares of Company B. The officials of the two companies stayed in session until 4 o'clock the next morning, when they finally reached an agreement and announced the tender offer. News came over the broad ticker at 9:30 A.M., before that day's market opened.

If you are an ordinary investor, you don't receive any *immediate* benefit from all this. You are not watching the broad ticker all day, ready to wheel and deal on the news of the moment. However, you obviously do benefit from having such agencies as the SEC and the NYSE and other exchanges insist that companies make public all pertinent information about their activities. This kind of policing is what makes it practical for you to invest at all.

Just how much advantage does an insider have over the public? Go back to the first two examples used in this chapter. Below and on page 59 are some selected figures on values that put the results of insider activity in perspective. By looking at these figure carefully you will see that insiders would have the advantage in cutting losses or in making profitable short sales when they had secret advance information on bad news. They also could make good profits on advance information on good news. On such quick profits, however, they would have to pay a full income tax. And if these actions turned out to be illegal, the full short-term profit would have to be paid to the company.

Value of 10 shares of Douglas Aircraft at various dates

Two years prior to insider coup	$300
One year prior to insider coup	450
Friday, June 17, 1966, the trading day before insiders started selling	830 to 880
June 24, 1966, the trading day after bad news was announced	690 to 740
Bottom of 1966 market decline, early in October	300
At time of merger with McDonnell, May 1967	600
Two and a half years after the insider coup	866

Value of 100 shares of Texas Gulf at various dates (adjusted for 3 for 1 split in 1968)

December 1961, two years before big ore discovery.	$800
December 1962, one year before big ore discovery	500
December 1963, just before the big discovery	700
While insiders were buying on basis of secret knowledge of ore strike	600 to 1100
April 17, 1964, day after public announcement	1350
May 15, 1964, one month after public announcement	1900
April 1965, one year after public announcement	2200
April 1966, two years after public announcement	4000

As you can see from the figures, the ordinary investor could not have competed for short-term profits, or perhaps avoided short-term losses, in these two stocks. But he still could have made out pretty well if he had bought either one of these stocks when they were historically low, or through a periodic acquisition program, and held them through the ups and downs until he had a substantial capital gain.

In addition to all this, the professionals and those supposedly on the inside of corporate news, are not all that good. Several years ago an official of one of the big stock exchanges told the author of this book the following story. The official had done a service for a big member firm and the managing partner said, "I am grateful for the favor and would like to return it. Buy stock in X company." The stock exchange official, being busy with his duties and having little time to study individual investments, but wishing to build up a fund to augment his retirement pension, bought several hundred shares in X company. The stock promptly went down. The broker thereupon called the official again and said, "Terribly sorry; very embarrassing. Sell your X stock and buy Y. We're pretty sure this is a good one." Unfortunately, Y also went down.

The partner in another firm, members of the New York Stock Exchange, told the author at a luncheon that he had investigated the advantages of dollar cost averaging in connection with a program developed by the firm for small investors. The results of his investigation had been rather disconcerting. He had concluded that if he had simply put a fixed amount of dollars into General Motors stock every month during all the years he had been on Wall Street, he would have made out better than he had with all his wheeling, dealing, buying and selling.

Admittedly, the small investor is competing against people who work at the stock market business eight hours a day. But in many cases they are too close to the trees to see the forest. If the small investor will adopt a good investment philosophy, stick to it and shun the tips and rumors floating around the financial community, he can make out well. One of the country's leading stock market analysts, Anthony W. Tabell, an associate of Delafield, Harvey, Tabell, an investment counseling firm in Princeton, N.J., says, "If good stocks are harder to pick, then investors have to spend more time at the job—maybe 30 or 40 hours a month, rather than two or three—or get professional help. The investor can manage his money. He is not stupid. If he doesn't do well, the reason is because he is lazy or he doesn't have the time to do the necessary research."

8

INDUSTRIES THAT CAN COPE IN THE SEVENTIES

The halcyon period for investors, in this generation at least, was from 1950 to 1965. Over that time span average earnings per share of the stocks in the Dow Jones Industrial Average nearly doubled. In addition, investors who were so leery of common stocks in 1949 when the Average was selling at only seven times earnings gradually turned into avid buyers. The growing demand pushed the P/E ratio up to the very high point of 24 in 1961 after which it settled down to around 17½ in 1965.

Thus, earnings nearly doubled and the P/E more than tripled. This leverage sent the average from 167 in 1949 to nearly 1,000 in 1965. A movement of this magnitude can wash out many mistakes. The investor who did only as well as the average saw his money increase sixfold in 15 years. The investor who concentrated on growth stocks—i.e., those whose earnings were growing faster than the average—was bound to have made out extremely well during almost any part of the period.

Beginning in 1965, alas, conditions changed. Earnings flattened out, and the price-to-earnings ratio settled down around the mid or upper teens. It is quite likely that earnings on good-quality stocks are resuming their long-term upward trend. But the prospects that the price-to-earnings multiple will double again is rather slim. Thus, the free ride, as it were, that came from the upward push of the multiple is largely gone. The increase that the investor can expect from his stock must depend mostly on an increase in company earnings. This makes it more important than ever that he select stocks that offer the best possible promise of earnings growth.

What industries, then, promise this future growth of earnings, and how will the changing conditions of the 70's affect them? First, note some general observations on the climate of the 70's and industries that may be expected to benefit or at least not be too adversely affected.

QUALITY OF LIFE

As mentioned in Chapter 1, there seems to be a turning away from big science, big engineering, big defense toward what might be called humanism—improvement of the quality of life, cleaning up the environment, better working conditions, more health services, more leisuretime and leisuretime activities, more personal care, and better and safer consumer products. It is significant that concern for the ecology defeated a proposed government subsidy for the supersonic passenger plane, the SST, in 1971. Even the exploration of space is becoming old hat. The 60's may be said to have been the decade of technology. The 70's may be the decade of the consumer. What about the young people who reject the heavy pattern of consumption that has characterized America and who are trying to return to a simpler life, making do with less? Actually, this movement is having little effect on retail sales. For one thing, proportionately fewer are involved than the publicity would indicate. For another, many of these young people are simply shifting their spending from stereos, tape recorders, records, etc. to blue jeans, bikes, skis, surfboards, knapsacks, etc. And these also cost money.

Fields in which industries may be expected to benefit include—

Leisure Travel, including motels and food-franchising operations; camping equipment; photographic equipment; vacation or second homes. (Some food-franchising operations have grown in a geometrical progression and overexpanded. Others have much growth potential. The field is like an ever-shifting kaleidoscope.)

Ecology Development and production of systems and products that will clean up the air and water and dispose of rapidly accumulating trash and garbage.

Health Drugs; automated and electronic devices to aid and monitor hospital patients.

Personal care Cosmetics, perfumes and other toilet preparations.

Convenience foods Ready-to-use foods for use by both the housewife and restaurants and institutions.

Banking New and varied financial and data-processing services.

FAMILY FORMATION

The big bulge of babies born during the years just following World War II are reaching the age when they are in the market for homes, appliances, life insurance and all the other amenities and necessities of settled-down married life. To many of these young families the old-fashioned hand-built house carries a price that is out of sight. Newer and cheaper types of housing will, as they are developed, offer a widespread appeal. Biggest buyers of life insurance, also, are men in their mid-20's and early 30's who have growing families to protect but only limited financial resources.

Fields in which industries may be expected to benefit include—

Homes Mobile and factory-built, or modular, homes.

General merchandising Chains, including mail order, department, discount and variety stores.

Autos
Appliances
Life insurance

ENERGY

Despite the shifting emphasis to humanism, today's society requires and demands an increasing supply of energy: fuel for autos and machines, electricity to operate a widening variety of appliances, air-conditioning and the like. Use of petroleum products, world wide, grows at an annual rate of about 7%. This is made up of growth in domestic demand of 4% to 5% and foreign demand at twice that rate. Consumption of electricity in the U.S. grows at 7% to 8%. Production of nuclear power is expected to grow ten times as fast during this decade.

Fields in which industries may be expected to benefit include—

Oils Companies that can maintain the best-working relationships with the politically unstable Arab nations.

Utilities Companies operating in fast-growing areas and especially those states with sympathetic regulatory agencies that tend to give generous rate increases.

Nuclear power Companies that supply nuclear equipment and fuel.

Electrical equipment Companies that supply generating and other equipment required for the expanding use of electricity.

BUSINESS GROWTH AND DEVELOPMENT

As long as the free enterprise system exists and flourishes in America, companies will compete and strive to expand and increase their profits. The battle goes on day and night to improve and speed up operations, to develop new products and markets and to cut costs.

All companies work to improve their own operations. Many also develop improved systems and machines that they sell or lease to other companies. Still others provide special business services —they lease fleets of cars to salesmen, guard plants, clean buildings or operate cafeterias.

The result is a vast and overlapping complex of operations that include electronic data processing, copying, bookkeeping, printing, addressing and mailing systems and machines, automated controls and measuring devices; materials handling equipment —strapping machines, conveyors, lift trucks, tractors, cranes, earth-moving equipment and a host of others.

Fields in which industries may be expected to benefit include—

Electronic data processing Although this industry is coming of age and growing more slowly than in the past, there is still a tremendous potential as businesses strive to cope with tremendously mounting paperwork, to speed up bookkeeping, billing, inventory control, printing, copying, addressing and mailing, record keeping—and to do it all with less cost and manpower. Smaller and cheaper equipment is being made available to smaller business units.

Laborsaving tools and machines Americans are an impatient lot. They want to get things done fast. This trait, combined with ever-rising costs of manpower, has led to the design and production of laborsaving tools—from the kits that enable the auto mechanic to change tires in a fraction of the time it used to take to gigantic machines that move tons of earth at a time. Machine tools can be programmed by computers to perform the most intricate shaping operations on metal. Pipelines move a varied assortment of materials with a minimum amount of human direction and control.

Cable television One of the great electronic expectations is a country-wide network of coaxial cables going into almost every home carrying what is known as cable television. The cables would carry much more than entertainment, news and ads. This electronic network would enable you to shop, bank, do mathematical computations and tell you about the weather, meetings and community events, all at the push of a button in the living room. There's even the possibility that mail might be delivered this way over facsimile machines.

INFLATION

There is the likelihood that inflation will continue despite all that government can do about it. And inflation is not good for profits, especially inflation in the range of an annual price increase of 4% or more. Inflation implies both wage and price increases, with wages going up faster. This means that when inflation is 4% or more, costs for many companies tend to go up faster than prices can be raised, and profits are squeezed. According to some analysts, this magnitude of inflation explains the fact that corporate profits were flat during the five or six years following 1965, despite the fact that GNP grew by 45%.

What kind of company can best keep earnings rising despite an inflation rate of 3% or 4%?

Research companies Those that continually come up with new products that have no price history, so prices can be set at a level that will bring in profits.

"Big ticket" companies Companies that produce goods or services where reliability is more important to the customer than price. Purchasers of such vital equipment as an expensive computer or an electronic medical device presumably would be willing to pay top price for complete reliability.

"Small ticket" consumer products Companies that produce consumer products in relatively small packages the price of which seems of little importance to the consumer. Examples might be soft drinks, cosmetics, specialty foods and the like.

Low labor costs As wage costs push up relentlessly, all companies strive to reduce manpower. Some, obviously, do better than others. Some industries by nature are more easily automated than others. Industries with built-in high labor costs are typically thought of as the steels and other metal fabricators and producers, autos, building and construction (notably home building) and the like. Industries that are traditionally thought of as having low labor costs are the oils and the utilities.

GOVERNMENT CONTROLS

Perhaps the most unmeasurable change that stands to affect the investment decision today is the degree to which the economy will be controlled by government. However it goes, big companies in the basic industries will be the likeliest targets for wage and price controls. This causes professional investment managers to steer clear of what they call "high profile" companies and to seek out "low profile" companies, by which they mean those that have maximum price flexibility, those that continually develop new products with no previous price base for comparison, and those smaller companies that, for example, produce consumer goods and services in relatively small units and whose price and wage policies are less likely to come under public scrutiny.

Fields in which industries may be least affected by government controls include—

Research and development Companies that plow back a sizable portion of their earnings into new products, and whose list of products for sale include a large proportion that were not on the market a few years ago, are least likely to be forced to hold down their prices to that of any previous base period. Actually, for new products, there is no previous base period.

Consumer-oriented industries It is significant that over a recent ten-year period the price of cola drinks rose 50%. Very little public complaint was made about it. On the other hand, if the price of steel or autos had risen by that amount, the public outcry would have been strident and there undoubtedly would have been a political campaign to have these big basic industries nationalized. Many other consumer-oriented companies can raise prices, either directly or by decreasing the contents of the package and keeping the price the same, without any particular notice on the part of the public.

COMPANY SIZE

There is a saying in Wall Street that "the tree does not grow to the sky." This applies to great and growing companies as well as to the market itself. Even the big growth companies that were so popular during the 50's and 60's should be re-examined. The bigger such a company gets in its field, the less likelihood that it can continue to increase its earnings at 12% or 15% a year. All other things being equal, the small or medium-sized growth company has the greater room for continued growth. Unfortunately, these companies are harder to spot than the giants with their established reputations and financial strength. And of course, many big glamorous growth companies are still dominant in their field and could have many years of good growth ahead of them before the competition catches up. This is a sticky problem of selection, and the prudent investor might want a mix of large, dominating companies that still have promising growth potential, plus some of medium size and a sprinkling of young and emerging companies that carry more risk and wider room for expansion.

SOCIAL RESPONSIBILITY

All companies, but especially large ones, increasingly feel the pressure of public opinion on their activities having to do with what might be called the public interest. Traditionally, company managements have felt that their primary responsibility—and in many cases their only responsibility—was to their stockholders. Today there is a growing feeling that corporations have an equal responsibility to the public at large. Demands are rising that managements improve their performance in terms of social, as well as financial, goals. We are talking here about three areas that cover consumers, environment and social responsibilities.

Consumers The consumer movement is widespread, spearheaded by vociferous leaders of organized groups that claim to represent the millions of Americans who are continually shopping and buying. The goals of these groups include safer products, as for example autos; unit pricing of groceries to permit easier comparison shopping; better warranties and guarantees; quicker and more sympathetic response on the part of manufacturers to complaints about quality and performance of goods or services purchased, and so on.

Environment Oil companies that have accidentally spilled oil in waters adjacent to beaches or wildlife preserves have come in for the major share of criticism. But it also extends to pulp mills, steel mills, smelters and others that pollute the air; chemical and other companies that discharge pollutants into streams and rivers; companies that package their goods in throw-away containers and so on.

Social responsibility This term covers a wide variety of pressures on corporations on the part of various political and religious groups. It should be remembered that educational and charitable institutions and foundations of various sorts hold millions of shares of stock in American corporations. Pressure is put on these institutions to exert influence in two ways: In some cases institutions have voted their proxies in stockholders meetings in favor of various corporate resolutions having social goals. In the famous GM case, some institutions advocated stockholder resolutions that would forbid the company to do business in South Africa and would require certain quotas for hiring employees from minority groups or granting them franchises. In the second instance, institutions have been pressured into investing only in the stock of companies that conform to certain criteria. Some institutions, for example, will not own stocks of liquor or tobacco companies, or those that produce weapons for the Department of Defense, or those that do business in proscribed countries, such as Rhodesia.

How much attention should the investor pay to these ideological controversies? Naturally, he wants to invest in companies that make good profits. This need not be entirely a selfish motive. Industry is the greatest source of employment and also the greatest source of revenue for the government and all the other social institutions, such as colleges and foundations. Most of the operations of the country at large are fueled by the wealth produced by industry and business. On the other hand, many analysts think that the best-managed companies are also the ones that are leaders in corporate responsibility. It would appear, then, that unless the investor is committed to certain political or religious convictions, he will make no mistake if he sticks to good-quality companies with forward-looking and responsible managements.

As an example of the attitude of an officer of such a company, B. R. Dorsey, president of Gulf Oil, has said, "Today maximum financial gain, the historical number one objective, is forced into second place whenever it conflicts with the well-being of society." And, to quote a leading investment counsel, David L. Babson, of Boston, Mass., "The companies which are the most responsive to changing social conditions are usually the best managed and turn out to be the best investments. And the least socially oriented firms tend to fall by the wayside over a period of time."

9

CHOOSING STOCKS

Picking individual stocks is the crux of investing. You can hire someone to do it for you—an investment counselor if you have $100,000 or more, or an investment company such as a mutual fund if you have less. But there is much to be said for doing the job yourself. It is challenging, it can be rewarding and you'll learn a lot.

First off, you must have an investment philosophy. No great job was ever done without a goal and a plan. Unfortunately, many people approach the market without a plan and without giving much thought to what they are trying to do. They usually have a fuzzy idea that they will somehow buy a stock that is going to go up. When it does go up, they will sell it, buy another and repeat the same pleasant experience. On a slightly more sophisticated plane, they expect to identify the low points of the market cycle, buy in then, and sell out at the highs, believing that somehow they can outwit the thousands of traders who are trying to do the same thing.

To this kind of person, stocks are simply symbols on the tape or abbreviations on the financial page, pieces of paper that are bought like lottery tickets. No one can make money in the long run by this kind of trading. Even professionals, with their charts and computers, can't do it consistently.

The sensible way to select a stock is not much different from the way you would shop for any product for which you expect to pay several hundreds or thousands of dollars. You want something of good quality that will perform well. Therefore you want to know quite a bit about it before you buy. In the case of a stock, when you buy you don't just acquire a piece of negotiable paper. You become part owner of a company that has management, employees, buildings, machinery, products and prospects for the future. It is these prospects for the future that you should be most interested in. And they are, of course, the hardest thing to measure. Here are some guidelines to help you select companies with good prospects.

Earnings growth A good company to own is one whose earnings per share of common stock may be expected to double, on the average, every five to eight years. This means a growth of 10% to 15% a year. The dividend, or yield, is less important because if earnings continue to grow, chances are the dividend will also. Some analysts express the hoped-for earnings growth in different ways. One, for example, tries to estimate the total earnings per share each year for the next ten, then adds them up and considers this to be a reasonable price to pay for the stock today.

The big problem, of course, is trying to estimate something that will happen in the future. No one knows what the future will bring forth. But one place to start is the record of past earnings. If they have been growing fairly steadily at, say, 10% a year for five or ten years, this is a good portent. You should also study the readily available information about the company's prospects. Is there anything impending that might change the trend?

Return on invested capital How much is the company earning on the money that the stockholders have put in and that it has borrowed long-term? This is not an easy calculation for the nonprofessional, but one investment analyst makes it roughly this way. He takes the total assets of the company, subtracts current liabilities, and uses this figure for the total money invested in the company. He then divides the current earnings in dollars by this total. A good return on invested capital might be expected to run from 10% to 20%.

Growth of sales A growth company naturally shows growth of sales. The figures should be examined. But remember that the proportion of these sales being converted into profit is extremely important.

Operating profit This is a ratio expressed as a percentage, obtained by dividing the company's net operating income by its net sales. Operating income is obtained by taking income from sales and subtracting operating expenses, which consist of the cost of goods sold and the selling and administrative expenses. Top-quality growth companies show not only a sales increase over the years but also an operating profit of, say, 15% to 30%. The operating profit of most listed companies is shown in Standard & Poor's Stock Reports under the heading "% Oper. Inc. of Sales."

Current assets versus current liabilities This is a ratio that analysts look at automatically. It is shown in most stock manuals. Sound companies usually have a ratio of two or three to one. Utilities can safely operate with ratios that are a great deal smaller since they have a steady and dependable income.

Equity-to-debt ratio All other things being equal, the less debt outstanding, the better for the holders of the common stock. A way to measure the debt burden of a company is to look up the dollar value of any bonds outstanding. Then look up the number of common shares outstanding, multiply this number by the market value of a share of stock to get the market value of the common stock. The equity-to-debt ratio is the value of the stock divided by the value of the bonds. Thus a company having outstanding $50 million of stock and $10 million of bonds would have an equity-debt ratio of five to one. Except in the case of utilities, a ratio of less than five to one would raise a question as to the quality of the company. Utilities, which have very steady and predictable income, habitually sell bonds for expansion money and the interest cost is taken into account in the setting of rates. Many manufacturing or service companies, it should be noted, have no debt outstanding at all.

Spending on research and development Large expenditures on R&D are the underpinning of most sustained growth. How this money is spent is also important. Generally speaking, money spent on developing new products gives more zip to growth than money spent on improving methods or existing products. Most iron and steel companies, for example, say the main purpose of their R&D spending is to improve existing products. But 70% of chemical companies say the main object of their programs is to create new products. One measure of the effectiveness of R&D, then, might be the proportion of a company's sales accounted for by new products.

Freedom from competition No company is completely free from competition. But a fast-growing, imaginative company often can develop so many new products and ideas that it can keep out ahead of the crowd. Such a company is like a football player who manages to get into the clear with the ball. The first few companies into a brand-new industry obviously have a wide field for growth. But remember, the newer the field or the product, the more risk is involved.

Low labor costs Since wages are the fastest-growing cost that companies have to bear, those that have been able to replace human toil with machines have an advantage in keeping costs down. A whole growth industry has been built up to fill industry's demand for laborsaving machinery.

Price flexibility Price controls combined with rising costs squeeze profits. Companies in the big basic industries with publicly posted prices are most likely to feel this squeeze. Yet there are degrees of controls. Utilities, especially in fast-growing areas —usually states where governments are keen for new industry— are generally allowed rate increases that permit an adequate and rising level of profits. Companies that produce consumer goods in small packages or provide services are least likely to come under rigid control of prices. But remember the other two great levelers of prices: competition and overproduction. For years the chemical companies suffered from both these ills despite research, development and new products galore.

Over-all quality This is hard to measure. It is a compounding of the characteristics mentioned above plus an indefinable aura of competence and success. Management should be young and aggressive, although the officers need not be young in years. Does the president of the company have a record of moving from one company to another; in other words, is he advancing himself? Or is he mostly interested in advancing the company? Do the officers and directors own stock in the company themselves? Is the company outstanding in its industry or field—a leader? What is the reputation of the products or services it sells? How do the advisory services rate its quality—excellent, speculative or what? Standard & Poor's *Security Owner's Stock Guide,* for example, rates companies as to stability and growth of earnings and dividends as follows: A-plus (highest); A (high); A-minus (above average); B-plus (average); B (below average); B-minus (low); C (lowest).

EXAMPLES OF COMPANIES TO LOOK INTO

The next chapter consists of a list of companies that have some or most of the characteristics mentioned above. It is not a recommended list by any means. But it is made up of companies that outstanding investment counseling firms, mutual funds and other large institutions—especially those that are growth-oriented—have judged to be promising enough to acquire and hold. It is basically a list to browse through and from which to pick perhaps ten or fifteen companies for further examination. The final choice must depend on the investor's situation and the conditions at the time he is ready to invest.

10

EXAMPLES OF INDUSTRIES AND COMPANIES

This chapter contains a very broad list of companies of the types that have been described in general terms in Chapters 8 and 9. Since there are over 200, this, obviously, is not a recommended portfolio or anything like it. The list merely encompasses a great many stocks that outstanding investment counselors have found attractive in the light of today's conditions and prospects. Thus, the list offers candidates for a possible portfolio. Which stocks you might choose will depend on many factors, not the least of which is each stock's prospects and price-to-earnings ratio when you happen to be reading this book!

You will notice that the companies have been grouped into industries. But there is too much crossover to permit any neat compartmentation. If you are looking for a company strong on pollution control, you might pick one of the smaller companies listed under the heading of environment, or you might prefer a bigger company, such as Merck, listed under drugs, that has strong pollution-control divisions, such as Calgon, Baltimore Air Coil and

Pacific Pumping. Some oil and paper companies are also real estate developers. Minnesota Mining and Manufacturing turns out so many kinds of products that it is almost impossible to classify. So it is best to use the industry classifications loosely and to judge each stock only after reviewing its products and prospects. Note, also, that most industry groups are split into two sections, A and B. This is simply an effort to indicate that some stocks in each group are thought to be superior by some investment counselors. "Superior" in this sense does not refer to quality alone but also to growth prospects. In other words, some group A stocks could be riskier than those in Group B. To many experts, the separation will seem arbitrary, but this is inevitable.

Keep in mind two other aspects of the list: Most of the stocks in the newer industries, such as environment, business services and recreation, are relatively small, and many are not comparable in quality to the large, seasoned and really top-quality companies listed in older and larger industries, such as office machines, consumer products and so on. Note, also, that both the industries and the companies are listed alphabetically.

The author is indebted to Standard & Poor's Corporation, 345 Hudson Street, New York, N.Y. 10014, for permission to excerpt the descriptions of companies from S & P's three sets of stock reports covering the New York Stock Exchange, the American Exchange and the over-the-counter market. Excerpts were made as of June 1972. Since these reports are revised four times a year, reference should be made to the most recent reports for more detailed and up-to-date information. Information has been obtained from sources believed to be reliable, but its accuracy and completeness and that of the opinions based thereon, are not guaranteed.

AUTOS

GROUP A

Monroe Auto Equipment NYSE. Sales $114 mil. Largest producer of auto shock absorber replacements. Also makes Load-Leveler stabilizing units as well as shock-absorbing equipment for railroad coaches, street cars, subway cars, locomotives, freight cars, tractor seats, airplane landing gear, automatic pinsetters, washing machines and dryers and outboard motors.

GROUP B

General Motors NYSE. Sales $18,752 mil. Largest producer of autos, trucks, buses and parts, this giant company also makes Frigidaire appliances, diesel and aircraft engines, locomotives, earth-moving equipment as well as products for space and defense.

Goodyear Tire & Rubber NYSE. Sales $3,195 mil. The world's largest rubber company manufactures new tires and tubes, retreads, repair materials, wheels, rims, automotive belting, hose, molded parts, foam, auto accessories, and products for defense and aviation industries. The company also buys consumer products for resale in its retail outlets.

BUILDING AND HOMES

GROUP A

Fleetwood Enterprises NYSE. Sales $154 mil. Produces mobile homes under brand names of Fleetwood, Broadmore, Festival and Barrington; travel trailers under the brand names of Terry, Prowler and Taurus; Pace-Arrow motor homes. The company also produces modular homes and modular home community developments.

Hobart Manufacturing NYSE. Sales $212 mil. Manufactures food machines, dishwashers, scales and packaging machines. Products for commercial use include coffee mills, food mixers, vegetables peelers, food cutters, meat and vegetable slicers, dish and glass washers, food-waste disposers, computing and noncomputing scales, systems for automatically weighing, computing, printing price labels and packaging foods, meat saws, meat tenderizers, patty molding machines, meat-fat testing devices, reach-in and walk-in refrigerators, high-speed steam-cooking equipment and medical and dental sterilizers. The company also makes Kitchen-

Air home dishwashers, food-waste disposers, food preparers and coffee mills.

Kaufman and Broad NYSE. Sales $152 mil. Major producer of mostly low-to-moderate-priced housing on its own developments in the areas of Los Angeles, Detroit, Chicago, San Francisco-Oakland-San Jose, New York-New Jersey, Paris, France, and Toronto, Can. Company also owns Nation Wide Cablevision, Inc., serving West Coast homes. It also manufactures mobile homes.

Lowe's Companies Over-the-counter. Sales $170 mil. Operates a chain of retail and wholesale stores, mostly in the Southeast, offering, at discount prices, building supplies, such as lumber, roofing, paint, heating equipment, plumbing and electrical supplies and builders' hardware; also consumer goods, such as refrigerators, television sets, sporting goods, lawn mowers and cooking utensils. Also sells mobile homes.

MGIC Investment NYSE. Leading private insurer of conventional residential mortgages, particularly those made by savings and loan associations.

Rouse Over-the-counter. Sales $36 mil. Develops commercial and residential real estate, such as shopping centers, office buildings, new self-contained cities, such as Columbia between Washington, D.C. and Baltimore, Md. Owns a mortgage banking company and an insurance agency.

GROUP B

Ceco NYSE. Sales $189 mil. Makes steel forms for concrete construction, reinforcing bars and steel joists, erects metal buildings, metal lathes for plastering, eaves, troughs, and steel and aluminum roofing and siding. Produces its own steel in electric furnaces.

International Paper NYSE. Sales $1,841 mil. World's largest paper producer. Makes pulp, containerboard, bleached board, newsprint, printing, writing and other bleached papers. The Long-Bell division produces lumber, plywood and insulating and building boards. Davol, Inc., another subsidiary, produces health supplies, including nonwoven fabrics for nurses and surgical gowns, patient drapes and other fabrics and reinforced tissue laminates. The company also makes facial and bathroom tissues, napkins, kitchen towels and disposable diapers. American Central Corp. develops and markets vacation homes and sites. Spacemakers is a designer and producer of leisure homes and condominiums.

Trane NYSE. Sales $258 mil. Manufactures air-conditioning equipment for homes and small industrial and commercial establishments: mobile air-conditioning equipment for trains, buses and aircraft; convectors, blowers, evaporators and condensers. Also serves the truck-trailer refrigeration field.

Weyerhauser NYSE. Sales $1,299 mil. Largest manufacturer of timber products, including lumber, plywood, particleboard and paneling. Also produces pulp, paper, paperboard, shipping containers and cartons, including corrugated shipping containers and milk cartons. Company operates a shelter division to develop land holdings, construct homes and provide mortgages.

BUSINESS SERVICES

GROUP A

Allied Maintenance NYSE. Operating revenue $69 mil. Provides maintenance and cleaning services for businesses, banks, buildings and specialized aviation services, including fueling of aircraft, ramp services, storekeeping of aircraft parts, etc.

ARA Services NYSE. Gross revenue $716 mil. Provides food and vending services to industrial plants and offices, schools, colleges, hospitals, airlines, travel and recreation facilities.

Automatic Data Processing NYSE. Sales $49 mil. Provides computerized data processing services for business, including payrolls and accounts receivable and bookkeeping for brokerage houses. Also provides services in graphic arts reproduction; publishes medical and scientific information, investment advisory information and handles personnel employment management.

Commerce Clearing House Over-the-counter. Annual income $52 mil. Publishes and distributes manuals and reports on taxes and business law and related subjects.

Dun & Bradstreet NYSE. Operating revenue $356 mil. Publishes business information and makes credit reports. Products include telephone directories, direct mail marketing and Moody's

Investors Services. The company also collects commercial accounts, publishes two business-management magazines and offers correspondence courses. A subsidiary, Fantus Co., makes economic and plant location studies. Another, Thomas Y. Crowell, publishes juvenile, college, reference, trade and paperback books. Corinthian Broadcasting owns and operates TV stations and publishes the Funk & Wagnalls encyclopedias.

Leaseway Transportation NYSE. Sales $251 mil. Operates through 150 subsidiaries, which run freight-trucking lines and lease trucks to others. One subsidiary, Anchor Motor Freight, has only one customer, General Motors, for which it transports autos.

Manpower NYSE. Sales $99 mil. Largest company providing temporary personnel help services for businesses, principally on an hourly, daily or weekly basis. Services include typing, secretarial work, filing, switchboard work, calculating, invoicing, bookkeeping, payroll preparation, mailing-list maintenance, addressing, mimeographing, packaging, etc. The industrial division offers warehouse work, loading and salvage operations, landscaping, home maintenance, inventory taking, car washing and parking, messenger and janitorial work. The company also provides sales, tax, printing and teaching services.

Peterson, Howell and Heather Over-the-counter. Sales $14 mil. Provides specialized management services for corporate fleets of vehicles, mainly automobiles. This includes purchasing cars for clients, selling used vehicles at replacement time, providing automobile expense-control reports and furnishing advice relating to financing, care and maintenance of cars. Company also handles leases between financial institutions and lessees. Reports are prepared on nonautomotive and entertainment expenses of field representatives for clients and statistical reports on car-repair incidence and expenses for auto manufacturers. Provides a purchase program for replacement tires and snow tires. Offers fuel purchase and billing service. A subsidiary offers house-hunting and related services for relocated personnel.

Prentice-Hall AMEX. Sales $128 mil. Publishes loose-leaf information on law, taxes, real estate, insurance; college texts, industrial, technical and vocational books; fiction, biography, travel and sport books and books of general interest; leaflets and booklets of an inspirational character for distribution by employers to employees; materials for supervisory, office and sales training.

GROUP B

Alexander and Alexander Over-the-counter. Revenues $53 mil. Acts as broker or agent to provide a wide variety of insurance services largely to business customers, including casualty, liability, property and marine insurance; does actuarial consulting; designs employee benefit and pension plans, etc. Also handles individual and group life, accident and hospitalization programs.

Brink's Over-the-counter. Annual sales $74 mil. Operates armored carrier service for transportation of money and securities for banks and other financial institutions in the U.S. and a limited number of foreign companies. Over three-quarters of the company's common stock is owned by Pittston Co., which is listed on the NYSE.

Marlennan NYSE. Income $159 mil. Operates insurance brokerage and agency businesses for all types of insurance and reinsurance for industrial, mercantile, utility and transportation companies and financial institutions. Company also owns Putnam Management Co., which is the adviser and manager of the Putnam group of eight mutual funds. Marlennan owns Marsh and McLennan, one of the largest insurance brokers in the U.S. and Canada.

A. C. Nielsen Over-the-counter. Sales $106 mil. Provides consumer-marketing services for manufacturers, such as point-of-sales information through cross-section samples of retail stores; a measurement of television audiences based on Audimeters connected to TV receivers in a selected sample of homes; and coupon redemption services for manufacturers and retailers. Also prepares statistical analyses of consumer response to product promotions; through an inquiry service helps magazine readers locate stores carrying advertized items; furnishes subscription fulfillment services for consumer magazines; furnishes the oil and gas industry with production histories to help make exploration more efficient; conducts custom-designed research on marketing problems and policies of manfacturers, wholesalers, retailers and transportation companies.

Pinkerton's Over-the-counter. Sales $135 mil. Provides security and investigative services for industrial, commercial and other clients, including sporting events, exhibitions, theaters and public gatherings. Provides uniformed guards and K-9 patrols using German shepherd dogs. Makes surveys and installs protection devices, such as alarm equipment.

CHEMICALS

GROUP A

Air Products & Chemicals NYSE. Sales $308 mil. Produces industrial and medicinal gases, including oxygen, nitrogen, acetylene, argon; cutting and welding torches, regulators, liquid nitrogen food freezing and rubber deflashing systems and anesthesia apparatus. Chemicals include alkylamines, anhydrous ammonia, exothermic compounds, fertilizers, fluorine, herbicides, catalysts, methanol, oxo-alcohols, pesticides, polyvinyl chloride, seeds and surfactants.

American Cyanamid NYSE. Sales $1,283 mil. This diversified company produces chemicals, drugs, fertilizers and building materials. Some of its many products include Formica, Sanitas and Wallclad wall coverings, acrylic fibers for clothing and carpets, rayon and polyester yarns for tire cord, Pine-Sol household cleaner, cosmetics and toiletries. Its Lederle Laboratories produces ethical drugs, including antibiotics, Myambutol oral antituberculosis drugs, biologicals, steroids, viral vaccines, diagnostic agents. Another division produces surgical sutures and hospital supplies. The company also is a supplier of fertilizers, animal feed supplements, pesticides and veterinary medicines. Two subsidiaries are engaged in construction of residential communities, apartments, shopping centers and office buildings.

Dow Chemical NYSE. Sales $1,911 mil. Large diversified company that manufactures over 1,100 products and services, including caustic soda, chlorine, fire retardants, solvents, fine chemicals, automotive coolants and fluids, phenol, urethane polyols, blasting agents, heat transfer agents and ion exchange resins. Among metals are primary magnesium and magnesium and aluminum mill products. The company produces plastics such as polystyrene, polyurethane, Styrofoam construction materials, saran film bags, molding and extrusion materials, coating materials, latex and packaging. Also weed, brush and grass killers, fumigants, insecticides, vaccines, feed additives and pharmaceuticals for animals. Consumer products include Saran Wrap, Handi-Wrap, Dow Bathroom Cleaner, Dow Oven Cleaner and Ziploc bags. The company also makes pharmaceuticals and biologicals. The Dowell division provides chemical service to the oil well drilling industry while the Industrial Service Division provides services in water and sewage treatment and industrial cleaning.

Lubrizol NYSE. Sales $187 mil. Developer and producer of additives to improve oil and gasoline used in various types of motor vehicles, boats and industrial motors. Additives inhibit oxidation, protect against wear and rust and so on, and are sold mainly to refineries and oil blenders.

GROUP B

FMC NYSE. Sales $1,354 mil. Manufactures machinery for food preparation and processing, agriculture and farm, pumps and waste disposal, power gardening, packaging, bulk material handling. It also makes chain for power transmissions and conveying, ball, spherical roller and sleeve bearings, speed reducers, power shovels and cranes, electromagnetic and mechanical vibratory equipment and solid-state power conversion equipment. Its American Viscose produces cellulose and synthetic fibers, yarn, staple, tire cord, cellophane and plastic packaging films, rayon cord and polypropylene strappings, microcrystalline cellulose. Other products include pulp for cellulosic fibers and films; inorganic chemicals, such as alkalis, barium, chlorine, peroxides and phosphates; organic chemicals, such as plasticizers, plastic material, phosphorous and glycerine. Also agricultural chemicals, such as industrial sulphurs and basic materials for pesticides. For the defense industry the company manufactures tracked vehicles, a deep-dive system for the Navy, shipboard gun systems, missile launching systems, patrol craft and rocket fuel.

Monsanto NYSE. Sales $2,087 mil. Produces plastics, coatings, resins, synthetic fibers, petroleum products, rubber and oil chemicals, feed ingredients, phosphates and detergents, crop protection chemicals and fertilizers.

National Starch & Chemical NYSE. Sales $149 mil. Manufactures adhesives used in packaging and paper converting, other adhesives used in packaging, woodworking, furniture plastics, building, auto and aircraft, bookbinding, shoes, luggage and insulation, makes cornstarch and other starches and dextrins, vinyl acetate polymers and copolymers. Company also produces corn oil used in food and gluten feed and meal for cattle and poultry.

NL Industries NYSE. Sales $916 mil. Formerly known as National Lead, this company produces products of which lead is the basic material, notably Dutch Boy paints. The company makes fabricated lead products, alloys, secondary or reclaimed lead and commercial grade antimony. It distributes zinc for die casting and processes precious metals for the electronic, jewelry and photographic industries. It makes precision bearings and special bearings for railroad industry, aluminum extrusions and sheet and cast aluminum tooling plates.

Also, titanium pigments, which impart whitening, brightening and hiding properties to paint, plastics and rubber; die castings of zinc, aluminum, magnesium and brass for autos, trucks, electrical appliances and office machines, anticorrosive pigments, flame retardants, castor oil derivatives and chemical specialties for the plastics, paint, ink and adhesive industries; battery oxides, custom injection moldings for office machines, autos and electrical appliances. The company supplies drilling muds and other weighted compounds to control oil and gas pressures, water treatment and corrosion inhibiting chemicals for the petroleum and pollution control industries.

The company owns the Lake View Trust and Savings Bank of Chicago.

Rohm and Haas NYSE. Sales $507 mil. Manufactures chemicals including resins for coatings, paper, varnishes, adhesives, oil and lubricants, as well as plasticizers and ion exchange resins. Products include Plexiglas for use in aircraft, signs, lighting, boat windshields, construction, auto taillight lenses and instrument panels, knobs and handles. Implex is an acrylic molding powder used in women's shoe heels, vending machines parts, etc. The company also produces chemicals for agriculture, including insecticides, miticides, fungicides, fertilizer ingredients, enzyme feed additives, antiseptics and detergents. Processing chemicals are made for the leather, textile and paper industries. Also produced are stretch fibers, nylon yarn and pharmaceuticals.

CONSUMER PRODUCTS

GROUP A

Avon Products NYSE. Sales $759 mil. Manufactures cosmetics and toiletry articles, which are sold door-to-door.

Beatrice Foods NYSE. Sales $1,827 mil. Produces dairy and other food products including milk, ice cream, yogurt, fruit drinks, candy. The company operates an institutional wholesale grocery business. Also included are home and garden accessories, recreation equipment, graphic arts, education equipment and specialty chemicals. Agri-products are sold to pet food manufacturers.

Carnation AMEX. Sales $1,148 mil. Processor and distributor of evaporated milk and other dairy products, frozen foods and instant food products, such as nonfat dry milk; operates fresh milk and ice cream plants and ice cream stores; produces packaged cereals and animal and poultry feeds. Also processes tomato, fruit and other vegetable products; produces dry and canned food for cats and dogs.

Chesebrough-Pond's NYSE. Sales $261 mil. Produces cosmetics, toiletries, fragrances, specialty foods, hospital products and proprietary medicines. Included are Vaseline Petroleum Jelly and Q-Tips Cotton Swabs as well as other medicated petroleum jellies, lip balms, cotton swabs, Pertussin cough syrup and vaporizers. Fragrances are sold under the Prince Matchabelli label and include Wind Song, Golden Autumn. Also Aziza eye make-up, Royall Lyme toiletries and Laszlo skin-care products. Hospital products include thermometers, surgical dressings and lubricating jelly. Ragu Packing Co. produces spaghetti sauces.

Circle K AMEX. Sales $94 mil. Operates convenience food stores in the West selling also alcoholic beverages, health and beauty aids, magazines and miscellaneous items. Many units also sell gasoline from self-service pumps.

Coca-Cola NYSE. Sales $1,606 mil. Largest soft drink producer, selling in the United States and 135 foreign countries, this company sells, in addition to Coca-Cola, Fresca, Tab, Fanta, Sprite and Simba. Subsidiary Minute Maid sells citrus products. The company also sells under the Snow Crop label and fruit drinks under the Hi-C label. Its food division processes, packages and distributes roasted coffee and sells tea and hot chocolate drinks and coffee-brewing equipment. The company also owns Belmont Springs Water Co., which markets bottled natural spring water, and Aqua-Chem, Inc., which produces water-purification equipment.

Colgate-Palmolive NYSE. Sales $1,210 mil. Makes toiletries and household products, over half of which are sold abroad. Household products include Ajax laundry detergents, Cold Power, Fab, Vel, Burst low-suds detergent, Axion and Ajax cleaners, Punch detergent, Palmolive Dishwashing Liquid, Baggies, Handiwipes and a food wrap, Stretch 'n' Seal. Toiletries include Colgate Dental Cream, Ultra Brite, Rapid Shave, Hour After Hour Deodorant, Brisk mouthwash, Halo, Lustre Cream and Bright Side shampoos. The company is the U.S. distributor of Wilkinson blades and razors. It also produces ethical drugs for treatment of mental depression, anemia, asthma, heart and stomach conditions.

Crown Cork & Seal NYSE. Sales $414 mil. Makes crowns, caps and other metal closures for food and nonfood products packed in glass containers, cans for the food, citrus, brewing, soft-drink, oil, paint, toiletries, drug, anti-freeze, chemical and pet food industries. Company also makes bottle washers and rinsers, bottle and can warmers, bottle fillers-crowners for beer and carbonated beverages, can fillers for beer and soft drinks, process equipment such as blenders, carbonators, coolers, deaerators and water treatment systems.

Federated Department Stores NYSE. Sales $2,358 mil. Operates over 100 general department stores and specialty shops, over 60 Ralphs supermarkets and ten discount stores all over the country. Department stores included Bloomingdale's, Abraham & Straus, Burdine's, Sanger Bros., Filene's, Bullock's and I. Magnin. Soft-goods stores include Gold Circle chain. Gold Triangle is a hard-goods discount chain.

General Foods NYSE. Sales $2,282 mil. Large producer and distributor of food and grocery products, including Post cereals, Jello-O gelatins and puddings, Gaines dog foods, Postum, Walter Baker's chocolate and cocoa, Franklin Baker's coconut, Calumet baking powder, Minute rice and tapioca, Swans Down flour and mixes, Kool-Aid soft drinks, Birds Eye frozen foods, and Maxwell House, Yuban, Sanka, Maxim and Bliss coffees. Burger Chef is a subsidiary. Viviane Woodard makes cosmetics, Kohner Bros. infant and preschool toys and games, and W. Atlee Burpee, seeds, lawn- and garden-care products.

Gerber Products NYSE. Sales $262 mil. Produces over half the baby foods consumed in the U.S., including strained and chopped vegetables, meats, soups, fruits, desserts, precooked cereals, juices, cookies, teething biscuits, egg yolks, a concentrated meat-base formula, and Modilac, a prepared milk formula. The company also makes waterproof plastic pants and bibs, stretchwear garments and nursery accessories.

Gillette NYSE. Sales $673 mil. Leading producer of razors and razor blades, home permanents, hair spray, shampoo, creme rinse, hair colorings and skin-care products under the brand names of Toni, Prom, Adorn, White Rain, Pamper, Tame, Dippitydo, Deep Magic, toiletries under the names of Right Guard, Foamy, The Dry Look, and Soft and Dri. The Paper Mate Division makes ball-point pens and refills, El Marko ink markers and Flair porous-point pens. The Autopoint Co. produces mechanical pencils, pens and other stationery items.

International Flavors & Fragrances NYSE. Sales $103 mil. Produces fragrance items used in the manufacture of soaps, detergents, cosmetic creams, lotions, powders, lipsticks, after-shave lotions, deodorants, hair preparations, air fresheners, perfumes and colognes. Flavor products are used by food and beverage industries in soft drinks, candies, gelatin desserts, cake mixes, dietary foods and dairy products as well as in pharmaceuticals, cordials and tobacco.

S. S. Kresge NYSE. Sales $2,559 mil. Operates variety stores under the Kresge name, small discount outlet stores in downtown areas under the Jupiter name and K Mart discount department stores. The company operates in Canada and Australia as well as the United States.

Examples of Industries and Companies

Nabisco NYSE. Sales $869 mil. Largest specialty baker; owns and operates biscuit and cracker bakeries, ready-to-eat cold dry cereal plants and makes Cream of Wheat.

J. C. Penney NYSE. Sales $4,151 mil. Operates Penney stores, which offer fashion and soft goods, hard lines and consumer services; makes catalogue sales; operates Treasury stores designed for self-service; food stores operated by Supermarkets, Inc.; Thrift Drugstores; sells insurance by mail; owns Great American Reserve Corp., which is engaged in insurance, banking, real estate and mutual funds.

PepsiCo NYSE. Sales $1,123 mil. Manufactures soft-drink concentrates and syrups to franchised bottlers for such products as Pepsi-Cola, Diet Pepsi-Cola, Mountain Dew, Teem and Patio. The Frito-Lay division produces snack items, including corn chips and potato chips. The PepsiCo Transportation Division owns North American Van Lines and National Trailer Convoy, a transporter of mobile homes and prefabricated building components and materials. The PepsiCo Leasing division provides leasing and financing services to third parties for electronic and office equipment and aircraft. Owns a majority interest in Wilson Sporting Goods Co.

Proctor & Gamble NYSE. Sales $3,178 mil. Largest maker of synthetic detergents, such as Tide, Cheer, Oxydol, Dreft, Dash, Joy, Ivory Liquid, Thrill; soaps, such as Ivory, Zest; cleansers, such as Comet, Mr. Clean, Spic & Span; and a fabric softener, Downy. Also produces edible products, such as Crisco shortening, Duncan Hines cake mixes, Big Top and Jif peanut butter, Folgers coffee. Toiletries include Gleem and Crest toothpaste, Scope mouthwash, Head & Shoulders and Prell shampoo; tissue-paper products, including Pampers disposable diapers.

Revlon NYSE. Sales $394 mil. Produces cosmetics and fragrances, including Ultima, Princess Marcella Borghese, Moon Drops, Natural Wonder, Norell, Réplique, Miss Balmain, Jolie Madame and Intimate. Men's scents include Pub, Braggi and Bill Blass. Products for beauty salons include hair-color preparations, furniture and equipment. Also produced are drug products; Arlidin, a peripheral vasodilator to improve blood circulation; Nitrolspan, a coronary vasodilator; Histaspan antihistamine; Liquiprin pain reliever for children; Mitchum Anti-Perspirant; Esoterica skin-toning cream and Asthma-Nefrin.

Safeway Stores NYSE. Sales $4,860 mil. Food chain operating stores mostly west of the Mississippi. Also operates, jointly with Holly Farms, a number of fried chicken outlets.

Sears, Roebuck NYSE. Sales $9,262 mil. Largest retailer of general merchandise through domestic stores and mail order. Offers Allstate property, liability, homeowners, auto and life insurance. Company also is in auto finance and motor club business, distributes a mutual fund and operates a savings and loan association.

Simplicity Pattern NYSE. Sales $85 mil. Leading manufacturer of paper patterns for women's and children's clothing; publishes *Simplicity,* a women's fashion magazine; *Modern Teacher,* for use of home economics teachers; *Simplicity Sewing Book* and *Simplicity Fashion News,* all designed to take advantage of the growing home-sewing market.

Southland NYSE. Sales $951 mil. Largest operator and franchiser of self-service convenience food stores. Processes and distributes milk, ice cream and related products; also manufactures cleansing agents, food additives, paint, industrial coatings, flavor compounds, candies, and block and processed ice. Stores go under names Pak-A-Sak; Speedee; 7-Eleven and Cabell's Minit Market.

Standard Brands NYSE. Sales $1,058 mil. Manufactures and distributes food products, such as Chase and Sanborn coffees, Tender Leaf tea, Royal desserts, Fleischmann's yeast, Planters peanuts, Fleischmann's and Blue Bonnet margarines and Hunt Club dog foods. Company also supplies coffee, yeast, corn syrups, eggs, frozen eggs, prepared fruits and other bulk food products to the restaurant, food service and bakery industries. A corn processing division sells starch, dextrins, syrup, sugar and related products to the food, confectionary, textile, paper and other industries. Chemicals include synthetic latexes and rubber, industrial adhesives, textile foam and compounds. The Fleischmann Distilling Corp. produces gin, vodka and whiskies and is the distributor for Black & White scotch in the U.S. Confectionary products include Baby Ruth, Butterfinger and Curtiss bulk candies.

GROUP B

R. R. Donnelly NYSE. Sales $331 mil. Country's largest commercial printer, prints *Fortune, Sports Illustrated* and *Time*. Also prints books including *World Book* and *Encyclopaedia Britannica*, as well as school, religious and legal books, and catalogues for such companies as Firestone Tire & Rubber, National Bellas Hess, Sears, Roebuck, Top Value Enterprises and Western Auto Supply.

Jewell Companies NYSE. Sales $1,629 mil. Operates several hundred supermarkets, mostly in the Chicago area under the Jewel Food Store name, plus Eisner Food Stores in Illinois and Indiana, Star Markets in New England, Buttrey Food Stores in Montana and Idaho, Brigham's snack-type restaurants in the greater Boston area, promotional drugstores under the Osco name, self-service family department stores under the Turn-Style Family Centers and a Direct Marketing division operating home service routes. Mass Feeding Corp. provides lunch service for elementary and junior high schools; White Hen Pantries are franchised convenience stores. The company prepares and markets sausage, ice cream, milk, tomatoes, eggs, bakery goods and aerosol items. It also has interests in Belgium and Mexico.

Kellogg NYSE. Sales $677 mil. Leading producer of ready-to-eat cereals marketed in the U.S., Canada and Mexico, including Corn Flakes, Rice Krispies, Special K, Sugar Frosted Flakes, All-Bran, Sugar Pops, Raisin Bran, 40% Bran Flakes, Sugar Snacks, Shredded Wheat, Pep Wheat Flakes, Krumbles, Corn Flake Crumbs, Cocoa Krispies, Concentrate and Stars. Newer products include Apple Jacks, Product 19 and noncereal items, such as Pop-Tarts, Frosted Pop-Tarts and Danish Go-Rounds. Salada Foods, Ltd., makes tea, baked goods and other grocery products. Fearn International, Inc., produces specialty food items for institutional and restaurant markets.

Scott Paper NYSE. Sales $746 mil. Largest producer of toilet tissues, paper towels and paper napkins. Also produces towel holders, facial tissues, wax paper, wax bags, table napkins, sanitary napkins and plastic and paper cups. The company also makes commercial printing papers, book publishing papers, converting papers for envelopes and wrappers, gummed labels, folding boxes, coating, converting and electrostatic paper and polyurethane foam. About 3 million acres of timberland are owned, managed or leased.

DRUGS

GROUP A

Abbott Laboratories NYSE. Sales $458 mil. Manufactures pharmaceuticals, hospital products, diagnostics, laboratory products and equipment, pediatric products and is in the consumer, animal health, agricultural and chemical fields. Brand names include Erythrocin and Compocillin antibiotics; Nembutal and Placidyl sedatives; Similac infant formula; Murine for eye care; Faultless hygienic rubber products; golf balls and clubs; and Sucaryl sweetener.

American Home Products NYSE. Sales $1,294 mil. Produces ethical drugs, including tranquilizers, vitamins, antibiotics, vaccines, steroids and veterinary drugs, as well as household products, housewares and foods. Some of its brand-name drugs are Anacin, Preparation H, Dristan, Kolynos toothpaste, BiSoDol, Infrarub and Dondril cold tablets, Household products include Griffin shoe polish, Wizard deodorizers, 3-in-1 Oil, Aero Shave, Aerowax, Sani-Flush, Black Flag, Easy-Off and Woolite soap. Food products include Chef Boy-Ar-Dee, G. Washington's seasoning, Franklin Dry Toasted Nuts, Jiffy Popcorn, Dennison's Hot Chili, Luck's canned foods and E. J. Brach and Sons candy. Kitchen products include utensils, aluminum food storage containers and stainless steel pots and pans under the brand names of Ekco, Flint, Geneva Forge, and Berkeley.

Bristol-Myers NYSE. Sales $991 mil. Produces toiletries and pharmaceuticals, including Bufferin and Excedrin, analgesics, Vitalis hair tonic, Ban deodorants, Pals vitamins, Sal Hepatica, Clairol hair products, Carmen and Kindness hair setters, and Luzier cosmetics, which are sold door-to-door. Abbot Tresses designs and distributes wigs. The company makes antibiotic drugs including Polycillin, Textrex tetracycline, Kantrex antibiotic kanamycin, Salutensin antihypertensive, and Naldecon, a nasal decongestant. Household products include Windex glass cleaner, Drano, Endust dusting aid and Renuzit spray starches. Mead Johnson division makes Enfamil, an infant formula, Metrecal and vitamins and other pharmaceuticals.

Eli Lilly NYSE. Sales $723 mil. Leading producer of pharmaceuticals, notably antibiotics for human and animal use and analgesics. The company also makes such drug items as antidepressants, antidiabetic agents, bulk chemicals, lawn and garden products, oral contraceptives and sedatives. The company owns Elizabeth Arden cosmetics, and another division specializes in custom packaging lines in paperboard and plastics for the electronics, automotive, textile, pharmaceutical, hardware and cosmetics industries, and the Indianapolis Stockyards, which happens to be adjacent to one of its drug facilities and which it leases to United Stockyards of Chicago.

Merck NYSE. Sales $748 mil. Leading producer of ethical drugs, including diuretics, antihypertensives, cortisone, steroids, drugs for mental depression, a nonsteroid antiarthritic drug, Sucret throat lozenges, vaccines for influenza, mumps, measles, German measles and a simultaneous treatment for rubella and mumps. The company also produces animal health and feed products. It is in the environmental field with Calgon, a maker of industrial water treatment chemicals and supplier of water-management and pollution-control services to industry, as well as Baltimore Air Coil and Pacific Pumping Co. The company spends heavily on research.

Pfizer NYSE. Sales $952 mil. Ethical drug producer that makes pharmaceuticals, including antibiotics such as Terramycin, Vibramycin, Rondomycin, Sinquan for coexisting anxiety and depression, Geopen semisynthetic penicillin, Navane for mental health, Diabinese, an oral antidiabetic, Marax for bronchial disorders and Antivert, an antinauseant. Also produces Coty fragrances and cosmetics, Leeming Pacquin health and beauty aids such as Visine eye drops, Desitin baby products, Ben-Gay ointment and the Hai Karate and Black Belt men's fragrances, Swedish Tanning Secret and Skinny Dip cologne. Also bulk penicillin, citric acid, benzoates, gluconic products, itaconic acid, caffeine, Maxatase detergent enzymes, flavoring products, lime and limestone items, talc products, iron pigments and metals for integrated circuits and cookware and refractory products for the steel industry, animal health items, feed supplements and ethical veterinary drugs.

Schering-Plough NYSE. Sales $391 mil. Produces ethical drugs, such as Garamycin antibiotic, Valisone cream and ointment for allergic and inflammatory skin conditions, Etrafon tranquilizer and antidepressant, Celestone Soluspan anti-inflammatory, Drixoral decongestant, Afrin nasal decongestant, Tinactin for athlete's foot, Coricidin for colds and A and D ointment for burns. Proprietary medicines include Di-Gel antacid, St. Joseph Aspirin, Solarcaine for sunburn, Correctol laxative and Aspergum. The company also makes Maybelline eye cosmetics, Coppertone and QT suntan products, Mexsana powder and the Sardo bath line. Household products include DAP glazing and caulking compounds, tub and tile sealants, gutter and lap sealer, waterless hand cleaner and cement patching and spackling compounds. The company also operates AM and FM radio stations and produces animal health products.

G. D. Searle NYSE. Sales $201 mil. Manufacturer of ethical drugs, including oral contraceptives Enovid, Demulen and Ovulen; Aldactone and Aldactazide for hypertension; Lomotil antidiarrhea agent; Flagyl for vaginitis and Metamucil for constipation. One subsidiary produces cattle medications and engages in artificial insemination of cattle. Another operates in the field of medical and biomedical instrumentation, including an advanced Pho/Gamma Scintillation Camera for detection of organ defects and tumors and other industrial and laboratory analytical instruments. The company also produce health testing and diagnostic systems.

Warner-Lambert NYSE. Sales $1,257 mil. Produces proprietary drugs, including Listerine antiseptic, Bromo-Seltzer and Anahist cold tablets; gums and mints including Dentyne, Chiclets, Clorets, Trident, Certs, Rolaids, Smith Brothers cough drops, Richard Hudnut and DuBarry cosmetics and fragrances. Also produces Efferdent Denture Cleanser, Pristeen feminine hygiene deodorant and Schick shave products. Parke, Davis is a subsidiary. Company also makes diagnostic reagents and blood fractions. Lactona Products division makes professional dental specialties. The Optical-Scientific group includes American Optical Co., making scientific and medical instruments, including Cool-Ray sunglasses.

GROUP B

Baxter Laboratories NYSE. Sales $188 mil. Produces intravenous feeding solutions, disposable blood containers for the collection, administration and processing of blood, disposable examination gloves, urological devices, disposable biopsy needles, disposable artificial kidney coil, heart-lung oxygenator, prescription drugs including Choloxin for reducing serum cholesterol levels and a heart-lung resuscitator. The company also makes enzymes for the drug, textile, brewing, food and dry-cleaning industries.

Smith Kline & French NYSE. Sales $357 mil. Produces ethical drugs, such as the tranquilizers Thorazine, Compazine and Stelazine; Dexedrine and Dexamyl stimulants; Eskatrol antiobesity; Cendevax German measles vaccine; and Ducon liquid antacid. Consumer products include Contac cold medicines; Sea and Ski suntan lotions; C3, a cold-cough capsule; Sine-Off, an analgesic and decongestant. The company also makes veterinary products, the Love cosmetics line and milk food products and other food products sold to airlines, supermarkets and dairy chains. Also medical services and instruments, including patient-monitoring equipment and clinical chemistry systems that perform biochemical assays. The company makes ultrasonic cleaning equipment and instrumentation for flaw detection and thickness and other testing.

Sterling Drug NYSE. Sales $652 mil. Produces ethical and proprietary drugs, such as Talwin, a nonnarcotic pain reliever; Neo-Synephrine nasal decongestant; NeGram for the urinary tract; Demerol pain reliever and Sulfamylon Acetate cream for severe burns. Also makes Bayer Aspirin; Midol, a pain reliever for menstrual distress; Cope and Vanquish for nervous tension headaches; Philip's Milk of Magnesia and Haley's M-O. Consumer products include Lysol and cosmetics such as Dorothy Gray, Tussy and Ogilvie. Other cosmetics and fragrances include Givenchy, Millot and Revillon lines. The company also produces color pigments, industrial chemicals, food enrichments and flavors and a wet-air oxidation process for disposal of organic wastes for municipalities and industry.

ELECTRICAL EQUIPMENT

GROUP A

Emerson Electric NYSE. Sales $656 mil. Manufactures electrical and electronic equipment, including motors and drives ranging from $\frac{1}{200}$th to 1,000 horsepower for such varied products as refrigerators, freezers, air conditioners, washers and dryers, ventilating equipment, pumps, heaters, tools and larger motors for industrial, commercial and agricultural use. Environmental products include items for the control of lighting, heating, cooling, sound, air distribution and temperature. In electronics and aerospace produces sensors and controls, radar and microwave equipment.

Essex International NYSE. Sales $589 mil. Manufactures wire and related electrical devices, operates a commercial trucking business and designs, produces and installs CATV systems. Customers include the auto industry, for which the company produces wiring systems, switches for turn signals, headlights, wipers and power windows; the construction, telephone and communications industries, for which it makes wire and cable products; the appliance industry, for which it makes insulated electric wire, switches, relays, thermostats and other controls.

Honeywell NYSE. Sales $1,921 mil. Produces automatic controls for residential heating and air-conditioning systems, environmental controls, security and fire protection systems; makes aerospace and defense products and systems, such as guidance and control systems for space vehicles, missiles and manned aircraft, antisubmarine torpedoes and photographic products. The company took over 81.5% control of General Electric computer operations, which makes it the third largest factor in the computer industry.

GROUP B

General Electric NYSE. Sales $9,425 mil. Largest domestic manufacturer of electrical equipment, including steam turbine generators, transformers, marine turbines and gears, gas turbines, meters, insulators, circuit breakers, batteries, capacitators, communications systems, controls, electronic tubes, industrial heating and insulating materials, medical systems, plastics, air conditioners, appliances, lamps, radio and TV receivers, stereo equipment, tape recorders, aircraft jet engines, armament systems, flight controls, missile re-entry systems, radar and space flight systems and engines for military and commercial aircraft.

General Signal NYSE. Sales $216 mil. Produces electrical, electronic, hydraulic and pneumatic control equipment, Regina vacuum cleaners, water and waste treatment products for industrial and municipal use, a process for sewage sludge treatment, hydraulic systems for farm and construction markets, fire and burglar alarms, lighting equipment, intercoms and teaching machines.

Square D NYSE. Sales $259 mil. Produces electrical control systems and control centers, motor starters, electronic welding controls and solid-state logic controls, circuit breaker and fusible load centers, safety switches, busways, wireways and underfloor ducts. The Heavy Industry Division makes crane and mill controls, high-voltage motor starters, electro lifting magnets, magnetic brakes and custom-designed controls. The company also produces switchgear, substations, switchboards, panelboards, transformers and steel transmission poles.

ELECTRONICS

GROUP A

AMP NYSE. Sales $226 mil. Manufactures solderless terminals, splices, coaxial connectors and pressure-crimping wiring tools.

Hewlett-Packard NYSE. Sales $375 mil. Manufacturer of precision electronic measuring instruments. Microwave equipment is used in research and development, production and maintenance of microwave communications, military and commercial radar, air navigation and guided missile control. Electronic counters and frequency-measurement equipment is used in electronics, nuclear science and industrial automation. Other products are oscillators, digital display tube voltmeters, oscilloscopes, graphic-recording devices, variable voltage power supplies for laboratory and engineering use, digital data and radio frequency systems, medical electronic apparatus, gas chromatographs, electronic calculators and computers.

Perkin-Elmer NYSE. Sales $171 mil. Produces laboratory analytical instruments to determine or measure the composition and molecular structure of matter, such as spectrophotometers, atomic absorption spectrophotometers, other spectroscopic instruments, gas chromatography instruments. Also a line of instruments for clinical, educational and industrial markets. Also precision optics and electro-optical systems for military reconnaissance, missile tracking, satellite surveillance, guidance alignment and astronomy, telescopes, laser reconnaissance sets. Also electronic components, digital equipment, laser products and vacuum systems, flame and plasma spray equipment for applying metals and ceramics on metals.

Tektronix NYSE. Sales $146 mil. Produces cathode ray oscilloscopes, which are testing and measuring instruments that give a visual presentation of electrical waveforms on the screen of a cathode ray tube similar to a TV receiver. Used to observe and measure electrical signals and nonelectrical phenomena that can be converted to electrical signals. Equipment is used by laboratories, computer installations, TV stations, repair shops, factory-inspection stations and missile-monitoring stations. Company also produces a line of programmable desk calculators for scientific and engineering use.

Texas Instruments NYSE. Sales $764 mil. Produces semiconductors, transistors, diodes, rectifiers and resistors. Company also sells ultrapure silicon to other semiconductor companies. Makes control devices, test equipment, recorders, petroleum-exploration instruments, minicomputers, radars for aircraft and antisubmarine warfare and air-traffic control systems. Worldwide geophysical exploration services are provided to the petroleum industry.

Varian Associates NYSE. Sales $187 mil. Produces klystron tubes and other radar-related components; microwave packages; power grid tubes; solid-state devices used in military electronics, communications and automation. Produces scientific and analytical instruments, including nuclear magnetic resonance, electron paramagnetic resonance, induced electron emission mass spectrometers, gas and liquid chromatographs, spectrophotometers, magnetometers, laboratory electromagnets and graphic recorders for the chemical, petrochemical, pharmaceutical and other industries. Also microwave processing equipment, accelerators and magnet systems used in radiation therapy and radiographic inspection; vacuum systems used in industrial coating and processing, semiconductor manufacture and testing. Produces small digital computers used in industrial processing; electrostatic writing instruments and equipment used in instructional television systems.

GROUP B

Motorola NYSE. Sales $927 mil. Largest producer of land mobile two-way radio equipment used by police, fire departments, utilities, railroads, taxis, etc. Produces closed-circuit television, microwave and remote signaling and control systems. Offers broad line of semiconductors, including diodes, transistors and digital, linear and hybrid integrated circuits. Makes black and white and color TV sets. Also, color electronic video recording Teleplayer for reproducing recorded cassettes through color TV sets. Produces sophisticated communications systems for government defense and space agencies. Also stero-tape players and radios for autos as well as solid-state ignition systems and alternators.

RCA NYSE. Sales $3,530 mil. Engaged in almost all phases of electronics; largest maker of color TV sets and major producer of black and white sets, radios, phonographs, stereo units, two- and four-channel cartridge players, records and pre-recorded stereo tape cartridges. Manufactures TV picture tubes, discrete semiconductor devices, integrated circuits and special vacuum tubes, broadcasting and communications equipment. The company makes and markets specialized data communications systems. A subsidiary, NBC, furnishes network television and radio services to independent TV and radio stations and owns and operates television, AM and FM radio stations. Electronic equipment and systems are made for military and space programs. Other subsidiaries are Random House, a book publisher, Hertz Corp., in car and truck rentals and a frozen foods producer.

Zenith Radio NYSE. Sales $573 mil. Manufactures television sets, radios, phonographs, hearing aids and television tubes for use by other manufacturers. Also medical electronics instrumentation and fuses, target detecting and safety arming devices for the military and radar and communications systems. Company has a system trademarked Phonevision that uses a decoding device connected to the TV receiver to unscramble a signal sent through the air designed for pay-TV.

ENVIRONMENT

GROUP A

American Air Filter NYSE. Sales $101 mil. Manufactures air filters, air-pollution control equipment, and air-conditioning, ventilating and heating equipment.

Beckman Instruments NYSE. Sales $137 mil. Makes analytical and test instruments for environmental monitoring and air- and water-pollution control, spectrophotometers and gas chromatographs and gas-sampling systems. Produces clinical instruments and equipment for use in medical research, such as diagnostic reagents, blood-sample analyzers, an automatic amino-acid analyzer and the Telesender, a system for transmitting electrocardiograms via telephone circuits. Laboratory research instruments include infrared, visible and ultraviolet spectrophotometers, centrifuges and gas chromotographs. Atmospheric monitoring and control products and systems are produced for space and undersea exploration and microwave technology.

Culligan International NYSE. Sales $50 mil. Makes equipment to treat water for hardness, turbidity, iron and manganese, disease-producing impurities, taste, odor, color, acid water and other contaminants. Its biggest market is for household products, but it also sells commercial and industrial products, such as softeners, deionizers, filters and deaerators.

Marley NYSE. Sales $79 mil. Manufactures water-cooling towers, such as those used by power plants to cool water discharged into streams and other bodies of water. Also engages in location, development and production of ground water and in soil engineering for public utilities, municipalities and industry.

Nalco Chemical NYSE. Sales $181 mil. Manufactures specialty chemicals for the petroleum industry but also for industrial markets, including water and waste treatments such as coagulants, coagulant aids, flocculants, corrosion inhibitors, scale preventatives, microbiocides, antifoams and ion exchange resins used in industry and municipal water and sewage treatment plants. Retention aids, antifoams, dispersants and slimicides are sold to the paper industry. Rolling oils, drawing and forming compounds, coolants, lubricants, rust preventatives, hydraulic fluids and refractories are sold to metal producers and fabricators. Other specialty chemicals include combustion aids, weed- and brush-control chemicals, textile treatments, rubber-process additives and industrial cleaners.

Research-Cottrell AMEX. Sales $103 mil. Produces air pollution control equipment, such as electrostatic precipitators, mechanical collectors, fabric filters and wet scrubbers; erects cooling towers and chimneys and provides related engineering services. Provides sewage and waste-water treatment, solid-waste disposal and architectural planning and engineering.

Zurn Industries NYSE. Sales $146 mil. Produces environmental systems and management, including valves, flow switches, hydrants, meters, retarding screening, drainage systems, strainers, filters and other water supply, waste and pollution controls. Also air and land pollution control equipment, including waste heat recovery systems, furnaces for burning noxious gases and land wastes, flyash arrestors, precipitators, fans and automatic regulators. Company also manufactures steam-generating systems for municipal and industrial electric-power generators, for heat transfer, space heating and as a heat source in desalination plants. Other products include mechanical drive flexible couplings and clutches, air-moving and ventilating systems, pipeline systems, acoustical equipment and automatic fire sprinkler systems.

GROUP B

Betz Laboratories Over-the-counter. Operating revenue $42 mil. Produces water-treatment equipment and chemical products for boilers, water-cooling and air-conditioning equipment. Also provides consulting services to industry and municipalities in connection with pollution abatement.

Buffalo Forge NYSE. Sales $59 mil. Manufactures air-handling and air-conditioning equipment, centrifugal pumps and heavy-duty machine tools. Air equipment includes blowers and fans for heating and ventilating, exhausters, coolers, dryers, humidifiers and mechanical draft apparatus. Pumps are made for marine and industrial use and for municipal water supply and sewage disposal systems. Tools include bar cutters, shears and machines that wrap and punch metal sheets or bars.

Carborundum NYSE. Sales $302 mil. A manufacturer of abrasives, this company has expanded into the pollution-control business. It produces grinding wheels, sandpaper and loose abrasives for industrial use, along with machines that use abrasive belts for grinding and finishing metallic and nonmetallic materials, also refractories and high-temperature electric heating elements for industrial furnaces. The company owns Spode, Inc., which distributes a line of fine china. Its pollution-control division makes systems and equipment for the control of air and water pollution.

Fischer & Porter AMEX. Sales $71 mil. Manufactures process-control instruments, including flow meters that measure, control and record various process variables, such as temperature, pressure, liquid level, viscosity and density for chemical, aircraft, petroleum and paper industries. Also active in water and waste treatment and electric power generation. Also in pneumatic control devices. Supplies complete systems for water filter and waste-treatment plants and chlorinating equipment to municipalities and industry.

Joy Manufacturing NYSE. Sales $301 mil. Makes mining and oil field equipment. Also produces environmental-control equipment and designs, supplies and erects air-pollution controls for the removal of particulate matter, including electrostatic precipitators, centrifugal collectors, filter systems, wet scrubbers and heat exchangers.

Neptune Meter NYSE. Sales $62 mil. Manufactures water meters and other meters used in petroleum and other industries; meter-testing equipment, automatic meter-reading and billing systems and liquid-measurement systems. Also produces meters for the gas industry and electric and gas meters involving telephonic meter reading. In environment, the company supplies equipment and complete installations for water and wastewater treatment, thermal waste-destruction units, industrial multi-hearth furnaces and spray dryers. The company also produces strain gauges for weighing and determining the center of gravity of aircraft, guided missiles, loaded railway freight cars; complicated molded electrical cable harness for jet aircraft engines and missiles; high-temperature wires and cables, and electronic warning devices for use in large construction cranes to guard against crane collapse or upset.

Peabody Gallion NYSE. Sales $59 mil. Manufactures truck equipment and garbage compaction devices, equipment for air-pollution control, water and waste-water treatment and solid-waste management. Products include wet scrubbers, centrifugal separators, efficient combustion equipment, fabric filter systems, liquid and fume incineration systems.

Rollins NYSE. Sales $127 mil. Operates largest pest-control business, the Orkin Exterminating Co. Also is in the wall-covering and decorating business, servicing retail stores, interior decorators and contractors. Operates a janitorial maintenance service for commercial buildings and an outdoor advertising business, and owns and operates AM and FM radio stations and VHF television stations. Company also owns a specialty chemical business, a data-processing service and a citrus grove.

Trans Union NYSE. Sales $255 mil. A holding company whose subsidiaries are engaged in railroad tank-car leasing, production of forgings, tank and pipe flanges, industrial and hardware fasteners; water and waste treatment for industry and municipalities; sewage-treatment plants and sewage-lift stations; commercial and domestic water softeners; liquid chemical feed pumps and water-cooling towers. A subsidiary owns three large land tracts near Los Angeles and another near Elmhurst, Ill.

U. S. Filter AMEX. Sales $31 mil. Manufactures filters for filtration of water for municipalities and industry.

FINANCIAL

GROUP A

H & R Block NYSE. Sales $62 mil. Operates income tax return services through its own offices and franchised offices. It is estimated that some 9% of total income tax returns in a given year are prepared in this manner. The company also operates schools and offers correspondence courses covering income tax subjects.

Western Bancorporation NYSE. Income $761 mil. Largest multibank holding company owning majority interests in banks in 11 western states, including the United California Bank, which, in turn, controls an international bank in New York City and a bank in Belgium.

GROUP B

Baystate Corp. Over-the-counter. Annual income $12 mil. A bank holding company that controls about a dozen small banks in the vicinity of the Boston metropolitan area.

Charter New York Corp. NYSE. Operating income $28 mil. Bank holding company that owns Irving Trust, seventh largest bank in New York City, and a number of upstate New York banks.

Cleveland Trust Over-the-counter. Net operating income $29 mil. The largest bank in Ohio serves Cleveland and northern Ohio with branch banks. Owns mortgage companies in Cleveland and Nashville, Tenn.

Society Corp. Over-the-counter. Owns banks in Ohio including Society National Bank of Cleveland.

GLASS

GROUP A

Corning Glass Works NYSE. Sales $594 mil. Produces over 60,000 products, such as TV-tube blanks, integrated circuits, resistors and capacitors, computer terminals, bulbs for lamps, reflectors and globes. Consumer products include Corningware, Centura, Pyrex and Corelle lines of heat resistant, unbreakable kitchen and tableware. The Counter That Cooks (a flat range with no external heating elements) and artistic crystalware by Steuben. The company also manufactures glass that darkens when exposed to light for use in photography and sunglasses, laboratory glassware, construction materials, aircraft windows and glass fiber optics assemblies. The company owns 28% of Owens-Corning Fiberglass, leading maker of fibrous glass, 50% of Pittsburgh Corning, which makes glass building blocks and cellular glass products, and 50% of Dow Corning, a manufacturer of silicone products.

GROUP B

Owens-Corning Fiberglas NYSE. Sales $537 mil. Leader in research and development in fibrous glass, producing Fiberglas wool for insulating homes, industrial and commercial buildings, automobiles, aircraft, refrigerators, tiles and board for acoustical insulation, textile fabrics, electrical equipment, wires and cables, plastic reinforcements with industrial, military and home applications. Produces filters for air-conditioning, heating and ventilating systems and mat products for use in storage batteries and for wrapping underground pipe. Also Fiberglas-reinforced plastic noncorrosive tanks, resins, coatings and chemical foams.

HEALTH CARE

GROUP A

American Hospital Supply NYSE. Sales $510 mil. Manufactures and distributes medical and hospital supplies, including intravenous and irrigating solutions, blood-typing serums, chemical reagents, gloves, syringes, surgical drapes, disposable trays for surgical use, laboratory and dental equipment and surgical instruments. Customers include hospitals, nursing homes, doctors' and dentists' offices, laboratories, educational institutions and blood banks.

Hospital Corp. of America NYSE. Net revenue $108 mil. Owns and operates general hospitals and performs hospital management services for others.

Johnson & Johnson NYSE. Sales $1,002 mil. Largest maker of surgical dressings and hospital products, such as ligatures and sutures, surgical instruments and specialties, Band-Aid and Johnson & Johnson lines, Red Cross tapes, Modess sanitary napkins, Meds and Carefree tampons, Micrin mouthwash, Bondex mending tape and Chux disposable diapers. McNeil Laboratories makes ethical drugs including Butisol, a sedative; Parafon, a muscle relaxant; Tylenol, an over-the-counter pain reliever; Grifulvin, an antifungal drug; Haldol, a sedative for mental patients; and Sublimaze and Innovar, used in hospital anesthesia. The company also makes birth-control pills and other contraceptives, a vaccine to prevent Rh disease in unborn infants and Sickledex, a test to detect sickle cell anemia.

Medtronic Over-the-counter. Sales $30 mil. Provides electronic medical instruments for surgical and monitoring use and artificial devices to replace internal parts of the body, the chief product being an implantable as well as a nonimplantable heart pacemaker to stimulate the heart electronically.

National Medical Enterprises AMEX. Operating revenue $26 mil. Operates general hospitals and convalescent hospitals in California.

GROUP B

Becton, Dickinson NYSE. Sales $255 mil. Manufactures medical, surgical and laboratory supplies, including reusable and disposable hypodermic syringes and needles, blood-collecting equipment, clinical thermometers, elastic bandages, blood lancets, bacteriological media, blood products, diagnostic reagents, tissue culture media, plastic laboratory ware, surgical blades, plastic medical tubing and diagnostic instruments. The company also raises laboratory animals and conducts research for others. Consumer products include an insulin syringe needle unit, Sportade action drink, vinyl gloves, Ace elastic bandages, fever thermometers and Green Thumb gardening gloves. Transducers, navigational instruments, medical electronic equipment, air-filtration systems and packaging services for cosmetic, pharmaceutical and food are also produced.

A. H. Robins NYSE. Sales $133 mil. Produces drugs for coughs, colds and respiratory ailments, including Robitussin, Robitussin-DM and Robitussin-PE, Dimetane Expectorant, Dimetapp, Dimetane and Dimacol. Donnatal is an antispasmodic drug, Donnagel, an antidiarrheal combination, and Donazyme, a digestant combination. Robaxin, Robaxisal and Skelaxin are for skeletal muscle relaxation; Allbee with C, a vitamin specialty; Robinul, an anticholingeric; Rybatran, a tranquilizer; Donnasep, a urinary antiseptic; Dopram, a respiratory stimulant; Sulla, a sulfanamide and so on. The company makes Chap Stick lip balm; Chap-ans medicated hand cream and other cosmetic, toiletry and household products. The company also produces perfumes and specialty foods, including potato chips, crackers, cookies and packaged nuts.

Rorer-Amchem NYSE. Sales $158 mil. Manufactures pharmaceutical products, including Maalox and Camalox, antacids; Quaalude, a sleep inducer; Ascriptin, a pain reliever; Parepectolin for diarrhea; Emetrol for nausea; Fermalex for iron-deficiency anemia and Neoxyn for poison ivy. Also surgical instruments and implants employed by orthopedic surgeons. The company also produces Ameben, a soybean herbicide; Weedone farm and garden herbicides, special weed killers and spray applicators. Metalworking chemicals include prepaint coatings. The company also engages in the treatment of process wastes and makes adhesives and mastic coatings used in thermal insulation.

INSURANCE

GROUP A

Pennsylvania Life Over-the-counter. Writes mostly accident and health insurance on an individual basis, concentrating on insurance against loss of income. Also writes life insurance and engages in sale of mutual fund shares.

Provident Life & Accident Over-the-counter. Writes individual and group life insurance, annuities, accident and health insurance and sells mutual fund shares.

GROUP B

Aetna Life & Casualty NYSE. A holding company, the largest investor-owned insurance enterprise operating in the life, property and liability fields. It sells variable annuities and with the Kaiser organization owns Kaiser Aetna, a real estate company.

Connecticut General Insurance Over-the-counter. This large insurance holding company owns Connecticut General Life, which specializes in reinsurance and large life policies; Aetna Insurance, which is a large underwriter of property and liability insurance; and Puritan Life, which writes group and individual life policies.

Government Employees Insurance Over-the-counter. Was formed to provide auto insurance to military and civilian government employees, but eligibility was broadened to cover professional, managerial and administrative personnel not in government service. Company also writes fire, homeowners, comprehensive personal liability and boat owners policies.

National General NYSE. Derives its major revenues from property, liability and automobile insurance, written by Great American Insurance. Publishing subsidiaries are Bantam Books and Grosset & Dunlap. NGC Theater Corp. owns theaters in the U.S. National General Pictures distributes film for Cinema Center and First Artists. Xebec Corp. is an electronics firm.

Travelers NYSE. Second largest insurance organization providing insurance to business and to individuals, including life, accident and health, property-casualty, auto, workmen's compensation and multiple peril.

LABORSAVING MACHINERY

GROUP A

Black & Decker NYSE. Sales $287 mil. Manufactures power tools and laborsaving equipment for industry, construction and home. Portable electric tools include drills, shears, nibblers, screwdrivers, impact wrenches, hammers, grinders, sanders, polishers, saws, routers, vacuum cleaners, valve refacers, valve seat grinders, lawn mowers and lawn and hedge trimmers. Portable air tools include drills, screwdrivers, nut setters, impact wrenches, die grinders, sanders, hammers, rammers and power chisels. Stationary woodworking and metalworking equipment include bench grinders, heavy-duty industrial and home workshop radial arm saws and panel saws.

Caterpillar Tractor NYSE. Sales $2,175 mil. Biggest manufacturer of earth-moving machinery, including diesel-powered crawler tractors, wheel-type tractors, bulldozers, scrapers, rippers, wagons to match wheel-type tractors, tool bars, cable and hydraulic controls, motor graders, pipe layers and traxcavators. Produces diesel engines, natural gas engines and electric generating sets. Supplies logging, oil, mining, agriculture, water-control projects and transportation. Sells worldwide. Makes Towmotor industrial and lift trucks.

Cincinnati Milacron NYSE. Sales $270 mil. Largest U.S. manufacturer of machine tools, including machines for grinding, milling, broaching, die sinking, cutter sharpening, lapping and metal forming. Its CM Chemical Division makes fluorescors, esters, lube conditioners, organo metallics, surface active agents, paint driers, plasticizers and stabilizers. The company also has entered the minicomputer field.

Clark Equipment NYSE. Sales $741 mil. Makes industrial

trucks, including fork-lift trucks, straddle carriers, towing tractors and powered hand trucks; construction machinery, including tractor shovels, bulldozers, scrapers and wagons, back-hoe loaders and logging equipment; manufactures refrigeration equipment, including food store display cases, walk-in coolers, food service equipment, condensing units, counters and shelving.

CMI AMEX. Revenues $44 mil. Produces, sells and leases construction machinery, such as sub-graders, base material spreaders and base trimmers, concrete layers, paving spreaders, asphalt pavers and precision graders. This equipment can complete up to two miles of dual-lane highway per day and is used in construction and paving of streets and airport runways. A subsidiary specializes in plant planning, plant modification, component manufacturing and custom-built plant installations. Also produces a hydraulically powered breaking and tamping machine designed for bridge and highway construction, repair and general demolition use.

Kearney & Trecker Over-the-counter. Operating revenue $36 mil. Manufactures numerically controlled machine tools that perform a wide range of machining operations, including milling, boring, drilling, threading, reaming, turning and tapping. Also makes standard milling machines that shape metals and special machines to order.

Signode NYSE. Sales $203 mil. Manufactures steel and plastic strapping and the tools and machines to use it for bonding or reinforcing shipping units, such as boxes, bales, crates, cartons and skids and to hold in place carload shipments or cargo aboard ship so as to withstand shocks. Company also makes staples and stapling equipment, nailing machines and strapping reinforced doors for retaining bulk commodities in freight cars.

Tecumseh Products Over-the-counter. Sales $388 mil. Manufactures compressors and condensing units for refrigerators and air-conditioning equipment, as well as Lauson and Power Products gasoline engines for lawn mowers, garden tillers and chain saws.

GROUP B

J. Ray McDermott NYSE. Sales $238 mil. Provides construction services for the petroleum industry, including engineering and construction of offshore drilling platforms, notably in the Gulf of Mexico; does dredging and lays pipelines in the sea and on land; drives piles and builds docks and bulkheads; designs and constructs plants to process oil, natural gas, petrochemicals and minerals; manufactures coolers and condensers for process and power plants.

Universal Oil Products NYSE Sales $318 mil. Engaged in engineering, construction, operation and maintenance services to the petroleum, petrochemical and chemical industries. Also manufactures catalysts, oxidation inhibitors, additives, antiozonants, aromatics and chemical intermediates to the petroleum, chemical, rubber, food and pharmaceutical industries. Produces tubing and aircraft seats. Makes industrial plastic laminates for electrical, mechanical, chemical and thermal applications. Supplies air-pollution control equipment, automatic chemical treatment of recirculating cooling water to prevent corrosion, scale formation or clogging; water-conditioning chemicals; acts as consultant on industrial water problems involving ground water and screens for water wells.

METALS AND MINING

GROUP A

Texas Gulf NYSE. Sales $283 mil. A leading supplier of sulphur for fertilizers and sulfuric acid, potash and superphosphoric acid. The company also mines zinc, copper and silver ore near Timmins, Ontario, Can. and produces oil and gas.

Utah International NYSE. Sales $104 mil. Engages in the mining of coal, iron ore, uranium and copper. Also dredging and California land development. Through affiliates conducts ocean shipping operations involving minerals and other bulk commodities.

GROUP B

International Nickel NYSE. Sales $789 mil. Produces about half the free world's nickel from mines in Canada. Properties also are owned in Guatemala, New Caledonia, Indonesia, Australia and the U.S. From its mines the company also produces copper, platinum, gold, iron ore pellets, cobalt and silver.

Reynolds Metals NYSE. Sales $1,093 mil. A fully integrated aluminum manufacturer that mines bauxite and makes ingot, semi-fabrications and finished products, such as sheet and plate, foil, extruded shapes and tubing, building products, cans and electric wire and cable.

OFFICE MACHINES AND EQUIPMENT

GROUP A

Avery Products NYSE. Sales $128 mil. Largest producer of self-adhesive labels and material for making them, as well as marketing tickets, tags and labels. Included are highway signs, emblems and decorative items for the graphic arts trade. The company produces equipment and systems for attaching labels and price markings, including a system for packaging luncheon meats.

Electronic Data Systems NYSE. Sales $74 mil. Designs, installs and operates electronic data-processing systems, including computers, for health care institutions, insurance companies, banking and other financial institutions and consumer-product companies. The distinguishing characteristic of this company is that it operates its systems for the customer.

IBM NYSE. Gross income $8,274 mil. Largest manufacturer of business machines. Makes computers for business, science and the military, electrostatic copiers, electric typewriters, dictating machines, magnetic tape typewriters, and cold-type composing equipment.

International Tel & Tel NYSE. Sales $6,131 mil. This large and widely diversified company produces telecommunications equipment, primarily in Europe, makes consumer electrical and electronic products including color TV, operates telephone companies in Latin America and has subsidiaries: Continental Baking, Throp Finance, Sheraton Corp., Levitt & Sons, Avis car rental system, Hartford Fire Insurance Company and other activities including mutual fund management. The company also supplies services and equipment to the defense and space industries in air navigation and communications. A subsidiary, Rayonier, produces chemical cellulose and lumber, while Pennsylvania Glass Sand produces silica.

National Cash Register NYSE. Sales $1,466 mil. Largest maker of cash registers; also produces bookkeeping, accounting and adding machines, computers and other business equipment. A subsidiary, Electronic Communications, designs, develops and manufactures electronic communication systems, subsystems and equipment, flight instruments and metal products for the military. Company also produces business supplies, including paper and magnetic tape, inks, continuous computer forms and carbonless paper.

Xerox NYSE. Sales $1,719 mil. Leading maker of xerographic and photocopying products. Also produces the Telecopier, which transmits and receives documents over normal telephone circuits; a printer that xerographically enlarges microfilm images onto ordinary paper; a viewer and hard-copy printer for microfilm. Company also produces education material including textbooks through Ginn & Co., periodicals, microfilm and learning products. Also computers and computer applications including timesharing for remote users.

GROUP B

Burroughs NYSE. Sales $932 mil. Makes adding, calculating and cash register machines, accounting machines, tape-perforating equipment, magnetic ink encoding equipment, electronic data-processing systems including computers and minicomputers, high-speed printers, card readers and punches, magnetic-tape readers, disc files, imprinters and encoders. The company also produces business forms and supplies for use with its various machines and systems.

Pitney-Bowes NYSE. Sales $301 mil. Sells and, in some cases, leases, letter-opening machines, a post-office canceling machine and parcel post meter, equipment for automatically facing and canceling mail, and a Tickometer, which counts and imprints tickets. Also manufactures coupons and sales slips, machines for folding letters and circulars, addresser-printer systems, electronic scanners, a meter system for paying federal documentary taxes, collators, price tags and labels, printed credit cards and desk-top copiers and computerized cash registers.

OILS

GROUP A

Arkansas Louisiana Gas AMEX. Revenue $235 mil. Produces natural gas, oil and extracted products and provides natural gas utility services to communities in Arkansas, Oklahoma, Louisiana, eastern Texas and Kansas. Also produces heating and air-conditioning equipment and cement products.

Continental Oil NYSE. Operating income $3,051 mil. Large crude oil producer and integrated marketing company, owns one-third interest in Oasis Oil Co. of Libya and about 55% of Hudson's Bay Oil & Gas Co. in Canada. Also owns Consolidation Coal Co. and makes chemicals and plastics.

Gulf Oil NYSE. Gross operating income $5,940 mil. International oil company with holdings in Kuwait, Venezuela, Iran, West Africa and Canada. Manufactures a wide range of organic, inorganic and specialty chemicals.

Louisiana Land and Exploration NYSE. Operating income $135 mil. Holds oil and gas properties from which it receives royalties and also develops oil and gas wells itself or in joint programs with others. Operations are in offshore Louisiana and in Texas, Mississippi and Alabama, as well as in Florida, Kentucky, Montana, New Mexico and Alaska.

Exxon Corporation NYSE. Gross operating income $18,701 mil. World's leading petroleum enterprise, accounting for about 15% of free world's crude oil production. Sells under the Exxon brand name. Has interests in pipelines and chemical production.

Texaco NYSE. Gross operating income $7,529 mil. Second in size among domestic refining oil companies and an important factor in the world petroleum industry. Also produces chemicals and petrochemicals.

GROUP B

Hudson's Bay Oil & Gas AMEX. Operating revenue $84 mil. Company acquires petroleum natural gas rights in Canada and explores for and develops hydrocarbons; is a major producer of crude oil, natural gas liquids and natural gas in Canada; also produces sulphur and is engaged in transportation, purchase and sale of crude oil and natural gas liquids and engages in mineral exploration.

Kerr-McGee NYSE. Gross operating income $603 mil. An integrated oil and gas producer that also does contract drilling in off-shore areas of Texas and Louisiana. Produces uranium nuclear fuels, potash, supplies railroad ties and other forest products, produces plant food, farm chemicals and coal.

Pennzoil United NYSE. Sales $731 mil. Produces, refines and markets oil, gas and petroleum products; operates natural gas transmission and distribution lines serving parts of Texas, Louisiana, Mississippi, Alabama and Florida; is a leading producer of Pennsylvania Grade crude oil; has interests in copper, molybdenum, sulphur and potash production.

Phillips Petroleum NYSE. Gross operating income $2,363 mil. Produces crude oil, natural gas, natural gas liquids, petrochemicals including synthetic rubber, Phiblack, butadiene, plastics, polyethylenes, polypropylene, fertilizers and other chemicals, paperboard and plastic containers. Markets Phillips 66 gasoline and oil products through retail service stations.

Royal Dutch Petroleum NYSE. Gross operating income $4,499 mil. A holding company that owns 60% of the Royal Dutch Shell Group, which, in turn, produces, transports, refines and markets petroleum products including petrochemicals, natural gas and so on. The group holds a strong position in foreign areas where petroelum consumption is increasing rapidly.

Standard Oil of California NYSE. Gross operating income $5,143 mil. International oil company that sells domestically and abroad through Chevron service stations.

Tenneco NYSE. Operating revenue $2,841 mil. Company operates natural gas pipeline systems; produces oil, and natural gas, industrial chemicals, polyethylene, foam and fabrics; is engaged in the machinery, equipment and shipbuilding businesses; owns Packaging Corp. of America, which produces paperboard and packaging; and is engaged in land-use operations.

RECREATION

GROUP A

Acushnet Over-the-counter. Annual sales $52 mil. A rubber company whose golf division provides a large share of net income. Golf products include golf balls under trade names of Titleist, Finalist and Club Special, Acushnet golf clubs and bags and Golcraft apparel. Rubber products used in brakes, power-steering units and windshield-washing and wiping devices are supplied to the auto industry.

Bell & Howell NYSE. Sales $298 mil. Produces cameras, business machines, educational equipment and electronic instruments. Recreation products include 8 mm, Super 8 and 16 mm cameras and projectors and 35 mm slide projectors; audio equipment such as cassette tape recorders and magnetic tape. The company also markets Japanese photographic products. Educational equipment includes textbooks and audio-tapes. The company operates schools offering programs in electronics engineering technology. Business equipment includes micro-imaging products, such as endorser-imprinters and microfiche cameras and readers, mail-handling equipment, motion-picture systems for airlines and 16 mm theaters, duplicating and copying machines, recording oscillographs, modules for analog computers, high-contrast chromium photoplates and special control valves.

Coleco Industries NYSE. Sales $36 mil. Makes above-ground, steel-wall swimming and wading pools, filters, Ping-pong tables, basketball backboards, low-priced pool tables, and toys such as action games. The company also produces polyethylene plastic wading pools, sandboxes, play boats, sleds and toboggans.

Coleman AMEX. Sales $144 mil. Produces outdoor recreation products including camping equipment, such as gasoline and LPG lanterns, gasoline and LPG camp and picnic stoves, portable coolers and picnic jugs, portable catalytic heaters, tents and sleeping bags and camping trailers, snowmobiles. Also makes heating, air-conditioning and associated equipment for mobile, modular and residential homes, light commercial buildings and recreational vehicles. Also CO_2-powered guns, fluorescent and incandescent lighting fixtures, compressors, water pumps and accumulator tanks for recreational vehicles.

Walt Disney Productions NYSE. Total income $176 mil. Produces motion pictures for world-wide distribution, operates amusement parks, produces television films.

Eastman Kodak NYSE. Sales $2,976 mil. Largest producer of cameras, including the Instamatic line, and photographic supplies, including films, still and movie cameras and projectors and equipment and supplies for photofinishing, the graphic arts and office copying. Synthetic fibers include Kodel polyester used in clothing and Verel modacrylic for carpets and draperies. The company also makes plastics and chemicals, military items including fire-control instruments, fuses and instrumentation tapes, vitamins, food additives and lasers.

Holiday Inns NYSE. Total revenues $605 mil. Operates the largest chain of motor hotels, manufactures furniture and equipment for restaurants, hotels, offices and institutions, provides food services for industrial customers and owns Continental Trailways and Delta Steamship Lines.

Host International NYSE. Sales $112 mil. Operates dining rooms, restaurants, cafeterias, coffee shops, airline clubs and inflight catering, cocktail lounges, hotel and other facilities serving food and beverages to the traveling public. The company also sells gift merchandise and periodicals at food establishments and gift shops and stands. Jim Dandy Fast Food division operates retail fried chicken outlets, and the company also operates Charley Brown's restaurants in California.

Howard Johnson NYSE. Total revenues $299 mil. Operates restaurants and motor hotels, including Red Coach Grills; sells frozen and packaged foods, ice cream, soft drinks; leases and sells restaurant and motor-lodge equipment and furnishings.

McDonald's Corp. NYSE. Sales $193 mil. Develops, operates, licenses and services a chain of some 1,900 self-service restaurants specializing in hamburgers, cheeseburgers, french fried potatoes, milk shakes and soft drinks.

McCulloch Oil AMEX. Revenues $78 mil. Developer of commercial, residential, recreational and resort communities in Lake Havasu City, Ariz.; Pueblo West, Colo.; Holiday Island, Ark.; Fountain Hills, Ariz., and Spring Creek, Nev. Company also holds interest in oil wells and participates in development of exploratory wells, owns interests in or operates gas-processing plants, owns and operates gas-transmission lines, owns coal mines and provides advertising, art and editorial services to newspapers. McCulloch International Airlines is a certified supplemental carrier.

Outboard Marine NYSE. Sales $353 mil. Produces outboard motors under Evinrude and Johnson trade names, inboard-outboard drives for boats, three- and four-wheel-powered vehicles under the Cushman name, including light industrial carriers, golf carts and pleasure scooters, Lawn-Boy power lawn mowers and garden implements, Pioneer chain saws, Ryan turf maintenance equipment, Evinrude and Johnson snowmobiles.

Polaroid NYSE. Sales $444 mil. Produces cameras and films that permit on-the-spot development and printing of pictures by dry process. Colorpack cameras are made for the company by outside manufacturers. The company spends heavily on research, most of which relates to the field of one-step photography, black and white, and color.

GROUP B

American Television & Communications Over-the-counter. Annual revenues $11 mil. Operates over 60 CATV systems in 25 states.

AMF NYSE. Sales $636 mil. Produces automated labor-saving machinery for the tobacco, clothing, tire-retreading and food-processing industries. Makes electrical products including switches, a device for inspecting gas and oil pipelines, emergency power equipment and electronic timing devices. Other products include rail car tanks, noise-abatement products, filters and strainers for liquids and gases, water-distillation machinery and high-speed welding equipment.

In the recreation field, the company makes automatic bowling equipment and accessories, including pinspotters, bowling lanes, pins, balls, bags and shoes. Also bicycles, sailboats, snowmobiles, golf clubs and carts, billiard tables and Harley Davidson motorcycles. The Head Ski division produces skis and tennis, archery, track and field equipment as well as sportswear.

Brunswick NYSE. Sales $514 mil. Produces leisure, health and science products. Recreation products include Mercury outboard motors, bowling centers, many of which the company operates, Brunswick and MacGregor brand products for golf, fishing, baseball, football, basketball and other sports. Medical products include disposable hypodermic needles and syringes, plastic surgical tubing, prepackaged medical procedure kits and computerized diagnostic instruments used for treating cardiac patients. The company also makes missile components for the defense industry.

Cox Cable Communications AMEX. Operating revenues $13 mil. Engaged in community antenna television, having investments in over 30 CATV systems across the U.S., the largest in San Diego. The company is a 56%-owned affiliate of Cox Broadcasting Corp.

Hyatt Over-the-counter. Gross income $125 mil. Operates a chain of hotels and motels mostly in California. Also operates Du Par's restaurants in Los Angeles.

Mattel NYSE. Sales $358 mil. Largest manufacturer of toys, including Barbie dolls, Hot Wheels racing cars and tracks, Sizzlers (miniature racing cars), education and preschool toys such as the Mattel-O-Phone, Talking Storybooks, Talking Picture Puzzles, Talking Clocks and a line of talking toys featuring Dr. Seuss characters, Monogram Model plastic model kits, aquariums and pet supplies and foods. Company also makes playground equipment, audiomagnetic tape and cartridges, cassettes and reels, family motion pictures, and owns Ringling Bros.-Barnum & Bailey Combined Shows, Inc.

Ramada Inns NYSE. Gross revenues $89 mil. Owns, operates and licenses others to operate motor hotels. The company also owns general hospitals, convalescent centers, medical office buildings, laboratories and pharmacies. Through a joint venture with The Bryn Mawr Group, Inc., the company is engaged in the recreational vehicle park field. A nitrogen reduction plant is leased to W. R. Grace & Co.

Rank Organisation Over-the-counter. Sales $449 mil. Leading motion picture enterprise in the United Kingdom, managing theaters in Britain and other countries; also operates hotels, restaurants, recreational facilities; operates film studios and laboratories and produces and exhibits movies. Also owns jointly with Xerox Corp., Rank Xerox, which has rights for making and distributing Xerox duplicating computer, office and medical equipment in the eastern hemisphere. Rank also makes scientific instruments, electronic equipment, color televisions and radios.

RESEARCH

Minnesota Mining and Manufacturing NYSE. Sales $1,829 mil. Spends heavily on research, which it translates into profitable products. Originally in the sandpaper and abrasive business, the company has diversified and produces a wide list of products, including Scotch and Magic Mending brand tape, surgical tapes, pressure-sensitive tapes for industrial use, drugs for relief of bronchial asthma, anticoagulants, muscle relaxers, pain relievers, etc., Thermo-Fax duplication products, paper products, microfilm cards and machines, electrical tapes, magnetic recording and instrumentation tapes, magnetic tapes used in space programs, ceramics, abrasives, adhesives, coating and sealers. An advertising subsidiary sells highway, shopping center and point-of-purchase advertising displays as well as Scotchlite reflective sheeting.

UTILITIES

GROUP A

Allied Telephone Over-the-counter. Annual operating revenues $10 mil. Serves parts of Arkansas, Missouri, Oklahoma and a small portion of Texas. Territory includes an area served by the recently opened inland waterway via the Arkansas River that connects Tulsa with the Gulf of Mexico. Through subsidiaries, the company manufactures telephone and CATV equipment.

Florida Power NYSE. Operating revenues $177 mil. Serves west coast of Florida from the St. Petersburg area north to the Georgia line and through the central area to Lake Placid.
Houston Natural Gas NYSE. Revenues $244 mil. Distributes natural gas to retail customers along the Gulf Coast area of Texas and provides wholesale gas service to utilities, pipelines and other companies for resale. Owns Liquid Carbonic Corp., supplier of carbon dioxide and other compressed gases. The company participates with Combustion Engineering and Ranchers Exploration & Development in exploration for uranium.
Texas Utilities NYSE. Operating revenues $453 mil. Through three subsidiaries furnishes electricity to an area in central and eastern Texas, including the cities of Dallas, Fort Worth, Wichita Falls, Tyler and Waco.
Virginia Electric & Power NYSE. Sales $375 mil. Provides electricity to most of Virginia, an adjoining small area in West Virginia and northeast North Carolina. Also provides gas service in the Hampton Roads area.

GROUP B

Florida Power and Light NYSE. Operating revenues $485 mil. Serves most of the east coast of Florida, with the exception of the Jacksonville area, but including Miami, Fort Lauderdale, Miami Beach, West Palm Beach, Daytona Beach, Hialeah, Coral Gables, Hollywood and Sarasota.
Houston Lighting & Power NYSE. Operating revenues $283 mil. Supplies electricity to south central Texas, including the ports of Houston and Galveston and an area containing widely diversified manufacturing, including production of magnesium sulphur, salt, natural gas, petroleum, oil tools, ships, steel, cement, paper, synthetic rubber, chemicals, building materials and food products. Agriculture in the area includes growing of cotton, rice, cattle and livestock feeds. In addition, there are numerous space-oriented firms established in the vicinity of the National Aeronautics and Space Administration's Manned Spacecraft Center.
Oklahoma Gas and Electric NYSE. Electric revenues $156 mil. Supplies electricity to Oklahoma and western Arkansas.
Southern Co. NYSE. Sales $822 mil. A utility holding com-

pany that controls Alabama Power, Georgia Power, Gulf Power, Mississippi Power and Southern Electric Generating Co., which supply electricity to a growing and diversified area covering parts of Alabama, Georgia, Mississippi and northwest Florida.

Tampa Electric NYSE. Operating revenues $101 mil. Supplies electricity to Tampa, the largest city of the Florida west coast and about 45 adjacent communities.

11

WHERE TO GET HELP AND INFORMATION

Before you can make an intelligent selection of a common stock, you need basic information. And most people want more—evaluations, judgments, recommendations. This is only natural. When you go into a hardware store, you expect the salesman to tell you something about the products he offers. The same goes for a women's dress shop, a shoe store and so on. But when it comes to stocks, you should be very skeptical about the advice you receive.

The stock market is compounded of so many ingredients that even its over-all course—the average of all prices—is completely unpredictable. And the future price action of any individual stock is more so. It is hard enough to forecast correctly the fundamental status of the economy. Even if your prediction of business conditions were to be accurate, the stock market doesn't go up and down with business conditions. Buyers and sellers have their own peculiar psychological motivations. They are trying to outguess each other and the public. Stocks very often go down on good news and up on bad news. Though the averages have historically anticipated changes in business conditions by about six months, these same averages make a lot of other sharp moves up and down that cannot be ascribed to any identifiable cause. In short, the market moves erratically a lot of the time. No one has been able to predict market movements consistently, and probably no one ever will.

Stock guides and reports The fact remains that the investor must get information and help from somewhere. Factual information comes from manuals, financial publications and annual or quarterly reports from companies themselves. Opinions and advice come from advisory services and from brokers. There is an overlap there. Some manuals also rate stocks as to their prospects, and brokers and advisory services often give factual information along with advice.

The most convenient place to find reference material is a broker's office. Many offices are run on an informal basis, and the reference books are out where anyone can use them. If not, a customer's man usually will be glad to make the reference books available for limited use by anyone who looks like a potential customer.

The two most widely used reference services are published by Moody's and Standard & Poor's. Each offers the basic material in several forms ranging from very abbreviated to very complete. For a quick rundown on a company, for example, you can try Standard & Poor's *Stock Guide*. This is a little booklet, measuring 5 by 8½ inches, that is crammed with information about nearly 5,000 stocks. (A similar booklet covers bonds.) On each company it gives the following information: ticker symbol, company name, where traded, quality rating, number of institutions holding the security, company's principal business, price range of previous years, trading volume and high, low and last price for most recent month, dividend record, abbreviated balance sheet, capitalization, and past and current earnings. If you wanted a personal reference book to carry around in your pocket, this little guide would fill the bill. It is published monthly. Moody's publishes a similar one, *Handbook of Widely Held Common Stocks,* quarterly.

Going up the line to a more detailed compilation, you come to Standard & Poor's *Stock Reports.* These are loose-leaf volumes kept up-to-date by quarterly substitution of new pages. The

Listed Stock Reports cover stocks traded on the New York Stock Exchange and the *American Stock Reports* cover stocks listed on the American Stock Exchange. The *Over-the-Counter Reports* cover a wide variety of unlisted stocks and the larger mutual funds. In each series the companies are listed alphabetically, and each company gets two sides of a sheet.

The typical *Listed Stock Report* begins with a recommendation as to whether the stock should be held or not. Then comes a graph showing prices for five or so years back compared with prices of similar stocks and with the Standard & Poor's *500 Stock Average*. Next come discussions of the company's recent sales or revenues, its near-term and long-term prospects, recent developments, and recent earnings and dividend payments. On the back of the sheet appears a table showing sales, profit margins, earnings, dividends and price ranges going back ten or more years. Balance sheet items, assets, liabilities, ratio of current assets to current liabilities and book value are covered for the same period. In addition, there is a description of the company and its position within its industry. The *American Stock Reports* and the *Over-the-Counter Reports* contain similar information.

For most purposes, Standard & Poor's *Stock Reports* are adequate. But for a really complete set of facts and figures about a company, you can refer to either of two voluminous references: Standard & Poor's *Corporation Records* and Moody's *Industrial, Transportation and Public Utility Manuals*. These are huge volumes covering thousands of companies in great detail. Information is kept up-to-date by the addition of new pages. To get a complete report on a company, you have to look up the basic material, then make considerable use of the index to find the various new items that are sprinkled through the most recently added pages.

For a quick picture of the past course of a stock's price, you can refer to a chart book available in most brokerage offices called *The Stock Picture,* published by M. C. Horsey & Co. It contains complete charts of 1,700 stocks plus abbreviated information on earnings, dividends and so on.

If you live in a large city, you can get some news about stocks from the financial pages of your daily newspaper. Such papers as the New York *Times,* the Baltimore *Morning Sun,* the

Boston *Globe,* the Chicago *Tribune,* the Los Angeles *Times,* and the Dallas *Morning News* give quite complete data on daily transactions on the New York and American stock exchanges. They also furnish selected quotations for investment companies and over-the-counter securities.

However, while it is interesting to know the price at which a stock changed hands the previous day, it is much more important to keep track of the company's sales, new orders, earnings and other measures of progress. Newspapers generally can provide such information only on the largest and most widely held companies. There are thousands of publicly owned companies that never get into the general financial news. The *Wall Street Journal* publishes the earnings statements of thousands of companies as they become available.

Weekly financial newspapers and magazines give similar but less complete coverage. Barron's *Financial Weekly* includes in its table of stock quotations both dividend rate and most recent earnings. Other publications to consider are *Forbes Magazine,* published twice a month, and *Financial World,* published weekly.

Most investors cannot devote full time to the study of economic trends and the statistics of industries and companies. They feel the need of a certain amount of professional advice. This need will vary from person to person. At one extreme is the man or woman who will want to assimilate facts and figures and make his or her own decisions with a minimum of outside help. At the other extreme is the investor who prefers to hand over all decisions to professionals. In between are those who want to make their own judgments but who welcome sound ideas and analyses. For all such investors, there are two baffling questions: Who is really competent? How can you tell the sound advice from the worthless?

The difficulty here is that there is more advice floating around on the subject of investing than on almost any other. The board rooms of brokerage houses abound in tips, rumors, and hearsay that are best disregarded completely. Brokers themselves, in order to acquire new customers and keep up the interest of old ones, feel obliged to furnish free market advice. In addition, there are advisory services that advertise their wares in financial publications, often by means of introductory offers that appear to be quite reasonable. Lastly, there are investment counselors who make their services available to clients much as do doctors and lawyers. But their fees are such that as a practical matter, only those with investment capital of $100,000 or in some cases even $200,000 or $400,000 can afford them.

Using your broker He (or she) is the person with whom you'll be in closest touch. The broker's main function is to execute your orders promptly and correctly. He also will give advice if you want it—sometimes whether you want it or not. If you have no idea of what kind of stocks you want to own, then your broker will be happy to suggest some. But you probably are better off deciding on your investment philosophy in advance, then telling your broker what you have in mind and checking your ideas of good stocks against his. Thus, in choosing a broker, it is well to try to find one whose investment philosophy is not too different from your own. Remember that one broker can keep thoroughly up-to-date on, say, half a dozen industries and only a certain number of stocks in each industry. Maybe, then, he will be familiar in detail with the doings and prospects of perhaps 50 companies. He will have only superficial or hearsay knowledge of the thousands of other companies whose stocks are available. So, if you are interested in owning top-quality growth stocks, you want a broker whose interests also lie that way, who instinctively, on his own hook, digs into the kind of information you need. If, on the other hand, your interests are more speculative, you want a broker who has a good feel for the faster-moving, riskier issues that often go up and down like a yo-yo on a string. What you don't want, if you are interested in long-term growth, is a broker who grabs the phone and calls you whenever he thinks a high flyer is about to move. Also, you don't want one who will be calling you and suggesting that you sell every time one of your stocks shows a paper profit. Remember that brokers make their money on the commissions from purchases and sales. This tends to give their advice a bias toward trading in and out. Beware of any broker who, in the jargon of Wall Street, is "hungry" for commissions.

Settling on the right broker probably is easier than finding a doctor or lawyer. You can move your account from one brokerage firm to another without feeling at all guilty. Some investors maintain accounts at several brokerage houses at the same time. So it's not a bad idea to shop around for a while, trying out this broker and that one, until you make a connection that is satisfactory. Always keep in mind that your broker is not infallible. If his advice were perfect, he would not be in the brokerage business at all. He would be a big, wealthy investor taking life easy and making calls to *his* broker.

Advisory services There is a wealth of published advice available to investors. You should try to make a judgment as to which is realistic and useful and which falls into the miracle or crystal-ball category. Although there probably are exceptions—generally speaking, the advice that is most flamboyantly advertised in financial newspapers and magazines is the the kind of advice to be most wary of. For example, how would you like to have the names of seven stocks likely to triple in value? Or a list of low-priced blue chips? Or 37 candidates for stock splits? Or a set of charts to tell you which way the market will go? All of this enticing information and more is offered for a few dollars—some of it even for free—in the ads that appear on the financial pages of newspapers. Probably you've wondered how good this information is. If the people who peddle the advice know so much, how come they aren't lolling on their yachts off the Riviera?

A realistic answer might be that no one can foretell the actions of the market as a whole or of an individual stock. About the best you can expect from an investment advisory service is a conscientious job of research, good factual material and sober recommendation. As to the services that offer tips for quick profits or charts that are supposed to foretell price actions—be wary. If that sort of information were reliable, it would be worth much more than a few dollars or even a few hundred. In fact, it would not be for sale. So if you do feel the need for some kind of investment advice, don't grab the service with the most exciting ad. First, take a look at the whole field. It may save you money and disillusionment.

The big financial services Moody's, Standard & Poor's, United Business Service, David L. Babson's, Value Line, Argus and Investment Counsel, Inc., of Grosse Point, Mich., are examples of the experienced organizations that have been in business for many years. Each provides a periodic report or survey covering business conditions in general and according to industry. Facts, figures and recommendations are presented on the stocks of selected companies. One issue of such a report may present a group of growth stocks thought to be attractive, another a list of stocks yielding good income and so on. From time to time reviews are made of stocks previously recommended. Some of these services also provide personalized consultation by mail. In some cases this privilege is included in the subscription price. In others it is not. Annual subscriptions range from $35 to $180.

If you are basically self-reliant and have the time to study, perhaps you can utilize the material that's available from market letters, investment services, and the like and be your own adviser. For many people this method is satisfying, but it could be expensive for someone who didn't have the knack.

Trust departments of banks About 26% of the banks in the United States have trust departments. These offer several possibilities. Depending on the policy of the bank, an investor with, say, $50,000, can either open an investment advisory account or set up an individual living trust. Banks that offer an investment advisory service will do the selecting of stocks subject to the customer's approval, furnish statements, collect dividends for him and so on. Fees generally match those charged by investment counselors, typically ½ of 1% of the market value of the fund and with a minimum annual fee of $500. In the case of a living trust, the customer turns the money over to the bank for investment and specifies how the principal and income are to be handled. A favorite arrangement is for the bank to pay the investor the income and to permit him to draw upon principal in emergencies.

Bookkeeping and handling charges are proportionately too great for a bank to accept small trust accounts. Many banks, however, have an arrangement for pooling small trusts and investing them as a whole in what is called a common trust fund. By this device, amounts ranging from $15,000 upward can be put in trust and the principal and income be paid out in the same way as they would be under an individual trust. A large bank may maintain several common funds to fit the different objectives of the individual trusts: a diversified fund of stocks and bonds for general use; an equity fund of stocks, and a fixed-income fund of bonds, notes and a relatively small amount of stocks. It may also have a tax-exempt bond fund.

In considering trusts of this kind, remember that a trust is not primarily an investment medium. People most often set up trusts to achieve some special objective—providing for the care of a dependent, minimizing taxes, assuring sound financial management for those who cannot or should not manage for themselves, letting someone have income from property without controlling the property itself and so on. Investing money is simply one of the duties that a trustee may be called on to perform in carrying out the purpose of the trust. And since a trustee is required by law to be particularly careful with the capital he has been given to manage, he must be prudent. Some states restrict trustees to a "legal list" of prescribed investments. Thus, trust funds may earn less than capital invested through other channels. The principal may be expected to grow during periods of rising stock prices, especially in the case of those that are more aggressively managed. (See Chapter 20 for more detailed information on trust funds.)

Investment counselors These professionals, like doctors and lawyers, are in the business of diagnosing and advising for a fee. Generally speaking, however, you do not consult an investment counselor on a one-time basis. The relationship is a continuing one. It rather resembles the fabled relationship between a Chinese patient and his Chinese doctor, in which the doctor is paid, not to cure a specific ill or disease, but to keep the patient healthy. The investment counselor treats each client individually. He determines the client's circumstances, needs and desires and selects a special bundle of securities to fit. This portfolio then must be continually reviewed and kept up-to-date. The investor may be consulted on all changes, or he may give the counselor carte blanche. Such constant supervision, plus research and overhead, costs money. Thus, investment counselors commonly charge a fee of ½ of 1% annually, based on the capital at stake. This percentage often is lower on assets valued at over $500,000. Since it involves as much work, and perhaps more, to supervise a small amount of capital than a large one, counseling firms generally set a minimum fee, in some cases $200 or $500 but in others

$1,000 or even $2,000 a year. Obviously, a person with only a few thousand dollars to invest cannot afford this expense. A very few counseling firms have made an effort to cater to the smaller investor; that is, one with capital of $25,000 or $50,000. Such firms, however, may simply have certain supervised lists of stocks into which they put clients' money rather arbitrarily without too much investigation of the individual's needs and his other assets. Also, the fee, as a percentage of the money being managed, is considerably above the ½ of 1% ordinarily charged on larger funds.

Selection of an investment counselor is difficult because it is hard to make a judgment on the firm's performance. One of the best ways, of course, is by personal recommendation of another investor who has been a client of one or more firms. Thus, if you were seriously considering opening an account with a firm of investment counselors, you would be perfectly justified in asking them for the names of one or two old clients whom you could consult. Many investment counseling firms publish advisory or market letters. A subscription to such a letter can give an idea of the soundness of the firm's recommendations. Also, many investment counseling firms manage investment trusts or mutual funds. The record of these funds is readily available in many publications. It might reasonably be assumed that a firm that can manage an investment trust or mutual fund competently can also manage an individual investment account at least as well. There also is a professional society, the Investment Counsel Association of America, located in New York City. It has high ethical standards but a rather small membership. You can write to the association to find what members are in your area.

Investment counseling services Some organizations that are not primarily in the investment counseling business will give investment management for a fee or, if the recipient is a good enough customer, without charge. Thus, an investor with substantial capital could open an advisory account with a large bank. Or if he were already a substantial customer of the bank, he might obtain free investment counseling without having to establish a formal arrangement. Similarly, a big investor can hire a brokerage firm to manage his portfolio. Or if he is a big enough customer of the firm, he can obtain a great deal of counseling without charge. It is assumed that the firm will be reimbursed by the commissions on the customer's purchases and sales.

Investment trusts For the person who does not have a substantial amount of money to invest, that is, he has less than $100,000, one of the most convenient and satisfactory ways to get professional management is to buy shares in a well-managed investment company or investment trust (two names for the same thing—mutual fund is another). This amounts to buying investment advice not on an individual but on a mass basis. The idea is that instead of owning stocks direct, you might prefer to own an interest in a bundle of securities selected by someone else—in this case the managers of the investment company. One advantage is that you spread a relatively small number of dollars over a number of different stocks or bonds and thus diversify your risk. Another is that if the fund is well managed, these stocks or bonds are selected on the basis of careful research by professional analysts. Quite possibly the professionals can do a better job of selecting than you could yourself. That is the investment trust or mutual fund theory, but the practice of it is not so simple. There are some 600 funds available so that the task of selecting the right one for any given investor, or even the one with the best record, is comparable to the job of combing through the stock market to find a good stock. Some advice on choosing a well-managed investment trust is given in Chapters 14 and 15.

12

PICKING A BROKERAGE HOUSE AND A BROKER

Many people think of a broker as one with inside information or at least enough financial background to know the names of some stocks that are going to go up. In real life, brokers don't have that kind of magic information. If they had it, they would be living in luxury and calling their own brokers. Brokers actually are trained to handle orders, to buy and sell in your behalf according to the rather complicated rules and customs of the financial markets. Brokers do have information about market conditions and the financial affairs of a number of companies listed on the exchanges or traded over-the-counter. But this information is provided them by their office research departments whose investigations are often supplemented by visits to plants and calls on company executives.

Most brokers will give advice if asked—some even if not asked. The quality of this advice varies with the judgment and experience of the individual broker. The broker's chief function, however, is to execute your buy and sell orders at the best available prices and to keep your account straight. This may sound relatively simple, but over the past few years there have been thousands of cases of mixed-up accounts, failures to deliver stock that has been paid for and, even worse, accounts that have been frozen for weeks or months when brokerage houses have gone bankrupt or been forced to merge with stronger competitors. You should keep in mind what happened during the period 1967 to 1971 so you can protect yourself in case of a possible recurrence.

The problem began in 1967 with a tremendous upsurge in trading. The market was rising, and as more and more people got on the bandwagon, some brokerage houses began to fall behind in their paperwork. Either old-fashioned "back office" methods simply could not cope with the staggering volume or else new computer systems broke down or were found to have been poorly set up in the first place. Despite these problems, however, all too many brokers greeted the upsurge in business as a sign that the millennium had come. They opened new branch offices, hired more salesmen and, as it turned out, overexpanded.

In the spring of 1969 one of the sharpest bear markets in history started and in two years had knocked stock prices down by 33% and volume to a mere trickle. Thus, not only did business suddenly fall off, but declining prices shrank that portion of brokerage firms' capital that is traditionally invested in stocks. The combination of mixed-up accounts, delayed deliveries, overexpansion, slow business, declining profits and shrinking capital took a heavy toll. Members of the New York Stock Exchange have always been considered, by and large, the best-run firms in the business. But during the two-year period of 1969 and 1970, a total of 129 NYSE member firms went out of business, merged or were otherwise acquired by other firms. Much to its credit, the New York Stock Exchange committed over $100 million to protect the customers of those firms that had encountered the most severe financial problems and were forced to liquidate. Thus, few customers actually lost their cash or their securities in the long run. But thousands found their accounts frozen while seemingly interminable inventories were taken as their firm was liquidated or merged with another. During this frozen period the customer could not obtain certificates for any stocks that the broker was holding for him, nor could he get cash out of his account.

The various stock exchanges, the National Association of Securities Dealers and the Securities and Exchange Commission all have been working on procedures they hope will prevent a recurrence. But the stock market is a volatile and unpredictable thing. If daily volume runs abnormally low for a long period of time, some firms will inevitably be in trouble. On the other hand, if volume runs abnormally high for a long period, some firms may again find back-office problems involving mistakes and mix-ups in accounts. Thus, selecting a financially sound and efficient broker is important if you are a beginner. And even if you are an old-timer, a checkup on your present broker may indicate that your best course would be to switch.

Choosing a brokerage firm In judging a broker, these are the two most important questions to ask: Is the firm financially sound? Is the firm profitable?

Soundness generally refers to capital position. NYSE member firms are required to maintain capital of at least one-fifteenth of their outstanding indebtedness. However, the NYSE, now under an early-warning system, begins investigating a firm's operational capital when the ratio exceeds 10 to 1. A good many firms got into trouble during the 1969–70 bear market because their capital, largely invested in stocks, shrank rapidly while their indebtedness stayed high. This put many in violation of NYSE rules and forced them into liquidation or merger. Even though the rule says 15 to 1, a lower ratio of indebtedness to capital is preferable, say 8 to 1.

A firm's capital position is set forth in its statement of financial condition, obtainable by asking. It would be desirable to receive a copy of the most recently *audited* statement. NYSE and AMEX member firms receive one surprise audit a year that results in an audited statement, as distinct from the firm's usual year-end statement of condition, which may or may not be audited. There's another catch. The firm may list as part of its capital, "subordinated" capital. This means that in addition to the capital the partners or stockholders have put in, the firm has borrowed money to use as capital, and this money must be repaid at some point. In some cases it can be called back upon six months' notice.

Profitability is important because if your brokerage firm is losing money, it may tend to skimp on service, take chances and perhaps give less-conservative advice in order to get business.

Probably the best way to evaluate both soundness and profitability is to go to a senior officer of your bank and ask him confidentially for the information you want. Your banker understands financial statements, and the bank may have a line of credit out to several brokers in town, in which case it checks into their condition as a matter of course.

As for other qualities, most investors need a "general store" type of firm; that is, one that caters to individual customers as well as institutions. In most places you have a choice of local branches of big NYSE firms that deal heavily in individual accounts—firms such as: Merrill Lynch, Pierce, Fenner & Smith, Inc.; Dean Witter & Co., Inc.; Paine, Webber, Jackson & Curtis; Reynolds Securities, Inc., and Shearson, Hammill & Co. Or there may be one or more local firms that have good records and reputations.

Unless you are a short-term trader, you probably want to avoid firms that specialize in underwriting hot new issues.

Once you select a firm, it is wise to ask the manager to recommend a particular salesman (account executive) whose interests correspond to your investment objectives. Thus, if you happen to be a long-term investor, you won't end up with a salesman who is all gung-ho for speculating in commodities.

You may have problems The commonest complaints about brokers have to do with back office or clerical problems. The rest involve misunderstandings between customer and salesman, or in a relatively few cases, such offenses as churning a customer's account.

One of the most common complaints involves delay in delivering stock certificates to a purchaser. Ordinarily, the procedure is this: You order the stock, probably by phone. By the fifth business day thereafter you settle; that is, pay the broker. At this point, wheels are put in motion to get you a certificate. The selling broker (who may be in a far-off city) is supposed to have sent the seller's certificate to your broker so he could forward it to the transfer agent (usually a bank, and frequently in New York City) for registration. The transfer agent will cancel it and issue you a new one, mailing this to your broker. In normal times this takes about a week or ten days, depending on the location of the transfer agent. In these times it can take anywhere from a week or two up to 30 days.

How much time should you allow, considering today's problems? Probably two and a half weeks for a round lot (100 shares) of a listed stock; perhaps three or four weeks for an odd lot or a stock traded over-the-counter. Some people who trade frequently get around the problem by having their stocks in "street name"; that is, the certificates are in the broker's name but credited to the customer in the broker's books. This will be discussed more fully in the next chapter.

Another way to get fast delivery is to buy through your bank. The bank will order the stock from a broker and pay for it out of your account when the certificate is delivered. This certificate will be negotiable (that's why the broker can deliver it so fast) and the bank will have to send it to the transfer agent and get a new one in your name.

Another common problem may occur when you buy a stock close to the dividend date. Even though you are entitled to the dividend, a delay in entering your name on the company's stockholder books may result in the dividend going to the old owner. In this case the broker should pay you the equivalent and collect from the seller. Any time you don't receive a dividend within a week after the payment date (as published in the newspaper or determined by your own records), you have grounds for a squawk.

If your firm merges with another, all accounts probably will be frozen until a complete audit of the books of both firms is made, and if one of the firms was in bad shape, this could take weeks. In the meantime, you can't withdraw cash or securities. You may, however, be allowed to sell a stock if it is going down and you want to stop the loss.

If your firm goes into liquidation, you might have to wait several months to get your cash or securities.

Suppose that in spite of all precautions, you have a legitimate complaint about your broker. You've waited and waited and still haven't got your certificate or your dividend. Or you put in a "limit" order to buy at 20 and your broker thought it was a market order and bought at 20½. Or you got somebody else's confirmation slip with a demand that you pay for stock you didn't order.

Some customers at this point want to write to their congressman. But the best first step, if you are dealing with a branch of a large firm, is to notify the branch manager. If this doesn't work, ask for a telephone conference with the regional or zone partner (who may be in another town or city). If there is a large amount at stake, you should formally put your complaint in writing to the regional or zone partner, with a copy addressed to "Managing Partner" at the firm's home office, usually in New York City. On the other hand, if you are dealing with a local firm, you should appeal directly to the managing partner.

If you don't get satisfaction from the brokerage firm, you can complain to the Securities and Exchange Commission (SEC), the New York Stock Exchange, the American Stock Exchange or, if over-the-counter stock is involved, the National Association of Securities Dealers. Here are the addresses to write to:

Division of Trading and Markets, Securities and Exchange Commission, 500 N. Capitol Street, N.W., Washington, D.C. 20549.

Complaint Division, New York Stock Exchange, Four New York Plaza, New York, N.Y. 10004.

Inquiry Department, American Stock Exchange, 86 Trinity Place, New York, N.Y. 10006.

National Association of Securities Dealers, 1735 K Street, N.W., Washington, D.C. 20006.

Probably the best bet is the SEC. It has regional offices around the country, and if you happen to live near one, a call there might help. The regional director may know the local manager of your brokerage firm and get matters straight in a jiffy. Otherwise, write to the SEC in Washington. Someone will phone long-distance or write to the main office of the firm in question and ask for an explanation within ten days. Such a call or letter often galvanizes brokerage firms into action.

If you get down to bedrock and decide you have real damages due you, then before you hire a lawyer, try putting your case before the NYSE, AMEX or NASD, as appropriate. These policing bodies have divisions for handling complaints and they also offer arbitration.

How to deal with your broker All this, of course, is best avoided by dealing with a broker who doesn't make mistakes (or not many, anyway) and who promptly straightens out mixups when they occur. You can do your part to help. When you phone in a buy or sell order, make precisely clear to your broker what you want and how you want it done. Ask him to call you immediately with a confirmation when the transaction has been completed. In this way you can quickly catch a mistake. Carry out your part of the deal on time by delivering certificates or payments within the five business days. If there are securities or cash in your account, get a monthly statement and go over it promptly to make sure it agrees with your records.

What can you expect your broker to do for you? Even if you have a relatively small amount to invest, you can expect the average broker to—

• Treat you courteously.

• Spend a certain amount of his time helping you clarify your thinking on what stocks you want to buy. (What *kind* should be decided by you in advance.)

• Offer the use of advisory services or manuals.

• Give you current quotations on stocks you are interested in.

• Make for you whatever purchase or sale you decide on at the standard commission rate.

You should not expect any broker to—

• Spend an hour of his time discussing a small investment on which the commission will amount to only a few dollars.

• Help you decide whether or not you should invest at all. (You should make that decision before you go in.)

• Tell you whether the market is going to go up or down. No one knows that.

No matter how fancy or simple it looks, a broker's office consists essentially of salesmen, a ticker tape magnified electronically so that anyone may see prices at which transactions on the New York and American exchanges are occurring, an electronic quotation set, like a miniature closed-circuit TV, on which you can obtain bid and asked prices of any listed stock and a number of over-the-counter stocks, the dividend rate, price-to-earnings ratio and so on, a Dow Jones broad ticker that carries continuous financial news and a teletype machine for sending orders rapidly to the floor of the exchange for execution. In addition, there may be a commodity board showing spot and future prices of commodities, metals, etc., and one or more traders who handle transactions in unlisted stocks.

Opening an account with a brokerage house is the simplest part of investing. (The hardest part, of course, is to make money at it.) If you walk into a brokerage house absolutely cold, the receptionist will introduce you to a customer's man (salesman) or "account executive." When he learns which stock you are interested in, he will get you a quotation, or current price. At the same time he will give you a "new account" form to fill out. The account form calls for your name, address, occupation, employer, social security number and bank reference, roughly the same information you would give in opening a charge account anywhere.

Several decisions are required at this point. Do you want a joint account with right of survivorship, similar to the joint account you and your spouse might have at your bank? Also, do you want the stock certificate put in your name, or names, and delivered to you, or do you want to leave it with the broker in "street name"?

If you open a margin account, you will automatically leave your stock in street name. Under present rules, you can buy stock on margin by putting up a sizable hunk of the purchase price and borrowing the rest from the broker at the going rate of interest. After you once own your stock, theoretically, under NYSE rules, it can decline until your loan is three-quarters of the price before you have to put up more margin. Many brokers, however, have house rules that permit a decline only until the loan is two-thirds of the price. New York Stock Exchange rules require the customer to deposit at least $2,000 to open a margin account. This is applied to your initial purchase.

When you give your order to buy, you must decide whether you want to buy "at the market," in other words, pay the going price, or put in a "limit order" specifying that you will pay a certain price and no more. Such an order may be "open"; in other words, you can leave it with the broker indefinitely so that if the stock ever comes down to your price, you'll get it. Most orders by individual investors, however, are put in at the market. If you give such an order, you will, if you request it,

Picking a Brokerage House

receive confirmation of your purchase, along with the exact price paid and the commission, within a matter of minutes. A written confirmation will come along later.

Commission rates Because brokerage houses got into so much financial trouble, as explained at the beginning of this chapter, in 1970 they were permitted to add a surcharge to commission rates on orders of less than 1,000 shares. In 1972 the basic rates were revised in accordance with the schedule below. These changes were based on the contention that brokers weren't making money on small orders. Even with the increase, commissions on orders ranging from $500 to $2,000 still run only between 2% and 3% on the average, which is not large compared with commissions charged for purchase of life insurance policies, annuities and most mutual funds.

Here is an abbreviated table showing the commission rate schedule adopted in 1972.

TABLE 2 MINIMUM COMMISSION SCHEDULE

Single Round-lot Orders		*Multiple Round-lot Orders*	
MONEY INVOLVED IN THE ORDER	MINIMUM COMMISSION	MONEY INVOLVED IN THE ORDER	MINIMUM COMMISSION
$100 to $799	2.0% plus $6.40	$100 to $2,399	1.3% plus $12.00
800 to 2,499	1.3% plus 12.00	2,500 to 19,999	0.9% plus 22.00
2,500 to 19,999	0.9% plus 22.00	20,000 to 29,999	0.6% plus 82.00
20,000 to 29,999	0.6% plus 82.00		

Subject to the provision that the minimum commission on single round-lot orders is not to exceed $65.

Plus
First to tenth round lot — $6 per round lot
Eleventh round lot and over — $4 per round lot

In no case shall the minimum commission per round lot exceed the single round-lot commission. Also, in no case shall the minimum commission for a round lot plus an odd lot exceed the commission on the next larger round lot.

Odd-lot Orders: Same as single round-lot rate less $2, subject to the provision that the minimum commission on an odd-lot order is not to exceed $65.

If in doubt, check the commission schedule in the back pages of a recent copy of Standard & Poor's *Security Owner's Stock Guide*.

Whereas brokers charge a uniform commission rate for listed stocks, they may charge a markup for purchases of stock in the over-the-counter market. This is because the over-the-counter market is not an auction market, but a negotiated market. When you buy an unlisted stock, your broker usually buys it for you from a dealer who is making a market in that particular stock. In other words, the dealer sells the stock to your broker who sells it to you at a higher price. This is different from charging a commission computed by a formula.

Here is how it works. Suppose you want to buy an over-the-counter stock known as First Consolidated (name fictitious). You ask for a quote from your broker. If the stock is that of a large and widely traded company, he punches in the symbol on his NASDAQ terminal and by this means projects on a televisionlike screen the bid or asked prices of all market makers in that particular security. Within seconds the broker can identify the best quote, put in a phone call to the appropriate dealer and buy the stock for you. If, on the other hand, First Consolidated is not one of those companies that is listed in the NASDAQ system, your broker will go the old-fashioned way and look up the stock in the quotation sheets, known as "pink sheets," to find which dealers make a market in it. He may then call two or three of these dealers to get a quote. He does not reveal whether his customer is a buyer or seller. Let us say that the quote is, in one case, 25½ bid, 26⅜ offered, in another 25½ bid, 26¼ offered. The stock, then, can be bought by the broker for 26¼. But in order to pay his overhead and make a profit on the deal, he will have to charge the investor somewhat more. Perhaps he will quote you a price of 27. If this is agreeable, the broker will buy the stock at 26¼, resell it to you for 27, and make a markup of ¾ of a point or roughly 2¾% of the purchase price. The same figures might apply if he had been able to get the various quotes over the NASDAQ system. According to guidelines of the National Association of Securities Dealers a markup, except in unusual circumstances, should not exceed 5%. Mostly markups are under 3%.

Instead of marking up the stock, the broker in the example could have resold it to you at the 26¼ price and charged a commission. Some brokers who are members of the New York Stock Exchange, and who do most of their business in listed stocks, do charge the NYSE commission rate no matter whether a stock is listed or over-the-counter.

In the case of a sale, the seller most often receives the bid price and is charged a commission, usually equivalent to the NYSE rate. The reason why there may be a markup in the case of a purchase and a commission in the case of a sale is this. When the dealer sells a stock to a customer, he may have gone to considerable expense to make the deal. For example, he may have done a lot of research in order to be able to recommend certain issues that he thinks are desirable. Thus, he may feel that a markup, which may be more than the NYSE commission rate, is justified. On a sale by a customer, however, no such merchandising is required. The customer simply has the stock and wants to sell. On the other hand, if the seller is a market maker in the stock, he must sell it as principal on a net basis; that is, the price would include all charges and commissions. Similarly, if the stock is purchased by a dealer for his own account, he will mark it down. The 5% guideline will apply in either case.

When you purchase or sell stock in the over-the-counter market, the markup or commission will depend on a number of factors: the kind of broker you are dealing with (big house, small house); the kind of security; how widely it is traded, etc.

The way the over-the-counter dealers quote the prices of the thousands of securities they deal in is coming to resemble the way quotes are furnished by the New York Stock Exchange. Each of these markets provides current bids and offers to potential buyers or sellers. Over-the-counter dealers provide them on their most widely traded securities. The NYSE provides them on all the securities it lists. The bid is what you might expect to receive, minus a commission charge, if you sold the security, while the offer is what you might expect to pay, plus the commission.

Here is how over-the-counter bids and offers are ascertained and published. There is a central organization known as the National Quotation Bureau. Traditionally, between two o'clock and four o'clock each afternoon, each over-the-counter dealer who makes a market in any given security sends in the bid and offered prices at which he is willing to buy or sell. The information is then tabulated on what are known as the "pink sheets." These are simply legal-sized sheets of pink paper on which are printed alphabetically the names of the most widely traded over-the-counter stocks. After each stock appear the names of the dealers who make a market in it, along with their current bid and offer. These pink sheets are kept by every brokerage house and usually are available on request. Selected over-the-counter quotations are listed in the daily papers. Widely held stocks are listed on what is known as the "National List." In addition, most papers carry a separate list of stocks of local companies.

In addition to the above, of course, the NASDAQ system provides almost instantaneous bid and asked quotes on a given stock (if it is large enough to be in the NASDAQ list) by all dealers making a market in that particular stock. The NASDAQ was developed by the National Association of Securities Dealers, and the letters stand for National Association of Securities Dealers Automated Quotations.

13

HOW TO BE A STOCKHOLDER

Leave it in street name? Once you have decided to be a stockholder, one of the first decisions you have to make is whether to have the certificate delivered to you or to leave it with the broker in "street name." Each course has its advantages and disadvantages. When you leave your certificate with the broker, he doesn't actually register the stock in your name. Instead, he carries the stock in his firm's name, along with hundreds or thousands of other shares in the same company, and makes a bookkeeping entry showing how many of those shares belong to you.

There are some advantages in this arrangement. The broker does a certain amount of bookkeeping for you. He receives dividends and credits them to your account, sending you a monthly statement. He also keeps the certificates in his vault and insures them against loss, fire, and theft. And even though the shares are in the broker's name, as long as you have paid for them and not borrowed against them, they are segregated; that is, the broker cannot lend them or put them up as collateral for loans.

Also, when your stock is in street name, it is somewhat easier to sell. There is no problem about hunting up the certificate, endorsing it and taking it or mailing it to the broker. A simple telephone call will complete the job.

Last but not least, most brokers provide these services free. They do it, of course, to accommodate the big investors who own hundreds of shares of stock and who buy and sell frequently. Because of this, if your account is fairly small and if you don't intend to do much trading (which you probably shouldn't unless you are quite sophisticated), your broker may be reluctant to hold your stock in street name. Although most firms do not charge for the service, a charge is permissible because the commissions the broker might get from you probably wouldn't pay for the cost of the safekeeping and the bookkeeping. So, while theoretically the service is available to all customers, large or small, in actual practice whether you can use it or not depends on the house policy of the individual broker.

Now note that carrying stock in street name may have some disadvantages. As your dividends accumulate, they will be put into your account and may lie idle for a while and won't be drawing interest. If you request it, however, dividends will automatically be paid to you when your broker receives them.

There is also this to be said for having your stock registered in your own name: Company reports, proxy material and dividends will come directly to you. When stock is held in street name, this material is forwarded to you by the broker and there can be some delay. Offsetting this, perhaps, might be the possibility that, as long as the broker holds your stock in street name, he'll remember you own it and may be expected to call you when he hears good or bad news about the company. Beware of the broker, however, who is always calling you up with good or bad news designed to persuade you to keep buying and selling.

Single or joint ownership? The next question to answer after buying stock might be whether to register it in a single name or in the joint names of husband and wife, mother and daughter, and so on. Registering in "joint name or the survivor" has three advantages. First, under the 1964 tax law revision, husband and wife can get a dividend exclusion of $200—as against $100 if the shares are in one name only. Second, if one person dies, the stock will pass directly to the other without going through probate. Since the executor's fees are generally based only on the assets in the probated estate, this will save on administration costs. Third, if the stock is in joint name, the survivor can get immediate possession. On the other hand, if the stock is in one name only, the survivor would have to wait for weeks or months to get the stock or the proceeds from its sale. Joint ownership also has disadvantages. If a married couple splits up, they may have bigger problems on property division. It is also conceivable that in a joint account, one party could sell stock without the knowledge or approval of the other party. However, the proceeds would go to both; i.e., either the money would be deposited in the joint account or the check would have to be made out to, and endorsed by both parties. Also, putting stock in joint names may entail a gift tax or at least a gift tax return.

Of course, even when a stock is in joint name and one owner dies, the broker may be reluctant to accept a sell order from the other party without a good bit of identification and explanation. Nevertheless, if, for example, a husband and wife own stock jointly and the husband dies, the wife has the right to sell it and receive the proceeds.

If you want to have stock registered in the name of yourself and another person, or the survivor, it would be sensible to introduce the other person to your broker at the time of purchase and make sure that he understands that the other owner is the one that has the right to sell the stock.

What records? Where? The best place to keep stock certificates, assuming they are not in street name, is in a bank safe-deposit box. Note that the box rental is deductible for income tax purposes. Before putting the certificate away, write down its number, the number of shares, the cost or value when acquired, and the name and address of the transfer agent. Put this information in a different place from the certificate itself. If you lose the certificate or it is destroyed, write at once to the transfer agent. You can get a new certificate, but you may have to buy an indemnity bond from a surety company to guarantee against some unauthorized person turning up with the original certificate and selling it by forging your name.

For tax purposes you should keep the confirmation slip you receive from your broker when you purchase or sell a stock. When you receive a dividend check, keep the attached explanation of the payment, if there is one, or the notification from the company.

In addition, it is well to keep a stock and dividend record showing the name of company, number of shares owned, serial numbers of certificates, date purchased, commission and tax charged, net cost, amount of each dividend paid and when, date sold, price, commissions and charges, and net profit or loss. You can make up a form or buy one ready-made at a stationer's.

Can you borrow? How much? Once you own stock, you can put it up as collateral for a loan. One advantage is that such a secured loan almost always carries a lower interest rate than an unsecured note or an installment loan. Your bank will make what it calls a "nonpurpose" loan of 50% to 75% of the market value of the stock, assuming it's of average or better quality. (The word "nonpurpose" means that the loan is not for purchasing stock or paying for stock already ordered. The customer usually must sign a statement that the loan is not for this purpose.) The percentage will depend on: (1) the policy of the bank, (2) whether the stock is listed on an exchange, (3) the stock's quality, (4) how good a customer you are of the bank.

Many banks do not like to make a loan on just one stock but prefer to lend on a diversified portfolio. One bank, for example, will lend 60% of the value of listed stocks and will go to 70% for its best customers, but will lend only 50% on unlisted stocks and then only to good customers. Another bank says it will lend 75% on good listed stocks and 66% on good unlisted stocks. Banks will also lend on mutual fund shares. The interest charged on nonpurpose loans is subject to negotiation between the bank and its customers.

If you have borrowed against your stock and it goes down, you don't necessarily have to put up money right away. But if it continues to go down, at some point the lender will want part of the loan repaid. Bank policies vary. Some banks insist that the loan not be allowed to become more than 75% of the value of the stock; others say no more than 60%. As an example of the 75% rule, if $700 were borrowed against $1,000 of stock and the value dropped to around $935, the bank might call for more collateral.

If you want to borrow money on your stock either to help pay for it or to pay for additional stock, you are making a "margin" loan. A margin account must initially have in it at least $2,000 of cash and/or securities. The Federal Reserve Board's margin regulations require you to put up a substantial amount of cash, which means that you can borrow much less on a margin loan than on a nonpurpose loan. The amount of a margin loan you can make depends on the economic climate at the time. In recent years the regulations have required the buyer on margin to put up 55% to 80% in cash, which means that you could borrow only 20% to 45% of the stock's value. Generally speaking, when the stock market is in the doldrums, the Federal Reserve Board sets margin requirements at a low level. The level rises as the market booms.

Not all stocks are eligible as collateral for a margin loan. Allowable stocks are those that are listed plus a certain number of over-the-counter stocks selected by the Federal Reserve Board.

The easiest way to make a margin loan is to do it through your broker. He will credit the money to your account and charge you the going rate of interest. Brokerage houses generally insist that a margin loan be no more than two-thirds of the current value of the stock. Thus, if you bought $1,000 of stock on margin, putting up $700 in cash and borrowing $300, the value of your stock could then decline to $450. At this point the loan of $300 would be two-thirds of the value, and any further decline would result in a margin call. It is possible, also, to make nonpurpose loans from your broker, but you should compare the terms and interest rate with a similar loan from your bank.

THOSE FINANCIAL REPORTS

To keep up on the affairs of a company, watch the financial pages of the newspaper and read the financial reports that are sent to stockholders. The financial reports in particular are valuable. They are audited, you can trust their accuracy, all right, but even so you can't be sure they'll tell you exactly what you want to know unless you can read between the lines a bit. Here's how.

Most annual reports look like magazines and are filled with pictures of the company's products and optimistic predictions for the future, but the heart consists of:

1. The balance sheet, which matches the firm's assets against its liabilities and shows the fundamental soundness of the company.

2. The income statement, sometimes called the statement of profit and loss, which shows how much the company made over the last year and, if you have the statements for the past several years, what the trend seems to be.

3. The footnotes, which might change the whole picture.

Probably the most commonly used stock-buying touchstones are the earnings per share and the price-to-earnings ratio.

Earnings per share—or rather the potential earnings per share—do most to determine the market price of the stock. To find the earnings available for common stock, start with the net income, subtract any dividend requirements on preferred stock, and divide what's left by the number of common shares outstanding.

To see how it works, look at the income statement of For Example, Inc., below. Net income is $505,000. Divide this by the number of common shares, 400,000 (from the balance sheet), and you get $1.26—earnings per common share. If the report had shown any preferred stock dividend requirements (say $700,000 at 5%, or $35,000), you would have subtracted that from the net income and then divided by the number of common shares to get earnings per share.

FOR EXAMPLE, INC., INCOME STATEMENT*

Net sales		$7,000,000
Cost of sales and operating expenses		
Cost of goods sold	$4,500,000	
Depreciation	900,000	
Selling and administrative expenses	600,000	6,000,000
Operating income		$1,000,000
Other income		
Dividends and interest		100,000
Total income		$1,100,000
Other deductions:		
Interest on bonds		140,000
Income before taxes		$ 960,000
Provision for taxes		455,000
Net income for the year		$ 505,000

* Copyright by *Changing Times*.

FOR EXAMPLE, INC., BALANCE SHEET, December 31

ASSETS

Current assets		
Cash		$1,900,000
Accounts receivable	$2,050,000	
less: provision for bad debts	150,000	1,900,000
Inventories		2,700,000
Total current assets		$6,500,000
Property, plant and equipment		
Land	200,000	
Buildings	4,000,000	
Machinery	1,000,000	
Office equipment	150,000	
	$5,350,000	
Less: accumulated depreciation	2,100,000	
Net property, plant and equipment		3,250,000
Deferred charges		150,000
Goodwill, patents trademarks		610,000
Total Assets		$10,510,000

LIABILITIES

Current liabilities		
Accounts payable	$1,500,000	
Notes payable	910,000	
Accrued expenses payable	200,000	
Income taxes payable	455,000	
Total current liabilities		$3,065,000
Long-term liabilities		
First mortgage bonds, 5% interest due 1970		2,800,000
Total liabilities		$5,865,000

STOCKHOLDERS' EQUITY

Common stock, $5 par value authorized, issued, and outstanding 400,000 shares	$2,000,000	
Retained earnings	2,645,000	
Total stockholders' equity		4,645,000
Total liabilities and stockholders' equity		$10,510,000

In a healthy company in a growth industry both net sales and earnings per share should increase yearly on the average. In cyclical companies sales and earnings should increase most of the time.

The price-to-earnings ratio is simply the ratio between the price of the stock and the earnings per share. To find it, divide the market price by the earnings per share. Say For Example sells for $18. Divide that by $1.26 and you get 14, which means that For Example's common stock is selling at 14 times earnings. This can be compared with the Dow Jones Average price-to-earnings ratio. A high price-to-earnings ratio might indicate the stock is overpriced, but a high ratio might be justified if the earnings have been increasing steadily and the trend can be expected to continue.

The current ratio tells you whether the company has enough working capital. Find it by dividing the total current assets by total current liabilities. In the illustration:

$$\frac{\$6,500,000}{\$3,065,000} = 2.1$$

Thus, For Example, Inc., has 2.1 times as many current assets as current liabilities. The ratio ought to be at least 2 for industrial companies; less, maybe, for industries that have no need to carry large inventories, like electric utilities.

It's not essential, but you can go one step further and check the quick assets—assets that can be turned into cash in a hurry, which leaves out inventories. To find quick assets, subtract the inventories from the current assets, which in For Example's case leaves $3.8 million. To find the quick assets ratio, divide this by the current liabilities:

$$\frac{\$3,800,000}{\$3,065,000} = 1.24$$

Thus, For Example has $1.24 in quick assets available to meet each $1 of current liabilities. This ratio, in most industries, should be over 1.

You find the operating margin of profit by dividing the operating income (the net sales minus cost of sales and operating ex-

How to Be a Stockholder

penses) by the net sales. Using For Example's report, that would be:

$$\frac{\$1,000,000}{\$7,000,000} = 14.3$$

A good company to buy into is one that is increasing its sales year after year and at the same time is converting a good percentage of these sales into operating profits. By "a good percentage" is meant one that is larger than that of similar companies in the same industry. The operating profit of a good growth company could be 15% to 30%.

The equity-to-debt ratio (sometimes called capitalization ratio) is the proportion of the company's long-term debt (represented by bonds it has sold) to the stockholders' equity. You find the ratio by dividing the value of the common stock (the current market value—$18 in this case—times the number of shares) by the face value of the outstanding bonds:

$$\frac{\$7,200,000}{\$2,800,000} = 2.57$$

Thus, the value of For Example's common is 2.57 times as much as its bond debt. For industrial companies, a ratio of 5 to 1 is desirable, but utilities and railroads may safely run as low as 1½ to 1.

Take note that in figuring the value of common stocks for this purpose, you have to multiply the number of shares by the current market value of the stock. Do not use the par value given under "stockholders' equity" on the balance sheet, as the par value generally has no relation to actual value.

Another way to evaluate the size of the company's debt is to relate it to the company's capitalization. The capitalization consists of long-term debt, preferred stock, common stock and surplus. The debt-to-capital ratio would be determined by dividing the long-term debt by the capitalization. In the case of For Example, Inc., it would be the long-term debt divided by the capitalization of $7,445,000 (long-term debt of $2.8 million plus stockholders' equity of $4,645,000), or about 38%. A complementary ratio would be the common-stock-to-capital ratio, which would be the stockholders' equity divided by the capitalization. In the case of For Example, Inc., this would be stockholders' equity of $4,645,-000 divided by capitalization of $7,445,000, or about 62%. A reasonable debt-to-capital ratio for industrial companies would be under 50%. For utilities, which traditionally raise capital by borrowing, the debt-to-capital ratio could be as high as 70% to 75%.

A company can be made to look good or bad simply by the accounting method used. For example, there are several ways of figuring depreciation, none of them particularly easy to understand. If a company switches from one method to another, it can make quite a change in financial results. A big vending machine corporation switched a few years ago, and the effect was to make a 4-cent increase in its earnings per share look like a 13-cent increase. If there has been a changeover, the footnote should tell you and alert you to check the significance.

Again, there are two basic methods of valuing inventories. One is called last-in-first-out (LIFO) and the other first-in-first-out (FIFO). While prices are advancing, the FIFO company will tend to look better; when prices are in a slump, the LIFO company will. Neither method is good or bad in itself, but you've got to know who's using which when comparing companies. And you should be aware of a change from one to the other. The footnotes should tip you off.

Occasionally, annual reports can be blatantly misleading. Until 1962, for example, one aerospace company issued "consolidated" reports—ones incorporating the performance of both the parent company and its subsidiaries—to the Securities and Exchange Commission, but not to the public. The subsidiaries were taking a licking and knocking total company profits out of the window, a detail you couldn't see in the glowing annual reports. Only the footnotes gave a hint that subsidiaries might be influencing the picture. The company eventually made peace with the SEC by making its reports to the SEC and to the public uniform. The SEC now requires a more detailed breakdown of earnings by product line in reports to the public.

Most companies give stock options to key executives. Too large a percentage of options in relation to the number of shares outstanding can dilute the value of the rest of the stock. A high percentage would be 10%. And the footnotes should tell the story. Convertible preferred stock, convertible bonds or debentures also are potential diluters of the common. Many companies report earnings per share on a fully diluted basis as well as on the regular basis.

Studying all of this may sound like a lot of work, but the money at stake should be worth the trouble. And sometimes you won't have to do all the arithmetic; the ratios and earnings per share may be figured out for you already—especially if it's been a good year.

TAX TIPS

Knowing the ins and outs of income tax regulations regarding stock ownership can save you many dollars. Here are some hints on how to handle your dividends and capital gains and losses.

Cash dividends You don't have to pay tax on all cash dividends you get. The first $100 of total dividends on your stocks is excluded from taxable income. If your wife (or husband) owns stock in her (or his) name, up to $100 of dividends she (or he) receives is also tax-free. If all your stocks are jointly owned, you pay no tax on the first $200 of dividends.

Suppose stock in your name earns $130 in dividends and stock in your spouse's name earns $60. You must declare $30 of your dividends as income. You would avoid paying any tax if the stock were in joint ownership. (But other considerations enter into joint ownership. Check it out with your professional adviser first.)

What if stock yielding $140 in dividends was owned jointly, while stock paying $50 was owned in your name alone? Half the dividends on the shares jointly held, or $70, are credited to you, half to your spouse. For tax purposes, you have $120 in dividends, of which $20 is taxable. Your spouse has $70 tax-free.

Dividends in stock If a company pays a dividend in the form of its own stock rather than cash, you pay no tax on the extra shares. But if you have the right to choose between cash or stock, then you must pay even if you take the stock. You list the stock's equivalent cash value as income.

Here are the rules that apply to stock rights (certificates issued by the company entitling you to buy your pro-rata share of a new stock issue). If their value is 15% or more of the stock's market value, you must allocate a proportionate part of your stock's cost to them. If their value is less than 15%, you may choose whether to allocate or not. If you don't, your cost of the rights is considered to be zero. There is no tax to pay when you receive the rights. When you sell, however, you will have a capital gains tax to pay if you receive more than the value you allocated to them.

A stock split is different. A two-for-one split, for example, means you get another share of stock for each one you own. You pay no tax on the extra shares.

If you have sold some stock Profits you make by selling stock are known as capital gains. The tax on such gains may be less than you would pay on ordinary income. If you hold the stock for more than six months, you've got a long-term capital gain (or a long-term loss if you sell for less than you paid). You've got a short-term gain or loss if you sell before six months. Net short-term gains are taxed just as your other income is—that is, at your regular tax rate. But long-term gains get favorable treatment. You are taxed, in effect, at only half your regular rate—and never more than 35% of the gain in any case. The gain is the difference between the actual cost of the stock (including buying commission and fees) and your selling price (reduced by sales commission, transfer taxes and similar expenses).

How do you treat capital losses? If you have no capital gains, then capital losses can be deducted from your income at the rate of $1,000 a year. Short-term losses are deductible dollar for dollar, but it takes $2 of long-term losses to offset $1 of ordinary income.

If you have a mixture of gains and losses, the tax is figured on a net basis. Divide your dealings into two sets: long-term and short-term. Subtract all your long-term gains from long-term losses, or vice versa. Do the same for short-term transactions.

Do you have a long-term gain and a short-term loss? If the gain is larger, the difference is a long-term gain. If the loss is bigger, the difference up to $1,000 can be deducted from your income.

Do you have a short-term gain and a long-term loss? If the profit is greater, the difference is a short-term gain. If the loss is bigger, the difference is deductible.

If you are thinking about unloading stock, here are a few pointers. Look at deals you've already made. Do you have:

• A short-term gain? It may pay to sell a loser to offset the gain, which would otherwise be taxed as ordinary income.

• A long-term gain? Even if you're bent on selling a loser, consider waiting till next year. That way, you pay only half your regular tax rate on the gain this year, but deduct the full loss next year up to $1,000 if no other gains are taken.

• A long- or short-term loss? You might simply hold onto your other stock and deduct the loss from your regular income. If you also have a short-term gainer that you're sure won't go higher, you can sell it now and take the profits tax-free—for these profits will be offset by your loss. But hold off selling long-term gainers for another year. In other words, let the losses reduce regular income one year, pay a long-term capital gains tax on profits the next.

If you haven't sold stock this year, check your "paper" gains and losses. Do you have:

• A potential long-term gain? Don't worry about the tax angle if your investment goal is to hold stocks for the long haul. But if you think you will be in a higher tax bracket next year, you might consider realizing part of your gains now. If your income will go down or hold steady, delay taking gains.

• A potential short-term gain? Hold onto the securities until you've had them for more than six months. The gain then is long-term.

• A short-term or long-term loss? You might consider selling now if your tax rate will be lower next year.

• Long-term gains and either short- or long-term losses? Avoid taking both gains and losses in the same year. The losses would offset your long-term gains, and only the net gain is taxed at the capital gains rate.

Mutual fund shares Mutual funds generally pay two kinds of dividends:

• Ordinary dividends; that is, income from dividends and interest on stock or bonds the fund owns. These are taxed just as other dividends on stock you own.

• Capital gains dividends. These are your share of the profits the fund makes by selling securities. They are taxed as long-term capital gains, even if you actually held the mutual fund shares for less than six months.

A small number of mutual funds retain capital gains instead of distributing them. They will then pay a capital gains tax directly to Uncle Sam on your behalf, at the maximum 25% rate. What if your capital gains rate is lower? You can recover the difference. Say the fund told you your share of the gains was $100 and it paid a capital gains tax of $25 for you. Report the $100 as a long-term capital gain. If your capital gains bracket is, say, 10%, you'd pay $10 on this amount. Then list the $25 under "income tax withheld" on page 1 of the tax form. Thus, you get a net credit of $15. One final step: Add $75 to the original cost of your investment for computing any future gain or loss when you sell the stock. (The law assumes you received the $100, paid $25 in tax, then reinvested the rest.)

Stock dividends when sold Say you sell some common stock that includes shares you had previously received as a tax-free corporate dividend. Generally, you'd first divide the total number of shares held after the stock dividend into the cost of the original stock. For example you bought 25 shares of American Box at $21 each, for a total of $525, then received five more shares as a dividend. The cost of each share, for tax purposes, then becomes $525 divided by 30, or $17.50. (You would pay the long-term capital gains tax rate on any profit from sale of the extra shares so long as the original shares were held at least six months.)

Stock splits You'd apply the same sort of arithmetic to figure profit or loss when you sell stock that's been involved in a split. A two-for-one split, for instance, would cut the cost of all the shares you then hold to half the cost of the original shares.

Stock rights Many stockholders are able to buy extra shares in a company at cut-rate prices by exercising rights issued by the firm. In most cases, the simplest way to figure the cost of these new shares, for tax purposes, is to use the price you paid for them. You would not then have to average out the cost of the old and new shares.

Stock bought in blocks Say you buy 30 shares of stock in a company in three installments of ten each, and each lot had a different price. How would you figure the gain or loss on one lot of ten you sell? If you can identify the particular lot, the gain is the difference between the original cost and your selling price. Tell your broker that this is a sale against the purchase of a particular date (you name it), and the broker will print this date on the confirmation even if the stock is held in street name. If, for strategic reasons, you want the least gain or the biggest loss, you would sell the lot that cost you most. To get the biggest gain or tiniest loss, unload the cheapest shares. What if you can't identify the particular lot you sell? Your gain or loss is the difference between the cost of the first lot you bought and the price at which you sell.

Gifts Perhaps your father gave you stock that originally cost him $1,000. If you sell it for more than $1,000, you pay capital gains tax on the difference—no matter how much the stock was worth when you got it. Suppose you sell the stock for less than $1,000. Then you take a capital loss for the difference between the selling price and the original cost, or the market value at the time of the gift, whichever is smaller. Say this same stock was worth $1,500 when you got it, then fell to $500 when you sold it. Your loss is only $500—the original cost of $1,000 less $500. Was it worth only $750 when you received it before dropping to $500? Your loss is $250—that is, the market value of $750 less $500.

Inheritance If you inherit some stock when a parent dies and then sell it later on, you figure the profit or loss, as a rule, on the value of the stock on the date of death. Exception: An executor may choose to value your parent's estate (for estate tax purposes) as of one year after death. In that case, your stock cost is the value at that date.

Deductions If you itemize on your return, you can deduct certain costs of buying or maintaining stock:

• State stamp taxes, usually imposed on the purchaser of stock. Note, however, that if you deduct this expense, you can't add the tax to your cost in computing profits or losses when you sell the stock.

• Safe-deposit rental if the box contains stock or other income-producing property, such as savings bonds.

• The cost of stock market newsletters, investment services and other professional advice—even newspapers.

• The value of stock donated to charity. Giving away stock that has appreciated in value can make sense. You don't pay any tax on the profit. And if the gain is long term, you can deduct the full market value as a contribution! If the gain is short term, you can only deduct the contribution's basis or cost.

14

DOLLAR COST AVERAGING

Here is one of the most foolproof ways of investing in the stock market.

First Pick out one or more sound common stocks or an investment trust e.g., a mutual fund. Do the best job of selection you can. That is all-important.

Second Pick a sum of money that you can conveniently invest once a month, once a quarter, twice a year or once a year. Don't be too ambitious. Choose a sum small enough to be spared even in bad times.

Third Buy monthly, quarterly, semiannually or annually as many shares of the stock or investment trust as your chosen sum will cover. As you go along, reinvest all dividends and capital gains.

Fourth Once you have started your program, keep it up, not for months but for years.

This method of investment is known as "dollar cost averaging." It is theoretically not as good as buying low and selling high. Unfortunately, however, the buy-low, sell-high method doesn't work. It is impossible to tell positively when the market is low and when it is high, or when it is about to go up or down. Even the so-called experts have been proven woefully inadequate in their efforts to forecast price movements. So dollar cost averaging is a substitute for guessing. And it works because it guarantees that the eventual cost of your investment will be reasonable.

HOW AVERAGING WORKS

Dollar cost averaging does even more than this. Note that when you invest a fixed number of dollars each time, this amount buys more shares when the price is low and fewer when it is high. Thus if you keep up your purchases over a long period of time, you will end up with a lower cost per share than if you had bought a fixed number of shares each time. If that sounds impossible, note this simplified example. Say you buy $100 worth of stock on the first of each month. The price, originally $100 a share, declines and then recovers to the original price. The following table shows that after seven months the stock you bought cost you $85.89 a share, or $1.25 per share less than the average price during the period.

TABLE 3 DOLLAR COST AVERAGING

DATE OF PURCHASE	PRICE PER SHARE	AMOUNT INVESTED	NUMBER OF SHARES BOUGHT	CUMULATIVE COST PER SHARE
Jan. 1	$100	$100	1.00	$100.00
Feb. 1	90	100	1.11	94.79
Mar. 1	80	100	1.25	89.29
Apr. 1	70	100	1.43	83.51
May 1	80	100	1.25	82.78
June 1	90	100	1.11	83.92
July 1	100	100	1.00	85.89
	$ 87.14	$700	8.15	$ 85.89
	Average price per share	Total amount invested	Number of shares bought	Cost per share

No matter whether the price of the stock rises, falls or just fluctuates, the use of this system ensures that you will pay less than the average price. And over a long period of time the saving in cost will mount up to worthwhile proportions. In fact, if you follow the dollar cost averaging method and the securities you pick turn out to be of average quality or better, your investment will grow over the long run at an average rate of 6% to 12% or perhaps more. Moreover, this kind of program can easily be started and maintained. Machinery for making such a bit-by-bit investment is available. Many brokers welcome the kind of customers who plan to make small regular purchases. Investment clubs—groups of ten to twenty-five investors who pool their money and knowledge—are flourishing. Almost all investment trusts also offer plans whereby shares can conveniently be bought at regular intervals.

Before starting such a program, however, you should note the reasoning behind the four precepts listed at the beginning of this chapter.

First, make sure your investment is of good quality. Obviously, if you buy into a company that is going slowly downhill, the longer you keep up your purchases, the worse off you are going to be. Choice of a poorly managed investment trust would be almost as bad. Your investment would not be growing as it should, and, in addition, the money you paid for professional management would be going down the drain. So long as prices go up and down, dollar cost averaging turns the fluctuations to your benefit and keeps your cost reasonable. But to profit in the long run, your stock should be of such quality that its value will rise. If the long-term trend is down, nothing will help you except a switch to another stock.

Second, don't be overly optimistic as to the amount you can afford to invest. One of the surest ways to lose money in the stock market is to commit money that will have to be used for something else. If you do this, you may find that you will have to suspend your program or even sell your stock at the worst time—when prices are depressed.

Third, don't cash in your dividends or capital gains. Plow them back. These small amounts are easily frittered away. But if reinvested, they give you the advantage of compounding, and over the years they will make your investment snowball.

Fourth, keep buying, rain or shine. It won't do to stop when the price of your investment goes down. In fact, that is the time to keep going because when the price is low your fixed sum will get you more shares. On the other hand, don't stop when the price seems high. While it may seem high in relation to past prices, it may actually be low in terms of what prices will be in the future. So don't try to second-guess the market. Just plug along with the averaging. It will guarantee you a reasonable cost.

A PLAN OF YOUR OWN

Save up first. The mechanics of buying stocks in regular installments are not difficult. Perhaps the cheapest way is to make one or two purchases a year. For example, you could deposit in the bank each week or month a sum that would amount to $500 on June 30 and $500 on December 31 of each year. Then on those dates you could order through a broker the number of shares of your chosen stock that $500 would cover. The New York Stock Exchange commission on a purchase of $500 would be around $16.50. If the purchase were an odd lot, you would pay only about $14.50 commission, but you would be charged the odd-lot price, which would be an eighth of a point above the last round-lot sale.

Note the smallness of the commission—less than 3%. It shows how you can keep costs down by accumulating the money yourself and buying direct through a broker. If, instead, you had started an accumulation plan and put a small amount into a stock each month, the commission might have been nearly twice as much. If you had bought the most common type of mutual fund, the commission might have been three times as great.

FORMAL PLANS

There are some advantages, however, to joining a formal accumulation plan.

- You usually make a cancelable agreement to invest so much a month or a quarter, and each time you invest, you receive a statement of account and often a reminder of the next payment due. For many people the agreement and reminders help keep the program going.

• In many plans the amount of each purchase, minus commission, is fully invested down to the fourth decimal place. This purchase of fractional shares is not possible in ordinary purchases of stock made through a broker.

• You may specify that your dividends automatically be reinvested in stock. In this way you never see the dividend checks and are not tempted to spend them.

MIP The most widely available plan for regular purchases of stocks is the Monthly Investment Plan of the New York Stock Exchange, offered by its broker members. Here is how it works. Go to a broker who is a member of the New York Stock Exchange with the name of your stock picked from among the more than 1,700 listed on the exchange. Decide how much you can afford to invest per month or per quarter. It can be as little as $40 or as much as $999. If you want more than one stock, you can split or alternate your payments.

When you decide what you want to do, you sign a cancelable agreement whereby you undertake to make the payments regularly. There is no penalty, financial or otherwise, if you miss a couple of payments, although the broker reserves the right to terminate the plan if you miss four payments in a row. The commission you pay will be 6% on amounts under $100; 2% plus $4.40 on amounts from $100 to $799 (with a minimum of $6) and 1.3% plus $10 on amounts above. Remember, also, the odd-lot differential. Each payment you make, minus the commission, will be invested in full and fractional shares of your stock to the fourth decimal place. Thus, if your payment is $50 and the odd-lot price of the stock is $18, the commission will be $3 and your account will be credited with $47 worth of stock, or 2.6111 shares.

You probably will want to leave your stock in the broker's custody until you complete your plan or purchase the desired number of shares. Or you can get free delivery after you have acquired 50 shares. If you want delivery beforehand, there may be a small handling charge. If you decide to quit the plan, you will receive the number of full shares in your account without delivery charge. Any fractional shares will be sold and a check sent to you for the proceeds. If you work in a company that will make payroll deductions for this type of investment, you can have as little as $4 a week deducted from your paycheck and sent in to buy stock.

For more information on this plan see a broker who is a member of the New York Stock Exchange or write to MIP, Box 209, Wall Street Station, New York, N.Y. 10005, for a free copy of *How to Invest on a Budget.*

Mutual fund accumulation plans Nearly 400 open-end mutual funds offer some kind of plan whereby their shares may be acquired by small, regular purchases. Of the funds offering accumulation plans, many require that the initial purchase be at least $100, $250 or more and that subsequent purchases be $25 or $50. Some plans, however, have no minimums, or minimums of $25 or $50, and investors may put in any amount subsequently.

One important detail about an accumulation plan is whether it is of the level-charge or the prepaid-charge type. In the level-charge type the sales commission is a fixed percentage, say 9% on every purchase. If you make 100 payments, the commission is the same on the first as on the last. In the prepaid-charge type, also known as the contractual or penalty plan, you agree to make to the firm sponsoring the plan a specified number of monthly payments. The sponsor will deduct sales commissions and other fees and invest the remainder. But a good portion of the sales commissions and other fees for the whole series of payments will be lumped together and loaded onto the first few payments. Hence, the prepaid-charge plan has what is known as a "front-end load."

As explained in Chapter 15, in many cases of the front-end load, less than half of your first year's payments actually is invested.

Although most contractual plans involve purchase of open-end funds, you can use this method to buy certain common stocks. In 1938 H. Dean Quinby, of Rochester, N.Y., worked out an investment contract plan with Lincoln Rochester Trust Co., whereby investors could purchase stock in Eastman Kodak. Later he added a plan for acquiring General Motors, AT&T, DuPont, Standard Oil of New Jersey, General Electric and Xerox.

Make sure you understand the ins and outs of the front-end load before you sign up.

Another thing to find out before starting an accumulation plan is whether the fund will reinvest your capital gains distributions without charging a sales commission. Most will, but in many cases a sales commission is charged for automatic reinvestment of dividends. Some funds will reinvest both kinds of distribution at net asset value; that is, without charging a commission.

INVESTMENT CLUBS

Have you ever thought that it might be fun for you and a few good friends to get together, pool your money, and use your combined knowledge and experience to select and buy some good stocks? You probably have thought of this and so have thousands of others. The result is there are over 50,000 investment clubs spread all around the country, and more are starting all the time.

An investment club is much smaller and more informal than an investment trust or mutual fund. Furthermore, club members do their own portfolio managing. Only occasionally do they ask for outside help. This can be all to the good because the members learn about investing by actual experience, and that is usually the best way.

An investment club provides an inexpensive way to invest. In most clubs, each member contributes $20 a month. (It could be more.) Twenty dollars, of course, is not a lot, but over the years it does mount up. The first modern investment club on record was started in Detroit around 1940. Using the $10-to-$20-a-month formula, each of the original members deposited $7,200 in 32 years. At the end of the period the securities this money bought for one member were worth $77,980, even though he had drawn out over $4,000. While this record might seem sensational, the average earnings rate of this club over its 32-year life has been slightly under that of the average club reporting its annual earnings to the National Association of Investment Clubs.

If, during a period when stocks appear to be attractively priced, you want to invest more than $20 a month, you can take advantage of the club's research program and buy extra shares for your own account. But if you do this and happen to buy when the market is high, don't blame your losses on the investment club idea.

One primary investment club rule is to stick to dollar cost averaging—investing a fixed number of dollars each month regardless of the level of the market. So if you have extra money to invest, consider using a similar dollar cost averaging plan and investing a fixed amount each month over a period of years. Otherwise you may buy high and suffer a loss.

An investment club is educational. A new research committee is appointed each month. In the course of a year or so, everybody participates in digging up facts and figures and deciding which stocks look most attractive.

Starting a club is not hard. Procedures are standardized, and model by-laws are available. Brokers generally are happy to accept a club account and give some organizational help, although after that a club ought to do its own stock selecting to gain the experience. It is probably easier to start a club, incidentally, than to try to get into an established one. Most existing clubs want to stay small and will take in a new member only when there is a vacancy.

If all this makes you think you might like to start a club, fine. But before you go ahead with the idea, consider also the possible disadvantages.

Looking at it from an investment standpoint, buying shares of a well-managed investment trust might be safer and more profitable than joining a club. The managers of the trust are professionals; club members are amateurs.

A club started when the market is relatively high could lose money if it disbanded within a few months or even a few years because the market might then be lower.

Unless members are congenial, a club could be wrecked by disagreement and wrangling.

Starting a club Now, if you still want to go ahead, here is how it is usually done. One person with imagination gets the idea and puts it up to two or three friends. All then sit down and

Dollar Cost Averaging

suggest names of four or five others who might be interested. When the group reaches six or eight, it meets again to round out the membership to about 15. In this rounding-out process, it is advantageous, although not necessary, to add a lawyer and an accountant. The more different interests and professions represented, the better.

Next step usually is to join the National Association of Investment Clubs and get an investment club manual. Annual dues are $10 per club. The cost of the manual is $3, which may be applied to the first year's dues. The manual covers the following ground: articles of agreement or by-laws, with an explanation of how to operate the club; investment policy; record keeping; reporting for income tax; stock study aids with a blank form; model agent agreement to be made with the broker handling the club's account.

Here is the address to write to: National Association of Investment Clubs, 1515 East Eleven Mile Road, Royal Oak, Mich. 48068.

When the club holds its first organizational meeting, it may invite a competent investment man to discuss the mechanics of investing and methods of selecting growth stocks. One member generally is appointed as agent. He opens an account with a brokerage house, puts in the actual buy and sell orders, and handles the money. The club's broker provides a safekeeping account, holds the club's securities, collects dividends and provides a monthly statement.

Guides for investing Now comes the most important part; the investing. At this point you will be interested to know that there is a set of tested investment principles that have worked out well for clubs over the years. The pattern was set by a pioneer club in 1940. Two Detroiters, Fred C. Russell, a purchasing clerk with the Federal Mogul Corp., and John Biscomb, a clerk with the Chrysler Corp., decided they wanted to accumulate enough money to go into business for themselves. They discussed the idea with a friend, George A. Nicholson, Jr., of Smith-Hague & Co., Inc., a Detroit brokerage firm. Nicholson suggested the club idea and laid down three guiding principles, which have now become famous.

The first is to invest each month all the money collected from members regardless of the level of the stock market or the business outlook. This gives the advantages of dollar cost averaging, as noted previously.

The second principle is to reinvest all dividends. This gives the snowballing effect of compound interest.

The third principle is to invest for the long pull and stick to common stocks of sound growth companies. Speculating is frowned on. Most clubs that have tried it have failed.

Acting on this good advice, Russell and Biscomb recruited six more young Detroiters—two clerks, an army officer, a salesman, a repairman and a foreman—and the club got under way. It succeeded from the start. As word got around about the new method of investing, club members began to get letters from people who wanted to start clubs of their own.

By 1951 the idea had spread so far that the Detroit club could hardly handle the mail. There definitely seemed to be a need for an organization to help would-be clubs get started and give them guidance. So three of the charter members of the original club in Detroit, Thomas O'Hara, Fred Russell and George Nicholson, organized the National Association of Investment Clubs.

Since selecting good stocks is probably the hardest and also the most important job that a club has, the NAIC has done considerable work on growth-stock selection methods.

There are several ways in which the investment club can get its information. The brokerage house where the club has its account will make available statistical market services. Sometimes it will allow club members to take out pertinent material overnight. The investment committee may also write directly to the president of any company in which it is interested and ask for the annual report and whatever other material is available. Such letters will usually bring in a raft of information, sometimes direct from the president of the company himself.

The ideal stock for an investment club has the following characteristics: a history of increasing sales and earnings; good prospects that sales and earnings will continue to increase; reasonable yield; a price that is also reasonable, considering quality, and that is likely to rise in the future.

To select the stock that comes closest to this idea requires that all stocks under consideration be broken down and rated uniformly as to sales, earnings, dividend, price, etc. When a club is new, a simplified table may be about all the members want to tackle.

Later, they can graduate to the more complicated *Investment Club Stock Selection Guide,* recommended by the NAIC. Filling out this form is somewhat like computing your income tax, but once a club gets the hang of it, it is really not so bad.

The first problem in using the Stock Selection Guide is to pick out those companies whose sales and earnings have grown by at least 10% a year for the past five years. A form is used for each company. Columns are provided for recording past years' sales and earnings. Figures are plotted on a ratio chart, and the lines projected to give an idea of how fast sales and earnings may be expected to increase over the next five years. A projected increase of 10% a year should be the club's over-all goal. And 15% is more desirable. The NAIC also recommends that 25% of the portfolio be in major companies in major industries where the growth may be more like 5% to 7%, and that another 25% be in smaller, faster-growing companies.

Growth stocks are not likely to pay as high dividends as stocks of more stable companies. Nevertheless, a prospective dividend rate of at least 4% within five years is desirable so as to enhance the effects of compounding.

Next problem is to answer the question, Is the stock a good buy at today's price? By use of the basic figures, a judgment can be made on the chances of the stock's going up in price compared with the chances of its going down. The NAIC's ideal ratio is three to one; that is, the price should theoretically be as likely to go up three points as it is to go down one point. Obviously, there is nothing hard and fast about such calculations. Their basis necessarily lies in estimates. But estimates based on known facts are better than guesses.

When a member resigns What happens if a member of a club wants to resign? Usually he need only give 30 days' notice, and he will receive his pro-rata share of the market value of the club's securities. The liquidation value of each share is calculated each month by dividing the total value of the club's holdings by the number of shares outstanding. The withdrawing member gets the liquidation value of his shares minus a 3% penalty and minus, also, any commissions the club incurs to sell securities and raise cash.

The club's broker All kinds of people have formed investment clubs: policemen, stenographers, bridge players, church groups. There are likely to be a few clubs in almost any given city, but in some places, Detroit, Mich.; Albany, N.Y.; and Indianapolis, Ind., for example, there are many more than you might expect. In those places live-wire brokers have contributed a good bit of their time and energy to encourage new clubs. This relationship between the members of an investment club and the broker who "sponsors" it—that is, who helps it to get organized—should be clearly understood.

A broker gets very little direct benefit from handling the account of the typical investment club. Assume that the club buys $250 worth of stocks each month. The broker's commission is around nine dollars. That certainly would not pay him for meeting with the club once during its organizational period and later making available his firm's market services, answering questions on specific stocks, etc.

There are certain benefits, however, that a young broker in particular gets from an association with one or more clubs. Club members will give him word-of-mouth advertising and help him widen his acquaintance. Also, there are usually some members who buy stocks for their own account, basing their selection on the monthly choice of the club. Young men and women in business who don't have much to invest today may turn into good customers in ten or fifteen years. Brokers like investment clubs also because they like informed customers. Investment club members become educated investors and quickly grasp points their broker is trying to make.

There is another reason why some brokers want to lend a helping hand in the investment club movement. They believe that the more people that understand the free enterprise system and have a stake in it, the more support it will get and the better it will work. So if you are starting a club, don't be oversuspicious of the broker's motives. He stands to get something out of it, sure. But chances are he will make a net contribution of his time and energy.

One more point about a broker: Get one with experience and

a reputation for good judgment. A young one is okay, but not a dumb one.

Whether you do your dollar cost averaging through an investment club, through MIP, through mutual fund accumulation plans, or just by saving up dollars and making periodic purchases directly in the market, you will benefit from certain built-in advantages. You won't have to worry about the ups and downs in the market. Your costs will be averaged out for you. If you have selected securities of good quality, you will begin to see your money snowball. If you started out putting $25 a month, or $300 a year, into good growth stocks and kept it up for 25 years, you should acquire an investment worth many thousands of dollars. Invest $1,000 a year and you should end up with a small fortune.

15

MUTUAL FUNDS AND CLOSED-END INVESTMENT TRUSTS

You turn your car over to the auto mechanic for repairs, your health problems to a doctor. Why shouldn't you turn your investment problems over to professionals and let them put your money to work? Maybe you should, especially if your capital is not large enough to warrant opening an individual account with an investment counseling firm. One way to achieve somewhat the same result is to buy shares in what is variously known as an investment company, investment trust or investment fund. You may be more familiar with the term "mutual fund." Mutual fund is the popular name for an open-end investment company. Most funds are open-end, but there are also closed-end investment companies.

When you put your money in an investment company, you buy an interest in a bundle of securities selected by the managers of the fund. Instead of owning stock in one or two operating companies, such as Eastman Kodak or Standard Oil of New Jersey, you own a tiny cross-section slice of dozens of companies.

You have automatic diversification, and all the while the managers of the fund are weeding out stocks they feel are doing poorly and substituting stocks they believe have more promise.

VARIOUS TYPES AVAILABLE

Fine and good. But shopping for an investment company is like shopping for anything else. There are many types and brand names on the market. Some are sold aggressively by energetic salesmen knocking on doors. Others are available only if you learn about them and seek them out. Some are available at a discount; others are sold strictly at the pro-rata value of their assets. Still others are obtainable only by paying a premium.

Some try for growth; others for income. Some invest in blue chips; others in lesser-known companies. Some are cautiously managed; others tend to shoot the works for big gains. Some have a splendid record of competent management going back over the years. And unfortunately, others seem to have been thrown together to give would-be managers something to manage and hungry salesmen something to sell. So it's well to be familiar with the field before you begin to narrow down your choice. Start with a few definitions and characteristics.

Net asset value per share This is the net dollar value of the securities the fund owns divided by the number of its shares outstanding in the hands of the public. Thus, on a given day a certain fund might own securities having a market value of $10 million. If it had outstanding in the hands of the public one million of its own shares, the net asset value per share would be $10.

Capital structure The two types here are the closed-end fund, which is the older, less prevalent and less publicized, and the open-end, or "mutual," fund, which is newer, more widely sold, and the kind you are more likely to hear about. Actually, both types are mutual funds in the sense that those whose money is being managed are also the stockholders. But in practice, the term mutual fund is applied only to the open-end type.

Closed-end funds Closed-end means that at some time in the past the fund has sold a block of shares to the public but makes no continuous offering of additional shares. Thus, the number of shares outstanding is constant. Most closed-end shares are traded on the New York Stock Exchange or over-the-counter just as are shares of manufacturing companies, railroads, utilities or banks. Examples are the Lehman Corporation, Tri-Continental Corporation and Niagara Share, all of which are traded on the New York Stock Exchange.

If you want to buy into a closed-end fund, you get in touch with a broker and through him buy shares from another investor who already owns shares and wants to sell. The price the buyer pays, or the seller receives, depends on supply and demand. It may be above or below the net asset value. If the price is above the net asset value, the stock is said to be selling at a premium; if below, at a discount. The commission is almost always at the New York Stock Exchange rate.

Mutual funds Open-end, or mutual, funds are based on a different idea. Open-end means that the fund stands ready at all times to sell new shares or redeem old ones. Thus, the number of outstanding shares of an open-end fund is always changing. While these transactions are usually done through a broker, there is no public trading. Thus, the law of supply and demand does not affect the price. When you buy, you usually pay net asset value plus a commission of commonly 8½% or 9%, although the percentage is scaled down for larger purchases. When you sell, you receive net asset value, usually without payment of a commission. Examples of open-end funds are Massachusetts Investors Growth Stock Fund, Chemical Fund and T. Rowe Price Growth Stock Fund.

As you can see, in one major respect closed-end and open-end funds are the same. They are in the business of investing money entrusted to them by the shareholders. In most other ways, however, they differ.

Discounts and premiums on closed-end funds In recent years many closed-end funds have been available in the marketplace at a discount from net asset value. This enables you to buy part ownership in a list of stocks, for example, DuPont, Union Carbide, Honeywell and IBM, at, say, 10% or 15% less than their market value. There's no particular gimmick about this except that, if you later sold your shares, you might have to sell at a similar discount. In the meantime, for every 85 or 90 cents you had invested, you would have a dollar's worth of capital working for you. Also, the discount could narrow, which would be an advantage. Discounts generally do narrow during booms and widen during declines.

There are several explanations for this discount. The main one, perhaps, is that there are no salesmen aggressively pushing the shares and creating a demand. The broker to whom you would go to buy closed-end shares can just as well sell you shares in any one of a thousand or more companies listed on the New York Stock Exchange. The commission would be the same either way. In fact, brokers have very little interest in selling you closed-end shares, since money put into such a fund is likely to stay there rather than move into and out of various stocks, thereby providing additional commissions.

Some closed-end funds at times sell at a premium over net asset value. The reason is that investors become enamored of particular funds, either because of their outstanding management record or because of favorable publicity or for some other reason. As a matter of fact, however, there is often no discernible reason why one fund will sell at a premium while another, which appears equally well managed, will sell at a discount. As in all free markets, investor psychology plays an important and mysterious role.

Mutual fund sales commissions Closed-end funds, having a fixed number of shares outstanding, can grow in terms of net asset value only. Mutual funds, on the other hand, can grow both in net asset value and in the number of shares in the hands of the public. Thus, mutual funds have in the past made up a very fast-growing type of security. One reason is that the salesmen have a greater incentive to sell open-end funds than almost any other form of investment. The sales commission generally runs around 9% of the net asset value. In the past it has not been stated as a percentage of the net asset value but as a percentage of the offering price, which is the net asset value plus the commission or "loading." If you wanted to buy one share of a mutual fund having a net asset value of $10 and the load was 8½%, you would pay

$10.93. (The 93 cents is the sales commission and is 8½% of $10.93, which is the sales, or offering, price.) Actually, of course, the 93 cents, in relation to the net asset value of $10, represents a commission of 9.3%. SEC guidelines set up in 1972 require the commission to be stated as a percent of the net asset value. Either way it is considerably larger than the 2% or 3% of the market price you pay when you buy closed-end shares or other listed stocks. And the salesman who sells you open-end shares receives about a third of the total sales commission—a return that makes it worth his while to seek out prospective buyers at office or home. It should be noted that on purchases of over $10,000 the typical sales commission begins to decrease until on a $100,000 purchase it may be only 3%.

Thus there has grown up a new type of security salesman who resembles the life insurance salesman and who is trained to sell open-end funds exclusively. This differs from the usual concept of a broker as being one who stands ready to sell you stocks and bonds, listed or unlisted, traded anywhere in the world.

Most open-end funds make no charge for redeeming shares. This is in contrast to closed-end shares, where you do pay a selling commission of 2%, 3% or some other amount, depending on the size of the transaction.

No-load mutual funds These are a strange breed of cat because they are not sold by salesmen at all. In fact, a no-load fund is one of the few things in this world that you can buy without paying a sales commission, directly or indirectly. The reason that you don't hear much about no-load funds is that no salesman knocks at your door trying to persuade you to buy one. Why should he? He wouldn't get any commission. Yet, except for the lack of a sales charge, these no-load mutual funds are run just the way others are.

You might wonder, then, what's up? Why should a mutual fund be willing to offer its shares at cost? And if it does, why doesn't everyone buy the no-load funds and save the commission?

For the answer, note that all funds, open-end as well as closed-end, whether a sales commission is involved or not, charge a management fee for handling the shareholders' money. In most cases, this fee is ⅓ to ½ of 1% per year of the capital under the fund's management, although it can be higher or lower. Thus, the managers of a fund having assets of $100 million might receive an annual management fee of $333,000 to $500,000.

Now while the managers of a no-load mutual fund receive no part of any sales commission, they still receive the management fee and thus are compensated for investing the stockholders' money. In addition, most managers of no-load mutual funds are investment counseling firms who handle large sums for private investors. For such firms the mutual fund may just be a side line, although it can be a useful one, as the following example will show.

An investment counseling firm ordinarily accepts only wealthy clients, charging a management fee, usually ½ of 1% of the money at risk. The smallness of the fee makes it uneconomical for such a firm to accept amounts of less than, say, $100,000, and it avoids the problem of charging a minimum fee of $500 or more a year. Such a firm may still want to accommodate the son of a good client or perhaps a young executive who promises to be a customer in the future. In many cases, too, wealthy clients want to establish small accounts for minor children or grandchildren.

One way to take care of the younger and nonwealthy investor is to set up a mutual fund. To such potential clients the firm can say, "Our mutual fund is managed in the same way as our big accounts. Put your money into the fund and you'll get the same treatment. There is no sales charge." Once such a fund gets started and begins to grow, it generally is offered publicly so that anyone can buy in.

This sounds like a good deal, but remember that you have a larger choice among the funds with loads because there are more of them. And the important thing is performance. One fund with a load might perform so much better over the years than one without a load that you would be foolish to buy the no-load fund merely to save the commission.

OBJECTIVES

Because the investment company field is such a desirable place for the person with, say, $500 to $25,000 to put his money, the investment community has developed many types of funds to provide an appeal to the large mass market.

There are, for example, balanced funds, which generally keep a quarter or more of their capital in cash, bonds and preferred stocks. There are funds that invest only in bonds, and others that try to provide the largest possible income to their shareholders and so on. Here are the several types.

Common stock funds These make up the greatest proportion of all funds. They can be either open-end or closed-end or no-load. In most cases the emphasis is on long-term growth. Generally known as diversified common stock growth funds, these usually keep more than 80% of their assets in common stocks, though in a declining market they may switch temporarily to greater holdings of cash or bonds. One type of growth stock fund puts more emphasis on income. While such a fund generally follows a policy of long-term growth, it aims for a greater income return from dividends than do the pure growth funds. Either type of growth fund is eminently suitable for most investors. Usually such investors already have enough fixed assets in the form of life insurance, a stake in social security and a pension plan, and perhaps savings accounts or savings bonds. What's needed is an investment in equities that will grow fast enough to outrun inflation, heavy taxes and the other burdens that beset the ordinary family. Another point: Why hire someone to invest your money in fixed assets such as bonds when you can do it so easily yourself?

Balanced funds These are useful to a person who wants complete management of all his assets, including fixed-income investments. Examples might be wealthier persons or those in retirement. But the investor who already has life insurance and savings or bonds may not need a balanced fund. Other disadvantages: The management fee takes a considerable slice of the income from the bonds and preferreds. This fee would be saved if the investor bought his own bonds or preferreds, which, generally speaking, are more easily selected than common stocks. Also, the balanced fund does not provide as big an opportunity for growth as does the stock fund.

Bond and preferred stock funds Income, rather than growth, is the objective and, again, the management charge can be a substantial part of the income.

Income funds These strive for a high yield and thus invest in companies that pay out a major part of their earnings in dividends. Such companies show little growth, and the risks in a free economy being what they are, a company that is not growing is in danger of declining.

Industry funds These spread their money over many companies in one industry. By buying into several such funds, you could obtain tremendous diversification. But diversification simply for diversification's sake is not always advisable. It is probably better to buy into a common stock fund that attempts to pick out a few of the most desirable companies in numerous industries.

Geographical funds These concentrate on one state, such as Florida, or one area, such as the Southwest. Since the managers are confined to one area, and yet must obtain diversification, they may be forced to buy stocks not as promising as others they could be buying if they were operating nationally.

Special situation funds These seek out companies in trouble financially or whose stock is available at a low price for some unusual reason. Results of this type of investment can be very good or very bad. Since these funds are so speculative, they would not seem to be desirable for the average investor.

Foreign securities funds In recent years, European, Japanese and Australian stocks have risen and also fallen, sometimes spectacularly. Thus, there is more risk in foreign securities than in those of American companies. One risk is political instability; another is unpredictable taxing policies. The investor who wants a stake in foreign operations can obtain it by purchasing shares in leading United States corporations that have interests abroad, such as Goodyear, Pfizer or IBM.

Performance funds In these funds the managers aggressively try for the maximum gain in the shortest possible time. The idea is to move nimbly into the market to catch a rise in a particular company or industry, then move nimbly out again and into something else. Performance funds are sometimes referred to on Wall Street as "go-go" funds because they put the emphasis on fast action and are likely to go up and down faster than other funds.

In some cases the portfolio turnover of a performance fund is five times that of run-of-the-mill mutual funds. The long-term growth, however, may be no greater than that of a well-managed growth fund.

Dual-purpose funds These have appeared in the United States in recent years, having originated in Europe. Such a fund offers two classes of stock to investors—preferred and common. The holders of the preferred receive all the income from the fund's portfolio, while the holders of the common receive all the capital gains. One problem faced by the managers of such a fund, of course, is how to select stocks that have equally attractive prospects of growth in asset value and income. To favor one type of investment over the other would be to favor one class of the fund's investors.

Leverage funds This is a rather rare type of closed-end fund that has several types of security outstanding in the hands of the public. Suppose a company is organized with assets of $15 million, one-third represented by preferred stock and bonds and two-thirds by common stock. The holders of the preferred stock and bonds would have a $5 million fixed interest in the fund, and the remainder would belong to the holders of the common stock. If the stock market dropped and the fund's holdings declined in value by 20%—to $12 million—the loss would be magnified on the common stock. The owners of the bonds and preferred stocks still would have claim to $5 million, so there would be only $7 million as equity for the common stock—a 30% drop from $10 million. On the other hand, if the market value of the holdings increased by 20%—to $18 million—the gain to the common stock holders would be magnified: Owners of the "senior securities" would still have a claim on only $5 million, so common stock equity would jump 30% to $13 million.

Most closed-end funds, such as Lehman Corp., have just one kind of stock—common. But a few also have issued senior securities, and these are said to be leverage funds. Many years ago, this feature made the common stock of such funds a venture strictly for the speculator. Today, though, the leverage factor usually is looked on as insignificant.

Hedge funds These were much in the news during the big bull market of 1968, although they had their origin 20 or 30 years earlier. Most hedge funds are operated for a small group of wealthy investors who have formed an investment partnership. Usually the managers are young and aggressive and have had business school training. They are adept in the use of computers and are not afraid to charge into and out of investment situations that would make an old-fashioned portfolio manager's hair stand on end.

The theory of the hedge fund is that you should always be long on the best stocks you can find and short on the worst. If the manager picks the right stocks, the longs will go up more in a rising market than the shorts; or the shorts will fall more in a declining market than the longs. Thus, either way the market goes, the hedge fund stands to make a profit. Needless to say, such funds must have large amounts of venture capital to work with so that commissions and managements fees are a relatively minor part of the operation. No small investor could afford the expense, not to speak of the risk.

PRICE QUOTATIONS AND MANAGEMENT FEES

Price quotations Prices of the larger mutual funds are quoted on newspaper financial pages under two headings, "bid" and "asked." The asked price is the offering price; i.e., net asset value plus sales commission. The bid price is simply net asset value. If the fund has no load, bid and asked prices are the same. Closed-end funds are quoted in the New York Stock Exchange and over-the-counter quotations. In addition, each Monday the *Wall Street Journal* and the New York *Times* list the prices of closed-end shares and the discounts or premiums as a percentage of net asset value.

Management fees and other matters How much do you pay to have your money managed by an investment company? The cost to the company of obtaining investment advice usually runs around ⅓ to ½ of 1% of the total net assets. Other expenses, such as commissions, auditing, legal and custodian fees, and overhead, are added to this percentage and may bring it up to ¾ of

1% or sometimes more for small funds. Expressed in terms of the gross income of the investment trust, expenses usually amount to 7% to 15%, sometimes to 25% or even higher. Since the largest item of expense in management is the advisory fee, it is important to know whether the percentage drops with the increase in the size of assets. In many cases the level does not decline, no matter how big the fund's assets get. This is contrary to the usual practice in the investment advisory field. Some funds do pay on a sliding scale; for example, a fee of ½ of 1% on the first $50 million of net assets, ⅜ of 1% on the next $50 million, and ¼ of 1% on the portion over $100 million. Note also that in some cases the investment company provides its own management, and when it does so, the expense ratio is likely to be very low. It can, in fact, be as low as ¼ of 1% a year, or ⅓ of the expense ratios of similar funds that pay advisory fees to outsiders.

Minimum investment Although quite a few funds have no bottom limits on orders, general practice is to require a minimum amount for initial and subsequent investments. The starting minimums range from $25 or less to as much as several thousand dollars. The funds normally accept smaller amounts for subsequent investments. Minimums are sometimes fixed in numbers of shares, so the dollar sum varies according to net asset values.

When you invest by dollar amounts, your purchase may include a fractional share. For instance, $1,000 will buy 61.728 ($61^{728}/_{1000}$) shares of a no-load fund with a $16.20 asset value.

Fund income A fund derives its revenues from dividends and interest on the stocks and bonds it owns and from capital gains made on the sales of those securities. Virtually all income left after payment of management fees and other expenses is distributed to shareholders.

You can arrange, either free or for a service fee, to have income and capital gains dividends automatically reinvested in the fund's shares rather than sent to you. Capital gains dividends are reinvested at the net asset value. Income dividends, though, are sometimes reinvested at the offering price, which includes the maximum sales charge.

Sales charge reduction options You can reduce sales charges simply by investing large enough amounts to take advantage of

Mutual Funds

the quantity discounts. Two other ways are to sign a "letter of intention" or buy shares in a fund that offers a "right of accumulation."

With a letter of intention, in its most common form, you indicate the sum you propose to invest over the following 13 months. The total has to be more than a prescribed sum, such as $10,000, $15,000 or $25,000. Each time you make a payment toward that goal, you'll be charged at the lower sales rate that would apply if you invested the total in one sum. Assume you set the target at $25,000, reducing the sales charge from 8.5% to 6%. If you make a payment of, say, $5,000, the fund will subtract a 6% charge of $300 rather than 8.5% or $425.

A letter of intention does not bind you to complete the pledged investment. But if you drop out, the fund will recalculate the sales charge at 8.5% and ask you to make up the difference. Some of the shares bought under a letter are kept in escrow to cover the higher charge if you fail to pay it.

With a right of accumulation, you ordinarily pay the regular sales charge for each separate investment, but the amounts are added and you qualify for a lower rate on later payments when the total passes one of the break points at which sales charges are reduced. Suppose the sales charge drops from 8.5% to 6% for investments over $10,000. The 8.5% will be deducted from all payments until the total reaches $10,000. Subsequent payments would be entitled to the 6% rate.

Mutual fund statements Traditionally, your evidence of ownership of mutual fund shares has been in the form of a stock certificate like a certificate showing ownership of any stock, such as General Electric or Standard Oil of New Jersey. But today most mutual funds do not issue stock certificates except on request.

Instead, you are sent periodic statements, such as the one below prepared by a major mutual fund that levies a sales charge. The account shows transactions of a client who invested $6,000 in three $2,000 installments and requested certificates for only the first $2,000. The fund issued 136 full shares and left 612_{1000}ths of a share on deposit. Both capital gains and dividends were reinvested. Dividend reinvestments are subject to a 40-cent service fee. **CTF** stands for share certificates, **REINV** for reinvested.

THIS IS A STATEMENT OF THE ACCOUNT

DATE	TRANSACTION	DOLLAR AMOUNT	PRICE PER SHARE	SHARES THIS TRANSACTION	TOTAL SHARES
	BALANCE FORWARD 1/27/70				.000
1–30	CASH INVESTMENT	2000.00	14.64	136.612	136.612
1–31	CTF ISSUED			136.000	
3–20	DIVIDEND—REINV	14.62	13.60	1.075	137.612
3–20	CAP GAIN—REINV	47.81	13.60	3.515	141.202
5–26	CASH INVESTMENT	2000.00	11.96	160.514	301.716
6–22	DIVIDEND—REINV	32.79	11.57	2.834	304.550
9–18	DIVIDEND—REINV	33.10	12.18	2.718	307.268
12–01	CASH INVESTMENT	2000.00	14.12	141.643	448.911
12–01	DIVIDEND—REINV*	45.69	12.84	3.558	452.469

* 15¢ PER SHARE ON SHARES OF RECORD 11–30–70 AFTER DEDUCTING .40 CENTS SERVICE CHARGE

THIS IS A SUMMARY OF THE ACCOUNT

Current Year's Activity			Shares Now Owned		
DIVIDENDS PAID	CAPITAL GAINS PAID	INVESTMENTS THIS YEAR	IN CERTIFICATE FORM	ON DEPOSIT	TOTAL
127.80	47.81	6000.00	136.000	316.469	452.469

Accumulation plans Two types of plans—"voluntary" and "contractual"—are used in the mutual fund field to encourage regular investment of small amounts. Both are called accumulation plans, but there are highly important differences between them.

In a voluntary plan you merely indicate that you plan to invest, say, $25 or $50 a month over a period of years until the investment builds up to any selected total. The standard sales charge is applied to each installment, and dividends and capital gains are reinvested by the fund. You can skip payments, reduce them (as long as you don't go below the fund's minimum) or stop when you like.

In a contractual plan, a substantial part of the first year's payments (in some cases, as high as 50%) are taken out to pay for current and *future* sales charges based on the entire planned investment—a practice called "front-end loading." You may lose a portion of those advance sales charges if you drop out of the plan early. You may lose out, too, even when you stay in, for this reason: The big front-end load reduced the amount actually invested in the fund's shares at the beginning. If share prices rise during the early stages of your investment, you won't gain as much as you would have if only the normal sales charge had been subtracted and you owned correspondingly more shares.

You may be able to avoid an early drop out by using a fund's emergency withdrawal plan. That gives you the right to sell most of your shares and replace them later without a second sales charge.

A recent change in federal law requires contractual plans sold on or after June 14, 1971, to use one of two sales charge arrangements:

1. The company can, as formerly, deduct up to 50% of the first 12 monthly payments for sales charges. The shareholder has the right during the first 45 days to cash in his shares and get a complete refund of the sales charges. Or, during the first 18 months, he can cash in his shares and obtain a refund of sales charges that exceed 15% of his total payments. But he would lose that 15%.

2. If a plan deducts no more than 20% from payments during any one year and no more than an average of 16% from the first 48 monthly payments, then it doesn't have to extend the 18-month refund right, only the 45-day one.

Contractual plans are sold by special companies that may be affiliated with a management firm or with the outfit that distributes a fund's shares. California, Illinois, Ohio and Wisconsin prohibit the sales of contractual arrangements.

Withdrawal plans To help shareholders who want a steady income for retirement or other purposes, most funds will make regular payments from an account once it has reached a prescribed minimum, usually $10,000. You can arrange to withdraw a fixed sum each month from the income and capital gains your shares earn or from a combination of income, capital gains and capital acquired from the redemption of shares. Some funds will adjust the sum for you according to current share prices to avoid selling off too many shares when prices drop. A complete description of withdrawal plans appears in Chapter 19.

THE PROS AND CONS

For a better idea of what those basic features of fund operations can mean to you as an investor, consider the principal advantages and disadvantages.

Diversification The fund gives you a chance to diversify your holdings. On your own you can probably buy securities of only a few companies. In a fund every dollar is spread over a wide range of stocks, thereby reducing the impact of a decline in any one security. On the other hand, weak stocks in a diversified portfolio may cancel out the gains of the winners, so you might make more by taking a chance on a few well-chosen stocks. Many people compromise by putting some money into funds and some into individual securities.

Professional management Your fund money will be managed by specialists with excellent sources of information and, often, sizable staffs of security analysts. Professional management, though, doesn't guarantee success. Some funds have not done as well as the stock market averages, particularly over short periods. Also keep in mind that you pay for that management service through the management fee charged by the fund.

Cost Investing very small amounts in a fund, even if it has an 8.5% load, won't cost much more than buying an equal amount of stock on your own. On larger investments, however, a stock exchange transaction may cost considerably less than a fund.

Systematic investment An investor can gradually build up a stake with monthly installments as small as $25, at no cost if he buys a no-load fund or at a reduced sales charge if he buys a load fund with a right of accumulation. But you can also set up a long-term program through the monthly investment program of stock exchange member firms, or by accumulating money for investment through regular deposits in a savings account.

To some extent, you can duplicate a fund's major services on your own. What makes the fund so attractive is that it puts these services all together into one convenient package. For the person who hasn't had much success selecting securities, or who can't spare the time and effort to manage his investments, a fund may prove to be the best way to participate in the stock market.

MAKING A CHOICE

There are a number of criteria in selecting an investment trust. The two main ones are these: First, are the managers of the trust trying to invest the money entrusted to them the way you would invest it yourself? For most investors this means putting the money into common stocks of good-quality and aggressive companies. Second, are the managers of the trust doing a bang-up job? In other words, is their investment record better than the average record of trusts with similar objectives?

Once these tests are met, there are other measures to apply. Is the sales charge reasonable? Is the annual management fee a modest one? Can shares be purchased in convenient amounts, assuming you do not wish to make a large lump-sum investment? In the case of closed-end funds, you can usually buy a few shares at a time through the Monthly Investment Plan of the New York Stock Exchange, as was explained in Chapter 14. In the case of open-end funds, there usually are minimum amounts that may be invested. For example, a fund may require a minimum initial investment of $250 or $500 and subsequent investments of, say, $50 at a time. Does the trust permit reinvestment of dividends and capital gains distributions conveniently and inexpensively? In many cases, funds permit reinvestment of capital gains distributions at net asset value, but charge the usual sales commission for reinvestment of dividends paid out of income. Other funds permit the reinvestment of both capital gains distributions and dividends at net asset value.

Here are other points to watch for.

Size The biggest and most widely known trusts are not necessarily the best. The managers of the very largest open-end funds with the hardest-hitting salesmen cannot confine their investments to a relatively few outstanding stocks. They have so much money coming in from shareholders that they must, perforce, spread it over many stocks. The largest open-end funds get so heavily invested in so many companies that they become, as it were, muscle-bound and cannot buy and sell with any freedom. Too often the diversification is so broad that the results are mediocre. This underscores the fact that only the best funds can beat the stock market averages.

Acquisition costs While not as important as performance, they do enter into the selection.

Sponsorship Who manages the trust and why? Selling shares in mutual funds has been a good business in the past although the industry suffered a slump in 1971 and 1972. The principle of investing through trusts has been sound, but unfortunately there is reason to feel that a few managers are more interested in the sales commissions and management fees than in providing the best possible results for the shareholders. Many such trusts have reduced management fees as a result of stockholder suits.

Performance An outstanding long-term performance record is important. In addition, the investor may feel better about putting in his money if he knows that the managers have thought enough of the trust to put in their own money. Of course, no one person could own a substantial interest in an investment trust with assets of hundreds of millions of dollars. However, a few could be mentioned, such as Lehman Corporation, Chemical Fund, State Street Investment Corporation and Tri-Continental Corporation, in which the managers and their families do have substantial holdings.

Which funds have done the best? This is the most important question and one on which many investors go astray. It is important because when you buy shares in an investment trust you are paying someone to manage your money. If you don't get good management, you get nothing.

Some investors go wrong because they buy the first trust they hear of. Or they may listen to some salesman without realizing that alternative, and perhaps better, investments are available.

Other investors buy a poorly managed trust because they see that it made money during a limited period. It is advisable to check on what management did over longer periods.

There are, in fact, several tests that should be applied to the management record of an investment trust. Ideally, the net asset value per share should go up with, or faster than, the stock market as a whole and decline more slowly. So one measure is to compare changes in net asset value per share with stock market averages during periods of rising prices and also during periods of declining prices. In addition to the rise and decline in the value of the shares, you naturally must take into account the amount of capital gains paid out. Most investors should reinvest these capital gains, but in some compilations of investment trust records, these gains are listed separately. Dividends should be considered of less importance by most investors.

Below are the names and descriptions of several books that will help you investigate various funds.

Investment Companies by Arthur Wiesenberger Services Inc., One New York Plaza, New York, N.Y. 10004, published annually, is crammed with information on the theory of investment trusts in general as well as detailed information on all open-end and closed-end trusts. The book may be examined in almost every brokerage house in the country and in almost every library.

Investment Trusts and Funds From the Investor's Point of View is another valuable publication put out each year by the American Institution for Economic Research, Great Barrington, Mass. The authors, using certain criteria, select a small number of funds, some open-end and some closed-end. These funds are then compared with their composite average.

Johnson's Investment Company Charts is perhaps the most intriguing gadget for judging the largest open-end funds (but not the closed-end type). It is published annually by Hugh A. Johnson, Rand Building, Buffalo, N.Y. 14202. Each fund gets a page. Its management record is measured by a line on a chart showing how much your shares would be worth today (including all capital gains distributions) if you had invested $10,000 in the fund ten years ago. You can look at this book in the offices of most investment dealers or in a library.

FundScope is a magazine devoted entirely to investment companies and statistics on their performance. Address is Suite 700, 1900 Avenue of the Stars, Los Angeles, Calif. 90067.

United Business Service also rates and comments on investment companies. Address is 212 Newbury Street, Boston, Mass. 02116.

EXAMPLES OF INVESTMENT COMPANIES

Remember, there are hundreds of investment trusts offering shares. You should look over many funds before making your selection. And generally speaking, this selection should be based on two considerations: First, do the fund's investment objectives correspond to your own? Second, is the management the best you can find?

The common stock funds listed below are not recommendations but examples of some that have done well over a long period of time. Their selection has been based on performance records, management costs and other factors. There are many other funds that have done as well, and some that have done even better if you consider only the record of the past year or two. So consider these funds as examples selected to show, among other things, the variety available. And keep in mind that the fact that a certain fund is not included in this list does not mean that it isn't a good investment.

The classifications below are those used by the Wiesenberger Financial Services, and have to do with asset size, investment objectives and volatility; that is, whether the fund's value may be expected to go up faster or slower than the stock market averages. Generally speaking, a fund whose value goes up faster than the averages in a bull market may be expected also to go down faster in a bear market. In each group the individual funds are listed alphabetically. Though most of the funds mentioned have long records by which to judge their performance, a few smaller, newer funds are listed for those who wish more action along with more risk. For more information on any of these funds, write for a prospectus and financial report.

GROUP A—LARGE OPEN-END GROWTH FUNDS, ASSETS OVER $300,000

Chemical Fund 61 Broadway, New York, N.Y. 10006, organized in 1938 and under the same management since then. Investment objective is growth of capital and income. The name implies that the trust specializes in chemical company stocks, but actually it has interpreted the field so broadly that it offers considerable diversification among industries as well as companies. Included are producers of drugs, nutritional products, toiletries and cosmetics, glass, rubber, paint, photographic materials, detergents, plastics, fertilizers, paper, petroleum products, synthetic fibers, etc.

Delaware Fund 7 Penn Center Plaza, Philadelphia, Pa. 19103, incorporated in 1937 and under same management since then. Investment objective is capital appreciation.

Enterprise Fund 1888 Century Park East, Los Angeles, Calif. 90067, formed in California in 1953 as the California Fund, became the Enterprise Fund in 1967. Present management has been in control since 1962. Investment objective is growth of capital.

Fidelity Capital Fund 35 Congress Street, Boston, Mass. 02109, organized in 1957 and under the same management since. Objective is long-term growth of capital.

Fidelity Trend Fund 35 Congress Street, Boston, Mass. 02109, organized in 1957 and under the same management since. Capital appreciation is primary objective; income is incidental.

Keystone Custodian Lower-priced Common Stock Fund (S-4) 99 High Street, Boston, Mass. 02110, organized in 1935 and under the same management since. Keeps as fully invested as practicable in common stocks selected primarily for growth but which may be expected to experience wide fluctuations in price in both rising and declining markets.

Massachusetts Investors Growth Stock Fund 200 Berkeley Street, Boston, Mass. 02116, organized in 1932 and under same management since 1935. Objective is long-term growth of principal and future income.

National Investors Corporation 65 Broadway, New York, N.Y.

10006, began operations in 1937 and has been under same management since 1942. Objectives are long-term growth of capital and income.

Oppenheimer Fund One New York Plaza, New York, N.Y. 10004. First offered in 1959 and under same management since. Maximum growth of capital consistent with a prudent investment policy is primary objective.

T. Rowe Price Growth Stock Fund One Charles Center, Baltimore, Md. 21201, a no-load fund organized in 1950 and under same management since. Objective is long-term appreciation of capital and income.

Technology Fund 120 South La Salle Street, Chicago, Ill. 60503, organized in 1948 as Television Fund, subsequently Television-Electronics Fund, and operating under present name since 1968. Under same management since 1948. Invests primarily in securities of companies expected to benefit from technological advances and improvements in aerospace, astrophysics, chemistry, electricity, etc.

Windsor Fund 3001 Philadelphie Pike, Claymont, Del. 19703, organized in 1958 and known as Wellington Equity Fund until 1963, has been under same management since 1958. Long-term growth of capital and income is the objective.

GROUP B—SMALLER OPEN-END GROWTH FUNDS—
OBJECTIVE: Maximum Capital Gain—
Volatility Generally High

Axe-Houghton Stock Fund 400 Benedict Avenue, Tarrytown, N.Y. 10591, organized in 1932 as Republic Investors Fund, has been under present management since 1950. Objective is long-term capital growth through common stock investments along with defensive investments in preferred stocks and bonds as conditions warrant.

The Chase Fund of Boston 535 Boylston Street, Boston, Mass. 02116, organized in 1958 and under the same management since. Basic objective is capital appreciation.

Equity Growth Fund of America 1900 Avenue of the Stars, Los Angeles, Calif. 90067, a relatively new fund initially offered in 1966 and under the same management since. Follows an aggressive investment policy for capital appreciation.

Ivy Fund 441 Stuart Street, Boston, Mass. 02116, organized in 1960, originally offered as Commonwealth Fund for Growth. Name changed to Ivy Fund in 1967 and has been under same management since. Primary objective is long-term growth of capital. The fund has no sales charge and has been a no-load fund since 1966.

Lexington Research Fund 177 North Dean Street, Englewood, N.J. 07631, the successor, through merger in 1959, to Research Investing Corporation, a closed-end investment company formed in 1939. Under same management since 1947. Long-term growth of capital is primary objective.

Mathers Fund One First National Plaza, Chicago, Ill. 60670, a relatively new, no-load fund, organized in 1965 and under the same management since. Primary investment objective is long-term capital appreciation and fund may invest in the securities of unseasoned companies or special situations.

The One Hundred Fund 1600 Broadway, Denver, Colo. 80202, a relatively new fund organized in 1966 and under same management since. Capital growth is primary objective. Fund managers say they will suspend sales of shares when total net assets exceed $100 million.

Rowe Price New Horizons Fund One Charles Center, Baltimore, Md. 21201, a no-load fund formed in 1960 and under same management since. Objective is to find growth stocks of the future before they attain sufficient stature to become attractive to institutional investors. The managers twice have suspended sales, believing that too rapid growth was not in the best interest of the shareholders. Minimum purchase was set in 1972 at $25,000.

Scudder Special Fund 345 Park Avenue, New York, N.Y. 10022, organized in 1956 and under same management since. Objective is long-term growth. Some investments may carry above-average risk and involve relatively new companies, and older companies whose earning power is being restored. A no-load fund.

Supervised Investors Growth Fund 120 South La Salle Street, Chicago, Ill. 60603, a relatively new fund organized in 1965 and under same management since then. Capital appreciation is fund's primary object.

GROUP C—SMALLER OPEN-END GROWTH FUNDS— OBJECTIVE: Long-term Growth of Capital and Income— Volatility Moderately Above Average

David L. Babson Investment Fund 301 West Eleventh Street, Kansas City, Mo. 64105, a no-load fund organized in 1959 under the name Associations Investment Fund. Name was changed to present name in 1968. Under same management since 1959. Objective long-term capital growth through investment in stocks of seasoned, high-grade companies, but also including some representation in smaller companies.

de Vegh Mutual Fund 20 Exchange Place, New York, N.Y. 10005, a no-load fund organized in 1950 by the investment counsel firm of de Vegh & Co. and merged in 1962 with the present NYSE member firm of Wood, Struthers & Winthrop, which has managed the fund since. Long-term capital appreciation is the primary objective.

The Johnston Mutual Fund 460 Park Avenue, New York, N.Y. 10022, a no-load fund formed in 1947 as a balanced fund and changed in 1959 to a growth fund. Management has been the same since founding. Primary objective is growth of capital and income.

Keystone Custodian Growth Common Stock Fund (S-3) 99 High Street, Boston, Mass. 02110, organized in 1935 and under same management since. Fund seeks capital growth through investments in common stocks of a class consisting of the better-quality stocks among those that characteristically move faster than the market during major price movements.

National Growth Fund 120 Broadway, New York, N.Y. 10005, one of seven funds making up the National Securities Funds, organized in 1940 and under same management since. Long-term growth of capital is the object.

Putnam Investors Fund 265 Franklin Street, Boston, Mass. 02110, organized in 1925 as Incorporated Investors, came under Putnam management in 1964, the name being changed to its present form in 1966. Growth of capital and income is the primary investment objective.

GROUP D—OTHER DIVERSIFIED COMMON STOCK FUNDS—OBJECTIVE: Growth and Current Income— Volatility Average

Fidelity Fund 35 Congress Street, Boston, Mass. 02109, organized in 1930, this fund has been under the same management since 1946. Objectives are long-term growth of capital and income and a reasonable current return.

Investment Company of America 611 West Sixth Street, Los Angeles, Calif. 90017, organized in 1933 and under same management since then, the fund was converted from closed-end to open-end in 1938. Long-term growth of capital and income are the primary objectives, with current income a secondary consideration.

Mutual Investing Foundation—MIF Fund 246 North High Street, Columbus, Ohio 43216, organized in 1933 as a common-law trust and reorganized in 1957 to be managed by a board of trustees. Present name was adopted in 1960. Objective is reasonable current income and possible growth of income through investments in common stocks, convertible issues or bonds.

Pioneer Fund 28 State Street, Boston, Mass. 02109, incorporated in 1928, present name adopted in 1951. Long-term growth of capital and reasonable current income are the objectives. Policy is to keep substantially fully invested with no attempt being made to speculate on broad price changes in the market. The fund seeks values in securities of companies that have not as yet become popular with the public.

GROUP E—OTHER DIVERSIFIED COMMON STOCK FUNDS—OBJECTIVE: Growth and Current Income, with Relative Stability—Volatility Below Average

Guardian Mutual Fund 120 Broadway, New York, N.Y. 10005, incorporated in 1950, is a no-load fund. A new investment policy adopted in January 1969 places emphasis on capital appreciation and, secondarily, current income. Previously the objectives were preservation of principal and reasonable income.

Istel Fund 345 Park Avenue, New York, N.Y. 10022, organized in 1945 and under the same management since. Policy is flexible and, depending on economic conditions, places varying emphasis on stability or appreciation of principal, and on stability or growth of income.

GROUP F—BALANCED FUNDS

Shareholders' Trust of Boston 535 Boylston Street, Boston, Mass. 02116, organized in 1948 and under same management since. Conservation of principal, reasonable current income and the possible enhancement of capital and income are the investment goals. Assets are distributed among bonds, preferred stocks and common stocks, depending on management's appraisal of the outlook. Not more than 75% of assets will be invested in any one class of securities.

GROUP G—INCOME FUNDS

Decatur Income Fund 7 Penn Center Plaza, Philadelphia, Pa. 19103, organized in 1956 and under same management since, was known as Delaware Income Fund until 1963. Investment objective is to earn the highest possible current income without undue risk to principal. Possible growth of capital is a secondary consideration.

Financial Industrial Income Fund 900 Grant Street, Denver, Colo. 80201, organized in 1960 and under the same management since. Primary objective is production of relatively high current income consistent with sound investment practice. Capital growth is an additional objective.

Provident Fund for Income 3 Penn Center Plaza, Philadelphia, Pa. 19102, began operations in 1960 and under same management since. Primary objective is liberal current income with secondary consideration given to long-term growth and need for protection of capital.

GROUP H—DIVERSIFIED CLOSED-END COMPANIES

General American Investors Company 60 Broad Street, New York, N.Y. 10004, formed in 1927 and under same management since 1960. Objective is long-term capital appreciation with lesser emphasis placed on current income.

Niagara Share Corporation 70 Niagara Street, Buffalo, N.Y. 14202, incorporated in 1925 and under the same management since. The Schoellkopf family of Buffalo were among the original sponsors, and members of the family have always been among the company's largest stockholders. Investment objective is long-term growth, investments being concentrated in a relatively few industries.

Surveyor Fund 90 Broad Street, New York, N.Y. 10004, organized in 1925 and originally known as General Public Service Corporation, this company's portfolio for many years was dominated by utilities. Since 1963 its holdings have become more diversified. Objectives are above-average long-range growth of capital value and investment income.

Tri-Continental Corporation 65 Broadway, New York, N.Y. 10006, organized in 1929, this is a leverage company having outstanding common stock, preferred stock and perpetual warrants to purchase the common. The corporation normally operates as a diversified common stock fund, but a small proportion of assets usually is invested in bonds. Objectives are conservation of capital values and growth of both capital and income, together with provision of reasonable current income.

16

MUTUAL FUNDS—
WHAT'S GOING ON?

If a group of people got together and said, "Let's pool our money, hire an expert in investment and pay him to invest our money for us," you would have a simon-pure mutual fund. This, however, is not how most mutual funds get started. It usually works the other way. A group of financial men get together and decide to start a mutual fund as a money-making business. There are four or five functions involved in managing, advising and selling most mutual funds. Not all mutual funds have all of these functions. In some cases the organizations that perform the functions are separate and distinct from the main management group. In other cases, some or all are combined. Here are the money-making functions:

• The sponsoring group, usually known as the fund's managers or advisers, makes money by charging the mutual fund a management or advisory fee. This is traditionally about ½ of 1%, but it can be more or less.

• The underwriter sells the mutual fund's shares to the public for a retail commission, commonly 8½% or 9%. Salesmen get most of this commission, but the underwriting group itself gets part.

- A broker, or several brokers, handles the buy and sell orders for the stocks in the fund's portfolio. If large funds turn over their portfolios rapidly, the amount of brokerage and the commissions generated are often tremendous.
- The management or advisory group has a contract with the mutual fund to manage or advise it (manage and advise are used interchangeably here). This contract, then, becomes a valuable asset. In some cases, contracts have been sold at big profits to other management companies. Or the management company with a profitable contract has "gone public"; that is, sold part of its stock to the public for a great deal more than the owners themselves originally put into it.
- The principals in these groups pay themselves good salaries and directors' fees.

As you can see, most mutual funds are organized by businessmen or entrepreneurs who have a variety of ways in which they can make money from the pool of capital provided by the fund's shareholders. And, obviously, there are possible conflicts of interest.

Now what defense do the shareholders of a mutual fund have against abuse by the managers, advisers and underwriters? In theory, the shareholders of the fund can elect a new set of directors. Or the shareholders can refuse to approve the fund's contract with the managing or advisory firm. But as a practical matter, such spontaneous action on the part of the fund's shareholders would be most unlikely. Since most mutual funds appeal to the small investor, ownership is widely diffused among many small holders. At many a mutual fund annual meeting, no shareholders show up at all, or at most, a handful. Shareholders vote almost exclusively by proxy and under these conditions, management control often is a virtually automatic counsequence of possession of the corporate proxy machinery by the promoting management or advisory group.

There are certain provisions of the law designed to protect the shareholder's interest in this welter of overlapping activities by management or advisory groups, underwriters and brokers. At least 40% of the fund's directors must be independent; that is, have no interest directly or indirectly in the fund's management advisory, brokerage or underwriting business. If the fund's underwriters are represented on the fund's board of directors, then a majority of the directors must have no connection with the underwriters. The same provision applies to the fund's brokers. And an investment banker, no matter whether he is connected with the fund or not, cannot serve as an independent director. Furthermore, the contract between the fund and its managers or advisers must be approved by owners of a majority of the fund's shares and also by a majority of the independent directors.

Despite these rules, the practice has been for the independent directors to go along with the directors representing the management, except in cases of patent mismanagement or improper conduct. Even without aggressiveness on the part of the public directors of mutual funds, shareholders have gotten quite a bit of action in recent years. There has been a rash of stockholder derivative suits instituted by law firms on behalf of mutual fund shareholders. In one case, for example, the prestigious Massachusetts Investors Trust and Massachusetts Investors Growth Stock Fund were sued by shareholders who charged that advisory fees paid by the two funds to Massachusetts Financial Services, Inc., which operates the funds, were grossly excessive. The two funds settled by agreeing to reduce fees over the coming ten-year period. Other charges involved the paying of excessive commissions to brokers who were selling the two funds' shares to the public. Part of these commissions, it was charged, should have been recaptured and paid back into the funds.

Right here, perhaps, is a good place to explain the practice of "give-ups." Mutual funds are required under the Investment Company Act to be continuously prepared to redeem their outstanding shares. This obligation is interpreted by the funds to require, or at least to justify, the continuous and unlimited offering of new shares. In most cases it is to the advantage of a fund's management to sell as many shares as possible. As more shares are sold, more sales commissions are generated, the advisory fee grows and so also does the brokerage business. Involved here is a method by which brokers who sell the fund's shares to the public can be rewarded not only by receiving a part of the sales commission but also by receiving buy and sell orders from the fund. These buy and sell orders, of course, generate brokerage commissions.

Up until recently, no volume discounts were permitted on the

New York Stock Exchange. An order to buy or sell 1,000 shares of a stock took very little more work than an order for 100 shares, but the commission was ten times larger. Commissions on very large transactions were so big that, in order to get the business, a brokerage house would even "give up" part of the commission. The practice arose whereby a mutual fund might do all its business with Broker A. But it also wanted to reward Broker B who was an outstanding retailer of the fund's shares to the public. So the fund would instruct Broker A to "give up" or pay out some of its commissions to Broker B. Broker A also might be instructed to give up some of its commissions to Broker C who was performing other services for the fund, such as providing it with research material or helping to calculate the fund's net asset value per share at the close of each day.

Give-ups were considered a bad practice by the SEC, and it outlawed them at the end of 1968. Early in 1972 the SEC, in a policy statement, also demanded that reciprocal brokerage for the sales of mutual fund shares be terminated. The argument against reciprocal business, of course, is that the giving of brokerage to those brokers who sell the fund's shares, increases the fund's size. This, in turn, increases the income of the managers or advisers without doing the fund's shareholders any good. On the contrary, a fund is considered more flexible if it remains at a moderate size. The biggest funds can be muscle-bound, so to speak, and as a practicality must confine themselves to a widely diversified list of large companies. In other words, some giant mutual funds generally show a performance about like the average of all stocks, while some smaller funds may be able to do better by investing in smaller companies that have an opportunity to grow from a smaller base.

Another well-known management company, Fidelity Management & Research Co., received a demand by a group of shareholders of Fidelity Trend Fund, led by the associate dean of the Georgetown Law School, to justify the size of the management company's annual fee. The Fidelity Management & Research Co. also was charged with "gross misconduct" because it gave up brokerage fees to brokers to encourage them to sell the fund's shares to the public, rather than conforming to the SEC's recommendations and recapturing part of the commissions for the benefit of shareholders of the funds. The court said, in fact, that the managers of the fund were guilty of a conflict of interest in not telling the fund's independent directors how such brokerage commissions could have been recaptured for the fund.

When the New York Stock Exchange changed its rules to permit commissions to be negotiated on large trades, it was expected that mutual funds would take advantage of competitive rates and thus be able to save their shareholders money. In some cases, however, mutual funds got around this by paying higher commission rates on the sale of large blocks through secondary offerings. In other words, when a fund decided to sell a large block, instead of negotiating a competitive commission through the exchange, it would hire underwriters who would set up a syndicate, break up the large block into smaller blocks, and sell them at retail at much higher commission rates than could have been negotiated on the exchange.

In other cases, mutual fund management companies have successfully been sued because they sold the management contract to another company, the entire profit going to the stockholders of the management company rather than a portion of it, at least, going to the shareholders of the mutual fund. For example, the investment banking firm of Lazard Frères & Co., which managed the former Lazard Fund, transferred the management contract by a merger with Moody's Investors Service. The fund's name was changed to Moody's Capital Fund, Inc. A class action suit was brought, claiming that the profit on the sale of the management contract should have gone to the shareholders of the fund, rather than to the management company, Lazard Frères & Co. A similar suit was won by shareholders of Dreyfus Fund against Dreyfus Corp., the fund's manager. In the Lazard case the judge ruled that ". . . If Lazard did not wish to continue as advisor and chose to recommend a successor and assist in the latter's installation, it was obliged to forego personal gains from the change. . . ."

Although these suits and other suits like them on behalf of mutual fund shareholders get little publicity in the newspapers, over a hundred actions have been filed around the country.

Other legal problems have arisen regarding the right of mutual funds and other institutional investors to hold membership on stock exchanges. Traditionally, the New York Stock Exchange and the AMEX have allowed only public brokers and dealers to be members. Nonmembers must pay commissions to members on purchases and sales. Naturally, some funds would like to hold memberships to avoid paying brokerage commissions to member firms. As a matter of fact, institutions can become members of some regional exchanges.

One of the reasons some mutual funds would like to have exchange memberships is that they turn over their portfolios faster than they ever have before. In fact, in recent years mutual funds have been buying and selling stocks faster than any other type of institution. In 1962 mutual funds turned over their portfolios at a rate of about 19% a year. In other words, each year, on the average, they sold about a fifth of the stocks they owned and replaced them with other issues. As the performance cult seized some investment managers, mutual funds began turning their portfolios over faster and faster until in recent years they have, on the average, sold and replaced well over half their stocks each year. This kind of turnover worried the SEC to such an extent that it began requiring each fund to make available to its shareholders its turnover rate. The range is tremendous. Some funds have a rate of only 6% a year while others have a rate of almost 500%, meaning that their whole portfolio of stocks could be completely replaced every ten weeks.

Other developments in the mutual fund field involve the rapid growth in the number of funds. This has been brought about primarily by the entry of life insurance companies into the field. Because life insurance values have been so badly eroded by inflation, the life insurance companies' share of the public savings dollar has fallen. To maintain their place in the economy, many insurance companies have acquired or started mutual funds so that their salesmen will have equities to sell as well as insurance. In 1972 some 60,000 life insurance salesmen were qualified to sell shares in over 200 life-insurance-owned funds.

For this and other reasons the number of mutual funds rose during the late 1960's until over 800 funds are available to the public in one form or another. Obviously, a good many funds were rather hurriedly thrown together to give salesmen something to sell. Many managements have turned in mediocre records or worse. Poor records of some funds have pulled down the average so that for a five-year period ending in 1971, the performance of the average mutual fund fell below the performance of the stock market averages.

As a result of all these problems—law suits, poor average performance, bad publicity and so on—shareholders began to turn in their shares in large numbers in 1971. In May of that year redemptions exceeded sales for the first time in 30 years. None of this is to say that a well-managed mutual fund is not a good investment. It can be. But shopping for a good fund whose managers keep the shareholders' interest foremost, and who have the competence to increase the value of his investment as fast as, and hopefully faster than, the stock market averages, has become a difficult task.

17

NEW ISSUES—SHOULD YOU BUY THEM?

How about freshly issued stock? Should you consider buying it? That depends a lot on your investment objectives and what kind of company is issuing the stock. There are three general types of new issue. First is stock issued by an established company that needs additional capital. From time to time even the biggest companies issue new stock to finance expansion, retire debt or for some other purpose. Buying such stock would be about the same as buying the company's stock in the open market. In other words, the risk of owning newly issued stock of a company like General Motors or General Electric would be no greater or less than owning GM or GE stock that had been on the market for some time.

Two other kinds of new issue, however, are in a different class. Stock often is issued by a brand-new company with only a short history of operations. There is considerable risk here because of the difficulties new companies always face. Then there is the stock issued by a company that has been operating for some years but that heretofore has been privately owned, or perhaps even family owned, but that has decided for some reason to "go public." Though such a company may be well established and profitable, buying a new issue of its stock may be quite risky because of the uncertainty as to where the stock's price eventually will settle. When underwriters offer a company's stock for the first time, they have to put a price on it, but they have no way of knowing whether their price will turn out to be higher or lower than the price that eventually will be put on it by the public.

In a sense all money raised from the sale of stock is "risk capital." But for the purposes of this chapter, risk capital will be considered to be the stock issued by new companies or companies that have only just decided to go public.

THE NEED FOR CAPITAL

Note that business can get money for expansion and development of new products in three ways: (1) by borrowing; (2) by plowing back earnings; (3) by selling stock.

A company has to be pretty sound and substantial to borrow big sums of money. A new, young company with a bright new idea can't do it. Also, when a company does contract a big debt and feels the weight of it hanging over its head, it is apt to be very cautious about using the money for any new venture, experiment or research that could but won't positively return the money intact.

Stockholders' money, on the other hand, whether it comes from plowed back earnings or from the sale of new stock, doesn't have to be paid out, or back, on any particular date—or ever, for that matter. So a company financed by its earnings or sales of its own stock is likely to feel freer to put that money to work in a way that may be somewhat risky but that also may bring in substantial profits. Remember, however, that a new company probably has few earnings to plow back, so it may have to depend on the sale of stock for its capital needs. A family-owned company, even though it may have good earnings, may also have good reasons for offering a block of stock to the public. Large stockholders may want to diversify their holdings or raise money for estate tax purposes.

Here is an example to show why risk capital is needed and how it often is raised. Say there are a couple of young men who have designed a new kind of computer component. The young men naturally want to sell this at a profit. In order to get into production, they need a building, machinery, workers, salesmen and working capital to meet payrolls and various other expenses. Where are they going to get the money?

You can be pretty sure of one thing. They are not going to get it from a bank. The banker might be the first person to approve of their plans and wish them success. He might even put some of his own money into the project. But he won't put in any of the bank's money. The bank uses its depositors' money very cautiously, for loans that are safe and fairly liquid. These might be short-term loans to well-established and successful businesses, or conservative loans to individuals backed up by improved real estate, sound stocks or the cash value of life insurance policies. So the bank is out.

How about the stock market? Can the young men incorporate and sell stock on the New York Stock Exchange? Positively no. Before a company's stock will be admitted to trading on the exchange, the company must have been in business a good many years, be large and prosperous, and have one million shares outstanding and 2,000 or more shareholders. So the stock exchange is out.

So where will the young men, with their bright ideas and their knowledge, turn for help? In the old days they would either work hard and save up enough capital to buy the machinery and equipment themselves, or they would go to one or two or more wealthy men in their home town and offer them an interest in the business in return for the capital to get started.

The original backers That is still the way it is today. If the computer device works, if the young men appear to have knowledge, skill and energy, then they may be able to arouse the enthusiasm of the local banker, lawyer and undertaker. Perhaps the banker, lawyer and undertaker will decide to "risk" $10,000 apiece. In return they will get shares of stock in the new venture. Note well that word "risk." The banker, lawyer and undertaker are not making the young men a loan. They are putting money into a business and getting a part ownership. If all fails, their money is lost. If the business prospers, they own a part of it and can share in the profits.

Assume, now, that the young men's idea is good, that the $30,000 capital put up by their financial backers is enough to buy the equipment and lease the building, that within a few months production gets under way and there is a real demand for the new device produced and sold by Computer Components, Inc. The young men and the banker, lawyer and undertaker then each own one-fifth of what promises to be a successful business. Assuming the contribution of the young men in ideas and knowledge is worth $20,000, the total capitalization is now $50,000.

Soon, however, a problem arises. Business improves so much that the young men can't meet the demand with the small building and few machines they have. The business needs more room, more machinery, a better location with a rail siding, and more working capital to expand their sales force. Where will the money come from?

The banker, the lawyer and the undertaker, although they are pleased with their original investment and want to keep their stock, don't feel like putting up any more money just now. On the other hand, the druggist has heard how well the young men are doing, and he would like to put up a little money himself. But who will sell him stock?

The banker and the lawyer can solve this easily. They recommend that the company create some new stock. Instead of five shares, there will be ten. The company will sell the five new shares, not at the same price as the old shares sold for, but for $15,000 a share. The increase is justified because the business is established now and no longer as risky as it first was, although, of course, there is still some risk. Each owner of an old share will get a chance to buy a new share at the new price. Any new shares not taken up by the original stockholders will be sold to anyone who cares to buy them.

So the druggist gets a chance to buy in. He realizes that even though the company is prospering, it can still lose out to a competitor with a better device, or the plant could burn down or any of a number of things could happen to jeopardize his investment. But still he feels that chances are pretty good that the business will keep growing and make a lot of money later, so he is willing to pay $15,000 a share for stock and will buy two shares. Further-

New Issues—Should You Buy Them?

more, his brother-in-law will buy another share, and the newspaper publisher will come in for two.

So now the young men have taken in new backers and have thereby brought in $75,000 of new money for a bigger building, more machines and more salesmen. Note that the original investors, who once owned the whole company, now only own half of it. But whereas they originally owned a company worth $50,000, they now own half a company worth $125,000, so they have already made a paper profit of $12,500.

So far so good. The company goes along selling its components until one day the newspaper publisher comes up with the news that in the next town there is an old, established company that makes electrical equipment. The elderly man who owns the company wants to sell it so there will be enough cash to pay estate taxes when he dies. He wants to sell to someone who will keep the company going, and if he finds the right party, he will sell at a reasonable price.

The directors of Computer Components, Inc., are interested. Here is a chance for them to add a new line and diversify their products. But they have no cash to offer. The banker suggests giving some stock to the owner of the electrical company in return for his building, machinery, patents and inventory. In case of his death, some of the stock could be sold to raise money for taxes.

Preferred vs. common stock When the proposal is put up to the elderly manufacturer, he demurs. Computer devices are brand-new to him. But the banker persists. What if he got "preferred" stock? That would give the old man or his heirs prior claim over the assets of Computer Components, Inc., if the company had to dissolve. And it would give prior claim to any money paid out in dividends. In other words, the preferred dividends would have to be paid in full before any dividends could be paid on the common.

That satisfies the owner of the electrical company, so the deal goes through. Computer Components, Inc., acquires the assets of the electrical company in return for 100 shares of Computer Components 5% preferred stock.

Stock splits When this news gets around, many townspeople begin to get interested in this prosperous new company run by the young engineers. A demand grows up for its stock. But there are so few common shares, only ten, that there seldom comes a chance for anyone to buy. In the meantime, the lawyer dies and leaves his stock to his two sons. Since it is only one share, it is hard to divide. The stockholders of the company, taking thought of all this, decide to split the stock 100 for 1. That means that the owner of every share of the original common stock will exchange it for 100 shares of the new common stock. Each new share will then be worth $\frac{1}{100}$ as much as each old share. But each stockholder will have 100 times as many shares.

After the stock split, Computer Components has 1,000 common shares outstanding. The original founders each own 100 shares, except that the lawyer's 100 shares are now divided between his sons. One decides to sell his 50 shares, so he drops in on the local broker. The broker has had inquiries about the stock and feels sure that he can sell 50 shares without any trouble. He figures it is now worth around $135 a share, and that is what the lawyer's son gets for it, minus the commission.

Making a market Pretty soon other shares come on the market and the broker is doing quite a business in it. The stock of Computer Components is then said to be traded "over-the-counter." Once trading is large enough to cross state lines, the company will be required to register its stock with the U. S. Securities and Exchange Commission.

The case history of Computer Components is a fictitious one, but there are many real companies that got their start in the same way. The Ford Motor Company had similar humble beginnings. When a company's stock is finally listed on a major stock exchange, there is always a ready market for any new stock that it might wish to issue for the purpose of raising risk capital.

Profit and risk Look back for a minute at the beginnings of Computer Components, Inc. Who made money on it? The early stockholders made the most. But remember, they took the most risk. They bet their money on two college graduates with an idea. The rest of the people in the town had their money safely stashed away in the bank or savings and loan association where they knew they could lay their hands on it, intact, any time they pleased. But they were getting 4% or 5%, while the investors in Computer Components ultimately received many times that.

As the company became established and better known, others bought its stock and they also prospered. But by that time the investment carried less risk, so the later investors made less. As the stock was traded more widely, it no doubt fluctuated in price, like all stocks. Some people probably bought it with money they really couldn't spare, had to sell later at a bad time, and thereby lost. But even the latecomers, those who bought after the company had become big and strong, could make 6% to 10% or more by buying and holding over the years. That assumes, of course, that the company kept its vigor, brains and wise management.

UNDERWRITING

Suppose, now, that at some point in its history Computer Components wants to raise additional capital by the sale of a block of new stock. The company probably would go to an underwriter. When a company sells its own stock to the public, the underwriter acts as a middleman. The underwriter buys the securities from the issuing company, holds them for the account of his own firm, at least temporarily, then offers them to the public. A broker, on the other hand, merely acts as agent for the buyer and seller. Many firms that do a day-to-day brokerage business also frequently underwrite new issues.

Established companies The biggest part of the underwriting business consists of the selling of new securities of established companies that need additional capital for modernization or expansion, so consider these first. Such issues are often so large that no single investment banker can handle the whole job. Syndicates are formed in which a dozen houses may join together, each buying a portion of the securities and reselling its share to its customers at a markup. This markup pays the overhead and provides the profit to the underwriter. The average markup in the case of shares sold by companies listed on the New York Stock Exchange is less than 4%. The financial pages of the newspapers carry ads every day for such newly issued securities—bonds, debentures, preferred stock, common stock, convertible debentures or preferred, and so on. An expanding utility company, for example, may offer a large issue of bonds to finance new power lines or generators. A large finance company may sell debentures to raise money to relend to auto buyers.

Rights Almost always in the case of common stock of established companies existing stockholders are given the opportunity to buy these additional shares. This opportunity is given via the issuance of "rights." As an example, suppose you own 25 shares of the ABC Company and you get a letter from the president saying the company is issuing additional stock and enclosed are 25 rights entitling you to buy two and a half more shares.

Here is how such rights come to be issued. Say the ABC Company wants to expand and needs more capital. It decides to sell additional stock, increasing its outstanding shares from 100,000 to 110,000. This decision affects you and every other stockholder because it threatens to decrease slightly your share of ownership and profits unless—and here is the crux of the matter —unless you buy your pro-rata share of the new stock. In that case you will maintain your original position.

For this reason many states require companies to offer new stock to their stockholders before they offer it to the public. Go back to your 25 shares of ABC. You have received 25 rights, one right for every share you own. Since the company is increasing its capitalization by 10%, you now have the privilege of increasing your holdings by the same amount, or of buying two and a half more shares. Your 25 rights will come in the form of two certificates. One will be a full certificate representing 20 rights and entitling you to buy two shares of new stock. The other will be a fractional certificate representing five rights and theoretically entitling you to buy half a share. As a matter of practice, you generally can't buy half a share. Your fractional certificate must be combined with others to make up a full certificate. Either you buy enough additional fractional certificates from someone else to make up a full share or you sell your fractional certificates for cash.

On each certificate there are instructions. If you want to sell the certificate for cash, you sign in one place. If you want to subscribe to new shares, you sign in another and make out a check based on the subscription price. If you have a fractional certificate and want to buy additional fractions to make up a full

New Issues—Should You Buy Them?

certificate, you can do that, too. You will be billed later for the cost. In all cases, you send your certificates back to the ABC Company's transfer agent, which may well be a New York bank.

How much are stock rights worth? In actual practice they are worth what other investors are willing to pay for them on the open market. But there is a formula by which their theoretical value can be judged. Assume that ABC is currently traded at $25 a share. The rights entitle you to buy two and a half new shares at $22 a share. The company has set this low price to encourage you to buy. But if you don't care to buy, what can you get for your rights?

To get the theoretical answer, write down the market price of the old stock, $25; subtract the subscription price of the new stock, $22; then divide by 1 plus the number of shares you must own to buy one new share, which in the example is ten shares.

The theoretical value of ABC rights, then, would be—

$$\frac{\$25-\$22}{1+10}=27\frac{1}{3} \text{ cents}$$

Since you have 25 such rights, their total theoretical value is $6.83. If you decide to sell them, you may get a bit more or less, depending on how brisk the demand is and what is happening to the price of ABC stock on the market.

Whatever you do about your rights must be done promptly. When ABC offers to sell new stock at $22 a share, or $3 under the market price, it is highly vulnerable. Suppose the stock market dropped suddenly, carrying the price of ABC down to $20. The right to buy new shares at $22 would be worthless, and the new issue would not get sold. Naturally, the ABC Company wants its stockholders to make up their minds in a hurry. Still, they must have time to read and understand the proposal, fill out the forms and mail them. The New York Stock Exchange therefore requires listed companies to give stockholders 16 days to use or sell their rights. Companies not listed on the exchange generally allow a comparable period. The stock exchange also sets a date at which the stock will sell "ex-rights." This ex-rights date is the date after which the stock no longer carries the right with it.

Whether you should exercise rights or sell them depends on how you feel about the stock in question and whether or not you should be buying more of the same or diversifying into other stocks. Don't be swayed too much by the appearance of a bargain. The price of the stock will be automatically reduced, as of the ex-right date, by the value of one right. So in the end you are about even with the board if you sell the right and take the money instead of subscribing to the new stock offering.

Warrants These are long-lived rights. Some have expiration dates; others are perpetual. They generally come into being as a "sweetener" to make an issue of stock or bonds more attractive. Usually the price at which a warrant entitles the holder to buy a specified number of shares of common stock is considerably above the market price of the stock at the time. But there is always a chance that the market will rise to a point where exercise of the warrant will be profitable. This gives it a speculative appeal.

Small or new companies Another part of the underwriting business is offering for sale the securities of new or privately owned companies that have decided to "go public." Such new issues, being smaller than offerings by established companies, require fewer underwriters and the underwriting markup is likely to be higher, 6% or 7%. In addition, the underwriter sometimes receives as part of his fee, cheap stock in the company or warrants, but this fact must be disclosed to prospective purchasers. As noted previously, when a small company offers securities to the public for the first time, it generally issues common stock. Its future, in all likelihood, is too uncertain for it to attract the type of investor likely to buy bonds. However, capital can be raised by making a bond convertible into common, which gives the bondholders the first claim against the company's assets and a chance to buy the common stock if the company does well.

In the case of a very small, new, speculative company, one underwriter alone may handle the whole issue. He may do it on what is known as a "best efforts" basis. In other words, instead of buying the whole issue and taking the responsibility for reselling it to investors, the underwriter may undertake only to sell as much of the issue as he can. If he fails to sell it all, the balance is left in the hands of the issuing company. When stock is offered on a "best efforts" basis, it often indicates that the underwriter is not too confident that he can place the whole issue, or it may mean that he does not have enough capital to swing the deal on the usual basis.

Underwriter's obligations Now, what are the obligations of the underwriting house when it offers securities to the public? It has a certain obligation to the issuing company. The job there is first to advise the issuer as to timing, price, terms, etc., of the issue, then to get the issue sold and the proceeds into the hands of the issuer at the least cost. The underwriting firm also has obligations to its customers, for it is to them, largely, that it expects to sell the securities. A reputable broker or investment banker doesn't want to recommend purchase of securities and then have them go sour and decline in price. That would be an excellent way to lose customers and go out of business. Finally, of course, the underwriting firm has a responsibility to its own partners, and this simply is to meet expenses and make a profit so that the business can prosper.

An underwriting firm with years of experience and a reputation to maintain will make every effort to offer its customers only sound securities reasonably priced with respect to the issuer's underlying assets and prospective earnings. Large issues of the securities of nationally known companies generally are offered by syndicates headed by large New York underwriters. Even so, there can be no guarantee that the securities so offered will turn out to be good investments.

When it comes to local issues, the prospective investor must be even more careful. In most cities there are local firms that have been in business for years and that exercise the greatest care in choosing which issues they will underwrite. However, in addition to outstanding and reputable local underwriters, there are also those who are less choosy about what they will do. The worst of these are simply looking for stock that they can unload on the public at as high a profit as the traffic will bear.

Gimmicks to beware of Here are a couple of notorious gimmicks designed to take your money. One is known in the trade as a bail-out. The following is an actual case with names omitted. A group of mining promoters organized a company having 6 million shares of common stock. They put in $10,000 in cash and 115 claims covering 2,260,000 acres in Utah, which had cost them $30,000. In return for their investment of $40,000 in the company, they received 3 million shares of stock and offered the other 3 million shares for sale to the public at 10 cents a share.

Right there you can see that if all went as planned and the public paid 10 cents a share for the stock, the promoters' own stock would have a market value of 10 cents a share or $300,000. Not only that, but they would be in control of a company having a quarter of a million dollars of capital (the $300,000 from the public sale of stock minus selling expenses). This is known as a bail-out because the public would have "bailed out" the promoters and acquired assets of dubious value.

Now how about the underwriters? In this case they agreed to sell the stock on a best-efforts basis. For this they received between 25% and 33% of the selling price. All they had to do was to ballyhoo the stock, and every time they sold 1000 shares, they raked in $25 to $30. They owned no stock themselves, nor did they agree to buy any. Therefore they took no risk. The big risk, of course, was taken by those who paid 10 cents a share for stock that had a true worth of a good deal less than that.

The other notorious gimmick used by small and unscrupulous underwriters is known as a "lock-up." In this case, the underwriters bring out a new issue of a glamorous-sounding stock and give it a big advance ballyhoo. They let it be known that this is going to be a "hot issue" and that the demand for it will be so great that the stock will have to be "allocated." In other words, eager customers who want 100 shares will be lucky if they get 10 or 25. To guarantee that the issue will be hot, the underwriters let their friends and relatives sign up for large blocks of the issue in advance, even though this is against the rules. The underwriters do, in fact, create an apparent scarcity. A would-be purchaser, finding that he cannot get any stock allocated to him on the day of the offering, starts bidding for the stock in the open market. This runs the price up. During the height of this price run-up, the insiders quietly begin leaking out their "locked-up" stock at perhaps double or triple the price they paid at the offering.

It is a well-known fact that many small underwriters have this reputation: If you are a good friend or customer and buy their new issues, they will get you in at the offering price and get you out at the top of the run-up. It's not hard to guess who is left holding the bag. It's the uninformed investor who buys at inflated prices and fails to get out in time.

Why is this sort of thing allowed to go on? you might ask. Actually, a great deal is being done to prevent it by both the Securities and Exchange Commission and the National Association of Securities Dealers. But it's a difficult job to police the 100,000 securities salesmen scattered over the country. The SEC requires the issuers of securities to make the most detailed advance disclosure of their assets, prospects, how the money is to be used and the risks involved, but the unfortunate truth is that a great many investors simply won't bother to read registration statements, preferring to base their decisions on what they hear from a salesman or someone else supposedly in the know.

HOW THE SEC PROTECTS INVESTORS

In regard to new issues, the basic SEC law is the Securities Act of 1933, sometimes known as the truth-in-securities act. When securities are first offered to the public, a summary of the company's business operations and its financial condition must be furnished to prospective buyers free. In the case of large issues of stock, this summary is known as a prospectus. When the amount of stock is less than $300,000, an abbreviated summary known as an offering circular may be used.

In either case, whether a salesman solicits an investor in person, by mail or by phone, a copy of the prospectus or offering circular must be furnished. If it is not, the nearest regional office of the SEC would like to hear about it. Sometimes the first written communication a prospect receives is the confirmation of an order he has given by telephone. Even at this late date, he may be able to cancel his purchase if the offering circular reveals information he was not given over the phone. If you ever cancel a purchase in this manner, however, be prepared to find a new broker.

Few purchasers of small new issues really study the offering circular or prospectus, so it's pretty hard to protect them from their own folly. However, the SEC and the NASD do have rules designed to prevent skullduggery.

When a new issue comes out, the underwriter and members of

his firm and his immediate family are not allowed to purchase any stock at the offering price unless such purchases are disclosed in the prospectus and conform to their past pattern of investing. Even if such persons have a history of investing in every new issue underwritten, they are supposed to receive only a reasonably small percentage of the issue and to buy it to hold for investment, not to sell for "a quick turn."

What is a reasonably small percentage, and what is a pattern of investing? These terms are susceptible of different interpretations. In almost every large offering of a hot issue, the NASD or the SEC, or both, has required the underwriter to fill in exhaustive questionnaires showing the disposition of every share of stock. Fines have been levied against culprits who violate the spirit or the letter of the rules.

The same rules apply to broker-dealers who may not be members of the original underwriting group but who have received expressions of interest in the stock from their own customers. If they receive an allocation of stock from the underwriter as an "accommodation," they must accept it at the offering price, less a selling group concession, and sell it to their customers at the same price.

Should you buy new issues? Despite all the pitfalls in the new-issue market, there are bound to be attractive opportunities for investment. In recent years the breakthrough in research has peppered the land with new, exciting ventures. Engineers, chemists, physicists, advanced mathematicians and young people with energy and big ideas have splintered off from established companies and started up new businesses with glamorous names and space-age products that mystify, and yet intrigue, the layman.

Many of these young companies have sold stock to the public and have achieved success so rapidly that their stock has skyrocketed. Naturally, the question arises in the mind of the investor, Should I try to participate in this space-age business and acquire shares in young companies that seem to be growing like Jack's beanstalk and outstripping even the old, established leaders?

This is a hard question to advise on. Undeniably, many of these little companies will grow and prosper and pay off handsomely for those who get in on the ground floor. Many more, however, because of lack of capital, lack of management know-how or inability to compete with the larger groups, will eventually fall by the wayside. The most difficult problem is selection.

The information is available to evaluate the prospects of a new enterprise. The Securities and Exchange Commission sees to that. But the average person hardly has time to read and compare the prospectuses of dozens of companies. And he probably should consider a good many before selecting even one. The large, reliable statistical services cannot evaluate the thousands of small new issues constantly appearing on the market. In the end, the investor is almost forced to ask for help. Chances are the person he will consult about a particular new issue will be the very underwriter who is trying to peddle it.

Unless you are prepared to take a rather high risk, you should leave small new issues strictly alone. Yet the business of raising public money for small, enterprising companies is a legitimate one. Every company from General Motors on down had its humble beginnings. If it had not been for courageous investors willing to finance promising new ventures, we would not be a great industrial nation with a high standard of living. Think what a service the backers of Henry Ford performed, both for themselves and for the public. They made themselves millionaires but also enabled Ford to begin mass production of automobiles.

If you are interested in trying to get in on the ground floor of small, new companies, you should do everything possible to avoid the pitfalls and realize also that these are more numerous than in any other kind of investing.

Guides to use Here are some ideas for investing in small, new companies.

Deal with a reputable underwriter. You can get names of good ones from your banker.

Learn everything you can about the company before you buy. Read the prospectus if the stock is already out. If it isn't, get what is called the "red herring." This is a preliminary prospectus containing what the company considers to be information required by the SEC. The selling price usually is left blank to be inserted later in the final prospectus. If the SEC does not raise any questions as to the adequacy or accuracy of the red herring, it becomes an effective prospectus. Otherwise, the underwriter revises it and resubmits it. All the facts about the company, and particularly all unfavorable facts and contingencies, are clearly set forth in the final prospectus. It would cost a potential investor thousands of dollars to buy such a complete and unbiased picture of a company's operations. The SEC makes the issuer and underwriter provide it to you free. So use it.

SBIC'S

There is another way to buy stock in new, small companies. That is to buy stock in a "small-business investment company," which invests its capital in selected small growth companies.

These small-business investment companies, or SBIC's, are privately organized but can borrow money at moderate rates from the government or the government can guarantee loans to the SBIC's. They can also receive certain tax advantages. In return, SBIC's must agree to lend to or invest in businesses having limited assets and net profits. Such small businesses historically have had difficulty raising capital or obtaining long-term financing.

After 1958, when Congress passed legislation fostering SBIC's, hundreds were organized. The movement was given a further boost in December 1971 when Congress amended the original act and permitted the Small Business Administration to guarantee debentures, both as to principal and interest, which SBIC's could sell to the public. The first underwriting, amounting to $37 million took place in May 1972.

Many SBIC's are closely held and difficult to buy into, but others have "gone public." Their stock is traded over-the-counter or on exchanges. By buying into one of these, you indirectly invest your money in the small companies that the SBIC itself selects, finances and, in some cases, advises. If these small companies prosper and grow, so will your investment. If they do not, chances are you'll lose money. The risk is there, and in some cases it may be more than if you invested in some small company yourself.

Here are the most pertinent facts about this kind of investment.

Professional management This probably is the most important single consideration. An SBIC may be organized by any group of people with capital. Many have been set up by banks. Others have been established by investment counselors or management men well versed in making large-scale investments. Many SBIC's, on the other hand, have been set up by obscure businessmen who operate on the local level. In such cases, the ability of the management is unknown.

Management policy If you are interested in small growth companies that may be on the verge of a large expansion, there are SBIC's that concentrate on this type of investment. Others buy into run-of-the-mill concerns. One SBIC, for example, invested in a chain of bowling alleys, a small iron and steel rolling mill, a clay-products company, a traprock company, a printing company and a string of motels.

Price When SBIC's first began selling stock to the public in volume, there was not much investor interest, and many SBIC shares were selling below net asset value. Later, the public became enthusiastic about SBIC's, and in 1960–61 and again in 1968–69 their stock soared. At other times prices have fallen and SBIC's have sold at a sizable discount from net asset value.

Any investor contemplating purchase of stock in an SBIC should ascertain the relation between the market price and the net asset value per share. All other things being equal, it is better to buy at a discount or at least not pay a very high premium.

Leverage This is a characteristic of investment companies that use borrowed money. Suppose an SBIC has X dollars of invested capital and borrows twice as much at a nominal rate of interest from the federal government (or from private sources utilizing government guarantees). If it then makes a large profit on its total capital, this profit (after interest is paid) accrues to those who put up the original money.

Tax advantages An SBIC and its stockholders receive preferential tax treatment. Dividends the company receives from investments are completely exempt from corporate income taxes. By comparison, ordinary corporations receive only an 85% exemption. If the SBIC suffers losses on its stock investments, these losses may be deducted either from ordinary income or from capital gains. Also, if stockholders in an SBIC sell their shares at a loss, this loss, too, may be deducted from ordinary income.

SBIC's resemble ordinary investment trusts, but there is one difference. An investment trust generally puts its money into well-established companies with a record of earnings extending back at least ten years. By contrast, an SBIC must confine its investments to small companies. Many companies that SBIC's invest in have never had any earnings at all and, at most, have what might be considered good prospects. As a matter of fact, there are on the market shares of investment trusts and mutual funds that also invest in glamorous growth companies. So if you want glamour, consider these trusts as well. And don't forget that a good many old, established companies are developing new products and new methods all the time. Sometimes the underwriters can make a brand-new little company sound pretty glamorous. But companies like IBM or Minnesota Mining and Manufacturing are pretty glamorous, too, and they have been in business a good long time.

18

SPECULATING

To speculate, according to the dictionary, is to engage in commercial operation that involves risk of loss, especially with an implication of rashness. Some gifted people speculate successfully. Bernard Baruch was a famous speculator and a successful one. But he never thought that the ordinary person had a Chinaman's chance at it. John Maynard Keynes, as will be shown later, made a fortune speculating in commodities. But he was one of the world's most brilliant analysts and economists. Most people, according to psychoanalysts, speculate because they have a compulsion to lose. So the ordinary investor should take warning. He can speculate easily enough. Perhaps if he devotes hours a day to studying statistics and if he has an instinct for sensing market trends, he can make a go of it. But he should realize at the start that all the odds are against him. He is competing with shrewd men who spend their time on the floors of the exchanges or in the commodity pits and rings, who are steeped in knowledge of the marketplace, who catch each bit of news seconds after it hits the wires. Some of these experts use computers to analyze the most intricate statistics on production, supply and demand. So speculation definitely is not recommended. For those who are interested, here are some of the ways it is done.

SHORT SELLING

In the old days many a fortune was made by selling short. Such famous figures as Joseph P. Kennedy, father of the late President Kennedy, and Bernard Baruch used this technique. After the excessive speculation of the 1920's, however, the New York Stock Exchange and the Securities and Exchange Commission adopted regulations that wiped out the opportunities for "bear" raids on the market. Today, short selling is still possible, but it is so hedged by restrictions that it is rather sparingly used, even by speculators on the floor of the exchange. Nevertheless, anyone still can sell short if he wants to.

To most people, short selling is a kind of upside down way of trying to make money. If a speculator bought 100 shares of stock at 20 and later sold it at 30, he would make $1,000 less commissions. Suppose, now, that he sells it first at 30, then buys it later at 20. He still would make $1,000 less commissions. In the second case, he would have borrowed the stock through his broker, sold the borrowed stock at 30, then later bought it back at 20 and returned it to the borrower.

In the old days when the stock market was much more volatile and when stocks surged up and down more rapidly, short selling was popular. In fact, speculators on the floor of the exchange sometimes ganged up on a stock, sold it short, drove the price down, and "covered" their short positions at much lower levels, making a pot of money in the process.

It is doubtful whether the small individual investor ever consistently made money selling short. To do so, he would have to guess correctly that the stock he borrowed and sold would, in fact, go down. If it went up, instead, he would be in a serious predicament. In the first place, when he borrowed the stock, he would have had to put up as security to the lender all the proceeds from the sale. If the stock later went up, the short seller would have to increase his deposit with the lender by an amount equivalent to the increase in his stock's value. If the stock kept going up, the day might come when the lender would want his stock back. In this case, the borrower would have to buy shares in the open market, take a loss and close out the deal.

Prudent short sellers, if there are any such people, sometimes hedge their short sales by use of a stop-loss order. Thus, if a speculator sold a stock short at 30, he might put in a stop-loss buy order at 32. If things went wrong and the stock began to rise, 100 shares would automatically be purchased for him at 32 and he would stand to lose only two points.

Short selling is a particular form of short-term trading that should be attempted only by the most sophisticated market operator. The ordinary investor cannot use it successfully.

COMMODITY FUTURES TRADING

"Have you heard the one about the country boy who wandered into the Coffee Exchange, blinked his eyes, scratched his chin, tugged at his ear and, upon leaving, learned that he had made $7,000?" So ran an ad some years ago in a financial newspaper. It went on to describe commodity futures markets as "the fastest-trading markets in the world—where you operate on as little as 10% margin—where fortunes have been made and lost in a matter of months."

Basically, this description is true. As a young man, John Maynard Keynes, author of the famous Keynesian theory of economics, was determined to be financially independent and never to "relapse into salaried drudgery." Shortly after World War I he began speculating, first in foreign exchange. He sold German marks and bought U.S. dollars. But early in 1920 the dollar began to decline and the mark rose, and Keynes soon found he had lost £13,000.

He borrowed enough to keep going and plunged into the commodity futures market, trading heavily on very small margins in lead, tin, copper, zinc, rubber, wheat, sugar, linseed oil and jute futures. Within four years he had made £58,000. During most of his life he continued to speculate in commodities and stocks, finally accumulating a £500,000 fortune.

Keynes, of course, was a genius. Unfortunately, the ordinary speculator in commodity futures may well have the opposite experience. A Department of Agriculture study some years ago indicated that three times as many small speculators lost money as made it. Still, the lure of quick riches is strong. Every large brokerage house has its contingent of men and women who are trying to outguess the weather and the professional commodity traders in New York, Chicago, Minneapolis and Kansas City. Here are the mechanics of it and the way the speculators figure their chances of success.

Hedging vs. speculation Suppose you overheard a wheat farmer say, "I've just planted my crop and I see that wheat is currently selling at $2 a bushel. I'd be happy to get that price for my crop when I harvest it next September."

At this point you might say to yourself, "This might be a good deal. The long-range weather forecast is for a hot, dry summer. Congress may raise the support price of wheat. By September the going price may be considerably above $2." So you say to the farmer, "Tell you what. I'll contract to take 5,000 bushels next September at $2 a bushel. And I'll give you 10% down to show good faith."

If you and the farmer made this kind of deal, you would, in effect, have bought a September wheat future, and he would have sold one. Every day thousands of transactions of this kind are made. Only instead of farmers and speculators meeting face to face, they give their orders to brokers who send them by wire to traders on the floor of one of the commodity exchanges. There the orders are filled on an auction market.

Visit the Chicago Board of Trade, and from the visitors' gallery you will see the pits, or trading areas, where contracts for wheat, corn, oats, rye and soybeans are constantly being bought and sold by quick signals of hand and finger. In Minneapolis there is the Grain Exchange; in Kansas City, the Board of Trade. In New York and Chicago there are the two Mercantile Exchanges, where egg, plywood, live cattle, hogs, platinum and silver coin futures are bought and sold. At the New York Commodity Exchange it's silver, mercury, copper and zinc.

There are only two reasons why a person would buy or sell a commodity future. One is to speculate. The other is to avoid speculation; in other words, to hedge. The farmer in the example just cited was a hedger. He knew wheat was $2 a bushel right then, and he wanted to establish the price for his crop once and for all without having to worry about future fluctuations.

Other examples of hedging: In January a chain of grocery stores wants to buy 100 carloads of flour to be delivered June 1. It asks a flour mill to quote a firm price. Now the miller does not want to buy all that wheat in January and store it until June. But in order to quote a firm price on the flour, he must know the cost of raw material, as well as overhead and profit. This means he must immediately establish the price he will pay for his wheat. He can do this by buying wheat futures. Who will sell them to him? Some speculator who thinks wheat is due to go down so that by June he can buy the futures back for less and make a profit.

When a country grain elevator buys wheat, it may sell an equivalent amount of wheat futures. Since it thus buys and sells wheat at the same time, it guards against a loss in case the price of wheat changes before it sells to the terminal elevator. The terminal elevator, in turn, may hedge when it buys wheat and so may the flour miller when he buys from the terminal elevator. Processors of cocoa, sugar, cotton and other commodities sell futures when they buy their raw materials to guard against inventory loss.

You can see that the speculator, by taking the other end of the deal from the hedger, is providing a public service. But that, of course, is not why the speculator is in the market. He buys and sells for only one reason, to make a profit.

Can he do it? Yes, say the brokers who handle such accounts, the speculator can profit if he has the capital, the nerve, and the will to follow certain rules of the game. But, at best, it's a risky business.

Rules of the game Here is how the brokers reason. In commodity futures trading, margins are very low, 5% to 10%. So while the risks are great, so are the potential profits. If a speculator buys on a 10% margin and the price rises 10%, he doubles his money. If he buys on a 5% margin and the price rises 10%, he triples his money. Although the speculator must pay close attention to daily movements, there are not so many basic variables to watch as there are in the stock market.

The two main ingredients of the commodity market are supply and demand. The figures on these are public information. There can't be any inside dope. Crop reports are jealously guarded against leaks until they are made public, and once public they are available to everyone. So are statistics on carry-over, exports, stocks under government loan and so on.

Then there are certain basic seasonal trends. Over the years, wheat prices, for example, tend to be lowest at harvest time in July and August and on the average gradually move up during the fall and winter until the new wheat comes in. Soybean prices usually hit their lows in the first two weeks in October.

Lord Keynes asserted that futures prices tend to rise 10% per year on the average. Professor Paul Cootner, of Massachusetts Institute of Technology, once made a study of the years 1954 to 1959 to determine what would have happened if, in June of each year, a speculator had bought a wheat contract calling for delivery in the subsequent May. A May wheat contract bought in June 1954 would have appreciated 9% by the time its delivery date came around in May 1959. The same future bought in subsequent years would have appreciated as follows: 11% in 1956, 1% in 1957, and 10% in 1958. But in 1959 it would have fallen 6%. The average annual appreciation would have been 5%.

Considering that the speculator could have bought such a contract on a 5% margin, you might assume that, if he had averaged out, he could have doubled his money. This assumption would be dangerous, however. For one thing, prices rise and fall from day to day, and the margin trader could easily have been wiped out on a series of temporary declines. Also, if he were pyramiding his profits, he would have been wiped out in 1959 anyway.

Just the same, brokers have certain rules of thumb that they think guard against some of these dangers. In the first place, no one should even think of speculating in commodity futures unless he is prepared to take losses. Some losses are almost inevitable. But the theory is that if losses are always cut short and gains allowed to run, a speculator can make money even if he is right only 35% of the time.

Most brokers recommend that whenever a speculator takes a position in a commodity future he immediately put in a stop-loss order. If he buys a wheat future for $2 a bushel, for example, he should put in a stop-loss order 2 cents below the market. Then if wheat falls to $1.98, he will automatically be sold out and his loss, hopefully, limited to only 2 or 2½ cents, although in a sharply falling market he could lose a lot more. If he sells a future short, he should put in a stop-loss order 2 cents above the market so that if wheat rises, instead of falling, he will again be sold out before he has lost much more than 2 cents.

In this way the speculator should attempt to cut his losses short. If by chance he catches a broad trend, then he should let his profits run. Thus, if a speculator bought wheat futures at $2 and wheat began to rise, going to $2.10, he should not take a profit but should move his stop-loss order up to $2.08. Then if the upward trend continued to, say, $2.20, he could move the stop loss to $2.18, and so on.

But what happens to the speculator who buys wheat at $2 and is sold out at $1.97 or $1.98? If he has bought one future, or 5,000 bushels, on a 5% margin, he has put up only $500, but has lost $100 or $150. If he tries it again, he may have the same luck. In fact, it may take several tries before he catches his trend. In the meantime, his capital is impaired.

That is why the larger and more conservative brokerage houses will accept as commodity trading customers only those who they think understand the risks and can afford to take them. Unless a new customer has a stock account (and on the average over half of them do), he usually must open his account with a deposit of at least $2,500 and sometimes as much as $10,000. Brokers generally shy away from women as customers. The reason given: Most women can't stand to take losses.

Trading in commodity futures is not expensive as far as costs and commissions go. The commission in and out for a 5,000-bushel wheat contract is only $30. It figures out that a three-eighth-cent rise in the price will compensate for the commission. Everything above that is gravy, at least on paper.

A good bit of free information is available to the commodity trader. The larger brokerage houses provide a wire service giving hourly price quotations and figures on stocks on hand, crop estimates and so on. Various advisory services also are on file in brokerage offices, or may be purchased on a subscription basis from the publishers, giving outlook and opinion on all commodity futures prices. Some brokers provide a free handbook giving an informal course in how to trade intelligently in futures.

As you see, it's easy to get into the futures market. Margin is small. Commissions are modest. And the same information is available to everyone. Then why don't more people make money at it? Here are the answers from account executives of several leading brokerage houses.

The risks The average trader won't make money in the long run because once he makes a few profits he begins to think he's an expert and doesn't bother taking the proper precautions, such as putting in stop-loss orders on every trade. Also, most people who trade in commodities also have previously traded in common stocks. They can't get used to the idea of cutting losses short. If the market goes against them, they tend to hold on and become stubborn. They apply stock market logic, which is that a good stock eventually is bound to come back. But this doesn't apply to commodities. The May wheat future can go inexorably down right until May. And at that point the owner must either sell and take his loss or take delivery of 5,000 bushels and make payment to the seller in full.

Amateur commodity traders have other faults. They are basically optimists and tend to take the long side of the market most of the time. In practice, according to the experts, a trader should be short about half the time.

Some years ago a group of Maine potato farmers got interested in the potato futures market. In theory, their role should have been that of hedgers. If the price was good when they planted their crop, you might expect them to sell futures and fix their year's income. Instead, many of them got overenthusiastic and actually bought futures. This meant, in effect, that the potato farmers had two crops to worry about instead of one.

Taking small gains is another pitfall. The successful trader must have nerves of steel and allow his profits to run. If he chickens out and takes small profits, they will be eaten up by the inevitable small losses.

And even though the information is available to everyone, the unexpected can easily happen. In the spring of 1960, eggs were firm, and the Department of Agriculture implied a short supply. But chicken farmers are not dumb. When they received this word, they simply reversed their usual practice. Instead of culling out their old hens, they let them live and keep on laying. As a result,

Speculating

September egg futures fell from around 38 cents a dozen to 30. Since there are 15,000 dozen eggs in a futures contract, every price drop of 1 cent meant a loss to the futures holder of $150 per contract.

Yes, it's fun to read about the country boy who wandered into the Coffee Exchange, blinked his eyes, scratched his chin, tugged at his ear, and made $7,000. That's a good old Wall Street joke. But here's another story, a true one.

An unsophisticated speculator bought a couple of coffee futures contracts, putting up $1,500 margin. The market turned against him and he decided to sell, but he couldn't the first day because coffee was down the allowable daily limit on the first transaction and there were no more trades that day. He put his sell order in the next day, and again futures were down the limit on the first sale and trading stopped. This went on for five days. By the time his position was liquidated, he had lost his $1,500 plus nearly $10,000 more.

And that's no joke.

BUYING STOCKS ON MARGIN

Initial vs. maintenance margins To cope with the subject, get firmly in mind the meaning of some stock market jargon. The "initial margin" is the percentage of the purchase price that the customer pays when he buys a stock. For a theoretical example, assume he buys a share of stock at 100 on margin. (In actual practice he could not margin one share, but it will serve as an example.) Assume also that the current margin requirement is 60%. (Margin requirements are changed from time to time, and the current rate when you happen to read this book may be higher or lower than 60%. This figure is used in the examples below because it is about the median rate.) In this case, where the margin is assumed to be 60%, the customer would have to put up $60 in cash and the broker would lend him $40. Once the stock is purchased, however, the margin begins to change as the market price of the stock goes up or down. It then becomes the "maintenance margin."

Suppose that the stock, purchased for $100, were to rise to

140. At this point the loan still would be $40, so the customer's equity would be $100 ($140 market value minus $40 loan), or 71%. On the other hand, suppose the price of the stock were to decline to 65. The loan still would be $40, so the customer's equity would be $25 ($65 market value minus $40 loan), or only 38½% of the stock's value. So the margin would be 38½%.

One reason it is important to keep these distinctions in mind is that the Federal Reserve Board regulates only the initial margin. Thereafter, the margin that the customer must maintain is determined by the brokerage house and the rules of the New York Stock Exchange. As a matter of fact, the maintenance margins that most brokerage houses and the New York Stock Exchange require are far below the level usually required by the Federal Reserve Board at the time of purchase.

According to New York Stock Exchange rules, margins must be maintained at 25% or above. In other words, as far as the stock exchange is concerned, the customer's equity can decline to 25% of the market value of the stock.

Most brokerage houses, however, are a little stricter and insist that margins must not fall below 33⅓%. In the example, the customer's stock, which he purchased at 100, putting up $60, could fall in price only to 60 before he would receive a "margin call." The value of the stock would be $60, the customer would owe $40 on it, leaving his equity at $20, or 33⅓% of the market price.

To sum up—under Federal Reserve Board regulations, assuming a 60% margin requirement (and remember, when you read this it could be higher or lower), a customer could buy stock by putting up 60% of the purchase price. Thereafter, under most brokerage house rules, the stock could decline 40% before the customer would be called for more margin. The margin at any time may be computed by this formula:

$$\text{margin equals } \frac{\text{market value minus loan}}{\text{market value}}$$

Margin calls What happens when the price falls to a point where a margin call comes? The customer can do one of several things.

Speculating

First, he can put up more money, thereby decreasing the loan and increasing his equity and hence the margin. To keep his margin at 33⅓%, he must put up two-thirds of a point for every point his stock falls below the minimum margin level. To check this in the example above, suppose the stock fell to 59.

$$33⅓\% \text{ equals } \frac{59 \text{ minus the new loan}}{59}$$

Solving the formula shows that the new loan must be $39.333, which means the original $40 loan must be decreased by 67 cents, or two-thirds of a point. Actually, if the stock falls below the 33⅓% margin level, the broker is more likely to ask for an increase in the margin of two or three points, bringing it up to 35% or 36%, to provide a little leeway.

The second alternative the customer has, of course, is to sell the stock, pay off the loan, and take his equity in cash. In the Roaring Twenties, when so many speculators were purchasing stocks on 10% and 20% margins, there was a popular saying, "Sell on the first margin call." This was another way of saying "cut losses short and let profits run." In those days, with small margins, a call would come after a rather small decline in the price of the stock. Under a 60% margin rule, a stock could decline 40% before touching off a margin call, so the old rule is not applicable.

A third alternative to the customer who receives a margin call is to buy more stock. This is a method of raising his margin since out of every dollar he pays for such stock, he must put up, under the example, 60 cents in cash. Say the customer buys at 100, putting up $60 and borrowing $40. His stock falls to 59 and he receives a call for more margin. If he buys $2.51 worth of stock, putting up 60% or $1.51 in cash and borrowing an additional $1, his margin then would be

$$\frac{\$61.51 \text{ (market value) minus } \$41.00 \text{ (loan)}}{\$61.51 \text{ (market value)}} \text{ or } 33⅓\%$$

Pyramiding So much for margin calls. Now take the more optimistic possibility. What if instead of going down the price of the customer's stock goes up? In this case, his equity and margin rise, and he can actually buy more stock without putting up any more cash. This is known as pyramiding. Assume that when the stock reached 120, the customer sold out, took his larger equity and used it to repurchase on a 60% margin. After paying off his $40 loan, he would receive $80 (disregarding commissions). Using this as his 60% margin, he could buy $133.33 worth of stock ($80 is 60% of $133.33). He would then owe $53.33 (40% of $133.33).

In actual practice it is not necessary for the customer to sell, take out his equity, and repurchase. He can acquire the additional $13.33 worth of stock by a paper transaction. If the customer pyramided once and the stock continued to rise, he could pyramid again. The table shows a succession of pyramids. It is assumed that each time the market value rises 20% the margin is readjusted back to 60%.

TABLE 4 PYRAMIDING ON MARGIN

	ADDITIONAL STOCK ACQUIRED BY BORROWING	MARKET VALUE	LOAN	CUSTOMER'S EQUITY	MARGIN
Initial Purchase		$100	$40	$ 60	60%
First 20% Price Rise		120	40	80	66⅔%
First Pyramid	$13.33	133.33	53.33	80	60%
Second 20% Price Rise		160.00	53.33	106.67	66⅔%
Second Pyramid	17.78	177.78	71.11	106.67	60%
Third 20% Price Rise		213.34	71.11	142.23	66⅔%
Third Pyramid	23.71	237.05	94.82	142.23	60%

Note that with pyramiding, the three 20% price rises would raise the customer's equity from $60 to $80 to $106.67 and, finally, to $142.23. If at the start he had invested his $60 outright, without borrowing, the three 20% price rises would have raised his equity from $60 to $72 to $86.40 and, finally, to $103.68. You see the theoretical advantage of pyramiding.

Margins for investment An investor can use margins for investment as well as speculation. One way would be to use the dividends from the stock to pay interest on the loan and, hopefully, to liquidate it. In the old days when stocks yielded 6% or 7% and interest rates were about half that, dividends could conceivably pay off a margin loan in a few years.

In recent years, however, there has been an inversion, and interest rates frequently have been twice the level of dividend yields. Of course, you get dividends on your whole investment while you pay interest only on your loan, which usually, depending on the particular margin requirement of the time, would be less than half the investment. Suppose, for example, you owned $10,000 of stock on which you had borrowed 40%, or $4,000. If the dividend yield was 3½% and the interest on the loan 7%, you would be receiving $350 a year in dividends and paying out $280 a year in interest. The balance could go toward reducing the loan, but it would be a slow process. On a stock with a higher dividend yield, say 7%, the advantage would be greater because $420 ($700 in dividends minus $280 in interest) would go toward reducing the loan. If all conditions remained the same, the loan would be liquidated in less than seven years.

Dangers The stock market crash of 1929 was not caused by margin trading, but low margins undoubtedly made it worse. After each of the awful days of the panic, Black Thursday (October 24, 1929), Black Tuesday (October 29) and the others, lights burned all night in Wall Street as clerks, fighting to catch up on their paperwork, sent out thousands and thousands of telegrams calling for more margin. The customers who could not put up the cash were sold out forthwith, adding to the terrible downward pressure on prices.

The crash brought to light the two great perils of low margins. First, many a small trader, using margins as a means to speculate, suffered a total loss of his savings, whereas if he had bought stocks outright, he might have salvaged something. In fact, if he could have held on, he or his heirs might have done very well, as many stocks today are selling at several times their 1929 high. Second, the pressure of forced liquidation contributed to the panic, which had such a depressing effect on business as a whole.

After the crash Congress undertook to prevent a repetition. Some experts wanted to abolish margin trading altogether, but this was overruled on the grounds that it would impair the liquidity of the great securities markets. Others wanted to have the privilege of trading on margin reserved for investors with accounts of $10,000 or more. This idea also was rejected.

In the end, it was decided that the problem could be solved by regulating initial margins. The Federal Reserve Board, in its discretion, can move the level upward or downward. Since 1934, when it received this responsibility, the board has changed the requirement many times, having set it as low as 40% in the late 30's and as high as 100% during the short boom of 1946. The board takes some satisfaction from the fact that no sudden drop in stock prices in recent years has developed into a downward spiral.

Brokerage houses themselves have a rule that to some extent deters the small investor from speculating on borrowed money. A margin account cannot be opened without a deposit of at least $2,000. According to the New York Stock Exchange, 80% of all margin accounts are held by people with incomes over $10,000.

Whether any individual should buy on margin is a question only he himself can answer. The theoretical advantages of buying on margin in a rising market have been shown. The disadvantage is that margins usually are a tool of the trader. And trading seldom works for the ordinary investor. His best bet is to buy top-quality stocks with a future and hold them.

If a man buys a house or a car or a washing machine with a small down payment, he gradually pays off the debt and eventually owns his purchase free and clear. Installment buying actually is a way of saving. But the trader who buys on margin seldom pays off his debt in installments. Whether he is ahead or behind, he is likely to liquidate his loan by selling the stock. And in either case he is a good prospect for another hot tip on a sure winner. Successful investors didn't make their fortunes in this way.

PUTS AND CALLS

Once upon a time, four office workers employed in a large eastern city ran into a broker they knew who asked, "Say, do you fellows want to make some money?"

There is only one answer to that question, and one of the group gave it, "How?"

"Buy some XYZ," the broker said. "I can't tell you the reason right now. It's confidential. But take my advice. Buy a hundred shares." He hurried on.

This cryptic recommendation was discussed at lunch. XYZ at that time was selling for 23½. It had sold over the past year or two as high as 45. In any event, a hundred shares would cost $2,350 plus commission, a sum beyond the capabilities of the four friends. But one of them had an idea. "Let's buy a call on it. Then if the guy is right, we'll make some money. If not, we can't lose much."

How a call works This idea was adopted, and by the following day a call had been purchased for $350, or $87.50 apiece, good for six months and ten days, exercisable at a price of 23¾. In other words, for $350 the group had acquired an option to buy 100 shares of XYZ at a price of 23¾ per share at any time during the ensuing six months.

The profit and loss prospects were as follows. The most the group could lose was $350. And they would lose it only if the stock declined and did not recover to 23¾ during the life of the call. In that case, the call would be allowed to expire. But if the stock went up, then the group stood to make $100 for every point it rose. However, the first 3½ points, or $350 of profit, would go to offset the cost of the call. Thus, if the stock rose from 23¾ to 27¼, or say 28 to cover commissions also, the group could count on breaking even. All it would have to do would be to sell 100 shares at 28, then exercise the call and buy 100 shares at 23¾. But if the stock went above 28, then the group really would stand to make a clear profit of $100 for every point of rise.

As it turned out, the company showed signs of invigorated

management, and the stock rose to 29 during the summer. But then it sagged off, and on September 18, when the call expired, it was 25⅞. The group got back $175 (cost of stock at $2,375 less two dividends: $2,350; sale at $2,587 less two commissions: $2,525; difference: $175). Nevertheless, the members were not dismayed. They had had the chance of making several hundred dollars apiece.

A put This example, an actual one, shows one way of using a call. A put is the opposite of a call. When you buy a put, you acquire the right to sell 100 shares of stock at a fixed price at any time during a given period.

Suppose, for example, you owned 100 shares of a stock that you had bought originally at 50 and that now was selling at 70. You might want to keep your stock in hopes it would go higher. On the other hand, you would like to put a floor under your profit. So you might buy a put for, say, $500. If the stock continued to go up, you would let the put expire and your ultimate profit would be reduced by $500. If the stock went down, you would exercise the put by requiring the man at the other end of the deal to buy the stock from you at 70. In effect, you would then have sold it at 65 (70 minus the 5 points for the put).

How to buy a put or call Puts and calls, as you can see, are simply options to buy or sell. They have been used by traders for hundreds of years, but nonprofessional investors seldom have taken the trouble to understand them. In recent years the public has shown a growing interest, and dozens of put and call options are offered for sale each day in the financial pages of newspapers. Buying such an option, however, is not the usual way of acquiring one.

If you wanted to buy a call on 100 shares of XYZ stock (puts and calls are seldom sold on less than 100 shares), you would not bother to shop through the newspaper ads but would go directly to your broker. He, in turn, would get in touch with a put and call broker in New York. There are only a few of these, but each one has a stable of clients who own many stocks and who are ready to sell, or "write," options on any of them at a price.

A typical option writer owns a large portfolio of the most commonly traded stocks. From experience he knows he can make money by standing ready at all times to sell any stock he owns for, say, three, four or five points above the current price, or by buying more stock for, say, three, four or five points below the current price. Therefore, at any time he will write an option on any 100-share block of stock he owns, charging a price equivalent to three, four or five points, depending on the length of the option, whether the stock is high-, low- or medium-priced and whether its price has been stable or volatile.

By shopping around, your broker eventually would be able to buy you the kind of option you wanted, provided the stock was that of a large company, widely owned. In such a case you would be buying a newly written option, exercisable at the market price at time of purchase. It could be made to run for 30 days, 60 days, 90 days or 6 months and 10 days, the extra 10 days in the last case being to ensure the buyer that any profit would be a long-term capital gain.

Prices vary, but the average cost of a 6-months-and-10-days call, for example, would be 14% of the total value of the stock. If you bought a call and sometime later decided to exercise it, you could sell it back to the put and call dealer direct, or you could actually acquire the 100 shares and sell them in the market. The result would be the same, and in either case you would pay the regular New York Stock Exchange commission on the sale of 100 shares.

Once you own a put or call, you can sell it at any time during its life. If you sold it well in advance of its expiration date, it might be resold by the dealer. The "special" put and call options advertised in the daily papers are such resales. While newly written puts and calls usually are exercisable at the then market price of the stock, those up for resale must carry the original price, which may be above or below the market price of the stock at the time of resale. The sale price of the option will have been adjusted to cover the difference.

How profitable? Now for the crucial question. Can you make money trading in puts and calls? Theoretically, yes. But in actual practice, the chances are against the nonprofessional. The Securities and Exchange Commission once concluded an exhaustive study of puts and calls. Here are a few of its conclusions:

• The buyers of puts and calls generally are individuals, mostly small investors. Calls are more commonly bought than puts.

- Approximately 43% of calls are exercised. The rest are allowed to expire.
- Of the 43% exercised, about one-half (21½% of the total) are exercised at a loss, the owner getting back, on the average, 40% of his cost and losing 60%.
- On the 21½% of calls exercised at a profit, the profit averages 150%.

Translated into briefer language, the above would seem to say that if you are a small investor and are considering buying a call, the chances are about four to one against your making money at it. But if you beat the odds and do make a profit, it might run as high as 150%.

CHARTS AND GRAPHS

There are two basic ways of selecting stocks and gauging the course of the stock market. One is known as the fundamental approach. It calls for a study of business conditions, of the relative position of industries, of the earnings of companies and the quality of management. It attempts to evaluate, to discover merits, weaknesses, potentials. This is the approach that has been stressed in this book.

The other method is known as the technical approach. Its premise is that stock prices themselves, as they move along from day to day, weave a pattern and tell a story of events to come. The technician, through his price charts, watches the interminable battle between buyers and sellers. He senses the rise and fall of investor confidence. From the actions of prices, he believes he can spot the time when supply or demand is winning out, and a stock, or the market as a whole, is about to break out and go higher—or lower.

Use of the technical approach is not recommended for the individual. For one thing, it requires a great deal of statistical work, more than the ordinary person can handle. And while most professional technicians use their charts to forecast the longer-term price movements, most amateur technicians are prone to use charts to try for short-term profits. This calls for trading in and out of the market, which seldom works for the ordinary investor.

Speculating

Nevertheless, the technical approach is of interest. At its best, and when combined with the fundamental approach, it can be revealing—sometimes startlingly so. And today, when it has become harder and harder to find bargains in the market, some big institutional investors, the managers of large funds, are paying a good deal of attention to the charts and prognostications of the really competent technicians.

Point and figure A point-and-figure chart shows only one thing, price movement. It neither shows volume of trading nor takes into account time in the usual sense. Time, says the chartist, is merely a measure of change. Therefore, unless the price of a stock changes by, say, one point, no entry is made on the chart even though weeks and months may go by.

Look at the chart below. It is based on one-point units and shows price movement of a stock that was first charted at 20. Once the chartist posted an X opposite the figure 20, he was interested in two things only—whether the stock sold at or above 21 or whether it sold at or below 19.

CHART 8 TYPICAL POINT-AND-FIGURE CHART OF A STOCK

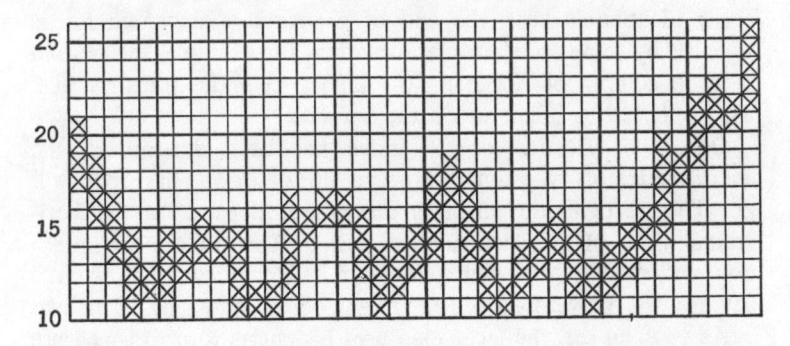

This stock subsequently sold at 19, so an X was made in the 19 square just under the previous posting at 20. This X established a down trend and, as long as this down trend remained in effect, all subsequent postings were made in the same column. In this case the down trend continued until a price of 17 was reached. The stock then reversed one point by selling at 18 and the chartist moved over into the next column to post 18.

Once this 18 posting had been made, a sale at 19 or 17 would establish a trend. The next recordable sale was 17 and the trend carried down to 15 in the second column. Subsequent fluctuations produced the pattern shown.

There are variations of this method—for example, the one-point unit, three-point reversal chart. In this case a reversal in trend is posted only if it extends three boxes up from the previous low or down from the previous high.

What does the chartist learn from his intricate pattern of X's? Chiefly he pays attention to "congestion areas." These are irregular horizontal bands in which the X's waver up and down but their main direction is sideways. These areas represent periods of accumulation by investors (perhaps insiders) who have confidence that the stock will go up, or distribution by holders of the stock who have reason to believe that it will go down. Eventually, once the sideways movement is over, the stock will break out either up or down.

The technician often can identify these periods of accumulation or distribution, although congestion areas take many forms and it requires experience and reference to other technical data to tell whether a given area represents a top or a base. In the most easily identifiable case, the end of a period of accumulation is signaled by some recognizable formation; for example, the bottom of each column of X's is a little higher than the previous one. This indicates a breakout on the up side.

Once the direction of the move has been determined, the chartist attempts to estimate how far up, or down, the stock will go. This vertical movement is thought to depend on the horizontal width of the accumulation period. Thus, if the accumulation period in a one-point unit chart had covered 15 horizontal squares, the upward movement might be estimated at 15 points.

As you can see, the technician uses his charts to try to measure the great intangible force of investor confidence that makes stocks sell at seven times earnings at one time and twenty times earnings at another. How do you measure the force that can push the price of a stock sharply up or down even though the company's financial situation would seem not to have changed?

Market charts The technician uses many charts. One shows the breadth of the market, in other words, the share volume of advancing stocks and the share volume of declining stocks traded daily on the New York Stock Exchange. Another shows the number of stocks traded that advanced in price versus those that declined. When volume is increasing and advances exceed declines, the market presumably is in for a rise.

Another intriguing way by which technicians attempt to measure confidence is by means of Barron's Confidence Index, published each week by *Barron's National Business and Financial Weekly*. There is a school of thought that the upward and downward movements of this index precede those of the Dow Jones Industrial Average by two to four months.

The Confidence Index is based on the assumption that professional bond traders can sense the coming changes in business conditions some weeks earlier than traders in stocks. The index measures the shifts back and forth between demand for high-grade, relatively safe bonds and the run-of-the-mill and, hence, more speculative bonds. If bond traders have confidence in the business outlook, they tend to buy speculative, high-yielding bonds. But if the outlook appears to demand caution, these traders shift into bonds of higher grade.

The Dow Theory You may have heard of the Dow Theory. It is based on the great law of action and reaction, which says that things do not move up or down in a straight line. A movement starts, gains momentum and goes too far. Then a reaction sets in. When this reaction is completed, the primary movement starts again. Once more there is a reaction. Thus, in a bull market stock prices seesaw upward. In a bear market they fluctuate downward. These wavelike motions are perhaps rough and irregular, but the technician attempts to gauge them.

One of the oldest attempts to interpret these undulating movements of the stock market was the Dow Theory, originated some 70 years ago by Charles H. Dow, first editor of the *Wall Street Journal,* and his successor, William P. Hamilton, and further developed by a financial writer, Robert Rhea. These observers of the Wall Street scene believed that the stock market was a relentless forecaster of business conditions. The market gives its bloodless verdict, say the Dow theorists, because businessmen are the chief buyers and sellers of stocks and each contributes what he knows about business. The market thus sifts and averages what all businessmen think about the future.

The Dow theorist, watching the continually moving lines of his industrial and railroad averages, thinks of himself as an observer on the beach watching the ocean. He measures the waves to determine whether the tide is coming in or going out.

The tides, or broad bull or bear movements, last several years. The ripples are the daily fluctuations and have no meaning. The waves that tell the tale are the short swings lasting for several weeks or months. If each new wave rolls up the beach a little higher than the last, and recedes not quite so far, there is a bull market. But at some point a wave will not go as high as the preceding one. It will also recede further. This might indicate that the tide had turned and a bear market begun.

The Dow theorist doesn't hope to catch the exact turn of the market. He knows that major trends run for several years. He expects to be late and doesn't mind as long as he's right. In October 1929, Hamilton wrote a famous editorial in the *Wall Street Journal* entitled, "A Turn in the Tide." It stated that a bear market was definitely under way. Jeers came from Wall Street because the industrials had already fallen 75 points and the rails 21. But, by 1933, industrials had dropped another 264 points and rails another 154 points.

Today the Dow Theory is considered by many to be somewhat archaic, but the technicians believe that the great law of action and reaction still operates.

Dangers of charting There are a great number of other indexes and charts that attempt to forecast price movements, measure intrinsic value, and gauge investor confidence. Almost every brokerage house has a chartist on its staff.

The great danger in all these charts and theories, of course, is that the layman tends to see in them the open-sesame to riches, the lazy man's easy road to wealth. They are far from that. Even the technicians handle these tricky tools with the greatest circumspection. The late Edmund Tabell, of Walston & Co., who worked with charts for over 30 years, admitted to around 30% of misses. And he used his charts, not in a vacuum, but as a check and a supplement to the fundamental approach to investment values.

"The layman who makes investment decisions based on fifteen minutes of chart work a day," he once said, "is simply playing financial Russian roulette."

Odd-lot statistics as forecasters of the market "The public is always wrong." This old Wall Street adage can't actually be proved to be true or untrue. But, as in many old adages, there seems to be just enough truth in it to make it worth pondering. Put another way, the adage says that the little guy is always pessimistic at the bottom and rampantly optimistic at the top. He sits suspiciously on the sidelines during a long bull market. As prices go higher, he realizes that he is missing the boat so he plunges desperately in just at the point when the professionals decide the rise is over and quietly sell out.

Then the coin turns over and the other side appears. The little guy holds his stock and watches it go down and down. In the beginning he won't believe he is wrong, and therefore won't sell out and take a small loss. No, he will ride the market down until at last he gives up in disgust and sells out at a big loss. This, according to the theory, marks the end of the decline, the point at which the smart professionals move in and buy. Then the cycle repeats itself with the little guy sitting on the sidelines watching the market rise again.

The proof of the pudding is supposed to lie in the "odd lot" transactions on the New York Stock Exchange, shown each day on the financial pages of newspapers. An odd lot is a block of stock of less than 100 shares. Most big investors buy and sell in round lots—i.e., blocks of 100 shares—while most small investors, having less money to work with, generally buy in odd lots of 10, 20, 50 shares, and the like.

The odd-lot figures reveal more than do the round-lot figures. Round-lot transactions are matched on the floor of the stock exchange, and there must be exactly as many sales as purchases. Therefore, round-lot transactions give no clue as to whether the trading is being initiated predominantly by buyers or sellers. But when a small investor puts in an order for an odd lot, the odd-lot dealer who receives the order either makes the sale out of his own inventory or, if necessary, buys a round lot, sells part of it, and puts what's left over into inventory. In the same way, when a small investor wants to sell an odd lot, the dealer buys it and adds it to inventory. Odd-lot transactions, therefore, are recorded either as buy orders or sell orders and, thus, are about the only available measures of what the public is doing.

Now for the $64 question. Do the odd-lot figures really show that the public usually buys at the top and sells at the bottom? Unfortunately, the statistics can be interpreted in different ways. Some of the shrewdest Wall Streeters believe that odd-lot transactions may have been useful market indicators in earlier periods when margins were low and there was a great deal of speculation. In those days, buying by the public meant that stock was passing into weak hands. Today, however, the small investor often is a young man with a family who buys sound stocks for the long term and hangs onto them. Nevertheless, many analysts believe that if either odd-lot purchases or sales, or particularly odd-lot short sales, took a very sharp jump or drop, they would sit up and take notice.

And some of the simon-pure chartists go a great deal further. They believe that the odd-lot figures do give an advance tip on market declines and rises. Actually, it may be that the actions of the steady, investor-type of odd-lotter do not reveal anything special about the market, while the actions of the emotional, speculative odd-lotter do give a warning worth heeding. In other words, sudden jumps or drops in odd-lot transactions may indicate that the public is getting impulsive and emotional and thereby contributing to instability.

What's the significance of all this? Probably, it's twofold. First, you may want to keep an eye on the odd-lot figures with the idea that there's a germ of truth to the theory that the public is usually wrong. Second, and more important, you should use the figures to keep your own perspective. Investors are like a flock of sheep: they tend to surge in one direction. This causes prices to go up too far in bull markets and down too far in bear markets. In the corrections that inevitably follow, those who bought at the top or sold at the bottom get hurt.

Perhaps the best way to handle your investments is to buy sound stocks at regular intervals, thus averaging out the price. But if you want to try to time your purchases, then better keep an eye on the odd-lot figures so you won't be infected with the spirit of the mob. After all, you don't want to help prove the old adage that you, as a small investor, are always wrong.

19

SAFETY AND INCOME

"Safety" is a deceptive word. Traditionally, in the investment field it means putting money into high-grade bonds, mortgages and savings accounts. In those places the dollars themselves are safe in the sense that the owner can be pretty sure of getting them back after a period of time, with interest. Unfortunately, those investments do not keep the dollars safe from loss of purchasing power caused by inflation and the continual upward creep of prices of goods and services. For this kind of protection, equities such as common stocks and real estate, with their fluctuating values, are supposed to be the answer.

Ideally, in order to get protection both from loss of the dollars themselves and from loss of purchasing power, a fund should consist of both fixed-dollar investments and equities. Many money managers not only keep their funds invested in both types, but try to shift into equities when boom and inflation appear likely and into fixed-dollar investments or cash when a recession appears to impend. Theoretically, this is an ideal way to handle money. When the stock market is rising, you own mostly stocks. When the stock market is falling, you own mostly bonds or cash. Or, to use another method, when the stock market seems abnormally high, you shift into bonds and cash. And when the market looks abnormally low, you shift into stocks. This kind of system doesn't work too well in practice because it is so difficult to forecast the trend of the economy or the stock market.

Here is an example of what can happen when you try to outguess the trend of the economy. Back in 1938 the Finance Committee of Vassar College decided to adopt a plan that automatically would cause them to shift their funds into fixed-dollar investments when the stock market was abnormally high and back into stocks when it was abnormally low. The committee studied the Dow Jones Industrial Average as far back as 1897 to decide on its normal level or median. This they put at 135. The higher the Dow Jones Average went above 135, the fewer stocks the fund could own. The further below 135 it went, the more stocks it must own. No stocks could be bought when the average was above 135 and none sold when it was below.

The plan worked all right for the first five or six years while the market was oscillating around the median level, which, incidentally, the Finance Committee adjusted at one time or another to 130, 140 and finally to 155. But along about 1945 an unpredictable thing happened. The market left its "normal" level, never to return (at least it hasn't yet). First it went up to 212, which forced the fund to sell its stocks and go 100% into bonds. Then the market bounced from 193 to 163 a couple of times but never came down far enough to permit the committee to buy back any stocks. Then the uncooperative averages took off, going up, up, up, hitting 200, 300, 400, 500, etc. And during this great bull market the plan, as originally set up, kept saying, "Don't buy, sell." But of course there was nothing to sell, as all stocks should have been sold out long before.

Naturally, the Finance Committee didn't stick with the orginal plan forever. The members were smart enough to see that the whole level of prices had shifted. In 1947 they bought stocks, using new money. And in 1949 they began basing the median level on a projected trend line of the averages that takes into account their long-term upward bias.

Some advocates of formula-timing plans have tied their formulas to an arithmetical trend line based on the Dow Jones Averages. Others have used a geometrical trend line. Still others have worked out moving averages. One expert has based his formula on the relationship between the current price-to-dividends ratio and that of the ten-year average. As you can see, it is easy enough to decide what ratio of stocks to bonds you want if you know when the market is high, low and normal. What throws the formula timers is trying to determine in advance what is going to be high, low and normal.

There are two reasons why the individual investor should be careful about trying to shift his investments back and forth between equities and fixed-dollar investments. One is the difficulty of knowing when to shift, as explained above. The other is that most families already have a sizable amount invested in fixed dollars. Life insurance, social security and most pension plans are of this type. Dollars paid in today will be returned in the form of a predetermined number of dollars sometime in the future. There is no opportunity for growth. So what most families need is an offsetting investment in equities. Nevertheless, for some investors bonds can have a place in the picture. In particular, there are instances where safety of the dollars themselves, rather than growth of principal, is the overriding consideration.

BONDS

Corporate, government and municipal bonds These are traded in the open market like stocks. The original buyers don't keep them forever and don't intend to in many cases. Millions of dollars' worth of bonds change hands every day. The price is determined by the law of supply and demand. You buy through your regular broker or through your bank. Commissions on bonds are extremely low. Most houses charge a minimum of $25 for a bond order. This $25 minimum would apply on orders of from one to five bonds. On 8 bonds the commission might still be $25; on 10 it might be $40 and on 20 it might be $80. As a percentage, the commission goes down as the size of the order goes up.

Remember that when you buy a bond, the issuer owes you a fixed number of dollars payable on a specific date sometime in the future. The issuer also promises to pay a specific amount of interest per year. If the issuer is a company and it doesn't make good on either of these commitments, the bondholders can force it into receivership. If the issuer is the federal or a local government of the United States, you don't have to worry too much about receivership.

Note the difference between bonds and common stock. When you own stock, you own part of the company and there is no promise that your money will be repaid or that you will even get dividends. You are essentially in the same position as is the owner of the corner delicatessen. The company will pay in dividends each year only what it judges it safely can at the time. Sometimes, if business is poor, it won't pay any. Other times it may pay large amounts, 6%, 8%, 10%.

If business booms, stock prices rise because of the prospect of big dividends. In bad times stockholders don't value their stock as highly because they expect that dividends will decrease. Stock prices thus move up and down pretty far and fast in anticipation of changes in business. Good bonds, however, with their fixed interest rate and promise to return a fixed number of dollars, don't fluctuate so much. When they do go up or down, it is usually because of a rather special set of circumstances. Bond prices sometimes go down when business is good or up when business is bad.

How bond prices fluctuate Here is an example of how bond prices can change. Back in 1962, the Duke Power Company issued a 4¼% bond due in 1992. The buyer of one of these bonds loaned the Duke Power Company $1,000. He was to receive 4¼% interest, or $42.50 a year, until the bond matured in 1992. Then he would get his $1,000 back. All very simple.

In the meantime, however, conditions changed. Consumer prices began to rise; inflation became a worrisome problem. The government tightened credit. Interest rates began to rise because lenders were no longer willing to put out money at 4¼%. In ten years the going rate for utility bonds had gone to 7¾%. In fact, on April 19, 1972, the Duke Power Company sold some new bonds, due in 2002, paying 7¾%. In other words, a buyer could put up $1,000 and get $75 a year, a great deal more than the investor who, ten years earlier in 1962, had put up $1,000 to receive only $42.50 a year.

Now what happened to that older 4¼% bond? Obviously, no one who could get a 7¾% return in 1972 was going to pay $1000 for an old bond that yielded only 4¼%. So the owner of the older bond, if he wanted to sell, was required by the laws of economics to accept less. And remember that bonds are being traded continuously just as are stocks. It so happened, then, that the law of supply and demand decreed that the older 4¼% bond fall in value to $665. At this price, a buyer would still receive only $42.50 a year. But this amount, based on a purchase price of $665, would amount to a cash return of 6.39% ($42.50÷$665). And in addition to this, the bond, bought at $665, would eventually pay off at $1,000 when it matured, so this $335 gain should also be figured into the yield. When so figured, it would raise the yield "to maturity" to about 7½%, or nearly as much as the newly issued bond.

During periods of falling interest rates, bond prices tend to rise. In some cases they go over 100; in other words, a $1,000 bond might sell for $1,050 or $1,100. Bond prices fluctuate inversely to interest rates. As seen in the preceding example, when the price of a bond goes down below par, the yield to maturity is made up of two parts: (1) the current yield, or cash that the bond pays each year, plus (2) the potential capital gain to be received when the bond rises to its maturity value of 100. Some investors who want to defer income prefer older bonds selling at a discount. The capital gain part of the yield to maturity will be received at a later date. Not only will this part of the return be taxed at the lower capital gain rates, but it will be deferred, perhaps until the owner has retired and is in a lower tax bracket.

Short-term governments If you bought a government bond on the open market that had only a few weeks to run, it naturally would sell almost at par. Buying such a bond would be like putting money in the bank, only safer. Similarly, government bonds due in five years or less usually sell pretty close to par. It takes a very large change in interest rates to change their value substantially. Since there is so little risk of their value changing, they are known as about the most riskless investment there is. And since the buyer doesn't take much risk, he ordinarily can't expect much yield.

Security. Investors buy bonds because they are safer and more stable than common stock. The stability, as we have seen, depends somewhat on changes in the level of interest rates in general. But there is another factor that can affect the stability even more and that is how much you can count on getting the full interest and principal when due. In the case of U.S. government bonds, there is no doubt about the issuer's ability and intent to pay. Corporate and municipal bonds are in a somewhat different class. To satisfy the purchaser, many bonds are secured by real property. A railroad may pledge so many miles of track. A manufacturing company may put up its machinery and building. Municipalities pledge future tax collections.

In cases where the interest or principal is not paid on time, the trustee for the issue, usually a bank, will take action in behalf of the bondholders. When a case of default goes to its ultimate conclusion, the pledged property is sold and the proceeds are distributed among the bondholders. This seldom happens in actual practice. The court usually permits the company to reorganize and to replace a defaulted bond issue with a new bond or with a combination of bonds and preferred stock and maybe some common stock.

A good many bonds are issued without any specific security. The issuer gives its word that it will pay, just as you promise to pay when you borrow at the bank on your signature. Such bonds are called debentures and although unsecured are often good investments. Thus, the debentures of a strong, profitable company earning enough to pay interest charges several times over might be safer than the first mortgage bonds of a company financially weak and able to meet interest payments only by the skin of its teeth. You don't want to end up owning a property that cannot earn enough to pay the interest on its bonds.

Put it this way. If the ordinary investor wants a speculative security, he might better buy a common stock. If he buys a bond, he presumably wants safety and stability, and therefore he should stick to the highest grades. That means either U.S. government or high-grade corporate bonds or municipals.

Quality To determine the quality of a corporate or municipal bond, the security analyst digs into the history and condition of the issuer. He also examines all features of the bond, including the indenture agreement (the contract between the issuer and the bondholders), the call price (price at which the issuer may call in the bond before maturity) and so on. But most investors don't have the time or the specialized knowledge for this type of test. The best bet for them is the bond ratings published by Moody's and by Standard & Poor's Corp. Moody's rates bonds as Aaa, Aa, A, Baa, etc. Standard & Poor's ratings are AAA, AA, A, BBB, etc. Unless you know exactly what you are doing, stick to the top grades. When you buy a bond, you don't want to have any doubt about the issuer's ability to make good. Usually, the higher the yield on a bond, the greater the risk. The lower the yield, the less the risk.

Like everything else, bonds have good and bad features. Your dollars are safe in high-grade bonds, but you have little protection against inflation. And you can lose money, even on bonds that are good. A good 3¼%, 30-year municipal bond that sold at par (100) in 1963 was selling for 76 ($760 for a $1000 bond) in 1972 because of the rise in interest rates.

There is another pitfall. If you buy a high-grade corporate bond when interest rates are high, at some future date when interest rates are much lower the company could take advantage of the bond's call provisions, pay you off at a small premium above par, and refund its debt at lower rates. You would lose your high-interest investment and be forced to invest your money somewhere else. The managers of the company are not interested in paying you one fraction of a percent more than they have to. Any savings in interest redound to the benefit of the common stockholders.

Tax-exempts So-called municipal or tax-exempt bonds are IOU's issued by states, cities, toll roads and similar revenue-producing public bodies. They promise to repay your money by a certain time and to pay a specific rate of interest. They are regarded as second in quality only to U.S. government bonds. The income is completely free of federal income tax and, in some cases, from the income tax levied by the state in which the bond is issued.

Municipal bonds fall into four categories. *General obligation bonds* are backed by the "full faith and credit" and, usually, the unlimited taxing power of the city, state, county or taxing district. *Limited-tax bonds* are backed by only part of the over-all tax revenue of the jurisdiction that issued them. As an example, bonds might be backed by a state's gasoline taxes or motor vehicle fees. *Revenue bonds* are secured by revenues from a particular source, such as a toll road, a community water, sewer or gas department, or even a ferry system. *Housing authority bonds* are issued by local public housing agencies to pay for building low-rent housing projects. Rents charged in the projects are not enough to pay off the bonds, so every year a federal agency, the Public Housing Administration, makes up any deficit with money granted by Congress.

Generally, municipal bonds have a face value of $1,000 and are bought and sold in units of five bonds. Thus, this type of investment normally means an outlay of $5,000. You can sometimes manage to buy a single bond, but it's a little bit risky—you may not be able to sell a single bond except at a sacrifice price if you have to liquidate.

When you buy or sell municipals, you don't pay a commission. The dealer is compensated by his markup; that is, the difference between what he pays for the bond when he buys it and what he receives for it when he sells it. Dealers often buy bonds and keep them in inventory for months before finding customers for them. In such cases the markup is not easy to ascertain, but it likely will average out at around ½% per bond.

Not only is the income from municipal bonds free of federal tax, but you don't even have to report that income on your federal tax return. State taxes are somewhat different. In many cases, you do not have to pay state income taxes on the interest from municipal bonds if they were issued in the state in which you file your income tax return. For instance, if you lived in New York, you would not have to pay state taxes on interest from New York state bonds, but you would have to pay state taxes on interest from, say, bonds of Richmond, Va.

Don't be dazzled by the idea of income without taxes, however. There is a catch: Tax-exempt bonds pay markedly lower interest rates than do similar but taxable bonds. The interest is so much lower, in fact, that most people can clear more after taxes from other investments than they can from a municipal bond without taxes. This is because the public bodies that issue municipals clearly do not have to pay as high a rate to compete for funds. They need only match or exceed the amount that the buyer would clear after taxes on other investments of comparable safety and liquidity. Tax-saving opportunities have the greatest appeal for high-bracket taxpayers, and for them the spread between pretax and aftertax income is sizable. So municipal bonds can often carry interest rates well below the going rates elsewhere and still find buyers. In actual practice, experts don't recommend tax-free bonds to investors unless they are in the 42% bracket or above.

However, it's easy to make your own calculation as to whether tax-exempt bonds are to your advantage or not. You start with a given tax-free bond. Say that you can buy one that pays 5%. What taxable interest rate is that equivalent to? To find out, you must first know the income tax rate you would be paying on interest. You can ascertain this, of course, by looking at your federal tax return, specifically what is known as your "taxable income." The income tax form gives a table showing what percentage you are paying. For example, if your taxable income is between $12,000 and $16,000 and you are filing a joint return, you pay $2260 plus 25%. The 25% is the tax rate you would pay on taxable interest. To figure what taxable interest return would be equal to a tax-exempt interest return, use this formula:

$$\frac{\text{tax-exempt interest return}}{1 \text{ minus tax rate}}$$

Thus, the taxable equivalent of the 5% tax-exempt bond would be .05 divided by 1 minus .25, or .05 divided by .75. The answer is .066667 or 6⅔%.

There are tables that give you the comparison between tax-exempt and taxable returns. The following is an example. Note that it applies only to married taxpayers filing a joint return. A different table would have to be used for single taxpayers, married taxpayers filing separate returns, and so on.

If the tax-exempt bond in question is free of state income taxes as well as federal, the state tax rate should be added to the federal rate and the combined rate used to go into the table. Thus, if your federal tax is 28% and your state tax 4%, use the 32% line.

Convertible securities The distinctive quality of a convertible bond, debenture or preferred stock is that it can be exchanged for common stock. Convertible securities thus resemble con-

TABLE 5 TAX-EXEMPT VERSUS TAXABLE YIELDS—MARRIED COUPLES FILING JOINT RETURN

Taxable Income		Federal Tax Rate	\multicolumn{5}{c}{Tax Yields on Tax-exempt Securities}
			4%	4¼%	4½%	4¾%	5%
OVER	BUT NOT OVER		\multicolumn{5}{c}{Yields Before Taxes on Taxable Interest}
$ 8,000	$12,000	22%	5.13	5.45	5.8	6.1	6.4
12,000	16,000	25%	5.3	5.7	6.0	6.3	6.7
16,000	20,000	28%	5.6	5.9	6.25	6.6	6.9
20,000	24,000	32%	5.9	6.25	6.6	7.0	7.35
24,000	28,000	36%	6.25	6.6	7.0	7.4	7.8
28,000	32,000	39%	6.6	7.0	7.4	7.8	8.2
32,000	36,000	42%	6.9	7.3	7.8	8.2	8.6
36,000	40,000	45%	7.3	7.7	8.2	8.6	9.1

Taxable Income		Federal Tax Rate	\multicolumn{6}{c}{Yields on Tax-exempt Securities}
			5¼%	5½%	5¾%	6%	6¼%	6½%
OVER	BUT NOT OVER		\multicolumn{6}{c}{Yields Before Taxes on Taxable Interest}
$ 8,000	$12,000	22%	6.7	7.1	7.4	7.7	8.0	8.3
12,000	16,000	25%	7.0	7.3	7.7	8.0	8.3	8.7
16,000	20,000	28%	7.3	7.6	8.0	8.3	8.7	9.0
20,000	24,000	32%	7.7	8.1	8.45	8.8	9.2	9.6
24,000	28,000	36%	8.2	8.6	9.0	9.4	9.8	10.2
28,000	32,000	39%	8.6	9.0	9.4	9.8	10.25	10.7
32,000	36,000	42%	9.1	9.5	9.9	10.3	10.8	11.2
36,000	40,000	45%	9.6	10.0	10.5	10.9	11.4	11.8

vertible automobiles. The car will keep you dry if it rains. But if it is clear, you can put the top down and let in the sun. Similarly, if business is bad, preferred stock and debentures will give you first call on the profits to the extent of a fixed return on your investment before dividends on the common are paid.

Safety and Income

If business booms, you share in the rise in price that may take place in the common. Of course, before you buy either a convertible car or a convertible security, you should assure youself of the soundness of the merchandise. If there is a drop in the price of the common into which a preferred, for example, is convertible, there may also be a drop in the preferred. But it shouldn't drop as much.

A convertible security can be exchanged for a fixed number of shares of the company's common stock. You make the conversion at your discretion by turning in the bond or preferred stock to the institution acting as the company's conversion agent. There may be a deadline on the conversion right, or in a certain number of years the "conversion ratio" may change so that you stand to get fewer shares than you would have during the security's early life. Many of the securities are "callable"; that is, they can be redeemed by the company before maturity, usually at a small premium, such as 3% or 4% over the face amount. The rights of the company and the owner of the security are spelled out in a document called the "indenture." It is vital to get these details before buying a convertible. Convertible bonds and debentures are usually issued in $1,000 denominations. Convertible preferred stock most often is sold in $50 or $100 units.

The right to convert a bond, debenture or preferred stock into common is potentially valuable, and investors usually are expected to accept a somewhat lower rate of interest or dividend on a convertible than on a nonconvertible security. As an illustration, suppose you bought a 4% bond convertible into 20 shares of common stock. If you paid the full face value for the bond and converted at once, you would, in effect, be paying $50 a share for 20 shares of common. When such a bond is issued, chances are the common will be selling somewhat under $50. But say the price of the common stock eventually goes up to $55. You could make a profit of $5 a share by converting the bond into 20 shares of stock and selling the stock for $1,100. In practice, however, it would not be necessary to convert because the bond itself would rise to reflect the higher price of the common. Suppose, though, that the common stock declines to $30. The bond will also decline. But it probably will not drop as much because as the bond's price goes down, the yield goes up and the bond becomes an increasingly attractive investment. This illustrates the defensive quality of a convertible security. When the common stock rises substantially, and causes a proportional rise in the convertible security, the convertible loses its defensive value. Thus, if you bought an older convertible for 175, the yield, based on this higher price, would be relatively low, and the security would have to decline substantially—perhaps to around 100—before the defensive feature would come into play. So the ideal price for the investor to pay for a convertible security is close to the price he would pay for a security of similar quality that was not convertible. This means that for all practical purposes, convertible securities should be bought when they are close to par and this usually means around the time of first issue.

A convertible security is a hedge. If you knew the market was going up, you would buy common stock. If you knew the market was going down, you would do better to hang onto your cash or buy good bonds. Investing in a convertible is sort of playing both ends against the middle. It's a good idea if it works, and it is working for many investors. They are the ones, however, who have taken time to study each security and get good advice on it before taking the plunge.

Savings bonds U.S. savings bonds are perhaps the safest dollar investment available. They are nonnegotiable; that is, the owner cannot sell or "give" them to another person. If he wants cash, he must turn them in to the government for the current redemption value. Other bonds are traded in the bond market and their values rise and fall daily. But the savings bond, with its guaranteed interest rate, is removed from the vagaries of the marketplace. You always know to the penny how much you can get for it.

The two chief types issued by the government are Series E appreciation-type bonds and Series H current-income bonds. Both earn interest at an average annual rate of 5½% if held to maturity.

Series E Current issues are sold with a five-year-and-ten-month maturity period. However, all E bonds now carry an automatic ten-year extension privilege. All will continue to draw interest during the extension period at the rate in effect at the time they enter the extension.

E bonds are now issued in seven denominations—$25, $50, $75, $100, $200, $500 and $1,000—and are sold at 75% of face value. Interest is added to the value of the bond each six months and at the original maturity date will equal the difference between the purchase price and the maturity value. The interest rate is low at first—4.01% the first year; thereafter the rate gradually increases; at maturity, a ½% "bonus" is added, raising the yield to 5½%.

Although interest on E bonds is subject to federal income tax (but not to state or local income taxes), you can defer paying the tax until the bond has reached maturity or until it is redeemed. But you have to defer payment initially. Once you start reporting the interest as annual income, you must continue to do so for the life of the bond, and for any others you purchase unless the Internal Revenue Service gives you permission to change.

You can buy up to $5,000, issue price, in E bonds in any calendar year, and you can redeem them any time after an initial two months' holding period. If you do cash them in, remember to redeem the most recently purchased ones first; they're drawing less interest. But don't cash any that are just about to reach the next six-month interest accrual.

Series H The purchase price of H bonds is face value, in denominations of $500, $1,000 or $5,000. Interest, which you must report annually on your federal income tax return (but not state or local ones), is paid to you each six months. You can purchase up to $5,000 in H bonds in any calendar year, and you can redeem them any time after six months at a Federal Reserve Bank or branch, or from the Treasurer of the United States.

You can also obtain H bonds in exchange for E bonds and U. S. Savings Notes (Freedom Shares). The $5,000 limit does not apply here. The exchange will enable you to defer the federal tax liability on accrued interest on the old E bonds or notes until the H bonds are redeemed; but you will have to begin paying tax annually on the H bond interest. H bonds you receive in exchange are not subject to the $5,000 annual limits on holdings. You can make the exchange only if your E bonds and/or notes have a minimum redemption value of $500.

Here are two ways to use the tax advantages of savings bonds. One popular plan involves purchasing bonds to help children meet their college expenses. If, for example, the father of a six-year-old girl decides to buy his daughter $56.25 worth of E bonds in her name each month, he may list himself as beneficiary and at the end of the first year file a tax return for his daughter showing the increase in bond value as income to her. With "intent" thus established, he need file no more returns as long as bond interest plus other income comes to less than $2,050. If the child's only income is bond interest and other *investment* income totaling less than $750, no further returns need be filed and no tax is due unless the investment income in any one year exceeds $750. If he sticks to his original plan, interest earnings by themselves on the annual investment of $675 will be too small to be taxed even during the later years, and since he continues to provide more than half of his daughter's support, he may still claim her as a dependent. Assuming that the 5½% rate continues in effect, when the child is 18 there will be $11,204 in the fund, including $3,104 of tax-free interest.

Another man, age 50, could set aside the same monthly amount to provide income in retirement, deferring tax on the interest until then, when his tax bracket will be lower. If over the next 15 years and ten months (the original maturity period plus the guaranteed ten-year extension) he buys $56.25 worth of E bonds each month and the interest rate doesn't change, he'll accumulate $10,688 in principal and $5,981 in interest, on which tax will be due. But he can exchange $16,500 of the $16,669 total for H bonds, taking $169 in cash, which would be taxable at the time, and receive an average of about $76 of monthly taxable income for the next ten years, and pay tax on the rest of the original E-bond interest accumulation when his $16,500 is returned to him upon redeeming the H bonds at age 75. By then, presumably, his wife will also be over 65, giving them four exemptions, two for age. As an alternative, he could add $331 to get $17,000 in H bonds. His original investment would remain intact and federal income tax on E-bond interest applied to purchase of H bonds would continue to be deferred until the H bonds were redeemed, reached final maturity or were otherwise disposed of. There is no guaranteed extension for H bonds issued currently, but earlier issues have been granted one or more extensions as they approached maturity or extended maturity.

INCOME

One of the best ways to get a high yield from your investments is to buy good growth stocks and hold them. While such stocks pay relatively small dividends based on the current price, the dividends tend to rise each year so that in a few years the yield will be quite high based on the original investment. Herbert P. Buetow, formerly president of Minnesota Mining & Manufacturing Company, has explained it this way. "What appears at first glance to be a conservative dividend policy may prove in the long run to be most rewarding for the stock owner. Any company dedicated to growth, but disinclined toward borrowing money or diluting its stock, must retain a substantial part of its earnings to provide funds for expansion of facilities and activities. This policy of 'postponed dividends' ultimately leads to appreciation of the stock as well as to greater dividends by stimulating sales and profits. Dividend policies of growth companies should not be measured in terms of a percentage of the current market value of the stock. Instead, current dividends should be expressed in terms of a percentage of the market value of the stock five or ten years earlier." A current Minnesota Mining & Manufacturing dividend may look conservative based on the current price of 3M stock, but in recent years it has represented a return of 30% to the investor who bought 3M stock 20 years ago.

Remember that though good bonds have been yielding more than common stocks in recent years, with a bond you are frozen into a fixed-interest return while in the growth stock your yield can increase indefinitely and eventually far outstrip the income from the bond.

Retired people, widows and others may have a need for more income than their investments yield. In such cases the income can be supplemented by drawing down principal. The most primitive way to arrange this would be for an investor to decide to pay himself a certain percentage, say 6%, on his investments each year. When dividends failed to make up this return, he could sell the least favored of his stocks, pay himself the necessary amount in cash, and reinvest the balance.

Withdrawal plans These offer several attractive possibilities. Keep in mind, though, that they are not annuities. An annuity guarantees you a fixed income for the rest of your life. You can't outlive it. On the other hand, a mutual fund withdrawal plan will last only so long as your capital lasts. If the underlying stocks in the mutual fund decline in value, instead of growing, your capital can diminish and eventually be entirely used up.

The risk of outliving your capital makes a mutual fund withdrawal plan most suitable as a supplement to a regular pension plan or an annuity, rather than as a sole source of retirement income. A withdrawal plan can also be used to make college tuition payments, to help pay off a mortgage or loan, or in other situations where you want to hold on to your equity investments but want regular income in larger amounts than dividends provide.

Here is how most withdrawal plans work. First you must have, or purchase, a minimum amount of shares in the mutual fund of your choice. This minimum in most plans is either $5,000 or $10,000; in a few cases it is as low as $4,000 or $3,000 and in at least one plan, $1,000.

Then you must decide on how much you want to pay yourself. Payments can be monthly, quarterly or, in some cases, semi-annually or annually. Most funds have a minimum limit on payments, typically $50 or $25 a month or a quarter. Some funds have no minimum. In others you may draw down any amount as long as it is in multiples of five dollars. In still others you may pay yourself a variable amount by specifying that a certain number of shares be liquidated each month or quarter. And some funds permit you to liquidate a certain percentage of each year's total value.

Safety and Income

The theory of the withdrawal plan is that your payment is made up first from the dividends the mutual fund pays and then, if that is not enough, shares are sold to make up the balance. In actual practice, some funds automatically reinvest all dividends and capital gains distributions, then sell enough shares to make up the entire regular withdrawal payment. Since the dividends and distributions are almost always reinvested at net asset value, this makes little difference in the amount received. But the distinction is important when figuring taxes. The fund should provide an annual statement showing how much income came from dividends and how much from capital gains. If you start a withdrawal plan by depositing mutual fund shares you already own, then be sure to tell the custodian bank or transfer agent how much these shares cost originally, so that at tax time you may be given a statement of your capital gains.

One advantage of withdrawal plans is their flexibility. You can change the amount to be withdrawn at any time, or add to the principal in specified chunks, or cancel the plan if you want to. It is advisable to review your plan periodically. If you started with a $10,000 plan and a 6% withdrawal based on the original amount ($50 a month) and if at the end of two or three years the shares had grown to a value of $12,000, you would then be drawing only 5% ($600÷$12,000). In this case, you might want to increase your withdrawal back to 6%, or $60 a month. Conversely, if the shares had decreased in value, you might want to cut your monthly withdrawal proportionately.

The most important ingredient of a successful withdrawal plan is having the right mutual fund. The "right" one, of course, is one that will keep your money growing fast enough so that your shares will never be worth any less than when you started. Statistics show that in many funds, a 6% withdrawal plan started ten years ago would have grown by 30%, 40%, 50% or even more. On the other hand, a good many funds would have shown a decrease in assets, in a few cases amounting to 50% or more.

There are hundreds of mutual funds, and most of them offer withdrawal plans. So the choice is wide. The best approach is to study the investment record of a number of funds. Borrow or buy a copy of *A Guide to Mutual Fund Withdrawal Plans,* published by Wiesenberger Services, Inc., One New York Plaza, New York, N.Y. 10004. The price is $20, but it is worth that to anyone who is thinking of putting $5,000 or $10,000 into a withdrawal plan.

A recent edition shows the results of a $10,000, $50-a-mouth withdrawal plan over a ten-year period, 1961–70, for large mutual funds. A breakdown of the results is interesting because 1970 was a down year for the market:

• 109 of the 171 plans showed a remaining value of over $10,000;

• 62 funds showed a remaining value of less than $10,000, and some were pitiably low: $3,391 in one case and $4,745 in another;

• 39 funds beat the Dow Jones Industrial Average (which rose 36% during the 1961–70 period) and showed a remaining value of at least $13,600.

Table 6, Part 1 shows the funds whose remaining values were $13,600 or more.

Note how many of the results fall near the median, which is about $14,900. It is also interesting to compare the top funds in Table 6, Part 1 with the top funds in the ten-year summary table of *Johnson's Investment Company Charts* (see Table 6, Part 2), which gives the results, as of December 31, 1970, of a $10,000 investment in each of 182 large funds. It is assumed that the money had been invested for ten years and that all capital distributions and investment income were reinvested. Table 2 proves that the best funds for a mutual fund withdrawal plan are simply the funds with the best over-all performance.

It should be noted, also, that the six funds in Table 6, Part 2 are all growth funds and do not stress income. Some funds that stress both growth of capital and growth of income and even funds that aim for high current income have also done well. But of the 39 funds listed in Table 6, Part 1, 21 have as their main objective growth of capital, while only ten aim for growth of capital and income, and only eight strive for income.

All the data on fund performance cited so far covers only the one period 1961 through 1970. What about other periods? Table 6, Part 3 gives a hypothetical example of a $10,000 withdrawal plan with Investment Company of America, starting every year from 1934 to 1962. Note that in only one ten-year period (1937–46) would the investor have ended up with shares having less value than when he started. Incidentally, periods of ten years have no significance except for comparative purposes. A withdrawal plan can last any length of time, just as long as the capital holds out.

As explained earlier, with some funds you do not have to draw down a fixed amount in dollars but can arrange to receive the proceeds from the sale of a fixed number of shares. This means that you would usually get relatively more income when the stock market was up and less when it was down. Table 7 gives a hypothetical illustration, using the David L. Babson Fund, of how a withdrawal plan would work if the owner had elected to receive the proceeds from the sale of ten shares each month. A comparison is shown with a $50-a-month plan.

There also is a way to start a withdrawal plan with a beneficiary. To obtain this advantage, you have to buy mutual fund shares through a contractual plan. Contractual plans have a bad

TABLE 6

1. Withdrawal plans in which the remaining value after ten years was ahead of the Dow Jones Industrial Average

FUND	REMAINING VALUE
*American Investors Fund	$16,040
American National Growth Fund	15,171
Axe-Houghton Stock Fund	19,504
Channing Income Fund	14,303
Chemical Fund	14,241
Colonial Equities	16,787
Composite Fund	13,622
Decatur Income Fund	15,980
Delaware Fund	15,058
*deVegh Mutual Fund	15,532
The Dreyfus Fund	14,089
Enterprise Fund	24,372
Fidelity Capital Fund	16,890

* no-load funds

FUND	REMAINING VALUE
Fidelity Fund	13,827
Fidelity Trend Fund	25,993
Financial Industrial Income Fund	14,656
First Sierra Fund	19,158
*Guardian Mutual Fund	14,486
The Investment Company of America	14,981
Investors Research Fund	14,204
Ivest Fund	23,156
*The Johnston Mutual Fund	14,674
Keystone Growth Common Stock Fund	14,644
Lexington Research Fund	15,151
Mutual Investing Foundation— MIF Fund	14,118
*National Industries Fund	14,872
National Securities Dividend Series	14,642
Oppenheimer Fund	21,974
*Penn Square Mutual Fund	21,714
*Pine Street Fund	14,686
Pioneer Fund	15,444
*T. Rowe Price Growth Stock Fund	14,744
Provident Fund for Income	14,341
Puritan Fund	14,401
Security Investment Fund	13,610
Southwestern Investors, Inc.	14,722
The Value Line Fund	15,449
Vanderbilt Mutual Fund	15,156
Washington Mutual Investors Fund	14,373

* no-load funds

2. Withdrawal-plan performance compared with straight investment performance, top six funds

Wiesenberger withdrawal-plan results—top funds
1. Fidelity Trend Fund
2. Enterprise Fund
3. Ivest Fund
4. Oppenheimer Fund
5. Penn Square Mutual Fund
6. Axe-Houghton Stock Fund

Johnson's charts ten-year performance results—top funds
1. Enterprise Fund
2. Fidelity Trend Fund
3. Ivest Fund
4. Oppenheimer Fund
5. Penn Square Mutual Fund
6. Axe-Houghton Stock Fund

3. Results of hypothetical withdrawal plans after ten-year periods, using Investment Company of America shares and $10,000, $50-a-month plans.

Period FROM — TO	Remaining Value
1/1/34—12/31/43	$21,264
1/1/35—12/31/44	20,749
1/1/36—12/31/45	10,875
1/1/37—12/31/46	4,582
1/1/38—12/31/47	15,604
1/1/39—12/31/48	10,975
1/1/40—12/31/49	12,864
1/1/41—12/31/50	17,075
1/1/42—12/31/51	23,457
1/1/43—12/31/52	22,759
1/1/44—12/31/53	16,568
1/1/45—12/31/54	19,934
1/1/46—12/31/55	15,342
1/1/47—12/31/56	19,355
1/1/48—12/31/57	18,369
1/1/49—12/31/58	28,322
1/1/50—12/31/59	30,762
1/1/51—12/31/60	26,674
1/1/52—12/31/61	27,693
1/1/53—12/31/62	21,822
1/1/54—12/31/63	28,605
1/1/55—12/31/64	18,556
1/1/56—12/31/65	17,431
1/1/57—12/31/66	15,928
1/1/58—12/31/67	27,035
1/1/59—12/31/68	19,098
1/1/60—12/31/69	14,655
1/1/61—12/31/70	14,980
1/1/62—12/31/71	13,109

name among some investors because most of them call for monthly payments over ten or twelve years, yet the commissions for all the payments are loaded onto the early payments. Thus, in the first few years as little as half the money paid in may actually be invested. You can, however, invest in a plan in which you make all the payments at once. This is called a single-payment contractual plan. It eliminates the front-end-load feature. The sales commission is practically the same as the 8½% commonly charged by most mutual funds.

The contractual plan offers these advantages: You can name a beneficiary who will receive the plan in case of your death. Under a contractual plan, you can also take out up to 90% of the money you have invested (only once each year, however) and pay it back later with no sales charge. So could your beneficiary if he received the plan.

Here's an example of how this might work. A man plans to retire and buy a single-payment contractual plan with his son as the beneficiary. He starts a withdrawal plan, paying himself so much a month. If anything happens to him, his son will receive the plan. If the boy is still in college, he can cancel the withdrawal option and draw up to 90% of the money for expenses. Later, if he begins to earn good money himself, he can repay the fund without charge and have an investment in mutual fund shares that still offers the advantage of the original plan.

Statistics indicate that withdrawal plans have done a good job in the past. They permit orderly liquidation of capital for those who wish to pay themselves more than their dividends alone would provide. But two points about withdrawal plans should be kept in mind.

First, drawing down capital is something generally (but not necessarily always) done later in life. Most individuals and families want to be building capital in the early and middle years.

Second, although a withdrawal plan offers intriguing possibilities, it is only as good as the underlying securities selected and held by the mutual fund. So picking a good withdrawal plan means picking the best-managed mutual fund you can find.

If you keep these points in mind, then a mutual fund withdrawal plan offered by a top-quality fund could be a way of having your cake and eating it, too.

TABLE 7 RESULTS OF TWO WITHDRAWAL PLANS USING SHARES OF DAVID L. BABSON INVESTMENT FUND

Plan A. Illustration of an assumed investment of $10,000 based on initial net asset value of $10,000 with ten shares withdrawn each month January 1, 1961, through December 31, 1970

amounts withdrawn

YEAR ENDED 12/31	FROM INVESTMENT INCOME DIVIDENDS	FROM PRINCIPAL	ANNUAL TOTAL	CUMULATIVE TOTAL	TOTAL VALUE OF SHARES HELD AT YEAR-END
1961	$ 95	$ 586	$ 681	$ 681	$10,812
1962	84	520	604	1,285	8,626
1963	171	471	642	1,927	9,684
1964	164	573	737	2,664	9,985
1965	150	531	681	3,345	10,914
1966	152	665	817	4,162	9,382
1967	255	643	898	5,060	10,411
1968	194	796	990	6,050	11,307
1969	179	897	1,076	7,126	10,359
1970	184	795	979	8,105	9,267
	$1,628	$6,477	$8,105		

Plan B. Illustration of an assumed investment of $10,000 based on initial net asset value of $10,000 with $50 withdrawn each month January 1, 1961, through December 31, 1970

amounts withdrawn

YEAR ENDED 12/31	FROM INVESTMENT INCOME DIVIDENDS	FROM PRINCIPAL	ANNUAL TOTAL	CUMULATIVE TOTAL	TOTAL VALUE OF SHARES HELD AT YEAR-END
1961	$ 95	$ 505	$ 600	$ 600	$10,896
1962	90	510	600	1,200	8,699
1963	172	428	600	1,800	9,816
1964	165	435	600	2,400	10,273
1965	158	442	600	3,000	11,490
1966	169	431	600	3,600	10,141
1967	244	356	600	4,200	11,643
1968	240	360	600	4,800	13,191
1969	150	450	600	5,400	12,690
1970	289	311	600	6,000	12,084
	$1,772	$4,228	$6,000		

Annuities One trouble with withdrawal plans is that you can't be sure you won't outlive your money. There is, of course, a way to guarantee that your money, in the form of monthly income, will last as long as you live. The vehicle for such an arrangement is an annuity. Most annuities are sold by life insurance companies. But insurance and annuities are two different things. When you buy insurance, you give the company a series of payments in return for its promise to pay a specific sum to your beneficiary if you die. When you buy an annuity, you pay the company a specific sum in return for its promise to give you a series of payments as long as you live. The annuity is designed primarily to protect you, not your dependents.

Actually, you can pay for the annuity either in a lump sum or in installments. Your money is invested mostly in fixed-dollar investments, such as bonds or mortgages, and earns interest. Then, when annuity payments begin, your investment plus interest is paid back to you periodically at a guaranteed rate that would theoretically exhaust your investment at the end of your life expectancy. But you keep on collecting even if you live longer. Your funds, keep in mind, are pooled with those of other annuitants. The money left in the kitty by people who die earlier is used to pay incomes for those who live longer.

You can arrange to have your income paid monthly, quarterly, semiannually or annually. Monthly payments are most common.

Annuities fall into two general classes. One type starts paying an income immediately after it's bought for a lump sum. The other, known as a deferred annuity, guarantees an income to start sometime in the future. You'd typically pay for it in installments, though a few companies will let you pay for a deferred annuity with a lump sum.

What if you die before you're slated to collect? In most cases, your beneficiary would receive a death benefit equal to the cash value of the annuity at the time of your death or the sum of the premiums paid, whichever is larger. If you surrender your contract before maturity, you'd collect the cash value.

You can also buy a combination insurance policy and annuity that provides more death protection during preretirement years while you're still paying for the annuity. That's called a retirement income policy.

You can choose to collect an annuity in one of five principal ways. (In each case, you receive an income as long as you live.)

Straight life annuity This is known as a "pure" annuity. All payments stop at your death. If you die shortly after the annuity starts, you will have gotten back only a small portion of your investment. But if you live longer than expected, you collect more than the purchase price plus interest.

Life annuity with installments certain If you die before a specified number of years, ten, for example, the payments continue to a beneficiary for the rest of the guarantee period.

Installment refund annuity If you die before you have received as much as you paid in, your beneficiary keeps collecting until total payments equal your investment.

Cash refund annuity Your beneficiary collects in a lump sum if you die before recovering the original investment.

Joint and survivor annuity Two people—usually a husband and wife—receive an income as long as either one lives.

Which way is best? Because a straight life annuity offers no guarantee that you will recover all or most of your investment, it is the least expensive. It furnishes the largest income for a given price. Thus, it is suitable for the person who needs maximum income and either has no dependents or has taken care of them through other means.

Perhaps you dislike the prospect of losing much of your investment if you die soon after your income begins. You might buy a refund or installments-certain annuity—if the income is adequate for your needs. (The argument for one of these annuities is stronger if you're in poor health.) But consider instead, buying the less expensive straight-life annuity and investing the difference elsewhere to pass on to your heirs. In that case, you'd still leave something even if you outlived the guarantee period of a refund annuity.

Are you counting on an annuity to support you and your wife? The joint and survivor annuity then makes sense. But if your wife is much younger than you, the payments may be too low for your needs.

The price of an annuity is figured on the amount of income it promises to pay. You can look at the price tag from two angles: how much income you get for a given premium, or how big a premium you must pay to buy a given income. You'll find typical rates on pages 274 and 275. Notice how costs vary with age and sex.

The older you are when you start to collect, the lower the cost. That's because your investment is returned over a shorter life expectancy. With a deferred annuity, the younger you are when you sign up, the less your annual premium will be. That's because your cost is spread over a longer paying period.

At the same age, women pay more than men for the same income. That's because women, on the average, live longer and collect more.

Income plan. A straight life annuity, as noted above, is the cheapest. The more generous the guarantee, the greater the cost.

Annuity rates are usually quoted in one of two ways: (1) the amount of income you get per $100 or $1,000 of premium; or (2) the amount you pay per unit, usually $10, of monthly income. The costs below were quoted by New England Mutual Life Insurance Co.

TABLE 8 IMMEDIATE SINGLE PREMIUM ANNUITY
(income to begin at once)

each $1,000 buys this monthly income   each $10 of monthly income costs

AGE MALE	STRAIGHT LIFE	10 YEARS CERTAIN	INSTALL-MENT REFUND	STRAIGHT LIFE	10 YEARS CERTAIN	INSTALL-MENT REFUND
50	$5.45	$5.40	$5.29	$1,835	$1,853	$1,892
55	5.93	5.84	5.69	1,685	1,713	1,757
60	6.58	6.52	6.33	1,520	1,534	1,581
65	7.48	7.26	7.07	1,337	1,378	1,415
70	8.72	8.08	8.00	1,147	1,237	1,251
AGE FEMALE						
50	$5.10	$5.08	$5.03	$1,960	$1,967	$1,989
55	5.50	5.46	5.38	1,820	1,832	1,860
60	6.04	6.00	5.88	1,656	1,667	1,701
65	6.81	6.68	6.52	1,468	1,496	1,533
70	7.88	7.51	7.36	1,270	1,331	1,359

TABLE 9 DEFERRED ANNUAL PREMIUM ANNUITY, 10 YEARS CERTAIN

each $100 a year buys this monthly income
Age at which payments begin

	MALE		FEMALE	
Age at Issue	65	70	65	70
30	$33.22	$47.14	$29.17	$41.13
35	26.32	38.08	23.11	33.22
40	20.30	30.17	17.82	26.32
45	15.04	23.26	13.20	20.30
50	10.44	17.23	9.17	15.04
55	6.43	11.97	5.65	10.44
60	3.05	7.37	2.68	6.43

Yearly dividends on the deferred annual premium annuity, if left with the company, might substantially increase the guaranteed monthly income. Insurance companies will not estimate the level of future dividend payments. The following table, however, shows the amount by which the monthly income would be increased based on 1970 dividend rates.

TABLE 10 ADDITIONAL MONTHLY INCOME FROM DIVIDENDS LEFT WITH COMPANY BASED ON 1972 DIVIDEND RATES

Age at which payments begin

	MALE		FEMALE	
Age at Issue	65	70	65	70
30	$16.61	$28.22	$14.58	$24.63
35	10.80	19.04	9.48	16.61
40	6.67	12.38	5.86	10.80
45	3.82	7.65	3.36	6.67
50	1.94	4.38	1.71	3.82
55	.80	2.23	.70	1.94
60	.20	.91	.17	.80

Annuity income is sometimes quoted in percentages. For example, the $5.40 monthly return that $1000 immediate single premium annuity would produce would be $64.80 a year, or about a 6½% return on the $1000. This is little more than a savings account would pay. And note that money in the savings account stays there while money in the annuity is being used up. This makes it not worthwhile, in the opinion of insurance men, to begin annuity payments earlier than age 55.

An annuity, basically, is an investment. True, it's a particular kind of investment. Nevertheless, you've got to compare annuities with such things as stocks and bonds, bank savings, etc., to pick out the advantages and drawbacks. These are the chief advantages:

• You're freed of the job of money management. No need to worry over investments—what and when to buy, what and when to sell.

• Annuities are the safest way to obtain a retirement income. (If you're uninsurable, they may be the only way.) You get guaranteed payments that can't be reduced by depression.

• You can never outlive your capital. You might develop your own system for tapping both principal and interest to finance retirement, but are you sure the capital will hold out as you grow older?

• A deferred annuity, paid for in installments, makes it easier to save for old age and more difficult to dip into your savings.

• There may be tax advantages. Your annuity premiums draw interest during your working years, but you pay no income tax on the interest until you actually collect it. By then your tax bracket may be much lower. Here is how the tax would be figured on annuity payments you would receive after you retired. The total investment would be divided by the total return expected during your remaining lifetime. If $50,000 investment were assumed to yield $75,000, some 66% of each payment would be nontaxable and continue so even after the full $75,000 had been received. Note that there are certain refinements of this formula in the case of refund annuities.

Annuities also have their disadvantages:

• You use up your capital and leave little if any for your heirs.

- You earn a relatively low rate of interest on your investment.
- Your investment value or income will not increase if inflation erodes the dollar's value. The dollars are safe; the purchasing power is not.
- Once annuity payments begin, you can't get at your investment in an emergency. An annuity, as a rule, has no cash or loan value after you start collecting.

Inflationproof annuities The trouble with the conventional annuity is that, once you begin receiving payments, they are fixed at the same amount for life. Rising prices could make that monthly income woefully inadequate after only a few years. To meet this objection, insurance companies have come up with what is known as a variable annuity. Theoretically, a variable annuity is close to the ideal retirement plan. It guarantees to pay you an income as long as you live. The size of the income is not fixed, as with a conventional annuity, but is designed to increase if prices increase and thus give protection against inflation.

The principle involved has been tested. For many years college professors and others in 1,500 institutions have participated in a retirement plan (called TIAA-CREF) that offers them both a variable annuity and a fixed-dollar annuity. They have been happy with the results.

Well, then, why isn't everyone rushing to buy variable annuities? Why aren't more retired people living off them?

For one thing, despite TIAA-CREF's record and the fact that several small variable-annuity companies have been in business for five or ten years, there still hasn't been a great deal of experience with them and they are thus viewed with caution by many people. There are no figures even approaching the wealth of long-haul data available to the buyer or seller of other investments, conventional annuities and life insurance.

An ordinary annuity pays you a fixed number of dollars per month for life. Thus, at age 65 you could hand an insurance company about $50,000 and receive a contract guaranteeing you a monthly lifetime income of $350. Month after month, rain or shine, you would receive that $350 regardless of economic conditions, the cost of living, or how long you lived.

But you know that for many years prices have been rising and the value of the dollar declining. As a result, you may be leery of a fixed income. That $350 a month looks fine now, but it could be inadequate in 15 or 20 years.

So instead of $350 a month, suppose you elected to receive each month one share of common stock now worth about $350 a share. You plan to sell it and use the proceeds as your income for the month. The value of stocks, on the average, has risen faster than the cost of living. So when prices rose, you would expect to get more for your share and thus be able to buy what you needed even at higher prices. For example, over the past ten years the price of IBM has grown at the average rate of 13% a year compounded. If it continued to grow at even half that rate, the income of a person receiving a share a month would be well protected against inflation.

A variable annuity does not pay off in shares of stock, but the idea is very similar. Instead of promising you a certain number of dollars a month as a conventional annuity does, your contract promises you a certain number of "units" a month. Each unit represents a proportionate share in a large portfolio of selected stocks. Every month the company will send you an amount of money equal to what your units are worth that month. Here is how the system works:

Suppose you sign up to buy a variable annuity with monthly payments during preretirement years for an income to start when you reach 65. When you send in your payment, you will be credited with "accumulation units" representing a stake in the investment portfolio. If the portfolio is then worth, say, $100 million and there are a million accumulation units outstanding, a $200 payment by you (forgetting expenses for the moment) would get you two accumulation units. If the fund's value went up to $120 million, your $200 would pay for only 1⅔ units; if it fell to $80 million, your $200 would buy 2½ units. Over the years, dividends and profits from the fund would be reinvested, and you would get your share in extra accumulation units.

Now comes age 65. You stop buying accumulation units and you start receiving "annuity units." The number of units you will get each month is fixed at that point and will never change. But the value of each unit will change with the value of the company's investments because each annuity unit, like an accumulation unit, represents a proportionate stake in the fund. Thus, you will never know in advance exactly what your retirement income will be. You will naturally hope that any variation will be upward, especially when prices are rising.

Once you get beyond the variable-value feature, you'll find that the structure of variable annuities closely resembles that of fixed-dollar annuities. You can buy one some years before retirement, with the income to start at a later date (a deferred annuity). Or you can choose to buy one at the time you retire, with the income to start at once (an immediate annuity).

You then have a choice of how you pay. An immediate annuity is paid for in a single, large lump sum. Thus, it is also known as a single premium annuity. A deferred annuity can be bought with a lump sum, too. Or you can buy it with regular monthly or quarterly payments until retirement (an installment annuity).

You will also have the usual choice of pay-out plans. You can elect a straight life annuity—it will pay as long as you live and then stop, no matter whether you live only a few years or decades. You can elect a joint-and-last-survivor annuity—it will pay until the last of a pair of beneficiaries (usually husband and wife) dies. You can elect a payments-certain plan—it will pay for a minimum of, say, ten or twenty years even though you yourself die sooner, but will continue for your lifetime if you live longer. The number of annuity units you will receive each month differs with each type of pay-out plan.

You can cancel a contract before the income period starts. You will get back whatever the value of your share in the fund is at the time you terminate, which may be more or less than you put in. You can usually borrow against this value, too. As with conventional annuities, however, you can't ordinarily cancel and get a cash value back after you have started receiving your monthly income, nor does the contract have a loan value then.

This is all well and good, but everything seems to ride on the assumption that common stocks will keep going up. All stocks don't go up, of course, even over the long pull. And those that do rise sometimes have sinking spells. For example, IBM fell sharply a couple of times during the last ten years, even though it was growing 13% a year "on the average."

Of course, a variable annuity is backed by a broad selection of common stocks. Therefore, the monthly income of annuitants moves pretty closely with stock prices as a whole. The long-range trend of stock prices as a whole has been steadily upward, and this trend appears to be continuing.

But even the stock market itself can go through some pretty wild gyrations. Furthermore, no one can rule out 100% the possibility of a protracted slump in the economy and, as a result, the market.

This is why most people and professional groups who use variable annuities team them up with a fixed-dollar annuity. In the TIAA-CREF plan for colleges, in fact, a participant must have at least a part of his contribution put into a fixed annuity.

The fixed annuity carries on even during stock market declines. If there should be a depressed period of falling prices, its dollars would be worth more. Meanwhile the variable annuity provides the kick that keeps the team ahead in what looks like a never-ending race with the cost of living.

There are other kinds of inflation-resistant annuities. One is a mixture, partly variable and partly fixed dollar. It is variable during the "pay-in" period—after deduction of expenses, the installments you pay during accumulation follows the level of stock prices. The pay-out, however, is in the form of a fixed-dollar annuity—the same number of dollars each month for life. Such a contract is generally not considered to be a variable annuity. For one thing, the whole point of a variable annuity is inflation protection during the retirement years, which the hybrid contract does not give. Secondly, such an arrangement is easily set up on a do-it-yourself basis; invest in stocks or mutual fund shares during preretirement years; use the resulting fund to buy a conventional annuity at retirement.

A recently introduced variation of the inflationproof annuity features an automatic increase in payments each year regardless of economic conditions. One such policy pays lower-than-average initial benefits but guarantees they will be increased by 3% a year indefinitely. If your monthly payment started at $100, for example, it would go to $134.44 during the 11th year and to $203.44 during the 25th.

Another innovation is the annuity that permits you to choose your own investments. During the accumulation period of a deferred annuity you establish a custodian account at a bank, consisting of stocks, bonds, savings accounts, mutual funds or other investments. You instruct the custodian to buy or sell whatever you wish and still have all dividends and interest (but not capital gains) accrue tax-free until retirement. Then you select any rate of return from 3½% to 9% and have the payments drawn against the value of your assets.

As you can see, there are many ways to provide safety of your dollars and income from them. The big question is, What kind of safety do you need most? If you can expect to live for a good many years, the biggest threat to your money probably comes from inflation. So you probably should have a good portion of your money in equities such as good growth stocks or sound real estate. And money so invested and kept invested over the years, eventually should provide a good income—more income, in fact, than you would get if you started out with income as your object.

20

TRUST FUNDS

A trust fund is a safe place to put assets, and it provides a way to make flexible arrangements for the disposition of the income from the assets. By definition, a trust is an arrangement whereby one person has the legal ownership of property but holds or manages it for the benefit of someone else. Here are the parties who are involved in such an arrangement.

Definitions First, there is the trustee. He is the legal owner who manages the property for someone else's benefit. He does not own it in the everyday sense of the word. He can do with the property only what the person who gave it to him has empowered him to do. He must dispose of the income from it and, sooner or later, the property itself, as instructed. He is accountable at law for mismanagement or failure to carry out instructions properly.

Actually, the trustee is likely to be not a person but an institution: a bank or a trust company. And there may be more than one. Many trusts are administered by cotrustees, such as a bank and an individual.

Next comes someone who appears in the definition only by inference. He is the fellow who owned the property originally and gave it to the trustee. He may have any of a number of titles—commonly creator, grantor or testator. He can, if he wants, name himself among those to benefit from the trust, directing the trustee, for example, to pay the income to him while he lives and then to his wife.

Finally, there is the person or group of persons or, perhaps, the charity or institution that is to receive the income and, eventually, the property itself. These are beneficiaries. Those who get money from the trust only while they live are life income beneficiaries. Those who get the principal of the trust when it is broken up are remaindermen.

So much for people. Two things round out the five elements that comprise a trust: the property itself and the set of instructions given to the trustee.

Your lawyer and banker will call the property placed in trust the principal, *res* or corpus of the trust. Almost any kind of property can be put in trust: real estate, insurance policies, patents, cash, stocks, etc.

The directions you give the trustee are the trust terms and are ordinarily set forth in a legal document called the trust agreement or, under certain circumstances, in your will. Some of the terms are fixed by law and public policy.

These terms will be examined at some length later. For now, simply note that they will outline the duties and powers of the trustee, say how long the property is to remain in trust, tell what shall and shall not be done with income and principal, and specify the rights of the beneficiaries.

Put all of these five elements back together again and translate them into an example. Mr. Green, preparing for retirement, assembles $75,000, garnered from the sale of his home, the cash value of his insurance and his savings. He creates a trust, with his bank serving as trustee. The bank's trust department agrees to invest the money and to collect interest and dividends. Mr. Green is to receive this income quarterly as long as he lives, and then it is to go to Mrs. Green in the same manner as long as she lives. After her death the bank is to reinvest the income and divide the total accumulation among grandchildren as they reach the age of 21.

As you can see, the trustee undertakes quite a job—investing, reinvesting, collecting income, parceling it out on schedule, keeping records, preparing tax information, keeping track of the grandchildren. Moreover, although the trustee does not by any means guarantee a fixed income or the absolute safety of the capital, he is legally responsible for managing the fund carefully and prudently.

Fees A trustee doesn't take all this on for the fun of it. He receives a fee. The amount varies with many factors, including state law. It may be a percentage of the income from the trust or a percentage of the principal or both. There ordinarily is a minimum charge when the trust is so small that it yields inadequate compensation on a percentage basis.

As a rule of thumb, fees, however computed, usually come to about ½ of 1% annually of the value of the principal. On a large trust a sliding scale is commonly involved in the computation, and the charge might be proportionately lower; on a very small trust the minimum charge commonly comes into play, and it might be proportionately higher. In one state the annual commission is limited to ½ of 1% on the first $50,000 of capital, ¼ of 1% on the next $450,000, and ⅕ of 1% on all over $500,000. There's an additional commission of 1% on any principal paid out of the trust fund. The trust also would be charged for legal fees, brokerage commissions and certain other expenses incurred by the trustee. Smaller trusts are subject to minimum annual fees such as $125 to $250 if the trust is invested in one of its common funds, and about double those rates if it is invested as a separate unit.

Basic types of trust Two basic types of trusts are available:

One is called a "living trust." It means a trust that you create during your lifetime, getting your lawyer to draw up an agreement and signing over some of your property.

The other kind is a "testamentary trust," also known as a "trust under will." Here you get your lawyer to incorporate the terms and the nominations of trustees and beneficiaries into your will. After your death the property is transferred to a trustee by your executor when he settles your estate.

Another kind of trust is sometimes treated as a third basic type, though it is really a subspecies. This is the life insurance trust, one in which insurance policies and the proceeds from them form the principal. It is a form of living trust. You draw up the agreement and make the trust the beneficiary of your life insurance. At your death the policies pay into the trust fund, which from then on operates just like any other trust. Sometimes the creator of such a trust continues to pay the premiums on the policies involved. Sometimes he puts into the trust, in addition to the policies, cash or income-producing property, which the trustee uses to pay premiums and keep the policies in force.

When you create a testamentary trust, you can't change your mind after it has started to operate, because you will be dead at the time. But when you create a living trust, you can leave yourself free to reconsider. You can make it a revocable trust by reserving the right to withdraw some or all of the property. Or you can make it an irrevocable trust by yielding all such rights.

Obviously, you want to think twice about making a trust irrevocable. One man put everything into an irrevocable trust, reserving to himself only a retirement income. When he later encountered a long illness, with heavy medical and convalescence costs, he couldn't touch the funds he needed to meet the emergency.

What a trust can do Here is a rundown of some of the things that must be or can be provided for.

• INCOME PAYMENT

The trustee can be told to hand over all income as he gets it or to make payments monthly, quarterly or annually. He can accumulate income for a time, as in a trust fund being built up to provide a college education. The trustee can be empowered to pay income only at his discretion. He can make payments on someone's behalf—college bills, medical expenses, insurance premiums.

• PAYMENTS FROM PRINCIPAL

Suppose you leave money in trust, income to your wife and principal to the kids at her death. Can she withdraw some of the principle, too, if she needs it? You can fix it either way. You can guard against emergencies or higher living costs by authorizing her to call for principal; or you can preserve the principal at all costs by forbidding her to. Or you can compromise by allowing withdrawals for stated purposes, within limits, or at the discretion of the trustee.

° DURATION

You must specify how long the property is to remain in trust before being distributed. The duration will be measured by lives, not by a period of years—that is, the property will be marked for distribution not after 10 or 20 years but, in most states, within 21 years after the death of any number of designated living persons. A lawyer or trust officer will be glad to explain why this is so, but you will be sorry you asked. It involved something called the Rule Against Perpetuities, which, to put it mildly, can be complicated.

° POWER OF APPOINTMENT

Instead of saying who gets the principal at the end, you can delegate someone else to choose later. Example: A man leaves a trust for his wife during her lifetime, to be divided among their children at her death. Should the money be shared evenly or will some deserve or need more than others? How many will be living? Rather than try to guess, he might stipulate that the money be divided as the mother directs in her will.

° INVESTMENTS

State laws limit what your trustee may do with the funds you give him. In most states he has reasonably broad discretion. In others he is limited to a "legal list" of securities, which is often restricted wholly or largely to such items as government bonds and gilt-edged utility bonds. You, however, can give him more or less leeway than the law prescribes. In a living trust you can reserve a voice in investment decisions for yourself.

° PROTECTIVE PROVISIONS

You can incorporate special provisions to protect what you feel are the best interests of beneficiaries. A spendthrift trust places a beneficiary's money beyond the reach of creditors. Benefits can be contingent on something happening or not happening. A man might leave money in trust for a son's widow but provide that his grandchildren get it instead if she remarries.

That doesn't cover all trust terms. Nor does it delve into the legal problems they present. It does explain and illustrate the common ones.

Note the variety, enabling you to adapt a trust to all sorts of circumstances and objectives. Note that most are concerned with putting a sum of money to work for one purpose while preserving the sum itself for another purpose—a basic idea of the trust. Finally, note that you can use the options to make a trust very rigid or very flexible.

In general, trust experts urge flexibility—broad investment authority, discretionary powers, ways to tap principal. You just can't foresee every contingency. Here are cases of too rigid trusts cited as evidence.

Early in the century a couple of successful businessmen gave trustees explicit instructions that they knew from experience would ensure sound, no-nonsense investment for all time. One said to invest his money only in first mortgages on Brooklyn real estate. Another specified the bonds of streetcar companies only.

Another man left money in trust for his son. To make the trust an incentive to his son's ambition rather than a drag on it, he decreed that payments from it were to match, dollar for dollar, the son's earnings. The more he earned, the more trust income. The less he earned, the less trust income. This scheme was greatly admired at the time. But the son contracted tuberculosis and was unable to earn a cent.

Ways to use a trust See whether any of these eight reasons for using a trust fund apply to your family.

1. To make up for lack of financial skill or interest. By using a trust fund, you hire a professional to do the job. Mr. A knows his wife is completely unequipped to invest skillfully the small sum he will leave. She might be overspeculative in her investments or overcautious. A trustee manages for her. Mr. B has little experience and less interest in handling invested capital. His small retirement fund is in a revocable trust for himself and his wife later.

2. For convenience. A trust can turn an irregular income into a regular one, eliminate record keeping and the bother of reviewing and reinvesting. And income continues at death instead of being cut off while an estate is settled. Mr. C works a trust

into his retirement plans simply so that he, and his wife after him, may relax and look forward to a monthly check in the mail. Mr. D, who supports a dependent sister, places a sum in trust with the income to go to her directly and thereby saves both of them bother and embarrassment.

3. To guard against waste. Money in trust can be partly or wholly safe from a beneficiary who would be likely to lose it or fritter it away. Mr. E was concerned over his wife's tendency to buy things "we simply must have" but that he couldn't afford. He left his money in trust. Mr. F had confidence in his daughter but not her husband. A trust gave his daughter the use of the money but kept it from his son-in-law.

4. To protect someone who is disabled or incompetent or a minor. The trust does the job they cannot. Mr. G wanted to leave money directly to a grandson but put it in trust until the grandson was old enough to handle it himself. Mr. H trusteed property for his own benefit, so that if in advanced age he became physically or mentally unable to manage for himself, there would be someone to look out for him.

5. To train and observe an individual or group slated to take over financial or business management later. A revocable living trust gives the creator a chance to do so. Mr. I wanted his two sons to carry on his business, first as trustees of controlling stock that would pay an income to his widow, and later as outright owners. He gave them control of the business as trustees of a living trust to gain experience and display their ability under his guidance.

6. For tax economies. Trusts can sometimes reduce income and estate taxes. The economies are usually of significance only to fairly well-off people, however, and should be worked out only with great care and in terms of the individual case. The man who gave his sister the income from trusteed securities may have removed that income from his own top tax bracket and placed it in her lower one. Mr. J is leaving $300,000 to his wife, who will leave it to their children. His estate will be taxed on $150,000, hers on $300,000. If half is put in trust, only $150,000 will be taxed at each stage.

7. To insure a future gift. This is another way of saying that a trust preserves capital. Mrs. K wants her sister to enjoy the

income from real estate that Mrs. K owns, but she is chiefly intent on leaving the property itself to her son. A trust achieves both goals. Mr. L uses an insurance trust to provide an extra inheritance for his grandchildren. He establishes a living trust to pay premiums on an insurance policy on his son's life. The grandchildren will eventually inherit insurance proceeds plus capital.

8. For flexibility in the future use and disposition of money. A trust is a way around too early or too rigid decisions. Take Mr. M, who provides that if his wife dies before him or with him, his life insurance proceeds will not be split arbitrarily among his children but will go into a trust, where the money can be used in the children's behalf at varying times, in varying ways and in varying shares.

A couple of alternatives In appraising the utility of a trust, you should always, of course, consider alternative ways of achieving your objectives. Trusts have advantages and disadvantages. Two alternatives are outright ownership of the property and life insurance settlement options. Compare these courses with a trust.

Outright ownership gives full control over the property, eliminates trustee fees, allows complete freedom in investment and reinvestment, and may produce higher returns and greater capital gains than a trust. Furthermore, the results obtainable from a trust will depend on the financial abilities of the trustee. They may be good or not so good. On the other hand, outright ownership leaves the burden and bother of management, makes funds vulnerable to loss and misuse. You cannot put conditions or limits on the use or disposal of the money. You can provide for one beneficiary but not a series of them.

Life insurance options and annuities offer a guaranteed lifetime income, guaranteed safety of principal, no trustee fees, and a unique system for the planned and orderly withdrawal of principal. Within limits you can impose restrictions on the use of the money. On the other hand, they do not have the flexibility of trust provisions, can include no discretionary powers, offer no chance of capital appreciation (except in the case of the variable annuity) and produce a lower return than an average trust. The interest element in an insurance-option plan works out to around 3%; an average trust will net, after fees, 4%—more or less, depending on the size and terms. Moreover, under settlement options your money is often scattered among several companies instead of being concentrated in a unified fund.

Common trust funds The common trust fund is a development in the banking field that has brought trusts down within the reach of average folks. Briefly, a common trust fund is a method whereby a bank combines the funds of small trusts into one single investment unit and thus obtains greater diversification for the trusts and operating economies that are passed along in lower fees.

If you walked into a certain big eastern trust company and established a $20,000 trust, the fee would come to $275 a year (it could be as high as $300 or $400 in other banks) under the standard system of trust management, which requires that the principal of each trust be kept entirely separate from the funds of every other trust. Moreover, the bank might have trouble maintaining average income, diversification and growth while balancing safety, yield and liquidity in a fund of that size. If it produced a 4% return, your beneficiaries would net only about 2½%.

But if you authorized your trustee to use the bank's common trust fund, the fee would drop to $105 a year. You could reasonably expect a net income for your beneficiaries of 3½% and somewhat more capital appreciation.

In another bank, of course, your charges might be different. But a return of 4% on your money and a 3½% net to your beneficiaries would be close to a national average. How are funds invested? At one extreme are funds invested exclusively in bonds; at the other are funds exclusively in common stocks. Some banks have a number of common trust funds with various objectives. Some are aggressively managed and do as well as, or better than, the stock market averages. However, a typical discretionary fund (which the majority are) might very easily be close to 50% common stocks, 12% preferred stocks, about 15% corporate bonds, 20% U.S. government obligations, and the rest scattered.

Do not, by the way, confuse a common trust fund with a mutual fund. It is easily done, but they actually are very different. The latter is a device by which a number of individuals pool their money for straight investment purposes. A common trust fund is a vehicle that a bank uses to invest money that it is administering as trustee. Your money can't find its way into a common trust fund unless you have a "true fiduciary purpose"—that is, unless you are thinking in terms of such objectives as are outlined on the preceding pages. There must also be a legal basis for the role of the bank; e.g., a will or a trust agreement. That is why, for example, banks are flatly prohibited from publicizing the yields earned by their common trust funds. They will quote current performance to a prospective creator, but to advertise yields would give the impression that such funds were investment plans, which they are not.

You may well have, perhaps to your surprise, a true fiduciary purpose. You may want to plan your life insurance under a more flexible program than options permit. You may want to preserve some hard-earned savings for another generation while you and your wife spend the income in retirement. You may want to make a gift to a grandchild or assure your heirs control of a family business.

Should these or any of the other objectives that a trust can meet sound familiar, pay a call on your lawyer or your bank's trust department.

They will examine your problem, explain how a trust can or cannot solve it, and fill you in on all the details. You just might walk out with one of the most valuable financial tools you have ever owned.

21

THE STOCK MARKET—
OLD STYLE

One of the wonders of modern business organization and communication is the ease with which you can buy or sell a stake in any one of some 50,000 publicly held companies. Anyone with established credit who can get to a telephone can buy or sell shares in the smallest or the largest publicly owned company in less time than it ordinarily would take to buy a ready-made suit or a week's supply of groceries. The stock market, in fact, is like a huge department store. The investor in stocks can have a charge account, can order by phone, and have the goods delivered or held in "will call." The "goods," of course, consist of part ownership in some manufacturing company, a railroad or a company that engages in any one of a thousand different kinds of business. Thus, for a given number of dollars you can become part owner of the company that produces your electricity or that made your auto, your television set or the popcorn vending machines at the neighborhood movie theater.

You should remember, though, that the price tags aren't fixed. You can return the goods, but you will not get back exactly the amount you paid. You may get less or you may get more. This is because once a company has sold a big block of stock

The Stock Market—Old Style

to the public, the shares keep circulating around. People buy them, hold them for a while, then sell them to someone else for whatever happens to be the going price. The amount of this buying and selling is almost unbelievable. In one day, fifty or a hundred thousand shares of one company's stock can change hands. And remember that there are thousands of these stocks being traded every day.

The ways in which stock transactions take place are undergoing very radical changes, largely because of the use of computers. This chapter will concern itself with the traditional methods of trading on exchanges and over-the-counter. The exciting innovations in computerized trading that will be seen in operation within a few years will be discussed in the next chapter.

Despite the new computerized techniques, there are only two basic ways that securities change hands. First, you may buy from or sell to another stockholder, the transaction going through two brokers, one representing the buyer; the other the seller. This kind of transaction takes place in the auction market on the floor of one of the exchanges. If you are selling, the floor broker representing you says, in effect, what will anyone pay? And he takes the highest bid. If he is buying stock in your behalf, he says, in effect, what is the stock offered at? And he takes the lowest price.

The second method of buying or selling involves, not an auction, but doing business with a dealer. This dealer has an inventory of the stock, much as a car dealer has an inventory of cars. He is constantly buying and selling and at any time stands ready to buy your shares at a price, or sell you similar shares at a higher price. The transaction, of course, will not be made by you directly, but through your broker. The difference between the dealer's buy and sell prices is his "spread," which pays him for his time, trouble, overhead and risk. While the auction market takes place on the floor of an exchange, the dealer trading is mostly done in the over-the-counter market, a network of dealers all over the country connected by phones and computers who do business in their own offices.

First, for illustration, consider a very simple transaction carried out in the old-fashioned way on the New York Stock Exchange without the use of computers. A man in Houston, Tex., gives an order to his broker to buy at the market 100 shares of XYZ Oil Company, which is listed on the New York Stock Exchange. The broker relays this order to his New York office, which, in turn, relays it to the firm's floor broker, who wends his way across the floor to the post at which XYZ is traditionally traded. These posts are horseshoe-shaped islands scattered around the floor and manned by clerks and specialists.

As the member from the firm with the buy order from Houston approaches the post, he sees several other members standing there, so he calls out, "How's XYZ?" Note that he gives no hint as to whether he wants to buy or sell. Someone answers with a price spread, for example, 52 to a quarter, meaning that 52 is the highest price that anyone is willing to pay for XYZ at the moment and that 52¼ is the lowest price at which anyone is willing to sell. If the member had a big block of XYZ to sell or buy, say quite a few hundred shares, he might ask for the size of the market—that is, how many shares were bid for at 52 and how many were offered at 52¼. But since his order is only for 100 shares, the minimum amount traded at the post, he likely begins to bargain by saying, "52⅛ for a hundred." Note that if he could buy 100 for that price he would better the market by an eighth of a point and save the purchaser $12.50. At that point an Exchange employee called a reporter at the post, hearing the new bid an eighth of a point above previous bids, puts the new information into the computer, where current bids and offers on all stocks are instantly made available electronically to inquiring member firms.

If nobody takes the member up on his offer to buy 100 shares at 52⅛, he may wait around for a while in hopes of buying at this price. Suppose, in the meantime, another member does arrive asking, "How's XYZ?" He has an order from one of his firm's clients in Jacksonville, Fla., to sell 100 at the market, although he does not reveal this detail. He is told, 52⅛ to a quarter. The newcomer says, "Sold a hundred at 52⅛." The Exchange reporter at once feeds this information electronically into the computer so that in a minute the transaction will appear on the high-speed tape, which is duplicated almost immediately in member-firm offices all over the country. Each member then makes a written notation to send back to his own firm, showing the name of the stock, the number of shares bought or sold, and the name of the firm on the other end of the deal. No written communication is exchanged between the members. They have made a verbal contract, and in all the history of the Exchange, while there may have been honest misunderstandings, no member has ever reneged. Following the transaction, the information is sent back to the respective investors by their brokerage firms. On the fifth business day following the transaction, in theory at least, actual shares of stock will be delivered by the selling firm to the buying firm and a certificate in the new owner's name issued by XYZ Company's transfer agent will be sent to Houston.

From that example you can see that the stock exchange is an auction market. The highest bidder, the member representing the buyer, bought from the lowest offerer, the member representing the seller. The deal was arrived at openly and audibly so that all members in the vicinity had an equal chance to interpose by making better bids or offers. Had two bid the same price simultaneously, the matter would have been decided by matching coins.

Not all transactions on the Exchange are quite as simple as the one outlined above. Suppose that a member wanting to buy 100 shares of XYZ arrives at the post and finds the lowest offer is 52¼. He offers to pay 52⅛, but no one steps up with 100 shares to sell. What does the member do? Since he has an order to buy at the market, the best he can do, obviously, is to buy at the offered price of 52¼. If he does so, from whom does he buy? Chances are in this case that he buys from the person who originally informed him that the market was "52 to a quarter." This person is "the specialist," a member whose main job is to maintain a fair and orderly market in certain stocks assigned to him by the board of governors. He stands at his post all day, furnishing current quotations and holding himself ready to buy and sell as required.

The specialist Each section of each trading post has its own specialist. Sometimes there are several members of a firm who specialize in the same stocks. From time to time the specialist provides current quotations so that a reporter may update the information in the Exchange's computer.

One reason for the specialist is that most large orders from professional money managers are not put in at the market but at a particular price. Thus, a trust fund officer, instead of ordering his broker to buy at the market might have ordered him to buy a block of XYZ at 51½. He would have realized that this was three-quarters of a point below the lowest offer, but he would have hoped to get his shares during a dip in the price. He could make his offer good for just one day, or good for one week, a month, or until canceled. Similarly, another investor, instead of ordering his broker to sell at the market, could have instructed him to sell at 53. Such orders at a particular price are known as limit orders.

Now when a member comes to the post with a limit order, say an order to buy XYZ at 51½, he can't stand around waiting for the market to dip to that level. That might take a day, a week or a month. In the meantime, he has other orders to fill at other posts. But the specialist, who is always standing at his post, will take the order for him and attempt to execute it if and when XYZ dips to 51½. In return for this service the specialist receives part of the member's brokerage commission. In this type of transaction he is a broker's broker. Thus, the specialist may have various orders to buy XYZ from 52 all the way down through 51, 50, 49, and even down to 40 if some investor is optimistic enough to think that someday he can get it for that price. On the other side of the specialist's book might be orders to sell starting at 52¼ and going up through 53, 54, 55 and so on, perhaps to 60.

The specialist's book also may contain sell orders *below* the market and buy orders *above* the market, called "stop orders." This happens in the following way. Suppose an investor had bought XYZ at 40 and it has risen to 52. He had a 12-point profit but did not want to sell because he hoped it might go higher. However, to protect his gain, he might put in a "stop" order instructing his broker to sell him out automatically if the stock went down and hit 50. This order would end up on the specialist's book. Conversely, a man who had sold short at 52, that is, sold the stock without actually owning any in the hopes that he could buy it back at a lower price, might put in a buy-stop order at 54. Thus, if he had guessed wrong and the stock began to rise instead of fall, his losses would be cut because his broker would have arranged for an automatic purchase as soon as the stock sells at 54 to cover his short sale. The member handling this stop-buy order would also give it to the specialist, who would enter it in his book.

As it turns out, then, the specialist has a book full of all kinds of orders "away from the market," that is, either higher or lower than the current trading level. Remember that limit orders are actually the majority of all orders placed. This may be hard to realize if you are a person who buys or sells stocks only occasionally because you probably do so "at the market." But professional investors and traders prefer orders at a specific price.

Ordinarily, then, even if there is no great activity in a stock, there are still plenty of actual bids and offers on the specialist's book, and even though there may be no other members around, the specialist is ready to give a bid and offer. The bid will be the highest bid he has in his book, which in the case of XYZ might be 52, and the offer might be the lowest offer, which might be 52¼. But what if there were so little interest in XYZ and so few limit orders in the book that the highest bid was only 51 and the lowest offer 54? That would seldom happen in a widely traded stock, but it might in an issue that was less active. Such a three-point spread would be undesirable in the view of the board of governors of the Exchange. The board prides itself on "close markets" and "continuity" in price movements. Thus, under ideal conditions there should be small fluctuations between successive trades. An investor hates to think that a stock he has just bought for $54 a share would, if sold back a few minutes later, bring only $51. So, if it happens that the highest bid on the specialist's book is 51 and the lowest offer is 54, the specialist is expected to do something about it. Specifically, he is supposed to "improve" the market by certain judicious buying and selling for his own account. Thus, he can arbitrarily narrow the 51–54 gap by offering to buy for his own account at 52 or sell at 53 or even 52½. Any customer will thereby be saved at least a point, or $100 per round lot (100 shares).

This combined role of the specialist as broker for others and dealer for himself caused considerable criticism in the years following the stock market crash of 1929. In the heyday of the boom, some specialists had participated in pools and helped rig markets. Today, however, the specialist works under stringent rules and the strict scrutiny of the board of governors of the stock exchange. He is supposed to trade "against the trend" most of the time. In other words, he is supposed to slow rapidly declining markets by buying stock for his own account even if he doesn't particularly want it. He also is supposed to slow rapidly rising markets by supplying stock, selling short if necessary. That means selling stock he does not own but which he borrows to deliver to the buyer. Later he must buy an equivalent amount to return to the lender. If the price goes up in the meantime, he is in the position of having to pay more for the stock than he originally sold it for.

Where, you might ask, does a specialist borrow as much as five or ten thousand shares of stock when he has to sell that much short? Officers, directors and large stockholders of a given company and institutions usually make large blocks of stock available for lending to specialists and other members.

Here are a few of the rules that a specialist must observe.

He may not, under pain of expulsion, buy or sell stock for his own account at a price at which he holds an order to buy or sell for a customer. He must pay an eighth of a point more or sell for an eighth less.

A specialist must be able to assume a position of 5,000 shares of each 100-share-unit of common stock in which he is a specialist. In actual practice, he has capital to buy or sell a good deal more. This is to enable him to offset temporary imbalances between supply and demand.

When a specialist wants to fill a limit order entrusted to his care by buying from or selling to himself, he must first send for and get the approval of the floor member from whom he got the order. Thus, if the broker doesn't think the price is fair, no trade is consummated.

A specialist may not show his book to other members.

A specialist makes money on commissions for executing limit orders and by trading for his own account. But he constantly runs the risk of losing back a slug of his profits in a very short time. One of the specialist's jobs is to "open" the market. That is, in the few minutes before ten o'clock in the morning of each trading day he studies his book and learns from other brokers in the crowd what orders they have to buy or sell. He determines from all this the fair bid and offer prices to be announced at the opening. Sometimes overnight news will have caused either a flood of buy or a flood of sell orders with no balancing sellers or buyers. It then becomes the specialist's duty to step in and make a market. This may require heavy buying or selling for his own account until bids and offers reach a balance.

As an extreme example, consider the dilemma of the specialist in Chrysler in the early morning hours of August 16, 1971, the day after President Nixon had frozen prices and wages and proposed repeal of the auto excise tax. Overnight buy orders for Chrysler had flooded in and stood at 670,000 shares. Sell orders, on the other hand, were only 269,000. Somebody had to come up with 400,000 shares to sell. Chrysler had closed the previous trading day, Friday, at 26⅜. Thus, the gap between buy and sell orders (401,000 shares) amounted to over $10.5 million. The specialist put in frantic calls and circulated Wall Street seeking sellers, telling potential sell cutomers holding Chrysler shares that the big demand could give them a good price. By about 3 P.M. the specialist had received orders to sell about 325,000 shares. He then went short (borrowed stock from others and sold it) to the tune of 75,000 shares, worth $2.3 million to make up an opening block of 670,000 shares at 31, up 4⅝ from the previous Friday's close. This same specialist had to risk additional capital to help open his other stocks. And it should be noted that Exchange rules require a floor governor's approval before a specialist can open a stock more than two points higher or lower than the previous closing price, or more than one point higher on issues below 20.

On this historic day, 32 million shares were traded on the New York Stock Exchange. There were 60,600 transactions, triple the pace of the previous trading day. More than 200 of the 1,300 common stocks listed had to be delayed beyond the time they would normally have opened. A few were not opened until the next day. This was not all bad. In the extreme cases, where buy orders exceeded sell orders by a large preponderance, the delayed openings gave the public an hour or two, and sometimes longer, to make decisions on whether to buy or sell a particular stock.

As you can see, the role of the specialist is vital. What makes it so is the size of the Exchange's business. Years ago specialists were not needed. The members originally sat around a table at their designated "seats" (a term still used to describe a membership) while the president read off the names of the stocks, one by one. If a member wanted to buy or sell, he shouted out his bid or offer. Gradually, this formal method broke down into a general auction at which brokers shouted their bids and offers at any time. Then, as volume grew, it became customary for members interested in particular stocks to congregate at certain definite points on the floor. The first specialist is said to have been a member who broke his leg and who, therefore, had to sit in one place. He offered to hold and execute order for other brokers.

Odd lots Suppose that you order not 100 shares but only a small amount such as 10—in other words, an odd lot. This order would come into the exchange in the same way as a round lot but would be routed to a level directly under the floor where the odd-lot firm, Carlisle deCoppet and Co., operates a business of breaking up round lots into odd lots for sale to customers while at the same time, purchasing odd lots that are offered for sale and combining them into round lots for resale to other firms.

Odd-lot prices are not determined directly by the auction method but are pegged to the price of the next round lot that passes over the tape. An odd-lot differential is added to the price on purchases or subtracted from the price on sales. The odd-lot differential is an eighth of a point. There is a slight compensation to the odd-lot investor in that his brokerage commission is $2 less than it would be on a round lot.

If the examples above had taken place not on the New York Stock Exchange but on the American Stock Exchange (AMEX), or on one of the various regional exchanges, the details of the procedures would differ, but the principle would have been the same. The trade would have taken place in an auction market.

Over-the-counter stocks Now for a sample transaction in the over-the-counter market. Suppose you wanted to buy shares in the ABC Company, which is not listed on any exchange. Your broker first would get you a rough bid and asked quote. Traditionally, each afternoon dealers who make a market in a given over-the-counter stock report their bid and asked prices to the National Association of Securities Dealers (NASD). These prices are printed on legal-sized sheets of pink paper, known as "pink sheets," and distributed each morning to brokers throughout the country. By glancing through these sheets, your broker can determine roughly which dealers are offering ABC at the lowest price. He will then get on the phone, or the teletype, and do some shopping to get the best price available. When the deal is consummated, the market maker, from whom you actually bought the stock, will mail the certificate to your broker, who will have the stock transferred to your name by ABC's transfer agent, who, in turn, will mail a new certificate to your broker, who will give it to you.

If ABC happened to be a fairly large and actively traded company, it might be listed on NASDAQ, which is an electronic communications system operated by the NASD. NASDAQ consists of small TV-like screens and in-put keyboards located in the offices of market makers and brokers. Your broker, by punching in the symbols for ABC on whichever quotation system he uses to get listed stock quotations, can immediately see the median bid and asked price for ABC. If you decide you want to buy, then the operation moves from your broker's desk into his firm's trading department, where a more sophisticated version of NASDAQ is in operation. When ABC's symbols are punched into this set, the screen lists all the dealers who are making a market in ABC anywhere in the country, along with their current bid and asked prices. Furthermore, these quotations are ranked according to the best offers (if you are a buyer) or the best bids (if you are a seller). Your broker thus can instantaneously determine where the best deal is for your proposed purchase of ABC, get on the phone or teletype and make the deal.

NASDAQ has one tremendous advantage over the pink sheets. NASDAQ bid and asked quotes are up to the second and the NASD requires each market maker to honor his quotes to the extent of at least 100 shares. The pink sheets, on the other hand, give the previous day's quotes, which may have changed overnight. Thus, if ABC is on NASDAQ, your broker's trading department can pick the best price and make one phone call to consummate the deal. Otherwise, he will have to call several dealers listed in the pink sheets to get their up-to-the-minute quotations before he can pick the one offering the best price. So NASDAQ, among other things, eliminates thousands of phone calls a busy broker would otherwise have to make.

As you can see from these examples, the auction markets that take place on the floors of the exchanges have some aspects of a dealer's market because the specialist is there dealing for his own account whenever there aren't enough bids and offers from the public to keep the auction market going. On the other hand, the over-the-counter market has some elements of auction in it since, especially through NASDAQ, dealers are bidding against each other for the customer's business.

THE EXCHANGES

NYSE There are, of course, other differences between the exchanges and the over-the-counter markets. Listed stocks are basically different from unlisted or over-the-counter stocks. The only shares that may be traded on the NYSE are those of companies that have been admitted to listing. Before a company can have its stock listed on the NYSE, it must meet certain requirements—have at least 2,000 stockholders owning at least 100 shares each; have at least 1 million total publicly held shares; have stock outstanding with a market value of $16 million and net tangible assets of the same amount; have shown a pretax profit of at least $2.5 million in its latest fiscal year and at least $2 million in each of the two preceding years. Once a company's stock is listed, it must maintain similar but somewhat lower qualifications. Other stock exchanges have similar listing requirements, but the figures are not as high, so that smaller and newer companies are eligible.

No one can trade on the floor of a stock exchange unless he is a member of the exchange. Here again, the qualifications are strict. Members are carefully examined before they are allowed to buy a seat. And member firms must maintain strict financial standards and have a certain designated minimum amount of liquid capital. Indebtedness, in proportion to liquid capital, is also strictly limited.

AMEX The American Stock Exchange is smaller than the NYSE and lists stocks that, on the whole, are more speculative. The AMEX has a colorful history. The first organized market in securities in New York sprang up 180 years ago under a buttonwood tree on lower Wall Street. The group that became the New York Stock Exchange moved indoors after about one year. Other markets formed in the street and on the sidewalks where robust traders sold stocks to each other and to the public, rain or shine, by shouting their bids and offers and making hand signals. There are people alive today who can remember when the American Stock Exchange, then called the Curb, operated outdoors. It was a colorful sight, the brokers wearing different-colored hats for identification and buying and selling by sheer lung power, all the while sending secret wigwagging, head scratching or hat-tipping signals to their clerks leaning out of office windows above. Eventually, in 1920, long after the more dignified New York Stock Exchange members had begun meeting around a table and making their bids and offers in orderly and quiet fashion, the Curb also moved indoors. Today, however, the AMEX still retains some of its early speculative flavor. The stocks it lists and trades are generally those of newer and less seasoned companies than those listed on the NYSE. In 1961 and 1962, the U. S. Securities and Exchange Commission, charged with regulation of the securities markets, made some telling criticisms of the way in which the Board of Governors, the standing committees and the specialists of AMEX operated their exchange. As a result, numerous reforms and organizational changes were made and the self-policing policies of the American Exchange were brought closer into line with those of the NYSE.

The exchanges The New York Stock Exchange handles 80% of the dollar trading volume in "listed" securities; that is, stock listed on any exchange. The American Stock Exchange, also located in New York City, handles another 11.5%. The balance of transactions in listed stocks is handled by regional exchanges scattered across the country. The chief ones are the

Boston, Midwest, Philadelphia-Baltimore-Washington, Pacific Coast, Cincinnati, Detroit and Pittsburgh stock exchanges. In addition, there are mining exchanges, specializing in shares of gold and other mines, and a few very small exchanges. There is one other exchange in New York City, the National Stock Exchange, founded in 1962, which lists the stocks of only a handful of companies.

Most of the regional exchanges have a long history. Those in the East were started in the early days of the republic. Those in the Midwest and the West sprang up to promote development of industry and commerce as civilization spread west. San Francisco's first exchange, for example, was opened in 1862 to help finance mining ventures. A Los Angeles stock exchange was organized in 1900 with the expansion of California's oil fields. The growing supply of local capital for midwestern enterprises led to the organization of Chicago's first exchange in 1882. After World War II many of the local exchanges began to consolidate. The present Midwest Stock Exchange represents the merger in 1949 of the Chicago, Cleveland, Minneapolis-St. Paul and St. Louis exchanges. The Pacific Coast Exchange was formed in 1957 by combining the San Francisco and Los Angeles exchanges. Today trading floors are maintained in both cities, and a modern communications system permits them to act as a single unit.

At first regional exchanges traded only local issues. As time passed, many local companies grew bigger and eventually listed their stock on the New York exchanges in order to acquire nationwide distribution of their shares and to attract investment funds nationally. Other companies switched from regional exchanges to the over-the-counter market for similar reasons. To compensate for loss of local issues, regional exchanges began to handle securities that also were traded on the New York and American exchanges. Now over 90% of the dollar volume of trading on the regionals is in stock also traded on the NYSE and AMEX. The regional exchanges manage to stay in business because smaller brokerage firms that cannot afford seats on the NYSE can afford seats on the regional exchanges. Their memberships in the regionals permit them to buy and sell many NYSE and AMEX securities, which they otherwise could handle only by turning transactions over to larger brokers and paying out part of the commission. The regional exchanges also provide a means of splitting up large stock transactions when the very size of the deal might distort the price per share. If, for example, an investor were to try to buy 3,000 shares of XYZ Company on the New York Stock Exchange, by the time he had purchased his first 1000 shares, the price might have begun to rise. Thus, he might obtain a better price on some of the remaining shares by ordering them through a regional exchange. Prices on the regional exchanges generally parallel those on the NYSE. Volume on regionals in dually listed issues, however, is generally light compared to volume on the two major New York exchanges.

There are other possible advantages to trading on regional exchanges. Because of the difference in time zones, the Pacific Coast Exchange is open two hours later than the New York markets. This provides the opportunity to trade on news released after the New York close. Some investors prefer to buy or sell national securities on regional exchanges because they can deal with local brokers whom they know and who offer special personal services. Trading on regional exchanges can save transfer taxes, especially when a large number of low-priced shares is involved, since the New York State transfer tax, generally levied on the seller, amounts to 1¼ to 5 cents a share. The rate for nonresidents of New York State is lower. Regional exchanges still provide a market for the securities of companies too small to qualify for listing on the big New York exchanges.

OVER-THE-COUNTER MARKETS

There are roughly 50,000 companies whose stocks are bought and sold by investors. Only some 2,500 of these companies have their shares listed on any stock exchange. Of the remaining issues, many are inactive, but some 30,000 are traded outside the exchanges in the over-the-counter market. In this market you find almost all kinds of securities, but they tend to be those that, for one reason or another, are less heavily traded. Over-the-counter dealers, in fact, will handle almost any kind of stock or bond for which there is any public demand. Thus, in the over-the-counter market you can buy a good many stocks that actually are listed on the stock exchanges, plus issues of thousands of small, medium-sized and fairly large companies that are traded locally or are not well-known enough or seasoned enough to be admitted to trading on the exchanges. Specifically, the following kinds of securities are traded over-the-counter: practically all government, state and municipal bonds; most corporate bonds; a large number of preferred stocks, many of them high grade; almost all stocks of banks and insurance companies, and, of course, the aforementioned common stocks of companies of almost every size and description from American Express Company to Revere Racing Association, which operates a dog track near Boston.

Most member firms who hold seats on the various exchanges also maintain over-the-counter departments. In addition, there are several thousand broker-dealers who do not belong to any exchange but who concentrate on over-the-counter trading. These broker-dealers are representatives of the oldest form of securities market we have. Over-the-counter trading began during the earliest days of the republic when the Continental Congress and canal and turnpike companies raised capital by offering their stock and bonds to the public. The actual offerings were made through banks. Thus, a bank generally kept a supply of securities on hand, and when a customer wanted to buy a particular stock or bond he would pay the bank by check or cash, and the banker in turn, would hand the security over the counter. The price would be a matter of negotiation between the bank and the buyer. In those early days, too, certain issues became very much in demand. It was natural that what the English called "stock jobbers" would begin buying and selling these popular issues as a full-time business. Two groups, which eventually became the New York Stock Exchange and the American Exchange, developed the formal auction method of trading. But the negotiated trading, engaged in first by banks and later by dealers, continued to flourish and the two markets grew up side by side. Their early differences persist even to this day.

The National Association of Securities Dealers (NASD) polices the over-the-counter market and maintains financial and ethical standards for its members. Since thousands of dealers, some very small, belong to the NASD and do business in the over-the-counter market, these requirements in no way resemble those of the large exchanges.

22

THE STOCK MARKET— NEW STYLE

The financial community today is in the midst of the most sweeping changes in its history. Within a few years the way stocks are bought and sold will bear little relation to the examples in the preceding chapter. Those sample transactions depended largely on direct verbal communication between parties, as well as telephone and mail. In the future most securities transactions will be handled by computers. Brokers and dealers will feed in the pertinent buy or sell orders. Computers will help set the price, and computerized bookkeeping will handle the actual transfer of ownership. In addition, instead of many exchanges and a separate over-the-counter market, all brokers and dealers may be organized into one nationwide system.

PAPERWORK CRISIS

These changes are only partly due to the invention of computers. It is conceivable that the stock market could have gone along for years using the old-fashioned methods. But beginning in 1967, a crisis arose that made drastic changes essential. The

The Stock Market—New Style

whole system of buying, selling and transferring securities began to break down. The cause was a tremendous increase in the volume of trading. Everyone, it seemed, wanted to get into the market at once. In the first quarter of 1967, 615 million shares changed hands on the New York Stock Exchange, 14% higher than for any previous three-month period and more than were traded in the full year of 1957, only ten years before. Each succeeding quarter of 1967 set a new record, and trading for the year was up 33% over 1966. So heavy was the volume that during the summer of 1967 brokerage firms began to fall behind in their paperwork. There were delays in delivery of stock to investors who had bought it. Accounts were mixed up. In August the NYSE felt it necessary to curtail trading for nine consecutive days by closing the exchange at 2 P.M. instead of 3:30.

As 1968 came along, stock prices were rising, a bull market was in full swing, investors and traders were doing more buying and selling than ever before in history. In 25 days in 1968 the volume exceeded 16.4 million shares per day, the previous record made on Black Tuesday during the crash of 1929. To many brokerage firms, this was the millennium. They began opening new offices and hiring more salesmen. Unfortunately, they spent more money and manpower getting new business than they did in expanding and improving the efficiency of their "back offices" —the organization of clerks and bookkeepers trying to handle the tremendous volume of business created by the salesmen up front.

Record keeping had never been a problem prior to 1967. Most of the energies of the governors had been spent guarding against fraud and manipulation and keeping member firms in sound financial condition. But now it seemed that thousands of irate customers were complaining of mixed-up accounts and failure to deliver stock certificates. A measure of the problem was the number of "fails," or failures to deliver securities to those who had bought them. By the end of 1968 fails among New York Stock Exchange members totaled $4 billion, and in July 1968 "aged fails"—fails 30 days old or older—totaled $837 million. While these figures refer to New York Stock Exchange member firms, it should be noted that conditions were no better, and in many instances worse among brokers and dealers who were not members of the NYSE.

As customers complained, the officials of the exchanges and the NASD began to take remedial action. In 1968 the NYSE imposed restrictions. It limited opening of new offices and hiring of salesmen by firms with operational problems. At the beginning of 1969 the NYSE went indefinitely on a four-hour day. The NYSE and the AMEX hired the Rand Corporation to develop a long-range plan of action. The exchanges and the NASD began plans to apply computerized automation to trading and record keeping.

FINANCIAL CRISIS

But then in 1970 a brand-new problem arose to plague the business. The stock market nose-dived. Investors lost interest and the problem shifted from one of too much business to not enough business. By April 1970 two-thirds of all NYSE members who did business with the public were showing a loss on the security-commission business. Lavish new offices were largely empty of customers. The new salesmen had few orders to fulfill. (Most firms, however, were still making money on their underwritings.) As the market dropped toward its low point in May 1970, many firms saw their capital, much of which was invested in stocks, decrease in value to the point where it was below NYSE requirements.

A number of these firms faced insolvency. For some years the New York Stock Exchange had a fund of $25 million to pay off customers of failing firms. Now the fund was taxed beyond its limits, so the Exchange raised the amount to $110 million by additional contributions. Congress also stepped in and passed the Securities Investor Protection Act in December 1970. By this time more than 160 NYSE member firms and an even larger number of non-NYSE member dealers had gone out of business. Most were either merged with or acquired by other firms. But some 80 NYSE member firms dissolved, retired from the securities business or self-liquidated.

REMEDIES

As 1970 came to a close, stock prices began to rise, volume increased, the surviving firms began to make money again and the crisis appeared to be over. But by this time a good many programs had been launched to make such a crisis unlikely again.

• The New York Stock Exchange had established a depository for stock certificates in New York City, known as Central Certificate Service, or CCS. In this depository brokers and banks deposited billions of dollars' worth of certificates. Thereafter, these various organizations could deliver securities one to the other, by computerized bookkeeping entries. Certificates would not have to change hands physically. In 1971, more than $100 billion worth of stock was delivered through CCS.

• The National Association of Securities Dealers started its own National Clearing Corporation to cut down on the physical movement of over-the-counter stock certificates. The NASD's system, known as "net-by-net," requires that brokers settle trades with the clearinghouse itself, instead of with each other *through* the clearinghouse, as in most clearing systems. Eventually, one way or another, stock certificates no longer will have to be delivered by mail but ownership will be guaranteed by a bookkeeping entry, just as your money is held for you in your bank.

• The NYSE began a study looking toward the "locked-in trade" whereby the trading floor would become an "electronic bridge" between brokerage firms and the clearance and delivery operations. An order to buy or sell a security would not only go electronically to the floor, but the succeeding steps, crediting one party with the cash and the other with the security, would be done instantly and automatically by computer.

• The NYSE started a program to computerize execution of odd-lot orders. This seemed like a natural way to save time and energy since the price at which an odd-lot transaction is effected is automatically determined by the price at which the next round lot changes hands.

• The NASD developed NASDAQ by which brokers can find

the best bid and asked prices for over-the-counter securities electronically. At the start some 3,000 over-the-counter stocks were "listed" on NASDAQ. A broker anywhere in the system could punch in a stock's symbol and on a miniature TV-type screen receive the bid and asked prices of all dealers making a market in that stock. Companies quoted on NASDAQ were required to have $1 million in assets, 500 or more shareholders, a minimum of 100,000 shares outstanding and at least two broker-dealers registered as market makers and continually quoting the stock in the system. Furthermore, these broker-dealers were required to buy or sell on order at least 100 shares of the stock at the price quoted. In order to change their bid and asked prices, market makers need only punch in new quotations on their NASDAQ input sets.

Both the New York Stock Exchange and the AMEX put into operation (on a trial basis at first) central computer systems by which member firms can send orders direct to the proper post, where they are executed automatically by computer. Initially, this system was used for round-lot orders only. The NYSE and AMEX systems differed technically, but were compatible.

THE MARTIN REPORT

Early in 1971 the governors of the New York Stock Exchange, under pressure from the public and the government to modernize, requested William McChesney Martin, former chairman of the Federal Reserve Board, to make a study of the constitution, rules and procedures of the Exchange to determine how, in his opinion, they might be improved in the public interest. The *Martin Report* was published in August 1971, and was widely hailed as a blueprint for a complete nationwide automated securities system. Mr. Martin's report, which concerned basically the New York Stock Exchange, started off by stating that the primary purpose of a securities market is to raise capital to finance the economy. The economy could not grow with it. In fulfilling this principal role, the market must also serve those who have already committed their capital to finance the economy. The marketplace must enable these investors to reconvert their securities into cash whenever their needs require. Investor confidence in the ability to resell their securities on fair terms is critical.

The following is a summary of the other important points of the *Martin Report*.

There are 31 million Americans who own common stocks directly and many millions more who participate indirectly in ownership through pension funds, mutual funds and insurance. The market thus should serve the public—the small investor as well as anyone else. It must be nationwide and it must maintain maximum liquidity. There must be centralized disclosure of all executions of buy and sell orders and other material facts. An auction market is best suited to perform this service.

Recent forces have disrupted the NYSE as an auction market. Institutional investors, such as mutual funds, insurance companies and the like, have acquired the power to influence the way markets are made. They have bought and sold NYSE listed securities in the over-the-counter market, seeking better prices and/or lower commissions and thus have by-passed the NYSE. (This is known as the "third market.") Institutions also have bought and sold directly with one another, again by-passing the floor of the exchange. (This is known as block positioning or "the fourth market.")

Because investors, and notably institutional investors, saw inflation and expected more inflation, they adopted "go-go speculation for short-term performance," which exploded volume, caused prices to soar, jammed the system with paperwork and later, when prices plunged, caused distortions and a breakdown in operations. The crisis receded after commissions were raised, the market began to rise and Congress created the Security Investors Protection Corporation to be financed by assessments on the members of the industry and backed by the federal government. Finally, the tremendous advantages of computers can improve the way markets operate.

To serve the interests of the public, a national exchange system must be developed to provide a single, national auction market for listed stocks. Such a system would include the New York Stock Exchange, the American Stock Exchange and the regional exchanges. The NYSE and the AMEX listing requirements might be used for two divisions of such a national exchange. Unlisted securities would continue to be traded in the over-the-counter market. No securities would be traded in both markets. (In other words, the third market would be eliminated.) The national exchange system should resemble the New York Stock Exchange, but pending establishment of such a national exchange, the NYSE should be reorganized to emphasize its quasi-public nature. The public should be represented on its governing board.

A liquid market—one in which the investor can readily convert his securities into cash at a price close to the last sale—depends, ultimately, as far as the NYSE is concerned, on the specialist system, which is designed to absorb the frequent imbalance between buy and sell orders. Increasing institutionalization (leading to tremendous orders of 10,000 shares, 50,000 shares and up) has placed heavy demands on the specialist. This also has led to the growth of block postioning—direct dealing between institutions and big broker-dealers, by-passing the floor of the exchange. There should be more specialists on the floor. And the block positioners should be subject to rules, regulations and qualifications defining their obligations to the public, and they should be required to work more closely with the specialists.

There should be complete uniformity among the various exchanges hooked into the national system. This would require Congressional legislation.

The primary purpose of every member of a stock exchange should be the transaction of business as a broker or dealer in securities. In other words, organizations that are primarily institutions, such as banks, mutual funds and insurance companies, should not be permitted to be members of exchanges. There are several reasons for this: Institutional membership could lead to a market dominated by organizations dealing for their own account, and tend to eliminate the agency relationship between broker and customer. Also, institutions might become too powerful in making markets on the exchange. Third, the separation between the securities business and other businesses should be maintained, not only to facilitate regulation, but also because of the unique role that the public exchange auction market plays as a very sensitive part of the mechanism of the free enterprise system. On the other hand, if institutions are denied membership in the exchanges, then present member firms should divest themselves of investment companies, mutual funds and investment advisory contracts.

The role of the small brokerage firm should not be overlooked. It has contributed to the health and strength of the economy by raising capital to finance new ventures and by serving the needs of small investors by broadening economic opportunity. Small firms should not be eliminated.

There should be a nationwide comprehensive depository of stock certificates. In the long run, certificates themselves should be completely eliminated. Brokers will then act as custodians for the "book entry" record of all of each customer's security holdings. The public must have assurance that ownership records will be transferred accurately and promptly.

There should be a single "consolidated exchange" tape that will provide complete disclosure of material information to all investors, including price and volume for every transaction in any stock listed anywhere. Eventually, stock prices should be quoted in tenths rather than eighths.

The *Martin Report* was widely and vehemently discussed throughout the securities business. As various points of view began to crystallize, two big issues emerged: (1) Who would be the leader in automating and streamlining the market? (2) Whom would the new type of market be primarily set up to serve, the individual investor or the big institution?

THE OVER-THE-COUNTER MARKET

In his report, Mr. Martin rather assumed that the New York Stock Exchange would be the dominating force and the model in tying all exchanges into a national system. The over-the-counter market was hardly mentioned. When it was mentioned, Mr. Martin's recommendation was that a substantial part of its business be eliminated; that is, the third market, or the trading done by over-the-counter dealers in stocks listed on the exchanges. It should be noted that historically the over-the-counter market has been a proving ground for unseasoned companies going to the public for new capital. No brand-new small company can have its shares listed on an exchange; the listing requirements forbid it. As small companies grow and become large and prosperous, they generally apply for listing and leave the over-the-counter market. The exchanges thus end up with the most widely traded stocks of the biggest and soundest companies, leaving the over-the-counter market with the smaller and more inactive issues.

Before World War II, very little business was done over-the-counter in listed stocks. The business that was done was in the slow-trading, high-quality issues, such as preferred stocks and also the common stocks of financial and utility companies. The more active stocks gravitated to the exchanges. During the 1950's and 1960's, however, institutional trading in common stocks grew tremendously. Mutual funds grew in size and number while insurance companies, pension plans and trust funds began to switch away from bonds and mortgages as investments and more toward common stocks. As these institutions traded more, they tended to do a growing amount of business over-the-counter, where deals are entirely negotiated, as distinct from the exchanges where transactions are effected in an auction market. Naturally, the over-the-counter dealers are reluctant to give up this lucrative third-market business in heavily traded stocks of big and prosperous listed companies.

One of the weapons the NASD has been able to use in its fight to keep its business in listed stock is its computerized quotation system, NASDAQ. NASDAQ has brightened up the image of the over-the-counter market by giving instantaneous quotes from all market makers in NASDAQ listed stocks and by guaranteeing that each quote is backed up to the extent of at least 100 shares. In the past, many complaints were heard about dealers who provided bid and asked quotes on a given stock but "backed away" when another dealer tried to buy or sell it at those prices.

In addition, NASDAQ has other fascinating potentials. It can give the bid and asked prices at which a given listed stock is being quoted not only in the over-the-counter market but on the New York Stock Exchange and all other exchanges at the same time. NASDAQ also has the built-in capacity to execute trades, notify all parties, and do the bookkeeping involved in crediting one party with the stock and the other with the money. So efficient and versatile is NASDAQ that soon after Mr. Martin had made his report, leading representatives of the over-the-counter market were challenging the traditional leadership of the New York Stock Exchange. They said, in effect, if a national securities exchange system is needed, NASDAQ, which serves over-the-counter dealers all over the country, is the logical vehicle.

With NASDAQ providing dealers with instantaneous quotes, and the capability of handling trading and bookkeeping, where is the need for exchanges? What is the good of having to go to the floor of the exchange to do business if shopping for the best price can be done from an office?

In the meantime, however, the NYSE has joined with the AMEX in developing the Securities Industry Automation Corporation (SIAC) which can make available to the public last sale data in all transactions in listed stocks in all markets across the country. The information would appear on ticker tapes at a speed of 3,600 trades per minute or on electronic interrogation devices such as desk-top recall and retrieval units.

Whichever system wins out, eventually all markets will be interconnected. Traders and market makers will punch their bids and offers into computers. Brokers will punch in their orders, and computers will seek out the best price, make the trade, do the bookkeeping. Evidence of ownership will be in the form of a statement, or perhaps a machine-readable card, such as an IBM card.

THE ROLE OF THE INDIVIDUAL INVESTOR

Volume of trading in the years to come will be tremendous. The New York Stock Exchange has made some projections.

• The number of shares listed on the NYSE, that is, the total number of shares that all the listed companies have outstanding, grows at the rate of 9½% a year and is expected to reach 24 billion in 1975 and 38 billion in 1980.

• Daily-average volume is expected to be in the 15–19–23 million share range by 1975 and in the 18–27–36 million share range by 1980. In 1971 it was over 15 million.

• The day of the year when volume of trading is highest is known as the high day. High-day volume is projected in the 26–33–40 million share range for 1975 and the 32–47–63 million share range for 1980. High day in 1971 was 31.7 million.

• Size of the average trade has been increasing and is expected to continue, as the following table indicates:

TABLE 11 AVERAGE SIZE
OF TRADE ON NYSE

1960	Under 200
1963	213
1965	224
1967	257
1968	302
1969	356
1970	388
1971	428
1975 (projected)	600
1980 (projected)	800

These figures give an indication of what is happening between the individual investor and the institution on the New York Stock Exchange. Bigger blocks of stock are being traded, a sure indication that institutions are doing more and more of the business. The question is whether or not the individual stockholder is to be crowded out of the market altogether and be forced to own stocks only indirectly—through ownership of mutual funds, pension plans, profit-sharing plans and the like.

The New York Stock Exchange maintains that about 60% of listed stocks are owned by individuals and about 40% by institutions and intermediaries and that this proportion has not changed greatly in recent years. But the proportion of trading done by individuals has declined drastically. Fifteen or twenty years ago, individuals did over 60% of the public buying and selling on the NYSE, excluding members' trading. In recent years this proportion has fallen to less than 25%. Institutions do the rest. Not only is the size of the average transaction going up, as shown in the table above, but the number of "large block" trades (trades of 10,000 shares or more) is rising very rapidly. In 1970, for example, there were 17,217 large block trades; in 1971 the figure had jumped to 27,000, an increase of 50% in one year.

The truth is that institutions have changed their investment philosophy 180 degrees in the past ten or twelve years. Their portfolio managers used to be rather conservative, buying good stocks and holding them. Around 1962 the average institution turned over its portfolio at a rate of about 12% a year. In other words, in an average year it would sell and replace only 12% of its stocks. In recent years, portfolio managers have caught the "go-go" fever and have turned to short-term capital gains as their objective. The turnover figure has increased to 36%, a rate that would have horrified portfolio managers of some years back. In fact, some conservative observers describe today's institutional turnover rates as nothing less than "churning."

This heavy institutional activity is bad for individual investors in two ways. First, the big blocks of stock that institutions buy and sell make more money for brokers. Naturally, brokers are much more interested in working with institutions and less interested in working with individuals. In recent years many brokerage houses have discouraged small investors by putting minimum limits on the size of orders or by refusing to open small accounts. The New York Stock Exchange has handled this problem by establishing an "investor service bureau" that helps the small investor find a broker who will take his business. The Securities and Exchange Commission, when it permitted the Exchange to increase commissions in 1971, insisted that firms that had traditionally handled small accounts must continue to do so. The Exchange was required to establish the service bureau in addition. The Exchange did establish the bureau and compiled a list of nearly 400 brokers who agreed to take small orders. You can get a free directory listing these brokers by sending a self-addressed card with the words "directory" on it to The Investors Service Bureau, New York Stock Exchange, P. O. Box 1971, Radio City Station, New York, N.Y. 10019. Any complaint on this subject should be sent to the same address.

The second way in which the rise in institutional trading hurts the individual has to do with liquidity. In the old days, the market was made up of millions of individual investors who had widely divergent objectives and opinions about various stocks and the market as a whole. When one investor wanted to sell a stock, there were plenty who happened to want to buy it at that particular time. Liquidity was also helped by the relatively modest size of the average transaction.

Today, with institutions dominating the market, the situation is different. For one thing, there is less divergence of objective and opinion. Communication has improved. It has been said, admittedly with some exaggeration, that young investment managers, uniformly trained in business schools, competitive and keeping check on each other's activities, all reading the same basic research material, hearing the same news at the same time, tend to try to beat each other into and out of the same situations. If the management of a big mutual fund decides to unload a large holding of a given stock (and it could amount to several hundred thousand shares), the word gets around pretty fast. Perhaps another manager who has been on the verge of selling the same stock will immediately decide to "kick it out." Soon, as the jargon goes, several institutions will be "running for the door" and the stock in question will take a steep and unexpected drop. Such a pile-up of sell orders not long ago caused a railroad stock to open at 47, off 14 points from the previous day's close. On another occasion a block of 226,000 shares of an electronic company was thrown onto the market, causing the price to fall from 42 to 33 in a few hours.

The ultimate fate of the small investor is hard to predict. It may be that when the market is completely automated, the cost of handling small orders will be less and the small investor's business will again be profitable. At least the New York Stock Exchange stoutly insists that individuals will buy and sell an average of 9.7 million shares a day by 1975 and almost 11 million by 1980.

23

REAL ESTATE—
GOING IT ALONE

"They're making more people, but they aren't making any more land." This remark, attributed to an old Texan, sums up the attractiveness of holding real estate in growing areas of the country. Certainly real estate is one of the oldest forms of wealth and has a solidity that sets it apart from the more intangible forms of ownership, such as stocks, bonds, bank accounts, insurance policies and the like. In addition, real estate is an equity that, if carefully selected, offers a hedge against inflation.

Against these advantages, of course, there are a few drawbacks. A venture into real estate usually takes a bigger chunk of capital than other investments. Since the market is slow and ponderous, buying and selling real estate must be a long-range proposition. Real estate is not as liquid as stocks and bonds. If you own a security listed on a stock exchange, you can sell it in five minutes. But to get your money out of a building or a vacant lot may take months or even years.

Real estate as an investment, then, is not something you can jump into and out of. To be successful, you need time and the patience to investigate every proposition. Also, you should have the common sense to seek out good advice and take it. Then, once you have put your money in, you should be able to leave it alone, usually for a period of years. You should have resources enough so that some emergency won't force you to dump your property on the market, sell to the first buyer that comes along and take a loss.

There are several ways of acquiring an interest in real estate. One is by means of a grass-roots enterprise in which an individual puts in his own money and time or in which a few friends, neighbors or business associates get together in a small group to search out local opportunities and invest in them. A quite different approach is to buy stock in a large real estate investment company or a real estate investment trust (REIT) or to buy a participation in a large syndicate set up by a professional syndicate manager.

This chapter will consider the grass-roots approach. It does involve risks and does take time and hard work, but the advantages are great. There is no big overhead expense, no one taking the cream off the top. If the enterprise is successful, the investors get all the rewards. In addition, they have the satisfaction of having done the job themselves. So if you feel you have the judgment, capital and persistence, either alone or with a few friends, to do your own real estate investing, here are some ideas.

Raw land It has been said that no one ever bought acreage on the outskirts of a growing city and did not make money provided he was willing to wait. There may be exceptions, but that statement is generally true. An oft-quoted rule of thumb for investing in vacant land is to go out a city's main thoroughfare until land is quoted for sale by the acre. Buy and hold until the price of your property can be quoted by the square foot. Another suggestion: Look for property on a thoroughfare linking a main business district to a high-grade residential district. Shrewd businessmen in every city have always purchased land in the path of new express highways or alongside them after they are built. Such property usually increases in value over the years, even though its initial purchase price may seem high.

If you do want to buy land, better stick to commercial possibilities. Residential lots seldom go up as much in value unless they can later be used for commercial buildings or unless they are located in a growing area where all houses are custom-built. Since the trend in building is toward mass production and prefabrication, the owner of a single lot in a community may have to wait a long time for the individual to come along who wants to build a home on that particular spot.

In buying vacant property, keep one rule uppermost in mind. It may be a long, long time before you find just the right buyer. So don't load yourself down with a mortgage that you may not be able to carry. And don't use money for a down payment that you may someday need in a hurry.

Lots by mail How would you like to buy some land in Brazil for two dollars an acre, or a bargain-priced lot in the West Indies, Florida, Arizona or California? Such property is often sold by mail at seemingly low prices, but don't let yourself be tempted into sending off a check. Experience shows that it's always advisable to inspect a piece of property in person and check out the identity of the promoter, the exact location, the value of similar land in the area, the legal status of the property, the financing, the availability of improvements and the zoning. The lots-by-mail business has been discouraged by various states and the National Better Business Bureau, but it still flourishes in some places. Many of those who went for schemes in the past have been bitterly disappointed. Many lots are now selling at 60% of their original offering prices. In some cases, the original owners lost their equity.

RENTAL PROPERTY

Houses Why not buy a house and then rent it? Won't the rental income greatly exceed the payments you will have to make on the mortgage?

Superficially, the answer is yes. Nevertheless, experienced real estate men believe that a house bought to be rented is not a good investment today. For one thing, there is no housing shortage. The renter has a wide choice, and the owner of a house for rent is also in competition with houses for sale on liberal terms.

There are other reasons why buying a single house and renting it may not pay off. The market price of an apartment house is generally based on the income it will produce. The price of a house, however, is not based on its prospective income, but on what home seekers in general are willing to pay for an attractive place to raise their families. You probably will have to pay relatively more for a house as an investment than you would if you, by yourself or with others, bought an apartment building.

One other point about a house for renting. There is no such thing as having a 5% or 10% vacancy rate. Your vacancy rate is either 0% or 100%, and when it is the latter, your income is suspended completely.

Lease-back Wouldn't it be wonderful if you happened to own a lot that an oil company, a bank or the postal service wanted to use? You might think that such a situation could come about only by chance, but you would be wrong. It is entirely possible for an investor to acquire a property, knowing in advance that someone will lease it. This comes about because many companies today generally want their capital available for expansion, operating capital and other purposes, not tied up in real estate.

It often happens that when a company picks a site but finds that the owner of the land is interested only in selling, it will look around for an investor who will buy the land, build on it and lease it to the company. If you happen to be known to the company's local manager as one interested in such investments, you might get the opportunity.

A lease-back arrangement with an oil company is a desirable investment for several reasons. First, you get a 10- to 25-year lease, so you take virtually no risk. Second, lenders have begun to look on such investments with favor and will generally put up a substantial portion of the money required to build a station. Third, you know in advance exactly what your rental will be. Generally, you can expect to get around 8% on the value of the land and 10% on the building provided the investment offers a tax shelter. You should get a larger return if it doesn't.

Some grocery and drug chains also use the lease-back method in building new stores. The size of the investment here is somewhat larger. Whereas a gas station could be built for, say, $35,000, a modern supermarket might cost as much as $180,000 or $250,000. But a good many stores are constructed these days as part of a shopping mall and are not available to individual investors.

In almost every case, lease-back investment opportunities are found by personal contact. You have to be in touch with local representatives of oil companies, drug chains or grocery chains. Sometimes these companies will retain a broker to find both the site and the investor to buy it and lease it back. Another good contact is the real estate department of your bank.

Apartment houses Owning and operating a four- or six-family flat or a small apartment house of, say, 18 units can be profitable for the small investor, but it is a tricky business. If you don't watch out, you may find yourself with apartments for rent in a part of town that is going downhill. Or a gleaming new modern building may go up across the street and attract many of your tenants.

Small apartment houses traditionally sell anywhere from eight to ten times gross rentals. Larger buildings, for which there are fewer prospective buyers, may sometimes be bought for six and a half times gross rentals, but this takes more capital.

SECOND MORTGAGES

Second mortgages and second trusts are treacherous, whether you lend on them or buy them as an investment. A second mortgage or trust is secondary or subordinate to the first mortgage or trust.

As an illustration, say Jones is anxious to sell his house for $15,000 to Smith, who has only $2,000 cash. The bank will lend $10,000 on the first mortgage, leaving a balance of $3,000 to come from somewhere else. Maybe Smith can borrow it on a second mortgage.

If Smith should default on either of the mortgages, his house will be sold at auction. If he has missed payments on the first mortgage, the proceeds from the sale first go toward paying off the first mortgagee. Anything left over goes to the holder of the second mortgage. Smith gets what remains. If payments on the second mortgage are in default, the house will be sold and the new buyer will assume the first mortgage. The price may or may not be enough to repay in full the holder of the second mortgage.

Thus, the holder of the second mortgage is in the riskiest position and is entitled to more interest than the holder of the first. (In case you are worrying about Smith, he doesn't count; he is merely the owner.)

Forty years ago, second and even third and fourth mortgages were common. Each mortgage would come due in toto on a given date instead of being paid off in monthly installments. Many mortgage holders were wiped out in the Depression. Then in 1935 the FHA began insuring first mortgages up to 80% and later 90% of the value of the house, thus combining the function of first and second mortgages. FHA mortgages, of course, are amortized monthly. Recently, however, home prices have been trending upward, putting more equity behind second mortgages and making them less risky. And the gap has been widened between the asking price for a house and the amount borrowable on a first mortgage. So second mortgages are back.

The mechanics of it Although second mortgages are known by various names, assume for clarity that a second mortgage involves two parties, the borrower and the lender, while a second trust involves three, the borrower, the lender and the trustees. If Smith defaults on a second mortgage, Jones must get a court order to have the house sold. But if Smith defaults on a second trust, Jones notifies the trustees and they sell the house.

There are two kinds of second trusts or mortgages, depending on who makes the original loan. If the seller of the house takes back a second mortgage or trust, the notes are known as deferred purchase money notes. If a third party, such as a mortgage company, makes the loan, the notes are known as money loaned notes. This distinction is important, as will be shown later.

The interest rate on the face of second mortgage or second trust notes might be 6%, 7% or more. However, hardly any mortgage company will take such notes for less than 9%, 10% or 11%. Here is how they work it.

Jones takes back a five-year second mortgage of $3,000 from Smith at 6%. Then Jones sells the note to a mortgage company at a 15% discount, or $2,550. This means that the first year the mortgage company will get a return of $270 (6% of $3,000, plus one-fifth of the $450 discount), or more than 10% on the $2,550 investment. Over the life of the mortgage the interest return will average 14%. This is legal even if the state usury law limits interest to 8% because Smith is still paying only 6% on the $3,000 he borrowed.

As a result of this practice, most second trust or mortgage notes are deferred purchase money notes taken back by the seller of the property. Mortgage companies buy such notes and do not generally lend money directly because if they did, it would be money loaned; there would be no discount, and the interest would be limited to the legal maximum. And, of course, they feel that because of the risk they must have more.

Frequently, the seller of a house won't want a second mortgage or trust but will take one anyway in order to make the sale. His intention will be to sell the note immediately. In this case he will naturally try to add the amount of the forthcoming discount to the price of the house, so as to avoid loss to himself. Thus, Jones might offer to sell Smith his $15,000 house for $15,000 cash or for $15,500 if a second mortgage or trust was involved. He would take back a $3,500 second mortgage or trust and sell it for $3,000, thus getting his $15,000 anyway. Smith, while nominally paying 6% interest on $3,500, would really be paying around 10% on the $3,000 he needed to buy the house for its true price.

Here are some points to remember about second trusts or mortgages:

When you are a seller, remember that a second mortgage or trust will deprive you of cash you might need as down payment on your next house. If you take a second mortgage or trust, don't expect to sell the notes for face value. Also, don't let the borrower get so far behind on his payments that he will never catch up.

Don't buy second mortgages or trust notes as an investment unless you know something about real estate.

If you do acquire a second trust or mortgage, immediately inform the holder of the first mortgage. Suggest that he notify you in the event he is forced to advertise the house for sale, so you can protect your interest.

PRECAUTIONS

Take nothing for granted That should be one of your mottoes if you plan to invest in real estate. Even the most seasoned operators in the business are extremely wary. One, for example, has made up a printed questionnaire of over a hundred questions. When considering the purchase of a property, he insists that every one of those questions be answered satisfactorily. If he cannot get the answer to a single question, he passes up the deal, even though all other aspects look favorable.

Take the case of a 70-year-old doctor and his wife who had saved up $100,000 on which to live in retirement. A real estate broker presented them with what appeared to be an attractive opportunity, an apartment house for sale for $800,000. An existing mortgage of $600,000 was held by a large insurance company, and in addition, the seller was willing to take back a second trust of $100,000. Thus, for $100,000 down, the doctor was able to purchase an $800,000 building, which presumably would have supported him and his wife indefinitely.

Now, the doctor did notice, when considering the purchase, that the first mortgage of $600,000 had less than one year to run. He questioned the broker, but was assured that there would be no trouble in getting a renewal. "What are mortgage companies for?" the broker asked airily. So the deal was closed.

For a few months thereafter the doctor and his wife enjoyed their retirement. But one day a reminder came from the insurance company, saying that the $600,000 mortgage would shortly fall due. The doctor turned this notice over to his broker, who again stated confidently that it could easily be renewed. A second and more urgent notice arrived. The doctor called his agent, and at this point the agent was worried. "They are all crazy," he said. "They won't renew."

What the doctor didn't know was that the $600,000 mortgage had been taken by the insurance company as a means of getting rid of a property it had acquired by foreclosure. After 20 years the building had depreciated, and the company felt that $475,000 was the most it cared to lend. If the doctor had been able to raise an additional $125,000 in cash, he could have renewed the mortgage and continued to live on his investment. But he had already used all his resources. He was unable to raise the money and lost the building and all his savings.

Using hindsight, you can easily point out what the doctor should have done. Before he bought the building, he should have gone to the insurance company and asked whether it planned to renew the mortgage. He would have received the correct answer, which was no, and he could then have looked further for a better deal. The moral of the story is: Let the buyer beware. Be sure the broker you deal with is reputable and competent and that all the facts are correctly presented. Then double-check everything yourself. And don't be awed by real estate jargon. Once you learn the technical language, you will find that the ordinary deal is not as complicated as it sounds.

Investigate thoroughly There are three main ways of getting knowledge and advice about real estate as an investment. First, the investor must depend heavily on the counsel of his broker. Therefore, he should take extra pains to ensure that he has a good one. The great majority of brokers are straightforward and ethical and have the best interests of their clients at heart. But a few are prone to cut corners and operate on the ethical fringes.

A new kind of expert in the field is the real estate counselor. For a fee he will give pure advice without acting in the capacity of broker or agent. Since he stands to make no commission on the deal, he is in an excellent position to give advice that is sound and disinterested. However, not many men in the country have enough counseling business to do it exclusively. Most members of the Society of Real Estate Counselors are brokers who will do counseling upon request and, when so doing, will not act as broker in that particular deal.

The second way to acquire knowledge of real estate values and legal and financial angles is to read the real estate sections of newspapers and talk to brokers, bank officials and property owners.

Third, and perhaps most important of all, check the details yourself before you sign any contract. Look at the property. Ask the tenants whether they intend to stay. Ask the mortgage holder whether he will renew, and, if so, get it in writing. Check on every angle you can think of, and think of as many as you can.

Good advice, some knowledge of the business and a thorough personal check of every deal—these should be the watchwords. Remember, also, that in real estate your money may be tied up for a long time. Don't use funds you may be needing.

24

REAL ESTATE—
REAL-LIFE EXAMPLES

Despite the assurances in the preceding chapter, you might ask, Can the ordinary person really get into real estate? Doesn't it take too much capital and too much know-how? Aren't the risks too big—risks of getting gypped or being foreclosed?

The answer to these questions is that ordinary people with relatively small amounts of capital can invest successfully in real estate in their spare time and are doing it every day. Here are a few real-estate examples to illustrate the point and also some of the problems. Names of individuals are fictitious.

A YOUNG MAN STARTING OUT

Take the case of 29-year-old Paul Knowles of Spring Valley, which is just east of San Diego. He says, "I had always wanted to start some kind of investment program, but because of a tight budget I knew that it would have to be something self-sustaining." Paul's tight budget was a result of his marrying and going to work right after high school and soon acquiring two children.

His job as a salesman for a wholesale grocery firm didn't provide him with much excess income.

Paul got his first break simply by learning that FHA would insure loans up to $39,600 with only 3% down on a small building containing four apartments known as a four-plex. Armed with this information, he began looking for a building that was basically sound but in need of modernization. The area he picked was East San Diego, which has good access to freeways and shopping and has been completely rezoned for apartments.

For several weeks Paul answered newspaper ads, read the Sunday paper listing of units sold with location and price paid, and spent much time examining apartments and talking to owners. When he finally felt he knew enough to make an offer, he bought a unit from an owner who was anxious to sell because one sale had already fallen through when the buyer couldn't qualify for the FHA loan. The price was $39,000 and the down payment was $1,300. Paul points out that FHA rules require that before it will insure a loan, the building must be appraised and meet requirements for construction, roof, drainage, plumbing and freedom from termites. On the other hand, it is entirely possible to acquire a property that for one reason or another might be hard to keep fully rented profitably.

When bought, the building was fully occupied except for the apartment reserved for Paul and there had been no rent raise for two years. Paul announced a ten-dollar-a-month increase. The difference between rental income and outgo, including insurance, taxes, interest (at 8½%) and principal, was $120 a month, which Paul spent on renovating whenever an apartment became vacant. A local firm installed carpet in the first vacant unit at a discount to get future business. Paul did the painting himself and bought paint, drapes and floor tile at sales. In two weeks, working evenings and weekends, he had the apartment refurbished and, after checking rents of comparable units in the neighborhood, easily rented it for $140 a month, an increase of $20 over the original rate. Over the next seven months he renovated the other apartments as they became vacant.

At this point Paul decided to trade his property for a larger one, but an ad brought no response. He then offered the unit for sale. After showing it for two Sundays, he sold it for $47,000 to a retired couple who were able to assume the FHA loan. He then ran an ad in the paper saying "Private party wants 6 to 8 units from owner." The response was good, and Paul bought a three-year-old, eight-unit building using his profit and assuming an 8¾%, 25-year conventional loan and giving the seller a small second trust. Now Paul has saved up enough to buy another four-plex and he hopes to continue his program of trading up. His advice is to buy older units and fix them up, rather than paying more for newer ones. He also says he saves $6,000 to $8,000 in commissions by buying direct from the owner.

A NEIGHBORHOOD SYNDICATE

Several years ago a group of neighbors got into a larger and somewhat less successful transaction. A doctor with a good income had asked the local banker for investment suggestions. The banker eventually came up with a waterfront farm some 100 miles distant consisting of about 925 acres selling for nearly a quarter of a million dollars. This sounded completely out of reach until the banker explained the following facts:
• Down payment was $80,000.
• The seller was willing to take back a first trust of $175,000 on which only the interest would be payable for five years.
• The cleared part of the farm was leased to a tenant who farmed it.
• A local sawmill operator was willing to pay $40,000 over a ten-year period for timber rights.
• The income would carry the taxes and interest.
• The depreciation on the buildings would give the owners a tax loss that could be applied to their other income.

So a syndicate was formed with ten units costing $8,000 apiece. The doctor took seven, leaving three, one of which was offered to John J. Bowdoin, who took it and, in turn, split it among himself and two friends. Thus, John, for an investment of only $2,700 ($8,000 divided by three) received a stake in a relatively large venture.

For about three years everything went well. An additional $10,000 was contributed pro-rata to purchase a bulldozer for clearing more land and for other expenses. After three years, however, the partners began to worry about what would happen when the "interest only" period elapsed and they would have to start paying down the principal of the mortgage. About this time they accepted an offer to buy the property for $361,000. This sounded good but then began the trouble.

It seems that the doctor, although nominally managing partner, was extremely busy with his practice and was relying on the banker to handle the legal details of the transaction. The banker, also busy, was not aware of how much the doctor was depending on him. So the ball fell between them. The sales contract gave the purchaser the right to occupy the property as of June 30. The tenant had agreed verbally to vacate the farm by that time. But it soon developed that under state law, he could require 90 days' written notice, and if it were not given, he had the legal right to occupy the farm for another year. On local advice he decided to exercise this right and the partners had to buy him off. Likewise, the timber cutter demanded reimbursement for all the timber that he could have cut had his contract not been canceled. In addition to cash payments to settle these claims and avoid lawsuits, the partnership had to pay $15,000 to a local entrepreneur to handle the negotiations.

Somewhere along the line, John discovered that the banker had been given a second trust note in the beginning representing a finder's fee of 10%, or $24,750, which was payable on sale of the property. As a result of all this, the capital gain was not as large as anticipated. But for each $9,000 invested, the partners received $13,338 representing a true annual growth rate of 10.3% compounded over four years. This return would not generally be considered adequate considering the risks involved.

Lessons learned—

• The managing partner, or at least someone, must be diligent in understanding every provision of every contract and making sure every loophole is closed and every loose end tied up. A lawyer should be in the group if possible.

• Each partner should read the original partnership agreement closely and understand every provision and every charge.

• No contract should ever be signed to sell a property until the seller knows he has all the legal documents signed and delivered guaranteeing that he can turn the property over to the buyer under the terms and conditions stated in the sales contract.

A NEIGHBORHOOD REAL ESTATE COMPANY

Some years back, ten men, neighbors and mostly members of the local Kiwanis Club, met with the idea of forming a small real estate investment company to take advantage of the rapidly increasing land values in two northern Virginia counties south of Washington, D.C. The group was an interesting one, consisting of a lawyer, a local banker, a retired accountant, a county building inspector, a highway inspector and a doctor who was a general practitioner and who, whenever a specific piece of property was mentioned, was likely to say, "Yes, I know where that is. I delivered a baby there once."

The minimum investment decided on was modest, $250 in cash and $25 a month for ten months. The lawyer drew up incorporation papers authorizing 5,000 shares of stock, and each incorporator was required to subscribe to a minimum of 50 shares at ten dollars a share. By the time of the first meeting of the incorporators and subscribers, word had gotten around so that the corporation actually began life with 27 shareholders owning a total of 825 paid-up shares and pledged to buy an additional 525.

Those of the group who had free time began scouting around the countryside and examining maps and records in the county courthouse. One summer evening, following a supper meeting of the Kiwanis Club, such officers and directors of the corporation who happened to be present were bundled into a car by the retired accountant, by then treasurer of the company, and driven over back roads to a rather inaccessible bit of scrub woodland. He recommended the purchase of three tracts totaling five acres because they lay in the middle of or close to what would be an interchange of Interstate 95 when it was extended south of Washington toward Richmond. The projected course of the highway was no secret, but no one had yet bought these tracts, perhaps because the asking price of $16,000 was considered too high. As some member reported scornfully, "It's only a pig farm and you could have bought the whole thing five years ago for $1,000." This remark illustrates one of the great dangers in the investment business—looking back instead of ahead. These tracts were sold some years later for over $200,000.

To illustrate some other dos and don'ts in this kind of investment, here is an abbreviated log of the company's doings over several years of its early history.

September 1960: Bought five acres expected to be on I-95 interchange. Price, $16,000.

December 1960: Bought 100 shares at 17 of the small local telephone company. Rumor had it that the commanding general of the Marine Corps base at Quantico, Va., having flown into a rage because he could not get an outside line, had ordered that the switchboard be yanked out and regular service taken.

April 1961: Bought 24 more shares of telephone stock at 14 through rights offering.

March 1962: Company permitted stockholders to buy more stock at $12, new net asset value.

June 1962: Bought 12 landlocked acres along Interstate 95 for $300 an acre with thought that access could be worked out later.

October 1962: Offered one-half acre on the I-95 interchange to several oil companies for $33,750. No takers.

January 1963: Received a 10% stock dividend on telephone stock.

May 1963: Offered stock to existing stockholders and interested friends at net asset value of $15 a share.

December 1963: Bought a house on 29 acres of land near Manassas, Va., for $17,000. Also bought two waterfront properties on the Eastern Shore of Virginia, one 60 acres and the other 150, on the theory that the bridge-tunnel complex being built across the mouth of Chesapeake Bay would open up the area to traffic from New York to Florida. (Unfortunately, no big pickup in traffic ever occurred and eight years later the company still had the two properties and had paid off the mortgages and lost its leverage.)

March 1964: Through rights, bought 96 more shares of telephone stock for 24, it then being traded in the market at 31.

May 1964: Put a price of $80,000 on half-acre I-95 tract. No takers.

November 1964: Increased authorized shares to 10,000 (since nearly 5,000 had then been sold) and set the net asset value at $20 a share.

February 1965: Made first sale of property—house and 29 acres sold for $27,750 net, a capital gain of over $10,000. Big celebration.

April 1965: Raised net asset value to $30 and bought an acre of land on a corner of U.S. 1.

August 1965: Bought 77 more shares of telephone stock through rights offering at $40 a share.

At about the same time, the real estate company found that it now had so many stockholders that it was necessary to apply to the U. S. Securities and Exchange Commission for registration of its shares before any more could be sold.

April 1966: After eight months of dealing with the Securities and Exchange Commission, was able to offer shares to the public at $30. Sold only 200 shares.

September 1966: Agreed to sell half acre on I-95 to Atlantic-Richfield for $90,000 but received no cash at this time.

November 1966: With only $12.40 in bank, necessary to float bank loan.

December 1966: Atlantic-Richfield, trying to delay settlement until it was ready to build service station, found a long neglected old county road on property. Since no title insurance had been obtained, it was necessary to go through time-consuming procedure of applying to the County Board of Supervisors to abandon the road.

March 1967: Delay in settlement with Atlantic-Richfield forced company to borrow $50,000 from bank at high interest rate plus two points.

August 1967: Settled with Atlantic-Richfield. Paid off bank loan.

December 1967: A stockholder who had bought in at 10, 15 and 30 determined the true annual growth rate of his investment to have been 27% a year compounded annually.

From here on, the company found the going easier. Its accumulated telephone stock appreciated because the area was growing rapidly. It eventually was sold for over $15,000. The company split its stock four for three, re-registered with the SEC twice, selling shares first at $30 ($40 on the old stock) and recently at $50 ($67 on the old stock).

Lessons learned were—

• It's easier to buy land than to sell it. And real estate deals almost always take longer than expected.

• Title insurance should be obtained on every piece of property at time of purchase.

• A small real estate company should have: (1) dedicated people who know the area and have time to search out bargains, (2) a lawyer, an accountant and, if possible, a securities man among the directors or officers, (3) a close association with one and preferably two local banks where lines of credit can be arranged.

• Many contracts to buy that real estate agents offer owners of property are phony. A typical provision in a contract says that the buyer is making an "earnest money" payment, but this money is to be put in escrow with a lawyer until settlement. Probably the check would not even be cashed but simply put away so that the purchaser would not put up real money at all. Another provision allows six months for settlement. Still a third states that if, prior to settlement, the buyer's engineers find the property "unsuitable," the deal is off and the so-called earnest money will be returned to the buyer. In other words, this so-called contract is nothing more than a free option for six months.

Other clauses sometimes found in purchase contracts offered to land owners provide that settlement will not take place until after rezoning has been obtained. There may not, however, be any provision that requires the purchaser to apply for rezoning at any given time, which could give him what would amount to a free option for several years.

ADVICE FROM AN ESTABLISHED INVESTOR

A very successful real estate investor who started with nothing many years ago and now owns over 2000 apartment units, an office building and other properties, gives this advice to those starting out.

"Expect to work hard evenings and weekends. Know everything you can possibly learn about the area you are interested in. When I started out I had a part-time secretary who cut up the real estate report service and filed each report by city block. Thus, I had a complete file showing who bought what, how much was paid and borrowed and so on, for every block I was interested in.

"Have the guts to follow through and put money on your judgments.

"Arrange all financing in advance. When I used to buy properties at auction, I would have the financing set. Sometimes, even though I was not high bidder, I got the property anyway because the high bidder couldn't swing the financing.

"When you sign notes, put above your signature 'without personal liability.' This means the property must carry the loan. If it cannot, don't buy it."

25

REAL ESTATE INVESTMENT TRUSTS AND SYNDICATES

If you want to make a real estate investment in which the properties are selected and managed by professionals, you have three choices: a real estate investment trust, a real estate investment company and a real estate syndicate. Probably the most suitable for the ordinary investor is the real estate investment trust, known by its initials as a REIT. A REIT is to the real estate investor what a mutual fund is to the stock and bond investor, an unincorporated association owning real property or mortgages. An investor can buy shares in such a trust and thereby become the owner of a small slice of all the property or mortgages held by the trust.

There are two kinds of REIT's. The realty or equity trust invests largely in real estate, such as office buildings, shopping centers, hotels, etc. The other invests primarily in mortgages, usually construction mortgages; in other words, it lends money on a short-term basis to builders and developers. The realty trusts are generally smaller, and most are traded over the counter, although a number are listed on the AMEX and a few on the NYSE. These trusts recently have had problems because of rising expenses, inflexible rents and flat earnings. As a result, many of them have converted into mortgage investments. The mortgage trusts, newer and larger, are mostly listed either on the AMEX or NYSE, with some traded over the counter. A few trusts combine mortgage and equity investments.

Back before 1960, real estate investment trusts were subject to the corporate income tax, which meant that they paid taxes on income and then their stockholders also paid taxes on the dividends received. Public Law 86-779, passed in the fall of 1960, gave to real estate investment trusts the special tax benefits already available to mutual funds. Thus, if a REIT distributes 90% of its income to shareholders, it pays no corporate income tax. The shareholders, of course, do pay income tax on their dividends. There are certain requirements to which a REIT must conform to receive this tax "pass-through" benefit.

• It cannot manage its own properties. It must be a "passive" investor, operating strictly as a conduit for investment income. Property must be managed by an independent contractor, who collects a management fee.

• It must have at least 100 shareholders, and no five or fewer individuals may own more than 50% of the shares.

• At least 75% of a trust's gross income must be derived from real estate or mortgages, and at least 75% of its assets must be in real estate (which includes mortgages), cash and government securities.

• Not more than 30% of the trust's gross income may be obtained from sales of securities held for less than six months or from sales of real property held for less than four years, apart from involuntary conversions.

While they operate under the same law and enjoy the same tax shelter, equity trusts and mortgage trusts take entirely different approaches to investing. You need a basic understanding of how both types work to decide which one would be more suitable for your purposes.

EQUITY TRUSTS

Since they are engaged primarily in the ownership of real property, equity trusts usually are paying off mortgages on the property out of rental earnings as well as passing income on to shareholders. This reduction of the mortgage debt coupled with inflation-boosted property values can give shareholders substantial real estate equity. A well-managed equity trust seeks good-quality real estate in which ownership value can be built up over a long period.

Typical holdings of equity trusts include office buildings, apartment houses and commercial property, such as shopping centers. But some hold such diverse properties as college dorms, motels, oil wells and vacant land.

Among the better-known equity trusts are Real Estate Investment Trust of America, the oldest of all REIT's; U. S. Realty Investments; Bradley Real Estate Trust; Greenfield Real Estate Investment Trust; and Pennsylvania Real Estate Investment Trust.

Right here is a good place to consider what is known as tax-sheltered income; that is, income on which no income tax must be paid, or at least on which income tax can be deferred for a number of years. Consider the example of a building that costs $120,000 of which $100,000 is attributable to the building itself and $20,000 to the land. Assume that the building is considered to have a life of 40 years. In other words, in 40 years it will be worn out or obsolete. Theoretically, at least, the building is losing one-fortieth or 2½% of its value each year. This 2½% of the building's original value, or $2,500 a year, is considered an expense just like taxes, interest, repairs and so on. Note, however, that unlike interest, taxes and repairs, the $2,500 depreciation is not actually spent. The owners have it. They can, if they wish, put it aside in a reserve fund where it will grow to an amount theoretically large enough to build a new building at the end of 40 years. But this is not required. In actual practice, part or all of each year's depreciation reserve can be paid by the owners to themselves as tax-sheltered income. This money, of course, is not really income; it is simply a return of the owners' original investment or capital. If they pay the full depreciation to themselves each year for 40 years, they will have used up the building entirely and have no money to replace it.

To go a bit deeper into this subject, the investor in a real estate property often can determine just how much of his income will be tax sheltered. Consider the example mentioned in the previous paragraph. Assume the following situation:

Cost of land and building	$120,000
Down payment in cash	40,000
Mortgage loan	80,000
Cost of building alone:	100,000
Annual depreciation, assuming life of 40 years:	2,500
Annual payment of principal and interest on mortgage:	7,200
First year interest payment at 7½%:	6,000
First year amortization, or payment on principal:	1,200
Gross income from rentals:	20,000
Operating expenses including taxes, insurance, maintenance, repairs:	9,200

With these figures, let us construct an equation showing the income and tax figures that are significant to professional real estate investors. What is known as the "cash flow" is the total amount of cash the owner receives after he has paid all out-of-pocket expenses. In this example, the cash flow is arrived at by taking the gross income of $20,000 and subtracting $9,200 of operating expenses, and the $7,200 payment on the mortgage, leaving $3,600. This is what the investor receives, but not the income that he pays taxes on. The $1,200 amortization payment is taxable, since it is not an expense but simply a payment by the investor to himself (since he is paying off a debt). Hence, for tax purposes this must be added to the $3,600 cash flow, making $4,800. From this, however, is subtracted the $2,500 depreciation, which is an expense, leaving taxable income at $2,300.

The formula: Cash flow plus amortization minus depreciation equals taxable income. In the example, $3,600 plus $1,200 minus $2,500 equals $2,300. Since the investor receives $3,600 in cash and pays taxes only on $2,300, then $1,300 of his income is tax-sheltered.

The depreciation taken in the example was arrived at simply by dividing the cost of the property by its estimated life in years. But it is permissible under the tax laws to load the depreciation so that more is taken in the early years and less later on. Two popular methods are the 150% declining balance and the 200% declining balance. In the 150% declining balance, assuming a life of 40 years, the first year's depreciation is 1½ times the "straight line" rate of 2½%; in other words, 3¾%. To compute the second year's depreciation, the dollar amount allowed in the first year is subtracted from the original value of the property ($100,000 minus $3,750, leaving $96,250) and 3¾% is then taken of the remaining value, in this case 3¾% of $96,250, or $3,609.

Assuming the 150% declining-balance method was used in the example, the formula for the first year would be $3,600 (cash flow) plus $1,200 (amortization) minus $3,750 (depreciation) equals $1,050 (taxable income). This would leave $2,550 tax-sheltered. If the 200% declining-balance method were used, the first year's depreciation would be 5% or $5,000 and the formula would be $3,600 (cash flow) plus $1,200 (amortization) minus $5,000 (depreciation) equals minus $200 (taxable income). In this case, the tax loss of $200 could be applied to other income the investor might have, and none of the income from his property would be taxable. It should be noted, of course, that the declining-balance method uses up the allowable depreciation much faster than the straight-line method, so at some point, the tax-sheltered income will be a lot less than it is initially. In such cases, the property often is sold and replaced by another.

Tax-sheltered income is available to REIT's. Some use it to the limit by means of declining-balance depreciation. In one case, a REIT has used it so that for every dividend dollar paid over a long period, only about 6 cents was taxable. Most, however, use straight-line depreciation. And many trusts do not pay out their depreciation at all but retain it in the form of reserves to cover remaining debt and to replace depreciated properties.

MORTGAGE TRUSTS

These REIT's finance just about every kind of real estate operation on a first mortgage basis, from raw land through construction to the completed building.

Mortgage trusts have no cash flow from depreciation since they don't invest in real property. On the other hand, their investment in long-term mortgages and short-term construction and development loans makes them more "liquid" than equity trusts. Many of their loans mature in a matter of months, and mortgages are usually easier to sell than real property. This liquidity allows mortgage trusts to react faster to changing economic conditions.

Though they can't claim depreciation—meaning their distributions are taxable as ordinary income—mortgage trusts do use a special financial tool: leverage.

Leverage involves the use of a small amount of equity to borrow money that then will generate larger returns. This provides the key to profits for mortgage trusts. They make their money on the difference between the cost of borrowed funds and the price at which they lend out these funds. The bigger the spread, the larger their profit. Construction and development loans in recent years have brought mortgage trusts good returns. They borrow at prime institutional rates or slightly above and lend at rates 3½% or 4½% higher. In tight-money times when banks and other lenders shy away from short-term construction and development loans, mortgage trusts are especially successful. The fantastic growth of REIT's between 1968 and 1971 was mostly in the mortgage trust field and resulted mainly from the tight money situation. When banks were forced out of high-risk construction loans, borrowers turned to the trusts and so did the attention of Wall Street. Mortgage trust stocks shot up accordingly. In later periods of easier money many mortgage trusts showed declines.

Questions arise about the risk involved in making construction loans. Certainly they involve more risk than insured home mortgages; that's why they bring a higher return. But well-managed mortgage trusts screen borrowers carefully and keep a close watch on builder operations. What about losses through default of builders? Since its loans are generally first mortgages, in the event of default and subsequent foreclosure, the trust is in a primary position for the recovery of the money it has advanced for the project. The older trusts, at least, have had little trouble with their loans. First Mortgage Investors, for instance, has lost only $31,000 from among the $509 million worth of construction loans it has put out over an eight-year period.

Lacking the bargaining power of such past performance, some of the newer mortgage trusts have trouble obtaining the low-cost lines of credit so vital to their operation. This is one reason analysts and brokers are wary when recommending mortgage trusts. They usually stick with the older, established associations. Most often mentioned are Continental Mortgage Investors, First Mortgage Investors and B. F. Saul Real Estate Investment Trust. The last named also owns property and is a combination equity-mortgage trust, with the potential to cash in on the benefits of each type.

A TRUST FOR YOU?

No particular type of real estate investment trust has a monopoly on success or lack of it. While a few newcomers have done very well, most impartial analysts suggest that the amateur investor will fare best if he sticks with established trusts that have good earnings records, whether they're in equities, mortgages or both. The managers of these trusts are proven performers, and good management, experienced in real estate and mortgage lending, is the basis for REIT success.

The caliber of its management is one of the few ways you can assess a newcomer. If it's a new equity trust, you can also ask what type of properties it is considering. With a new mortgage trust, you'll want to know whether it can obtain sufficient credit to utilize leverage properly and whether it can expect good customers for its loans.

Most investors must rely on a broker for information about REIT's and their management. Because REIT's are essentially a new business oriented more toward real estate than the stock market, many brokers haven't yet dug deeply into their complicated fundamentals. Some knowledgeable brokers recommend against investing in a REIT altogether, though that advice may often be a matter of preference for another specific form of investment rather than an indictment of the trusts. Others see a well-managed trust as an excellent, double-barreled (real estate plus stock) hedge against inflation.

If you're interested in real estate investment trusts, check your broker first. After getting his recommendation—if he has one— try to do some checking on your own. Ask any real estate or mortgage banking contacts you have about the trust and the people running it. At the least, find out what type of trust it is and what properties it's dealing with.

Buying stock in a REIT without investigating it first is like buying a coat without trying it on. You could very easily get one that doesn't fit you. If you are seriously interested in REIT's, there is a book you should read by all means. It is *Handbook of Member Trusts,* published by the National Association of Real Estate Investment Funds, 1101 Seventeenth Street N.W., Washington, D.C. 20036. This book, while quite expensive, gives the pertinent information on all the largest and most successful trusts, both the equity and mortgage type. Another book on REIT's, also quite expensive, is *The Real Estate Trusts: America's Newest Billionaires,* Audit Investment Research, Inc., 230 Park Avenue, New York, N.Y. 10017.

REAL ESTATE INVESTMENT COMPANIES

Since 1960, when Congress passed the law giving real estate investment trusts the special tax benefits, well over a hundred REIT's have been formed. The number of real estate investment companies, on the other hand, has not grown at all. The reason is obvious. Real estate investment companies must pay the corporate income tax, which for large companies amounts to around 50%. Then dividends paid to stockholders are again subject to income tax.

There are, however, a few real estate companies with shares outstanding in the hands of the public. These can be of three kinds: (1) The small company, such as the one described in Chapter 12, that has fewer than 100 stockholders and, therefore, cannot qualify as a REIT; (2) the big company that cannot qualify as a REIT for other reasons—for example, because too much of its income comes from sources such as construction or sale of building materials, rather than from real property holdings; (3) the company that uses depreciation to offset corporate income and thus defer income taxes to such an extent that it does not need the pass-through advantage available to REIT's. Tishman Realty, Uris Buildings and Del E. Webb are examples of real estate companies. All are traded on the New York Stock Exchange. In addition, a good many other big industrial companies have extensive real estate interests—Gulf Oil, IT&T, McCulloch Oil and other companies mentioned in Chapter 10.

REAL ESTATE SYNDICATES

A real estate syndicate offers tax advantages similar to those obtainable from a REIT. The syndicate itself pays no corporate income tax. The distributions to the partners are taxable to them as income or capital gains. Syndicates can be small, such as the one described in Chapter 24, or they can be very large and professionally managed. Like REIT's and real estate investment companies, a syndicate enables a person with a few thousand dollars to become part owner of property requiring a down payment of perhaps $100,000 or $150,000. At this level there are few potential buyers and therefore better chances for a bargain. One disadvantage of a syndicate is that it usually owns but one property and therefore lacks diversification.

A syndicate usually consists of one general partner and a number of limited partners. The limited partners' liability is "limited" to their original investment. And they have no rights to involve themselves in the management of the property. That is left to the general partner or managing partner. Sometimes a syndicate is put together spontaneously by a group of investors, but more often it is set up by a syndicator, a professional real estate man who locates a property, arranges for the financing and so on. At some point in the arrangements he has a syndicate agreement drawn up and offers limited partnerships either to friends or business associates or to the public. Large syndicates with a number of partners usually must be registered with the Securities and Exchange Commission and with the state regulatory authorities. Sometimes syndicate shares are offered without payment of a commission or underwriting fee. Larger ones offered through brokers usually carry an underwriting fee of 10%.

The syndicator may simply sell the property to the syndicate, or he may remain on as managing partner. He may buy into the syndicate himself as a way of convincing other investors of his good faith. More likely, however, he will get a free share for his compensation. As a professional real estate man he may act as broker in selling the property to the syndicate and thus receive a commission. He may also sell insurance on the building and receive a contract to manage it.

One way a real estate syndicate can make money is to find a building that is currently unprofitable because it is not being put to its best use, buy it cheap and convert it to a new and profitable use. Thus, a syndicate might buy an old apartment building with old-fashioned four- or five-room suites, modernize it, and chop each suite in two. It would then contain twice as many units, and the gross rental might be doubled or increased by 50%. One syndicate bought an old out-of-the-way hotel, modernized it, arranged space for stores on the ground floor and converted the balance to apartments. Another bought an apartment house in a downtown location and converted it into an office building, increasing the rents substantially. Larger syndicates often are formed to tear down obsolete office or apartment buildings and replace them with modern structures. Such an operation obviously requires a large amount of capital.

Along with lack of diversification, lack of liquidity is a disadvantage for limited partners in a syndicate. An elaborate legal agreement must be drawn, outlining the procedures a member or his estate must use to dispose of his interest. There generally is no organized market for syndicate memberships. In some cases a fund or its partners will repurchase a member's share at a 5% discount from his original cost, perhaps with a provision that such a repurchase will be made only if the financial condition of the syndicate, as determined by the managing partner, permits it. In other cases where there is no buy-back agreement, if a partner wants to sell his share, the other partners will merely help him locate a buyer. One of the problems in selling a syndicate share is obtaining an up-to-date appraisal of the properties so the seller will know approximately what kind of price to ask. If the syndicate doesn't obtain professional appraisals at regular intervals, the seller would either have to pay for an appraisal himself, usually an expensive proposition, or expect to dicker over the value with any prospective purchaser of his shares.

Generally speaking, because of its lack of diversification, its lack of liquidity and its emphasis on tax-sheltered income, a syndicate is most suitable for a person in a relatively high income bracket with a good bit of money to invest—money that he definitely won't be needing for a good many years.

26

REAL ESTATE— HOME OR FARM

A carefully selected house bought with the help of a mortgage can do three things for you. It can help you accumulate money by providing a forced savings program. It can make you a profit over the years if you happen to own it during a period of economic expansion, shortages or inflation. It is one of the few investments that can be used as well as held.

For most people, buying a house represents the biggest financial commitment they will ever make. Therefore, every detail of the transaction is important.

The house should be sound, attractive, usable and marketable.

The mortgage will probably run for years, so every fraction of a percent in the interest rate means hundreds of dollars lost or saved.

The monthly payment should not be so large as to be risky or so small as unduly to protract the term of the mortgage and pile up interest.

The price, although sometimes brushed off as unimportant compared with the size of the monthly payment, is obviously very important. Overpaying could result in a substantial loss.

Here are three questions to ask yourself before buying a house:
Is the house attractive and a good buy at the price?

Can I afford to buy it under the financial terms offered?
Will I save money by buying instead of renting?

The neighborhood Choosing a good neighborhood is probably the first step in choosing a house. Naturally, you will consider availability of shopping facilities, schools, churches, transportation. But there are other things to consider.

Suburban and rural areas attract many. They provide that "spacious living" out with the trees and bees. They also present their problems.

Unincorporated communities don't always develop the way the ads and the real estate salesmen predict. So if you move into such a community, don't expect miracles. Sewage and water systems may be a long time reaching you. When they do, it will cost you money to connect with them.

Fire protection should be carefully studied. If it is not adequate, fire insurance may cost as much as $2.50 per $1,000 annually, instead of the $.90 to $1. rate available in many communities with organized, full-time fire departments.

Cost of transportation is another item that can eat into the savings you make by living in the suburbs. You may have to drive your own car to work and pay to park it every day. That soon runs into money.

Main traffic arteries through better-class residential sections usually are good guides to follow in picking a suburban homesite. Lots close to such highways, including those beyond the developed areas, are likely to have fairly stable values.

Zoning restrictions may be sharply changed as economic pressure develops in future years. Even if no one puts a glue factory on your street, you may unhappily discover that your neighborhood is losing its original residential character. So ask your public planning officials about the prospects.

Restrictions running with the property may cause unpleasant surprises unless you know about them when you buy. You may suppose they merely keep the neighbors from doing things like erecting unsightly chicken houses in their back yards. But they also may prevent you from fencing your garden to keep out the neighbor's dog.

The house itself Think ahead about the house you are buying— five years, ten years ahead. If you have growing children, the question of separate bedrooms will come up in due course. Are there likely to be elderly parents or other relatives sharing your home in the future? If so, a first-floor bedroom and bath may be desirable.

The whole question of the livability of any house may be considered in terms of the family's needs. Will it accommodate without friction the hobbies of the individual members, their need for privacy? Is a recreation room a vital requirement?

Settle as many of these questions as you can in family conference or in your own mind before you start looking at specific houses. It will save you time, perhaps save you from being talked into buying something that doesn't really meet your needs.

For people who build their own houses, structural soundness is largely a question of good specifications and competent supervision to see that they are carried out. Buying an existing house, especially an older one, is a different matter.

The roof line, to take an obvious starting point, should not sag. Such a condition is difficult to correct. Don't let anybody tell you it's a minor matter.

The chimney is important. Some of the extra-wide chimneys being built for single-story ramblers or ranch-type houses have been causing trouble. The only way to check on the chimney draft is to light a fire in the fireplace.

Gutters and downspouts should be checked carefully. Are they rusted through or clogged? Do they drain away from the foundation? Those of copper are more durable than those of galvanized metal. If the metal is painted, Junior's toy magnet will help you identify it. The magnet won't stick to copper.

There should be a copper shield between the top of the foundation walls and the sill in termite territory, chiefly in the South. Slender earthen tubes running up the foundation from the ground to the wood framing suggest the presence of termites. Stick a knife blade into suspected beams or joists. If the wood is powdery, buy some other house.

The steel beam or wood girder giving mid-support to the floor joists is the key structural unit in the house. At least eight inches of each end of it should rest on the foundation walls.

Floor joists ought to be at least two inches thick, spaced evenly about 16 inches apart and bridged about every eight feet of their length with cross braces. The braces stiffen the joists, help distribute heavy loads.

Subflooring is one item on which some builders skimp. It is not visible in the upper rooms, but you can usually check it in the basement. The boards should not be more than eight inches wide, preferably laid diagonally across the joists.

A floor drain in the basement is important. Lack of it sometimes betrays a careless or inferior builder. If the basement has an outside areaway, this should have a separate drain.

Crawl space between the house and any unexcavated portion of the foundation is a must to allow for repairs of pipes, electric wiring and ducts. The crawl space should be at least two and one half feet deep and well ventilated.

Basement leakage can be a major headache. Remember that it is very difficult to do waterproofing effectively from the inside. Wet patches on the foundation and basement walls are danger signs.

Foundation walls ought to be eight inches thick if made of concrete block, poured concrete or tile, 12 inches thick if brick, and 14 inches if stone. Vertical cracks in the walls denote settling and often reveal that the concrete footings on which the walls rest are not strong enough. If the house is built on filled land, it may take years for the ground to stabilize. That could mean recurrent cracking of plaster, higher upkeep bills.

Automatic heating systems are the most convenient type. But the important question is whether the furnace is efficient. You may have to check that with a heating specialist.

Adequate hot-water storage tanks are essential. For the average family, a 30-gallon storage tank is the absolute minimum. If the laundry is done at home, a 50-gallon tank may be needed.

"Economy" equipment may actually prove very costly. Speculative builders often install the cheapest furnace, water heater and storage tank they can. If there are no written guarantees on this equipment, don't accept it.

Plumbing that makes loud gurgling noises is probably not vented properly. A country sewage system should have a septic tank with a disposal field rather than a cesspool.

Water pressure is often a source of trouble in older houses. Turn on all the faucets in the house; then see if there is pressure enough in an upstairs tap. Examine the water pipe where it enters the house; the diameter should be at least an inch.

Overloaded electrical circuits are dangerous. Ordinary lighting circuits take a 15-ampere fuse and are designed for lights or appliances using a total of 1,725 watts. Look at the fuse box. If larger fuses have been installed in order to accommodate more lights or appliances, the circuits are overloaded and there is a risk of fire.

If the house has picture windows, remember that even expensive thermal glass does not counteract the tendency of cold air to flow off large glass areas. Moreover, big windows on the street side may drive you frantic, what with the lack of privacy and the glare from headlights of passing automobiles.

Insulation of outside walls and roofs is fairly standard in the building of houses now. But insulating material that is pumped into wall spaces may settle. It generally is not as desirable as insulation that is nailed in place.

What should you pay? Generally speaking, the real estate business tends to operate in the interest of the seller wherever there is leeway for any breaks. On residential property it is customary for the salesman's 5% or 6% commission to be paid by the seller. So the higher the sales price, the more the salesman makes.

Prospective house buyers usually are unaware that they can hire a real estate agent to work exclusively for them. As an inducement for the agent to negotiate the lowest possible price, a deal could provide for a bonus payment—say $100 for every $500 he succeeds in knocking off the asking price.

Most real estate men will tell you that it is not necessary for a buyer to hire an agent to get a residence. They say that, although the seller pays the commission, they are actually working just as much for the buyer because there can be no sale unless the buyer is pleased, too.

Weigh the costs and advantages of each method and use the one that seems best to you.

There's another service available that many buyers are not aware of. Experienced professional appraisers can be hired almost anywhere. They will examine a house and tell you whether it is structurally sound and worth what the owner wants for it. Their fees range from $15 to $35 for each appraisal. But wait until you've got your mind pretty well made up before you call in an appraiser.

TABLE 12 MONTHLY PAYMENTS ON $1000 MORTGAGE

TERM	5%	5½%	6%	6½%	7%	7½%	8%
5 years	$18.88	$19.11	$19.34	$19.57	$19.81	$20.04	$20.28
6	16.11	16.34	16.58	16.81	17.05	17.30	17.54
7	14.14	14.38	14.61	14.85	15.10	15.34	15.59
8	12.66	12.90	13.15	13.39	13.64	13.89	14.14
9	11.52	11.76	12.01	12.26	12.51	12.77	13.02
10	10.61	10.86	11.11	11.36	11.62	11.88	12.14
11	9.87	10.12	10.37	10.63	10.89	11.15	11.42
12	9.25	9.51	9.76	10.02	10.29	10.56	10.83
13	8.74	8.99	9.25	9.52	9.79	10.06	10.34
14	8.29	8.55	8.82	9.09	9.36	9.64	9.92
15	7.91	8.18	8.44	8.72	8.99	9.28	9.56
16	7.58	7.85	8.12	8.40	8.68	8.96	9.25
17	7.29	7.56	7.84	8.12	8.40	8.69	8.99
18	7.04	7.31	7.59	7.87	8.16	8.45	8.75
19	6.81	7.08	7.37	7.65	7.95	8.25	8.55
20	6.60	6.88	7.17	7.46	7.76	8.06	8.37
21	6.42	6.70	6.99	7.29	7.59	7.90	8.21
22	6.26	6.54	6.84	7.13	7.44	7.75	8.07
23	6.11	6.40	6.69	7.00	7.30	7.62	7.94
24	5.97	6.27	6.56	6.87	7.18	7.50	7.83
25	5.85	6.15	6.45	6.76	7.07	7.39	7.72

Does it make any difference when you buy? Of course it does make some difference, but if you are thinking of waiting for prices to fall, you might have a long wait. And the long-term trend of prices seems to be up, not down. So unless you are pretty lukewarm about the whole business and would like to look around for a couple of years, don't worry too much about the timing.

Shopping for terms Once you've decided on the house and the price, there remains the problem of paying. To most people that means a mortgage running for 15 to 30 years. It used to be that the borrower paid only interest during the life of the mortgage, no principal. The whole mortgage then would fall due every three or five years and have to be renewed. Sometimes the lender would not renew and the borrower had to scurry around and raise the money somewhere else. Thanks to savings and loan associations and the FHA, most home mortgages written today are self-liquidating. That is, monthly payments include both interest and principal.

You probably will have to deal with a bank, a savings and loan association, a mortgage company or an insurance company to finance your purchase. Terms and interest rates vary, so shop around. Use the table on page 356 to guide you in relating size and length of mortgage, interest rate and monthly payment. Select the appropriate term and interest rate and then multiply the amount shown by the number of thousands of dollars you expect to borrow. These figures cover both principal and interest. As you repay, a little more of each payment applies to principal and a little less goes for interest.

You can be reasonably sure that reputable professional lending agencies will not permit you to borrow more than your income warrants. But the ordinarily accepted rule is that the purchase price of a house should not exceed twice your income.

Try to have a clause in the mortgage permitting prepayment without penalty. That will enable you to pay off a chunk of the principal any time you wish. Note how prepayment can save you money. If you repaid a $20,000 loan at 7% in 20 years instead of 25 you would save $5,172 in interest.

Other pointers on financing:

Extras and changes made in the course of construction of a house should be itemized in the purchase contract.

Special assessments for street paving or similar public works often take property owners by surprise. Your local tax office can tell you of such assessments already authorized. The more complete your community is with respect to curbs, gutters and utilities, the less chance there is that special assessments will be imposed.

Title insurance is a prudent investment. A lawyer can give you a certificate of title, and he accepts responsibility for any outstanding claims he fails to find. But he may die ten years from now. Insurance of the title, costing around $60 per $10,000, protects you in that event, or you may get a title certificate and insurance from a corporation that specializes in this field.

The full cost of owning your house includes more than the monthly payments you make on the mortgage principal and interest. You will also have taxes and insurance, repairs, replacements, utilities and fuel. As your own landlord, you'll pay all the bills. The total of the annual costs should not exceed one-fourth of your income.

Taxes on your land and house ordinarily should not be more than 2½% of the purchase price. If they are, you should be leery. They will be a regular and recurring burden, so inquire about them at the outset.

Look at it this way. Buying a home makes you save more, so in that way it's a good investment. But it also makes you spend more. To make a decision to buy or not to buy, first make a bare bones financial comparison of buying and renting. Then try to weigh the intangible benefits against the extra money you know you will spend.

HANKERING TO BUY A FARM?

Do you have a yen to be a gentleman farmer? Want to buy a place in the country as a haven from the atomic bomb, a hedge against inflation and maybe as a justification for having some losses to write off on your income tax return?

If so, here is what the experts advise you to do: Go ahead and dream of wide verandas, lush fields, grazing cattle and an expanding bank account—and then just keep on dreaming. Don't put any money into the idea. If you are city-bred, buying a farm will probably turn out to be simply a romantic way of losing your shirt.

A farm, generally speaking, has been a good inflation hedge. In the past 30 years land has increased in value faster than the dollar has declined in value. This does not mean, however, that any farm you buy will do that and also make a net profit.

On that tax-deduction point, you may be able to deduct the farm's losses from your income for several years if you are seriously trying to operate your farm as a profitable business.

But the Internal Revenue Service knows that no legitimate business operates in the red perennially. Eventually, you may be told you are running not a farm but merely an expensive hobby, and your write-offs will be disallowed.

Now, if you are a stubborn optimist who won't take advice and still want to buy that farm, all right. Grab a pencil and your reading glasses, and get ready for a lot of figuring and frustration. Maybe a miracle will happen, and you will turn out to be one of the few city folk who can actually make a farm pay.

First, what is a farm? For the purposes of this discussion, it is a real business in which you invest money and on which you try to make a profit. It's not a fancy country place where you raise a few vegetables and hang up a rustic sign with the word FARM on it.

Buying a farm is like making any other investment. You should know something about it before you start.

One man, a department head in a large company, is getting set for retirement in two years. He is going to buy and operate a farm, so he has already started studying. He says that by the time he retires he will know almost as much about farming as he does about his own business. Maybe he will. At least he is beginning with the right idea.

Advice There is plenty available, free. You won't have any trouble finding sources of information. Next to veterans, farmers get more help from the government than does any other large group. The Department of Agriculture publishes pamphlets, maps and instruction books galore on every phase of farming, and much of the material is free. In every county there is a county agent who represents both the federal and state agricultural agencies. His sole job is to give free advice and help to farmers. At every state college there is an agricultural extension service that studies agricultural problems and makes the findings available to farmers.

As a starter, write to the Superintendent of Documents, Washington, D.C. 20402 for a pamphlet called *Facts for Prospective Farmers,* Farmer's Bulletin 2221. Price is 15 cents. It gives a long list of sources of information. Then go have a talk with your county agent. He probably knows more about the farms in your area than any other single person.

When you begin to look for a farm, keep one thing in mind.

You are buying dirt. You can fix up a broken-down barn or a run-down house. You can make a lot of other changes above the surface of the ground. But the soil underneath was built up over the centuries by crumbling rock and tiny deposits of dead grass and leaves. You can't make much of a change in it in your lifetime without spending an awful lot of money. So when you buy a farm, buy good soil. And know it is good.

Soil maps covering two-thirds of the farm counties in the United States are available. The types of soil are shown in colors, and with each map comes a booklet explaining what each type of soil will grow best and about how much it will yield. Some of the newer soil surveys also give suggestions for managing each type of soil.

Get the soil map for your area and study it before you start looking for a farm. You will then know in advance where to look for the kind of land you want. County agents have soil maps. Maps are also available at state colleges and at libraries, or they can be obtained by writing to your congressman or to the Soil Conservation Service, U. S. Department of Agriculture, Washington, D.C. 20250.

Other things you want in a farm (make your own check list) are a good neighborhood, good roads, nearby churches, market and shipping points, electricity, phone, school bus, farm help. When you look at a farm for sale, cast an eye on the adjoining farms, too. Note whether your prospective neighbors use good farm practices and conserve their soil. If their land is full of weeds and gullies, yours probably will be, too. If they can't make a go of it, can you?

Farm management It is no accident that farmers in your area concentrate on certain kinds of crops and livestock. By continual experiment generations of farmers have found out what is best suited for each type of land and climate. So be smart. If most prosperous farmers in your area grow corn and hogs, lay off the mink ranches and shade-grown tobacco.

The shortage of farm labor makes it hard to keep a good farm manager and to get hired help. So try to stick to simple farming that requires neither skilled labor nor large numbers of seasonal workers, such as fruit and vegetable pickers. A dairy farm, for example, requires skilled farm workers who will stay on the job for a 14-hour day, seven days a week. Good dairy hands are scarce.

A cattle farm devoted largely to pasture takes a minimum of labor. Such a farm could have cultivated fields rented out on a one-half share basis, which means that the renter would grow the grain and give you one-half as rent. You would use the grain to carry the cattle over the winter. This type of operation, however, would require a good bit of capital. The breeding herd might well cost as much as the land itself.

The size a farm should be is not measured by whether it contains a certain number of acres, but by whether it is an operating unit. The ordinary unit is a farm that can be managed by one farmer and a hired hand or a farmer and his son.

Make it a business proposition. Don't try to run your farm catch as catch can. Hire either a dirt farmer or a management agency to operate it. Here is one arrangement that is common between the owner of a grain farm and his tenant. The owner gets half the grain crops and pays half the production expenses plus all the costs of maintenance of machinery and buildings. The tenant pays a small cash rental for use of hay and pasture land.

On a Great Plains wheat farm, the owner might get from a fifth to a third of the wheat crop but would pay none of the production expenses. In general, if a landlord takes his rent in cash, he gets only one-half to two-thirds of what he would get if he took his rent in crops. The poorer the land, the smaller the landlord's percentage.

Most tenants or renters won't take as good care of your land as they would of their own. So when you make an arrangement, specify the soil conservation measures you want carried out. Probably you will have to pay for these yourself, since the tenant may not see any benefit coming to him.

A farm management agency generally charges 5% of the gross income from the farm—perhaps more if the farm is very small. That will probably amount to 10% of the owner's net income, but in most cases it will be well worth it. Most management agencies not only will operate your farm but will help you buy and stock it.

Financing You can buy a farm at almost any price. But you'll probably get just about what you pay for. When farm income is high, professional farmers working good land are able to get a return of about 8% on their investment. Of course that doesn't apply to the family that buys a run-down piece of pasture at what looks like a bargain. It does mean that a fertile farm, properly managed can be a good investment.

Borrow money to buy a good farm rather than pay cash for a poor one—that is the advice of agricultural experts. So the next step after finding a farm may be a search for a lender. If you can pay off a mortgage in five years or less, you can probably get a loan from the person who sells you the farm or from the local bank. In such cases you might pay one-third to one-half down. If you want a long-term loan, there are two possibilities: the local farm loan association or an insurance company.

Farm loan associations are co-operatives authorized many years ago by Congress and originally financed by 12 federal land banks. There are now nearly 1,000 of these associations owned and run by farmers. They make "land bank" loans ranging from five to forty years.

You don't have to operate your own farm to get a land bank loan. But you must have control of the operation and participate in the management. Loans are limited to 65% of the normal appraised value of a farm. A farm that sells for $30,000 may have a normal, appraised value of only $20,000 and thus be eligible for a land bank loan of not more than $13,000.

Insurance companies lend millions of dollars on farms, and in many parts of the country they meet land bank terms. One advantage of getting a land bank loan or an insurance company loan is that in the process you will get a good, sound appraisal of your farm. You can also get such an appraisal independently by paying a fee to a farm real estate appraiser or a farm management agency.

Farm valuation How do you know what a farm is worth? You can figure it out yourself by a method known as capitalization of expected net income. This will take some careful figuring and estimating. First you decide what return you think you can get on your investment. You probably won't get it, but you can hope.

Say you want to get a return of 5%. The next step is to figure carefully and realistically the expense, gross income and net income you can expect from the farm. This will take a good many hours of study and calculation and probably will require the help of an expert, such as your county agent. Nevertheless, do it. If you don't, you are being extremely impractical.

The rest of the problem is simple. If you figure you will make a net income of $10 per acre over the long run, divide this by 5% to get a valuation of $200 per acre. Checking back, a 5% return on an investment of $200 is $10 per acre net income.

So if you seriously mean to buy a farm, get every cobweb out of your head, and don't waste time dreaming of country air and home-cured ham. You'll have to work like the devil and use all your ingenuity. If you can make a go of it, you'll have a good investment, a hedge against inflation, a healthful avocation that will keep you outdoors, and probably a safer place to live in this dangerous world. Furthermore, you'll have the last laugh on the experts.

27

INSURANCE

A Prerequisite to Investing

This chapter describes a financial commitment that most families should make before stocks, bonds or real estate are even considered.

There are two basic reasons why a man works hard and tries to accumulate money. First, he wants to acquire wealth for himself. It may be that he desires to use it to obtain an independent income, luxuries, a business or the wherewithal to retire in his old age. Second, he wants to provide an estate to leave to his family upon his death.

LIFE INSURANCE

Building up wealth is a slow and arduous process. But creating an estate can be done overnight. Life insurance does it. So life insurance should definitely be acquired before a man plunges into the long and hazardous task of saving and investing money. After he has made his pile, his insurance needs will change.

Until then he should cling to enough to take care of his dependents in case something should happen to him.

Buying life insurance is not always easy because the buyer is apt to let his emotions sway his judgment. Some life insurance salesmen deliberately, or unwittingly, play on these emotions and cause the buyer to get more insurance than he can afford or the wrong kind for his particular purposes.

The young man in the market for life insurance and the family man who may already have some protection should know the fundamentals of insurance and how it works. They should understand the different kinds of insurance. They must be able to get and use expert advice. They must know how to build a program of family security, tailored to fit their individual needs. Get these things clear in your mind to start with:

The basic job of life insurance is protection It has certain investment features that should be remembered. But concentrate on safeguarding your family against possible loss of your earning power. Don't take on such things as retirement and college educational plans, at least not in the beginning.

The subject of death should not be evaded Some people, including a lot of young wives, are squeamish about dealing bluntly and openly with the chances of death. That attitude is a luxury you can't afford. Sit down and thoroughly and rationally explore the problems your dependents would have if you died.

How insurance works Insurance is highly technical. You can't expect to be an expert and you don't need to be. It will help, though, if you understand the underlying theory.

First, picture a set of statistics known as a "mortality experience table." It takes a million persons at the age of one year and then proceeds to tell you approximately how many of them are going to die every year from age one to 99.

This table is the precision tool that makes life insurance possible. You, as a buyer, are concerned with *who* is going to die; all the insurance company cares about is *how many*.

To see how this works, imagine a group of 10,000 young married men, all 29 years old. These men realize that some of them will die during the coming year, leaving widows without income. Why not get together and raise a fund to guarantee each widow a $5,000 nest egg?

A glance at the mortality table shows that eleven of their number will probably not live out the year. That means that eleven widows will need $5,000 apiece—so the fund must contain $55,000. Each man puts $5.50 into the kitty and is assured that his wife will not be left destitute if he should be one of the eleven.

The association will have to tack on a little extra to pay for time and paperwork. On the other hand, it will also allow for the fact that some money can be invested for a while and produce income.

There you have the equivalent of a life insurance company writing one-year-term life insurance policies.

The basic pattern is as simple as that. A big national insurance company works with a varying number of people of all ages and walks of life. The investment of collected funds plays a big role in its operations. Most insurance is not written on the simple, one-year, revolving-fund basis. But the theory is the same.

Study that example and you will see that if you live, you cannot expect to get back all the money you have paid in unless you have a type of policy specifically designed for investment values. Some or all of your premium has gone into the common fund to pay beneficiaries. You have not thrown this money away, however, for you received something in return. It paid for protection against something that might have happened but didn't.

There are four basic kinds of life insurance policy, but no one can tell you which kind to buy without a careful look at your individual case. Each has its special uses.

Term insurance You buy it for a specified period only—usually one, five or ten years. At the end of that time you stop paying and the protection stops, too. You get nothing back if you are still living at the end of the term, and little or nothing if you drop the policy before that. As you grow older, the cost of term insurance gets higher. Term insurance is relatively cheap, as far as annual expense is concerned. It is usually recommended when temporary protection is needed or when the buyer needs protection but just can't afford higher-priced insurance that might be more desirable for the long pull. Some term policies provide level amounts of coverage while others provide decreasing coverage and are particularly appropriate for protecting your mortgage, etc. Also, look into certain types of term "riders" (these are attached to "permanent" policies) that give you the option to buy additional amounts of insurance as you get older without having to produce evidence of insurability. Note that other kinds of term insurance are convertible during the life of the policy into more permanent types. Here again, the insured person can convert without the necessity of taking another physical exam and thus is guaranteed insurability.

Ordinary life This is a permanent, lifetime policy. You must pay an annual premium as long as you live, or at least until you are about 85, to keep the full amount of protection. The premium is higher than for a term policy bought at the same age, but the premium always stays the same, instead of going up periodically, as the premium on term insurance does. Some kinds of ordinary life policies, however, call for lower "graded premiums" for three to five years before leveling off, the presumption is that salary increases will enable you to meet the higher premium later on.

Part of what you pay goes to build an increasing cash value. You can borrow against this cash value. If you cancel the policy, you get the cash value back or exchange it for a certain amount of paid-up protection or you can use the cash value to extend your full protection for a specified number of years.

Ordinary life—often called straight life—is the standard, most popular kind of insurance. It gives permanent protection and contains an element of saving. It does, in a smaller way, all the things that fancier, higher-premium policies do.

Limited payment This policy is like ordinary life except that you pay premiums only for a fixed number of years—usually 20 or 30. After that the full amount of insurance remains in force without further cost to you. In effect, you simply telescope the payments on an ordinary-life policy into a fixed period of time. While you *are* paying, therefore, the premium is higher than for ordinary life. The cash values are higher, too.

Endowment This policy is written for a fixed number of years, say 20, and for a certain amount, say $10,000. If you die before the policy matures, your beneficiary gets the $10,000. If you live out the full period, you get it—in a lump sum or in monthly installments. The cost is necessarily heavy. At age 30, for instance, you must pay over twice as much for a 20-year endowment policy as for ordinary life in order to get the same amount of protection.

Note that these last three types of "permanent" insurance, ordinary life, limited-payment life and endowment, provide cash values that can be regarded as fixed-dollar portions of your estate. They are very similar to savings bank deposits, are fully as liquid, and actually have a tax shelter because they defer taxation until the point of surrender. The interest rates credited in dividends in mutual companies in recent years have been in excess of 4.5%.

TABLE 13 WHAT VARIOUS POLICIES COST

Here are premiums and cash values per $1000 of insurance to show how they vary with the type of policy. (Figures are for sample non-participating—guaranteed price, no dividend—policies and, of course, would not be the same for all companies. Participating—dividend paying—policies have higher initial premiums but also have certain advantages that deserve your attention.)

Age at Which Policy is Issued:	25 ANNUAL PREMIUM	20TH YR. CASH VALUE	35 ANNUAL PREMIUM	20TH YR. CASH VALUE	45 ANNUAL PREMIUM	20TH YR. CASH VALUE
Five-yr. renewable term	$ 3.46	—	$ 4.30	—	$ 8.43	—
Term to 65	7.30	$ 87	10.60	$ 86	15.99	—
Whole life	12.44	236	17.81	325	26.94	?
Life paid up at 65	15.29	273	22.40	411	37.59	$ 696
Endowment at 65	19.39	351	28.41	550	47.91	1000
20-payment life	21.27	459	27.48	574	36.51	?
20-yr. endowment	42.45	1000	43.81	1000	46.31	1000

There are special policies that are combinations or adaptations of the four basic types.

A family-income policy, for example, is an ordinary-life policy (or some other permanent policy) with term insurance on top of it. The amount of term insurance coverage starts high and gets smaller every year until it finally runs out. The whole thing is rigged to guarantee that if you die while your children are young, the policy will pay a certain income until they are grown. Then your wife will collect the full value of the permanent policy. A family-income rider attached to a permanent policy can give a finely balanced protection to a young married couple.

Sometimes special policies of this type are what you want, sometimes not. The trick is to understand just how they work. The most frustrating thing of all about this subject is the discovery that there is no real answer to the fundamental question, How much insurance does a man need? It has been said—not at all helpfully—that the man who died yesterday didn't have nearly enough, while the man who will die next week needs none at all today. You hear of families being "insurance poor," meaning that so much goes for premiums that living standards actually suffer. Yet the late Mayo Adams Shattuck, a lawyer who was a top authority on estate planning, once wrote, "I have yet to see my first client who has enough life insurance."

How much is enough? A number of formulas have been offered as solutions to the riddle of how much is enough, but none are really useful. The most familiar is the one that says 10% of your income should go into insurance premiums. Another says a man should carry at least $10,000 for a wife and $5,000 for each child. Another says he should provide enough to assure half of his present income.

The fanciest ones are those that treat Pop as though he were a capital sum, hired out at interest. Estimate his probable future earnings over his life span, says one such theory, and subtract his personal expenses. Calculate the sum of money that, if invested at a reasonable rate of interest, would produce the same sums in yearly payments of principal plus interest. Buy that much insurance.

Most of these attempted formulas ignore your budget. All ignore the fact that every family is in some way different from all others. And all ignore the fact that there is no such thing as "enough" insurance for the same reason that there is no such thing as "enough" income or "enough" years to a lifetime.

The best way to decide how much insurance you need is to forget all such systems and work on your own individual situation.

First, estimate how much immediate cash would be needed to wind up your affairs This amount should include funeral and medical bills, unpaid income and property taxes, death taxes if any, outstanding bills and debts, estate costs and the general expenses of getting the family re-established.

Next, work out an estimated budget This will involve some long, sober husband-and-wife talks—for the basis of such a budget is what she and the kids would most likely do should something happen to him. Reckon, item by item, the minimum amount the family would probably need for housing, clothes, food and so on.

Third, fix the amount desired for special lump sum needs or goals For example: the mortgage, an emergency fund, college educations.

Then go back and find out how much of this ready cash and steady income your present resources will provide Social security will, in most cases, provide a good chunk of income while children are around and, later on, after the wife reaches 62 or 65. Social security will pay a small lump-sum benefit, too. You may have group insurance where you work. You may have health insurance to provide cash or produce income, or to do both. If you are a veteran, your widow and minor children may be entitled to benefits, even if your death is not attributable to any service-connected disabilities. The family may have or be due to inherit an independent income of some sort.

Between the sum you have figured the family would need and the sum your present resources would supply there will be a gap. The amount of insurance you need is the amount it will take to fill that gap. Your insurance agent or broker can help you calculate the monthly income that a given face amount of insurance could provide your family, or he may have access to new computer services provided by leading insurance companies that do an excellent job of "programming" your present assets, social security, veteran's and other benefits and accurately assessing your needs.

Don't be surprised if you have to compromise. You may very likely find that you can't afford enough insurance to fill in the entire picture all at once. You may have to let one item slide for now, concentrate on another, weigh one need against the other.

You're the only one who can say what your household budget can and should absorb.

There are over 1,700 companies that write life insurance in the United States. Which one should you buy from?

Don't buy from a small or relatively new company unless you are thoroughly familiar with it That may sound tough on young and struggling outfits, but the prudent thing is to make them prove they can give you the economy, safety and experience of the large, well-established and well-known organizations. Strength, not size, is important. Check out a small company in *Best's* or some other rating manual.

Don't buy by mail Many companies advertise by mail. Some special operations—for ministers, for example—are conducted by mail. But a regular mail-order outfit probably just isn't licensed to have offices in your state, and a prudent buyer deals with one that is. Also, you don't get the services of an agent.

Do take group insurance if you're eligible for it or the special insurance that is sometimes available to such groups as teachers and ministers Also, if you live in Connecticut, Massachusetts or New York, look into the advantages of insurance sold by savings banks in those states. There are no salesmen; therefore no sales commissions to be deducted from premiums.

Do ask around among your friends and relatives and find out how they feel about companies with which they have had experience When they are dissatisfied, find out why. Remember those companies that are consistently praised or recommended.

Companies vary in the premiums they charge for their insurance, in the benefits their policies provide, and in various practices connected with the sale and execution of their contracts.

If you shop costs, be guided for the most part by general reputation; look upon cost estimates as approximate, don't fuss over slight differences, and don't think in terms of price tags only.

Life insurance may be either "participating" or "nonparticipating." In the former case, the annual premium contains a considerable safety margin, which will ordinarily be returned to the policyholder at the end of the year as a so-called dividend. How much will be returned can't be foretold, however, since the amount depends on such factors as investment yields, expenses and death rates during the course of the year. Participating insurance is sold by mutual companies, those owned co-operatively by policyholders, and sometimes by stock companies, those owned privately by stockholders.

Nonparticipating insurance is sold by all stock companies, and many sell only that. The premium is noticeably lower than that on participating policies, but no dividends are paid to reduce it. Historically, participating life insurance has proven to be cheaper than nonparticipating, in the long run. The participating premium, which usually is larger initially, can be shaved in early years of the policy by use of an Economatic type of policy where the face amount for the first year or so is at a higher level than in later years, with the dividends after the first or second year used to bring the face amount up to the original.

How to buy insurance The fact is that you will probably do best to choose an agent rather than a company. Again, go after the word-of-mouth recommendation. If an agent comes to you cold without being sent by a mutual acquaintance, ask for references—that is, get the names of clients who can tell you how they have fared in the agent's hands, what kind of job of analysis and planning he has done for them.

Most agents (who like to be called "underwriters," by the way) are both honest and competent. An agent who has attained his Chartered Life Underwriter (C.L.U.) designation should have better advisory and planning capabilities because of the training required to obtain the C.L.U. designation. But they are also salesmen. They have a special knowledge of and a natural bias for the policies of their own company. If you buy from an agent, you will probably have to rely on his advice and counsel to a very great extent, even though you are well aware that he is no "impartial expert." There are also "brokers" who do not represent one company exclusively. They can sell you a policy from any one of several companies, depending on your individual needs.

Don't be pushed, pressured or rushed. Make sure that the agent or broker takes time enough to examine your needs and resources carefully, time enough to work out an individual solution to your individual problem. Make sure that you take time enough to furnish him all the information he needs, as well as time enough to think long and carefully before you sign up.

The transaction is not over when you have decided to sign. You should expect your agent or broker to furnish you with a written summary of the plan you and he have worked out for using the insurance proceeds in case anything happens. You should expect him to handle or guide you through any routine paperwork that may be required. It may be necessary, for example, to fill out various settlement agreement forms in connection with the policies of other companies that you have bought in the past. He should also be able to supply information on your social security benefits.

And finally, you and he should go over your program at least once every five years to see what adjustments or additions may have become advisable.

The day may come when you have accumulated enough wealth by hard work and shrewd investing to enable you to begin cutting down on your insurance, or to change your coverage to meet different needs, such as estate taxes. That will be a happy day if it comes. But the truth is, even the men who make the big fortunes seldom find it advisable to dispense with their insurance.

HEALTH INSURANCE

Today there is a wider variety of good health insurance available than ever before. The policies themselves are easier to understand, containing less of the old-time "fine print" of which the comedian said, "The big print gives it to you and the little print takes it away."

Nevertheless, a good bit of this excellent coverage is wasted because too many people insist on insuring against expenses they could pay themselves. At the same time, they fail to cover themselves against the shattering, once-in-a-lifetime expense that could use up years of savings and wreck the family finances.

Partly this is due to a misunderstanding of what constitutes real insurance. Think of fire insurance as an example. Thousands of people in a community pay premiums year after year, and once in a while someone's house burns down and he is fully compensated. The others don't expect anything back from the insurance company. They are happy that their houses didn't burn down.

Ideally, health insurance should operate the same way. A family with good coverage should pay in without expecting anything back unless the worst happens—some huge expense that couldn't possibly be handled by the family's regular finances. Medical expenses caused by appendicitis operations, having babies or a week or two in the hospital certainly could be handled as easily as an automobile is bought or a vacation paid for.

Unfortunately, millions of people tend to measure their health insurance coverage by how much they can get back from the insurance company. They want policies that will consistently pay them back as much as they have paid in—more if possible.

This attitude defeats the insurance principle. If everyone in an insurance pool of this type gets his money back in benefits, no one, in the long run, can get more than he contributed. This kind of insurance policy must have severe limitations that prevent it from covering the heaviest expenses that, logically, should be insured against. Buy such a policy and you are merely paying the insurance company to handle your medical budgeting. The company collects, deducts expenses and overhead, and regularly pays you back 80% or 90%. That simply isn't insurance.

To test the adequacy of your own health insurance, dream up a couple of very serious health situations, then figure out whether your insurance would take care of them. Suppose, for example, the breadwinner in the family was injured or became seriously ill and was unable to work for 18 months. What would happen? Or suppose that another member of the family, wife or child, had a mental breakdown, required many months in a sanitarium, the total bill running to $5,000 to $10,000. Where would the money come from? These situations, you might say, are improbable. Yet it is these very improbable events that should be insured against. Probable events should be budgeted for.

Failure to make this distinction between the role of insurance and the role of budgeting has caused millions of families to waste part of their insurance dollars. So the first, great principle in health insurance is to have *real* insurance that will handle the worst health problems you can think of.

The second principle, just as important, is to know exactly

what you have. Know what your policy does and does not cover, who in your family is eligible, whether it will ever expire or its benefits be narrowed. Although most policies nowadays are clear and explicit, too many people don't even bother to read them carefully. Group policyholders especially are negligent.

One man recently retired after working for years in a company that had a group health insurance plan covering employees and their families. Upon retirement he was informed that he was still covered. He assumed that his wife also was still covered, but she wasn't. Very shortly after this man's retirement, his wife became seriously ill and spent the remainder of her life in a hospital. The resulting financial strain could have been averted if the couple had realized the facts. But they had never read the company's policy carefully.

Even Blue Cross or Blue Shield basic plans can be full of surprises if you don't read the policy. There are dozens of Blue Cross plans in effect across the country. They vary widely in coverage. One will pay for a semiprivate room for 180 days, if needed. Another cuts you off after 31 days. So no matter what kind of coverage you think you have, know for sure by reading the policy. If necessary, ask questions.

Income protection Protection against loss of the breadwinner's income is thought by insurance men to be the most important kind of health insurance a family can have. The vice-president of a large company puts it this way, "Even the individual of limited means can eventually pay big bills and big debts if only he retains the ability to work and earn a living. When that is lost, all is lost unless funds are available to replace the earnings."

Disability income insurance, as it is called, protects the policyholder by guaranteeing to pay him so much a month while he is disabled. A variety of policies is available. The program most often recommended would pay the insured something less than his regular income. The amount, generally ranging from 75% to 50%, is based on the belief that most families can get along on less than full pay if they have to, particularly since the first $100 a week, after 30 consecutive days of disability, is not subject to income tax.

Two important considerations in disability insurance are the waiting period and the maximum period during which the policies pay. The longer the waiting period, within reason, the more economical this kind of insurance becomes. If the waiting period is only one week, the insured person will be putting in a claim every time he is sick for more than seven days. Small claims cost insurance companies money in paperwork and overhead. If the waiting period is one month, the insured person handles the shorter periods of disability himself. His premiums then will pay for a larger monthly income during any long period when he is unable to work. Many people work for companies that will pay for a certain period of disability so that the waiting period is no hardship. Also, employers can make available group long-term disability coverage with larger benefits and lower rates, perhaps 25% to 30% lower, than individual policies. Even if the employee pays the entire cost of the plan and the employer simply sponsors the plan, significant cost savings are available. However, the product is different; for example, it is cancelable.

The longer the policy guarantees to pay for disability, the better. Some guarantee to pay only up to one year per disability; others guarantee five years, and so on. The best policies pay to age 65, when pension benefits normally begin. These long-term policies cost the most, but then if a man were to be disabled for life, he would want a continuous income. Your own disability policy should, of course, be merged into social security and/or any plan your employer may have. Professional men often can get coverage through their professional association.

It is particularly important that disability policies be noncancelable and guaranteed renewable up until the day the policyholder retires. Otherwise, if the insured person becomes a poor risk because of deterioration of health or because of having been through a disabling illness or having suffered an accident, the company can refuse to renew the policy on some anniversary date.

"When you have a policy that is noncancelable and guaranteed renewable," one insurance company executive says, "you own the policy and regardless of the number of claims you may have, you still exercise policy control. But when a policy is renewable at the option of the company, it means you rent the policy and you can be evicted any time the company wishes."

In calculating the need for disability insurance, keep in mind the disability payments available under social security. Persons who meet the qualifications and are totally disabled can draw, at the time they are disabled, the same amount of benefits they would have received had they been 65 and entitled to retirement. The requirements governing disability benefits are these:

• If you're disabled before 24, you need credit for a year and a half of work in the three years before you are disabled.

• If you're disabled between 24 and 31, you must have credit for half the period between 21 and the time you are disabled.

• If you're disabled at 31 or older, you must be fully insured *and* have credit for five years in the ten years before disablement. (This rule is designed to limit benefits to people who work regularly. It would exclude, for example, a woman who worked briefly after she was married and then dropped out of the labor market.)

Note, though, that if you do work regularly, you don't need much work experience to qualify for disability. A young man injured only a few years after he begins work can qualify for help for himself, his wife and his children.

Guard against the big bills Catastrophe insurance, or major medical, also is the kind of "real insurance" that most insurance experts think it important to have. A wide variety of policies is available.

The principle of major medical is that it leaves the smaller medical expenses to be handled by the individual himself. There usually is a deductible, say $100, $200 or $500 or more. The deductible is least when major medical is bought along with a "basic" hospital and surgical policy. Unless the medical expenses rise above the deductible, the policy does not begin to pay. But when medical bills soar above the deductible, the major medical policy pays 75%, 80% or sometimes 100%, depending on the terms, of all legitimate expenses.

A good, broad major medical policy covers hospital bills, doctors' bills, nursing bills, treatment for mental illness and just about every medical expense. It may have a co-insurance feature, which means that the company pays 75% or 80% of all covered expenses, while the insured pays the other 25% or 20%. The purpose of this is to give the policyholder an incentive to keep bills to a reasonable level. Note that coverage for out-of-hospital expenses for psychiatric treatment usually is limited, and sometimes in-hospital benefits are also limited.

Although most major medical policies are good and broad, each policy should be read carefully. There are always some limitations and exclusions. Some limit the amount to be paid for hospital room; some exclude mental illness; most exclude expenses for practical nursing, and so on.

Here are some criteria for purchasing major medical coverage.

• Get broad coverage with the fewest possible exclusions. Don't buy a policy that covers you only against certain named diseases. Buy one that covers you in general. Be sure that mental illness is not excluded.

• Have the limit per illness plenty high, say $25,000 to $50,000. The whole purpose of this kind of insurance is to keep you prepared for the worst. Also, know the cut-off period for any one illness if there is one. Three years is not any too long.

• Make sure members of the family are covered. It's just as expensive for a wife to be sick as for a husband.

• Get a policy that will be noncancelable and guaranteed renewable until Medicare would take over. It should be noted that even hospital and major medical policies that are guaranteed renewable are subject to upward premium adjustments on a class basis. On the other hand, individual long-term disability coverage is available on a completely noncancelable and premium-guaranteed basis.

• Buy fairly early in life. Many policies can be first purchased only at ages below 50.

• If you have a group policy, check to make sure that all members of your family are covered and can continue to be covered if you leave the group or retire. Those who leave the group should have the privilege of converting their policies to nongroup policies without medical examination. The premiums would, of course, be higher. Many group policies, too, continue coverage on employees and their families even after retirement, although the coverage may be somewhat narrowed.

Hospital bills and surgery Most insurance experts think hospital and surgical insurance are number three in importance for health insurance. The reason is that these policies generally begin repaying the first dollar that the insured person spends. Usually there is no deductible. "First dollar" policies are designed to help pay for even short stays in the hospital, for obstetrical care, or for operations that do not result in prolonged expense. In effect, these policies perform a budgeting task. But apparently millions of people are willing to pay to have someone do the budgeting for them.

The truth is that people tend to be lax about providing even for routine expenses. Doctors' bills often go unpaid; patients go to the hospital unprepared to settle up in cash. So years ago doctors and hospitals joined together to make what amounts to a budgeting service available. Today it is very widely used.

Blue Cross and Blue Shield plans differ from other coverage in that benefit payments are made to the hospital or participating surgeon, not to the insured. The terms of these policies should be read carefully. Most Blue Shield plans pay full surgical costs if the insured person is in a low income bracket because the participating doctor will accept as his full fee the amount that the Blue Shield payment schedule allows for the particular operation. For those in higher brackets, the plan usually pays only part of the cost because the doctor is free to charge his regular fee, which is ordinarily higher than the allowances made by Blue Shield.

Even those not in a group can buy Blue Cross or Blue Shield plans, though enrollment may be open only at certain periods during the year, and applicants must prove they are in good health. Those who cannot get into group plans can buy individual hospital or surgical policies from insurance companies, but a health examination or medical questionnaire is required. These plans are more economical if bought with a deductible. Also, individual medical care is very expensive compared with Blue Cross or a group medical plan available from one's employer.

What should you spend? How much should a family logically spend on health insurance? An official of one company says, "I would think that the average family should spend somewhere between 2½% and 4% of its income on health insurance, depending on the amount of group insurance provided by the employer, salary-continuance policies of the employer, and the amount of other assets that might be called upon to meet emergency costs." Another company says that a family in the $7,500 to $15,000 income bracket might spend 3½% to 5%.

A family's health insurance needs vary during its life span. In early and middle years the family should guard the breadwinner's earning power with disability income insurance, noncancelable and guaranteed renewable up to retirement. There should be broad catastrophe insurance on all members of the family, renewable at least to the point where Medicare begins. When retirement age approaches, the need for disability insurance disappears. Catastrophe insurance definitely should be continued at least until Medicare takes over. If it is not available, good basic hospitalization and medical coverage are musts.

Here, briefly, is how the two parts of Medicare work.

Part A is hospital insurance It pays for such things as drugs furnished by the hospital, operating room charges, semiprivate room and regular nursing services.

You get Part A automatically, whether or not you retire, when you become eligible for social security or railroad retirement benefits. Coverage is figured in benefit periods, which start the day you enter a hospital for covered services. You become eligible for a new benefit period when you have been out of a hospital or place that mainly provides skilled nursing care for 60 days in a row. (Note: Even noncovered care, such as custodial care in a place devoted mainly to skilled nursing care, can keep a new benefit period from starting.)

There's no limit to the benefit periods you can use. However, days within one benefit period do accumulate. Keep this in mind when figuring what bills you can get stuck with.

• You pay the first $60 in hospital expenses each benefit period. After that you're covered for 60 days of hospital expenses in the benefit period.

• After the first 60 days you have partial coverage for 30 more days in a benefit period, but you co-pay $15 a day. Use all of the 30 days and you'd owe $450.

• Beyond the basic 90 days of coverage in each benefit period you have 60 days in a lifetime reserve, but you co-pay $30 a day when you use these lifetime reserve days. Use all 60 and you'd owe $1,800.

You can choose not to use the lifetime reserve benefits. You may not want to use them if you have additional insurance that will pay 100% of your hospital expenses, or some amount greater than $30, beyond the basic 90 days per benefit period. Another reason to save the lifetime reserve days is that once they're used, they're never replaced.

• You also get 100 days of coverage in each benefit period in an extended-care facility (ECF) if you need skilled nursing care following covered care in a hospital. The first 20 days you get full coverage, but for the other 80 days you co-pay $7.50 a day. Use all 100 days and you'd owe $600. Medicare does not pay ordinary custodial care.

• Some things Part A won't pay a penny for include personal comfort items (television and telephone), private-duty nursing, private room in a hospital or ECF (unless it's medically necessary), or, except in emergency cases, care in a hospital not participating in Medicare or care in a hospital outside the U.S. Nor will Part A pay for doctor bills; they're covered under Part B.

Part B is medical insurance It pays surgical and medical fees no matter where the doctor treats you—hospital, office, home. Part B is open to almost everyone 65 or over whether or not they're eligible for social security or railroad retirement benefits. However, you must enroll for Part B and pay monthly premiums, now $5.60. If you wait a year or more to enroll after you turn 65, you'll pay a higher premium. And after three years' delay you won't be able to sign up at all.

• You pay the first $50 of medical expenses each year. Thereafter, Part B covers 80% of reasonable medical expenses and you pay the remaining 20%. Say that after you've paid the first $50, you have medical bills of $1,000. You'd owe $200.

• Part B doesn't pay for drugs you take yourself even if prescribed by a doctor. Nor does it pay for cosmetic surgery or exams or for fittings and purchases of hearing aids, glasses or false teeth, all of which can be expensive.

If you were lucky, you might not need any more coverage than Medicare provides. Don't count on it, though. You could end up owing thousands of dollars to hospitals and doctors. Spend 150 days in a hospital in one benefit period and you'd owe $2,300 in hospital bills alone.

The average hospital stay for people 65 and over is 13 days. Even if you are there for only a week or two, you would still need some way to pay for what Medicare doesn't—balance of the medical bills, private-duty nursing, etc. An estimated 40% of the medical bills are more than the Medicare allowances. Since many insurance plans will pay only the remainder of the "customary and usual fees," and generally won't pay for any custodial care, you can still be left with a hefty bill not covered by Medicare or supplementary insurance.

You can try to fill the gaps in Medicare in a number of ways: by dipping into personal savings; through group health insurance you have from work; or through supplementary insurance available from one of the more than 70 Blue Cross and Blue Shield plans, from commercial insurers or as a member of such groups as the National Council of Senior Citizens.

How much of your savings you should set aside depends on what you can afford and how much of a gamble you want to take. At the least, you should have $100 for the deductibles and, if you don't have supplementary insurance, maybe another $500 to $1,000 for the Medicare co-pays. Even if you do buy additional insurance, chances are it won't cover all the gaps in Medicare. Many policies merely *extend* coverage on items covered by Medicare, and won't pay for things Medicare wouldn't.

For insurance, start checking where you work. Some employers let retired workers continue their group health coverage. Usually you'd get the plan's benefits minus the coverage you get through Medicare. You'll probably get the same kind of deal even if you don't retire at age 65.

Check also with unions, fraternal organizations or other groups you belong to.

The cost and coverage of supplementary insurance varies widely. The supplementary Blue Cross and Blue Shield plan in Arizona costs $7.30 a month. It fills most of the Medicare gaps but doesn't pay the $7.50 a day toward ECF benefits and pays only $10 toward the $50 medical service deductible. But it will pay $30 a day from the 91st to the 150th day whether or not you use the lifetime reserve days and continues paying $30 for another 215 days.

The Florida plan costs $7.10 a month and pays the Medicare

deductibles under Part A and all co-pays, including the ECF. After a $50 deductible it will co-pay and extend coverage under Part B up to $5,000 when you no longer have coverage under Medicare. It will also pay for services in a hospital not participating in Medicare or in a hospital outside the U.S.

The Wisconsin Physicians Service plan is one of the most costly and most comprehensive of all the Blue Cross and Blue Shield plans. Cost is $14.70 a month. It pays all the Medicare deductibles and co-pays plus drugs prescribed by a doctor, in-hospital private-duty nursing services, and up to $22,500 for hospital and medical services for six years for each illness after Medicare benefits are exhausted, but it won't pay for custodial care or for any services not eligible under Medicare.

From commercial insurers you can choose two basic kinds of policies: income plans and reimbursement plans.

Income plans pay a stated dollar amount when you're in the hospital. Sometimes you can pay extra and get options that extend benefits in an ECF or add surgical benefits.

One company's income plan pays $100 a month for up to 12 months. You can get the policy no matter what your age (some companies offer plans regardless of your health). Cost ranges from about $20 a year for people 65 to 69 years old, up to $31 a year for people 80 years or older. If you stayed the average 13 days, you'd get about $40. The policy is renewable only at the option of the company.

Another company pays ten dollars a day for each hospital day for up to 365 days. It's open to people between 65 and 79 and is guaranteed renewable for life. Cost is about $37 a year.

Reimbursement plans pay a stated dollar amount or percentage of expenses for certain health services in or out of the hospital. Benefit periods usually are limited, often to a year, or benefits are limited to a certain maximum.

These plans do more than income plans and they cost more.

One company pays 80% of charges not covered by Medicare in a hospital, up to $15 a day from the first day to the 90th day and $40 a day thereafter. It also pays 80% of surgical and physician services not covered by Medicare as well as 80% of charges in an ECF not covered by Medicare. The plan is guaranteed renewable and there's no limit on entrance age. Depending on the deductible, benefits are limited to $10,000 up to $20,000. Cost is $144 a year.

Below are the kinds of questions to ask when you shop for health insurance to supplement Medicare. Remember, though, few policies will cover *all* your health expenses. And you should keep abreast of the changes expected in the Medicare program.

• Does the insurance pay the Medicare deductibles?

• Does it pick up the co-pays; that is, the $15 a day for the 61st to 90th day per benefit period in a hospital, the remainder of medical services not covered by Medicare, and so on?

• What does it do about lifetime reserve day benefits?

• Is there a maximum amount of benefits the company will pay or a time limit on benefits?

• Does it pay for drugs not covered under Medicare?

• Is the policy renewable at your option or can the company cancel it?

• Are you covered in U.S. hospitals not participating in Medicare or in hospitals outside the U.S.?

• Is the initial premium low as a come-on, with higher premiums thereafter?

• Will the policy cover pre-existing health problems?

LIABILITY INSURANCE

Big damage suits have become so common, and juries have become so prone to award large sums to the complainant, that a prudent family is obliged to carry a certain amount of liability insurance. Otherwise, a successful suit might wipe out the family's entire financial assets—home, savings, investments.

Usually the most needed type is auto liability insurance. Most states require a minimum coverage of $10,000 per person injured, $20,000 per accident and $5,000 property damages, but this is hardly enough in the light of the size of awards often made by juries. Awards of $100,000 have become common. The extra cost for raising the minimums to $100,000 per person, $300,000 per accident, and $10,000 property damage is well worth the relatively small additional premium.

Perhaps the second most dangerous area is around the home.

If a visitor or even a stranger stepped into a hole in your yard or fell on a broken step, he could sue you for plenty. Fortunately, your Homeowner's Insurance policy, which covers fire, windstorm and other damage, probably carries a $25,000 liability clause covering bodily injury and property damage. This could be raised to $100,000 for a very small four or five dollars additional premium. It probably would not cover you, however, if you were sued for libel or for causing a false arrest or if you are a professional man and were sued in connection with professional activities. If there's any likelihood of this happening, you can buy what is known as an "excess liability" policy, which will cover you up to a million dollars. Normally such coverage will cost $65 or $75 a year.

For most people auto and Homeowner's policies, if the minimum amounts are high enough, provide all the coverage that's reasonably necessary. But extra coverage could be worth the cost if you have any doubts.

The main things to remember in all three kinds of insurance —life, health and liability—is to avoid the gimmicks and stick to coverage against the most likely *big* losses. In other words, buy real insurance against expenses that you never could manage to pay yourself.

28

MONEY MANAGEMENT

If you are the head of a family, you are in fact a businessman. The family has all the elements of a business. It makes and sells something—usually in the form of the services of the breadwinner. It has income, expenses, overhead, invested capital, working capital and surplus. This may seem a dull and mundane way of looking at a family, with its wealth of relationships that are not merely material or financial. And yet, whether it irks you or not, you cannot escape from the reality that any family is a form of small business.

A family is probably tougher than a business. A family can survive and even prosper with slovenly internal methods that would send any other business to the wall. The family is more flexible. For this reason it is actually not necessary for a family to manage its business p's and q's as carefully as a regular business must. But it is desirable. It is a way of getting along better and making the available family money go further.

In this discussion an attempt is made to show any head of any family how to stretch the money and make it do more. The methods are essentially business methods. Some may be too complex for the average family or unsuited to the nature of the family head. In this case, the full dose of guidance may be cut to half a dose. The whole thing need not be swallowed, but it would do no harm to swallow a little bit of it.

Young men, especially, face the problem of learning how to finance a family. Eventually they learn it, usually by trial and error. When young men get to be older men, they think in arrears of how much better off they would have been if they had followed certain stricter financial courses in their younger years. That's the benefit of hindsight.

Even older men, even businessmen, do not always run their family affairs on a "businesslike basis." They may be crack administrators at the office, but they often are loose with the personal and family budget.

BUSINESS METHODS FOR THE FAMILY

First, then, take a look at the way a business is run. It must make a profit or die. So at the beginning of each year it estimates its gross income, expenses and net profit, and then plans on how to use the profit most effectively. Month by month during the year, the businessman eagerly compares his accomplishments with his forecast. If he is doing better than expected, he may expand; if worse, he may have to trim his sails and set a new course. But at all times he knows where he is and what he is aiming for.

The same cannot be said for many families. Their finances are run on a hit-or-miss basis. The hit-or-miss family always has to strain to get the things it really wants because it has let its money leak away on less essential stuff bought on impulse. The husband gets a good salary, but he tries to operate on too little working capital. This causes him to worry and fuss at his wife and the children. Often he has to borrow to tide the family over a crisis, and this causes unnecessary fees and interest.

The wife sees plenty of bargains in clothes and appliances, but seldom takes advantage of them because she knows only in the vaguest way what items she is going to need and when. Eventually, necessity forces her to buy in a hurry without much chance to shop around.

The husband always thinks things are going to be better next month, and this causes him to start investment programs that he usually has to give up. The last time he bought stock it was not long before he needed the money. Unfortunately, at that particular time the market was down. He had to sell, although if he could have held on, he would eventually have had a nice profit.

Several times the family has gotten a little ahead and bought savings bonds only to have to cash them in within a few years. The interest received was thus only a percent or so instead of the more than 4% they would have received had they held on for the full seven years.

Net worth and cash forecast charts It is not hard to see that a little financial planning would do this family a world of good. Maybe it would do your family some good, too. Are you game? If so, here is the way to start. Examine the sample charts on pages 389 to 391. They may look a bit complicated at first glance, but don't let that worry you. The theory is very simple. You are going to make one chart to keep track of your net worth. Your net worth, of course, is the value of your major assets, such as savings, stocks, bonds, real estate, etc., minus your debts. If you are getting anywhere, your net worth should be increasing a little bit each month. Your net worth chart is going to show you how much.

The other chart is to be a cash forecast. It will show you how the cash is going to flow through the family coffers during the coming year, with no regard to whether it goes toward increasing your net worth. It may show that in certain months you will be pinched and in others you will be loaded with cash. But in the latter case, it may be cash that will be sorely needed for heavy obligations later on.

An example will show the difference between the two charts. Say that you know that in February you will pay a life insurance premium of $191, which will cause the surrender value of the policy to increase by $118. This $118 is a saving and will show up as an increase in net worth. The remaining $73 is an expense and will not appear on the net worth chart. Your cash forecast, on the other hand, will show an outgo of the whole $191.

Now note that each chart has one wide column for each month. Each wide column is divided into three narrow columns labeled *Last year, Estimate for this year* and *Actual*. This is a device to help you estimate the figures for 12 months ahead, then compare actual results with your estimates. The reason for recording last year's figures is that they are usually the best basis for making estimates for this year.

Cash forecast The cash forecast is the one to do first. Take a big sheet of drawing paper, leave a three-inch margin on the left, then divide the rest of the sheet into 12 wide columns, and finally divide each wide column into three narrow columns. Or you can buy sheets with columns already marked. They are obtainable at stationery stores and are known as accountants' worksheets or ruled columnar sheets. Another method is to use one 8½"×11" notebook sheet for each month. Divide it into three columns.

Label the columns as indicated in the sample, one wide column for each month, and the first narrow column for the same month a year earlier, the second for this year's estimate, the third (to be filled in later) for this year's actual figures.

The cash forecast, in its simplest form, is going to enable you to look ahead at the coming months and make four estimates about each one: how much cash you will have on hand at the beginning of the month; how much money you will take in during the month; how much you will spend; and how much you will have at the end of the month. Just how detailed you want to

CHART 9 CASH FORECAST*

	January				*February*	
	LAST YEAR	ESTIMATED FOR THIS YEAR	ACTUAL FOR THIS YEAR	LAST YEAR	ESTIMATED FOR THIS YEAR	ACTUAL FOR THIS YEAR
Cash on hand and in checking account, end of previous period	$167	$150		$ 78	$165	
Receipts:						
Net pay	518	552		518	552	
Borrowed	100					
Other				26	26	
Total cash available during period	$785	$702		$622	$743	

* Copyright by *Changing Times*.

	January			February		
	LAST YEAR	ESTIMATED FOR THIS YEAR	ACTUAL FOR THIS YEAR	LAST YEAR	ESTIMATED FOR THIS YEAR	ACTUAL FOR THIS YEAR
Fixed payments:						
Mortgage	$ 70	$ 70		$ 70	$ 70	
Life insurance				191	191	
Fire insurance	26	26				
Auto liability insurance						
Savings bond	19	19		19	19	
Real estate taxes						
Loan		8		8		
TOTAL	$115	$123		$288	$280	
Variable Payments:						
Light	$ 7	$ 7		$ 6	$ 6	
Gas	23	23		28	28	
Telephone	7	7		6	6	
Medical	12	5		8	8	
Car	17	17		15	15	
Food	140	140		132	132	
Clothing	25	25		40	40	
Nonrecurring large payments						
Airline tickets	193					
Christmas bills	80	100				
Other	88	90		75	75	
TOTAL	$592	$414		$310	$310	
Total payments	$707	$537		$598	$590	
Recapitulation:						
Total cash available	$785	$702		$622	$743	
Total payments	707	537		598	590	
Cash balance, end of period	$ 78	$165		$ 24	$153	

CHART 10 NET WORTH FORECAST*

	January 31			February 28		
	LAST YEAR	ESTIMATED FOR THIS YEAR	ACTUAL	LAST YEAR	ESTIMATED FOR THIS YEAR	ACTUAL
Assets:						
House	$16,000	$15,750		$16,000	$15,750	
Car	1,138	875		1,116	857	
Life insurance cash value	354	472		472	590	
Savings bonds	220	440		240	460	
Cash	78	165		24	153	
TOTAL ASSETS	$17,790	$17,702		$17,852	$17,810	
Liabilities:						
Mortgage	$ 8,750	$ 8,450		$ 8,725	$ 8,425	
Loans	100			92		
TOTAL LIABILITIES	$ 8,850	$ 8,450		$ 8,817	$ 8,425	
Net Worth	$ 8,940	$ 9,252		$ 9,035	$ 9,385	

* Copyright by *Changing Times*.

make those estimates is up to you. The number of categories used in the sample cash forecast on page 389 has proved about right for many people. But yours can have more or less, depending on your needs. Here is a warning, however: Don't try for too much detail at first. A simple worksheet kept up-to-date is better than an elaborate one abandoned.

The next step is to label the horizontal spaces in the left-hand margin. The top line should be *Cash on hand and in checking account, end of previous period.* That shows what you start each month with. On the next lines list receipts during the month, including all cash coming in, paycheck, money borrowed, gifts and so on. The total of all the first few lines, then, will give you all the money available during that month.

The next section covers fixed payments, the ones you can positively expect to be a certain amount. They will include rent or payments on the mortgage, various insurance premiums, regular savings and so on.

Then come variable payments, the ones you know are coming

but can't tell exactly in what amount. They will be bills for telephone, light, gas, doctors, food, clothing and so on. In this section, inevitably, there will be a large sum of money spent but not easily accounted for. It will include all kinds of cash payments and incidentals too numerous and bothersome to record. This item is probably going to look pretty big, but don't worry about it and don't try to break it down—at least not at first. You will only involve yourself in needless paperwork. Label it *Other*.

Here also leave a few lines for large nonrecurring payments, such as Christmas bills, vacations, out-of-town trips. If you threw these into the *Other* category, it would distort it and make it jump around from month to month. You want it to be stable so you can estimate it accurately.

Now come the critical spaces. Devote the bottom of the sheet to a recapitulation. Label one line *Total cash available*, the next, *Total payments*, the last *Cash balance, end of period*. That, of course, will be the amount with which you will head the column for the next month.

Your blank cash forecast is now ready and you can start entering figures. If you have never done it before, this is going to be very revealing. Before you start, here is a trick that is strongly recommended. Use three differently colored pencils: red, green, blue. Red will always be used for last year's figures. Green will be used for future estimates. Blue will be used later for actual results.

To start, get out your checkbook stubs and receipted bills for the past 12 months and whatever other financial records you keep. Start with whatever month it happens to be when you read this. If it is June, start with your records for last June and enter them in red. Probably you won't have accurate figures for every category for last June, but fill in every category anyway, guessing where you have to. Your check stubs should give you most of the data you need.

This is the time to take up your green pencil and begin making estimates for this month. You know how much you had at the beginning of the month, so enter that. You also know what the monthly paycheck is and you can figure the fixed expenses. The variable expenses you can't know, but here is where last year's figures come in handy. If you don't know the size of the electric bill you'll get this month, just assume it's going to be the same as the one you got a year ago. When it comes in, you can pay it and then enter the correct amount in blue under *Actual*. And that will give you help in making the estimate for next month.

Don't stop now, however. Still going through your old check stubs, fill in the red figures for the other 11 months. All 12 months will then have a column of red figures filled in. Next, begin filling in the rest of the green estimates. Keep in mind that they are only estimates and don't rack your brain too fiercely. By all means resist the temptation to decide right now that you are going to change your normal pattern of spending. This is a forecast, not a New Year's resolution. You are trying to make a hardheaded judgment on what lies ahead.

As you go forward in your estimate, you will spot in such upcoming items as mortgage payments, insurance premiums, tax bills, Christmas spending. Each month you should have about the same big *Other* items. And you will be able to see pretty clearly how much cash you will have on hand at the beginning and the end of each period. The average of these two figures for any month is your average working capital. If it is under $100, it is probably too low.

Here are a few tips that will make record keeping easy in the future. When you come home from a shopping trip, throw store receipts for cash payments into a box. Collect them and tot them up at the end of the month. Pay by check whenever you can. Make sure all family income goes first into the checking account, then out into other channels by check. Use charge accounts and credit cards if you can handle them conservatively.

Net worth forecast The net worth forecast comes next. It is comparatively easy to make because, unfortunately, most people have very few items to list. Forget about your income and your living expenses. A pipe doesn't care how much water flows through it. All you are interested in now is what you are catching in the reservoir.

Take your net worth forecast sheet and list in the left-hand margin your major assets. Omit minor items such as personal possessions, clothes and furniture. Stick to such things as the market value of your house, car, stocks and bonds, the amount in savings accounts, the cash value of life insurance policies, and the actual cash you have on hand at the end of the period. Use the sample on page 390 as a guide.

Next list your liabilities. These will include the balance you owe on the mortgage, the balance you owe on other debts, such as the loan on your car, and bank loans. Again use red pencil for last year's figures, green pencil for this year's estimates, and blue pencil for actual results.

To get your net worth at the end of each month, simply subtract total liabilities from total assets. The month-to-month increase probably won't look very large, but let's face it, that's all it was. Maybe you can do better, but don't yield to the temptation to start a brand-new savings program on the spur of the moment.

There are a couple of tricky things about your net worth. Theoretically, your house is depreciating, losing value because of increasing age. But maybe over the past years the actual market value has gone up because of inflation. Here is the way to handle this part of your net worth forecast. For all last year's months simply list what you consider the market value to have been at the beginning of last year. To get this year's figure, make a new estimate in the light of the condition of the house and the real estate market today. Use this figure for all months of this year, and plan to revalue again at the beginning of next year.

Your car is another item somewhat hard to assess. A car loses value much faster than a house. Depreciation plus obsolescence (going out of style) reduces a new car's value by 30% to 40% the first year, 15% to 20% the second year, 10% to 15% the third year, and around 10%, 9% and 6% in the years succeeding. The man who buys a new car every year has an average annual depreciation expense about twice that of a man who keeps his car four years. This is a real decrease in net worth, which shows up unmistakably in the trade-in allowance.

Figure how much your car has depreciated from its original cost. If it is two years old, it has depreciated 45% to 60%. So for its present worth put down between 40% and 55%. The exact figure will depend on the condition of the car. At the beginning of next year its value will have dropped another 12½% on the average. So during this year lower the value by one-twelfth of this amount each month. Say you figure it is worth

$875 now, but will be worth only $656 in a year. Each month its value will drop around $18.

Using your records effectively When you have completed your cash and net worth forecasts, you are in business. Maybe it has taken a couple of afternoons to get everything figured and entered, but it will be worth it. You have created a wonderful tool that has many uses.

First of all, you now have a pretty good idea of where the money has been going. As months go by, you can begin to form a pretty shrewd guess as to where it will go in the future. By anticipating future demands, you should be able to cut overhead. All life insurance premiums can be put on an annual basis. Bank service charges can be cut. Borrowing can be kept to a minimum. Maybe in the months ahead you will be saving a bit more. If so, fine. If, on the other hand, you are spending more, you should be able to spot where it is going.

HOW TO GET THE FUNDS YOU NEED

If you want to invest or build a reserve fund, you must have money, and, to get money, most people have to save. Saving in this sense means the building up of a cash fund that can be invested or stashed away in a reserve fund. Broadly speaking, an increase in the cash value of a life insurance policy or a decrease in the size of the mortgage on your house is also a saving. But for the purpose of this chapter, saving means accumulating cash or the equivalent.

Saving isn't easy and it isn't much fun. Basically, there's only one way to do it: Hold down your outgo and keep up your income. There are, however, some tricks that make the job a little more intriguing and less of a chore. Here are half a dozen of the most common.

The marked-money method is the oldest known to man and is nothing more than a piggy bank with a rule book built in. Pick a coin, anything from a penny to a half dollar. Say you decide on nickels; from then on, nickels are unspendable. Every nickel you get goes into the sugar bowl. Keep this up for a little while and it easily becomes a habit. You'd be surprised at how quickly small-change savings can mount.

The short-take method is based on the theory that it's easy to be strong-willed for a week or two at a time. You can manage a lot of economies for a few months that you couldn't stand indefinitely. Many families have successfully used the technique of setting a brief period, say three months, and just saving their heads off. They'll cut expenses to the bone, knowing that the end is always in sight, and sock away a tidy sum of cash. When it's over, they blow themselves to a celebration and resume their unthrifty living (but with cash in the bank) until they feel strong enough for a repeat.

The windfall method is one for which the circumstances have to be just right. Every once in a while you are likely to "find" some money. Perhaps you get a raise. Perhaps you finish paying an installment debt. Perhaps the doctor orders you to quit smoking, or the cleaning woman quits and you can't find a replacement. Wherever it comes from, there's suddenly a certain amount of money lying loose. Grab it quick, or part of it, for savings, before it gets absorbed by living expenses. You got along without it before, and you can continue to.

The even-swap method requires real determination. Pick one specific regular expense. Trade it for savings money. Make it a sacrificial lamb and deposit its cost in the bank each month. This is a bit easier than more general kinds of budget-cutting because the dramatic twist helps morale. Managing a cut in the entertainment budget, for some mysterious reason, is generally harder than depositing the price of the midweek movie in a tin can as you settle down to a quiet evening at home.

The self-service method calls for discovering a job you pay other people to do that you might do yourself. Laundry? Car washing? Lawn mowing? Repair work? Kids' clothing? Do it yourself and bank the saving.

The elbow-grease method means you save more by earning more. It's not as hard as it sounds. If your goals are modest enough, say ten or twenty dollars a month, there may be plenty of opportunities for a little spare-time earning. For example, the apartment developments of the country are full of housewives who save up for this or that by baby-sitting for their neighbors.

Look around. If you can spare a couple of days or evenings a week, there may well be a way to cash them in.

None of these tricks contains any magic. But any one—or another of your own invention—might prove a shot in the arm to make the flesh as willing as the spirit.

PROGRAMS TO HELP YOU SAVE

The financial people who make a business of safekeeping other people's money have devised a number of more formal schemes to add a zip to thrift. Here are some samples of how they work.

Some savings banks offer packaged plans designed to help the saver reach any goal. For residents of the bank's own state the package can include savings bank life insurance, E bonds and a savings account.

Suppose a state resident, aged 35, decides that in ten years he wants to have $1,000 in E bonds, $1,000 in a savings account and, during the whole period, $3,000 of ordinary life insurance. All he has to do is send this information to the savings bank and its statisticians will figure out how much he should send the bank each week. In this case, it comes to about five dollars. The bank will take the money, make the deposits, and buy the insurance and E bonds, all in the customer's name.

The statistician of such a bank will figure out a similar package plan for anyone anywhere. Tell him how much you want to have in E bonds and a savings account at the end of X number of years, and he will figure the correct weekly or monthly rate of savings. You can also state how much you want to save each week or month, and the bank will tell you how much you can expect to have at any given time. All computations cover interest on savings at the current rate. One advantage of this plan is that there are no commission or service charges. Also, there is no penalty if you miss a payment.

Commercial banks, with their variety of services, make it possible for a bit-at-a-time investor to work out several interesting programs. For example, a good many banks now issue savings certificates similar to E bonds but maturing in a shorter period of time. You could deposit so many dollars a month in a savings account and, every time you get up to $100, buy a savings certificate. These certificates vary from bank to bank. One type is payable on a certain date; another after a certain length of time; a third only after the owner has given written notice of intention to cash it in. These certificates pay 4%, 5% or more if held for the full term, but less if cashed prior to maturity. You can also instruct your bank to buy you an E bond at any regular interval, deducting the money from your checking account.

Ordinarily, banks will not agree to deduct money from your account for any purpose unless you are a good customer and have a special problem stemming from a trip abroad or something of that sort. (California banks are an exception. They will automatically pay mortgage and certain utility bills from your checking account.) The reason is, obviously, that the bookkeeping is expensive, requiring the use of a tickler file to remind the bookkeeper to make each deduction. In some cases, however, banks have agreed to deduct a fixed amount periodically from a depositor's checking account and send it to a designated place. If this appeals to you, it is worth looking into.

Thousands of large companies have also made it possible for employees to have money deducted from their paychecks and invested in E bonds. The advantage is that what you don't see you won't miss. Some companies will make similar deductions for the purchase of their own stock or shares of mutual funds.

There are several other ways by which you can invest a small amount each month in common or preferred stock or the shares of mutual funds. These are discussed in Chapter 14, Dollar Cost Averaging.

An interesting but expensive way to save is to make an installment loan at your bank, use the money to buy an E bond or to make some other investment, and then pay back the loan out of current income. The advantage is that the bank will put the heat on more strongly to make you pay back the loan than you would to make yourself save. The man behind the note teller's window is a more compelling personage than the one behind the window marked "Savings."

Some people have even borrowed from a bank and used the money to buy stocks. You have to be careful here to stick to the rules. You cannot put up listed stocks as collateral and use the proceeds to buy more listed stocks. This would be a violation of the Federal Reserve Board's margin requirements. For this reason, when you borrow on listed stocks you must fill out a form stating the purpose of the loan. These requirements, however, do not apply to all unlisted stocks. And you can put up as collateral assets other than listed stocks—a life insurance policy, for example—or borrow on your signature, and use the money to buy stocks, whether they are listed or unlisted.

Choosing a goal One great way to help yourself save is to keep continually in mind the goal that lies ahead with all its glittering promises and feeling of security. It is also comforting to note your progress from month to month. Here, then, are two tables, one to tell you how much to put away each month in order to reach a particular goal, the other to show you how a certain amount put away faithfully twice a year will snowball.

Table 14 is for use in setting up a regular monthly saving program, and it shows the sum you must put aside each month, at various rates of interest, to build up a given amount in a given time. If your goal is larger than $7,500 or is an in-between amount and you want to avoid multiplying or moving decimal points, split your objective into two or three smaller ones. Treat a $9,000 goal, for example, as a $4,000 one plus a $5,000 one.

The required monthly investments have been figured as exactly as possible and will hit your objective almost on the nose. Therefore, you're safe in rounding them off a bit or in using them as minimums.

The table is based on two assumptions: (1) Interest is compounded semiannually. (2) Money starts to earn interest the same month it is deposited or invested.

Table 15 shows how regularly deposited savings grow over the years. The assumption is that deposits are made in two equal amounts, one at the beginning of each six-month period. Interest is compounded semiannually.

RAINY-DAY MONEY—WHERE TO INVEST IT

One of the first precepts in investing is: Don't use money that you may need for something else, because even the most care-

TABLE 14 REGULAR SAVINGS NEEDED TO REACH A GIVEN GOAL

Find your savings goal in this column	\multicolumn{6}{c}{Here is the regular monthly saving needed to reach that goal if your money is invested at . . .}
	2½%	3%	3½%	4%	5%	6%
$1,000 in 5 years	$15.64	$15.44	$15.24	$15.05	$14.66	$14.29
10 "	7.33	7.15	6.96	6.78	6.43	6.10
15 "	4.58	4.40	4.23	4.06	3.74	3.44
20 "	3.21	3.05	2.88	2.73	2.44	2.17
30 "	1.87	1.72	1.58	1.44	1.21	1.00
$1,500 in 5 years	$23.45	$23.16	$22.86	$22.57	$21.99	$21.43
10 "	11.00	10.72	10.44	10.17	9.65	9.14
15 "	6.87	6.60	6.34	6.09	5.61	5.16
20 "	4.82	4.57	4.32	4.09	3.66	3.26
30 "	2.80	2.58	2.36	2.17	1.81	1.51
$2,000 in 5 years	$31.27	$30.87	$30.48	$30.09	$29.33	$28.58
10 "	14.67	14.29	13.92	13.56	12.86	12.19
15 "	9.16	8.80	8.46	8.12	7.48	6.89
20 "	6.43	6.09	5.76	5.48	4.88	4.34
30 "	3.74	3.43	3.15	2.89	2.41	2.01
$3,000 in 5 years	$46.91	$46.31	$45.72	$45.14	$43.99	$42.86
10 "	22.00	21.44	20.88	20.34	19.29	18.29
15 "	13.74	13.20	12.69	12.18	11.23	10.33
20 "	9.64	9.14	8.65	8.18	7.31	6.52
30 "	5.60	5.15	4.73	4.33	3.62	3.01
$4,000 in 5 years	$62.54	$61.75	$60.96	$60.18	$58.65	$57.15
10 "	29.33	28.58	27.84	27.12	25.72	24.39
15 "	18.32	17.61	16.91	16.24	14.97	13.77
20 "	12.85	12.18	11.53	10.91	9.75	8.69
30 "	7.47	6.87	6.30	5.78	4.83	4.02
$5,000 in 5 years	$78.18	$77.18	$76.20	$75.23	$73.31	$71.44
10 "	36.67	35.73	34.80	33.90	32.16	30.48
15 "	22.90	22.01	21.14	20.30	18.71	17.22
20 "	16.07	15.23	14.41	13.64	12.19	10.86
30 "	9.34	8.58	7.88	7.22	6.04	5.02
$7,500 in 5 years	$117.27	$115.77	$114.31	$112.84	$109.97	$107.16
10 "	55.00	53.59	52.20	50.86	48.23	45.72
15 "	34.35	33.01	31.71	30.46	28.07	25.82
20 "	24.10	22.84	21.62	20.46	18.28	16.29
30 "	14.01	12.88	11.82	10.84	9.06	7.53

fully selected investment probably won't appreciate in value all at once. It may take years for it to fulfill your hopes. In the meantime, as the stock market fluctuates, the value of your stock may at times be below what you paid for it. If during such a dip in price you happened to need money desperately and had no reserves for emergencies, you might be forced to sell out at the worst time.

That's the reason that the first thing to do with your savings is to sock away a certain amount of money in an emergency fund. If you have such a fund, plus adequate insurance, you can approach the problems of investing with a freedom from pressure and worry that will enhance your good judgment.

Strictly speaking, an emergency fund is not an investment, since investing implies converting money into stocks, real estate or something other than cash. Nevertheless, an emergency fund can earn interest or dividends and grow in value. So it is an investment in a sense. Several questions arise about a fund of this kind. What's it for? How much do you need? Where do you put it?

How big a reserve? An emergency fund should obviously be reserved for bona fide emergencies: serious illness, loss of job and so on. It should never be borrowed from for such relatively unimportant uses as the purchase of a car, house or TV set. It should not be loaned even to close relatives except in cases of dire need.

As to how big the fund should be, an old rule of thumb says a family should be able to live for six months if its regular income were cut off. Interpreted conservatively, that would mean that a family's liquid savings, minus its short-term debt, would equal one half its annual take-home pay. Interpreted very liberally, it might mean that a family should be able to lay its hand on enough cash by various means to live six months. In addition to liquid savings, certain other assets might be counted: cash value of life insurance policies, stocks conservatively valued, the amount fully vested in a company pension plan. Note the dangers of this practice. The cash value of a life insurance policy might be needed to keep up premium payments. Stocks might go so low, in a recession for example, that it would be a shame to sell them. The amount vested in a company pension fund might be obtainable only by quitting. So, for defense against a financial crisis,

TABLE 15 HOW REGULAR SAVINGS GROW OVER THE YEARS

Yearly Savings	After 5 Years EARNINGS TO DATE	TOTAL	After 10 Years EARNINGS TO DATE	TOTAL	After 15 Years EARNINGS TO DATE	TOTAL
$100 at 1%	13.95	513.95	54.20	1054.20	122.07	1622.07
$100 at 1½%	21.95	521.95	82.62	1082.62	187.70	1687.70
$100 at 2%	28.34	528.34	111.95	1111.95	256.63	1756.63
$100 at 2½%	35.69	535.69	142.25	1142.25	329.03	1829.03
$100 at 3%	43.16	543.16	173.52	1173.52	405.08	1905.08
$100 at 3½%	50.74	550.74	205.81	1205.81	484.99	1984.99
$100 at 4%	58.43	558.43	239.16	1239.16	568.97	2068.97
$100 at 4½%	66.25	566.25	273.60	1273.60	657.23	2157.23
$100 at 5%	74.17	574.17	309.16	1309.16	725.01	2250.01
$100 at 5½%	82.22	582.22	345.89	1345.89	847.56	2347.56
$100 at 6%	90.38	590.38	383.82	1383.82	950.13	2450.13
$200 at 1%	27.91	1027.91	108.40	2108.40	244.14	3244.14
$200 at 1½%	42.19	1042.19	165.24	2165.24	375.41	3375.41
$200 at 2%	56.68	1056.68	223.91	2223.91	513.27	3513.27
$200 at 2½%	71.39	1071.39	284.50	2284.50	658.06	3658.06
$200 at 3%	86.32	1086.32	347.05	2347.05	810.17	3810.17
$200 at 3½%	101.48	1101.48	411.63	2411.63	969.99	3969.99
$200 at 4%	116.87	1116.87	478.33	2478.33	1137.94	4137.94
$200 at 4½%	132.49	1132.49	547.20	2547.20	1314.46	4314.46
$200 at 5%	148.34	1148.34	618.32	2618.32	1500.02	4500.02
$200 at 5½%	164.44	1164.44	691.78	2691.78	1695.12	4695.12
$200 at 6%	180.70	1180.70	767.64	2767.64	1900.26	4900.26
$300 at 1%	41.86	1541.86	162.60	3162.60	386.21	4866.21
$300 at 1½%	63.28	1563.28	247.86	3247.86	563.11	5063.11
$300 at 2%	85.02	1585.02	335.86	3335.86	769.90	5269.90
$300 at 2½%	107.08	1607.08	426.75	3426.75	987.09	5487.09
$300 at 3%	129.48	1629.48	520.57	3520.57	1215.25	5715.25
$300 at 3½%	152.22	1652.22	617.44	3617.44	1454.98	5954.98
$300 at 4%	175.30	1675.30	717.49	3717.49	1706.91	6206.91
$300 at 4½%	198.75	1698.75	820.80	3820.80	1971.69	6471.69
$300 at 5%	222.51	1722.51	927.48	3927.48	2175.03	6750.03
$300 at 5½%	246.66	1746.66	1037.67	4037.67	2542.68	7042.68
$300 at 6%	271.14	1771.14	1151.46	4151.46	2850.39	7350.39

Money Management

	After 5 Years		After 10 Years		After 15 Years	
Yearly Savings	EARNINGS TO DATE	TOTAL	EARNINGS TO DATE	TOTAL	EARNINGS TO DATE	TOTAL
$600 at 1%	83.73	3083.73	325.20	6325.20	732.42	9732.42
$600 at 1½%	126.57	3126.57	495.72	6495.72	1126.23	10126.23
$600 at 2%	170.04	3170.04	671.73	6671.73	1539.81	10539.81
$600 at 2½%	214.17	3214.17	853.50	6853.50	1974.18	10974.18
$600 at 3%	258.96	3258.96	1041.15	7041.15	2430.51	11430.51
$600 at 3½%	304.44	3304.44	1234.89	7234.89	2909.97	11090.97
$600 at 4%	350.61	3350.61	1434.99	7434.99	3413.82	12413.82
$600 at 4½%	397.50	3397.50	1641.60	7641.60	3943.38	12943.38
$600 at 5%	445.02	3445.00	1854.96	7854.96	4350.06	13500.06
$600 at 5½%	493.32	3493.32	2075.34	8075.34	5085.36	14085.36
$600 at 6%	542.28	3542.28	2302.92	8302.92	5700.78	14700.78
$1,000 at 1%	139.55	5139.55	542.00	10542.00	1220.70	16220.70
$1,000 at 1½%	210.95	5210.95	826.20	10826.20	1877.05	16877.05
$1,000 at 2%	283.40	5283.40	1119.55	11119.55	2566.35	17566.35
$1,000 at 2½%	356.95	5356.95	1422.50	11422.50	3290.30	18290.30
$1,000 at 3%	431.60	5431.60	1735.25	11735.25	4050.85	19050.85
$1,000 at 3½%	507.40	5507.40	2058.15	12058.15	4849.95	19849.95
$1,000 at 4%	584.35	5584.35	2391.65	12391.65	5689.70	20689.70
$1,000 at 4½%	662.50	5662.50	2736.00	12736.00	6752.30	21572.30
$1,000 at 5%	741.70	5741.70	3091.60	13091.60	7250.10	22500.10
$1,000 at 5½%	822.20	5822.20	3458.90	13458.90	8475.60	23475.60
$1,000 at 6%	903.80	5903.80	3838.20	13838.20	9501.30	24501.30

a family should certainly rely largely, if not wholly, on liquid savings.

There are four qualities you want your savings to have. These qualities will pretty well determine where the money is to be kept. Listed in order of importance, they are:

Safety—You want your money to be reasonably secure against depression, panic and theft.

Liquidity—You want to know that you can withdraw your savings without too much delay or red tape even during a possible banking crisis like that of 1933.

High earnings rate—You want your money to earn interest at as high a rate as possible consistent with safety and liquidity.

Convenience—You want your savings to be located where you can take care of them with minimum trouble.

No one institution provides the maximum safety, liquidity, earning rate and convenience all in one package. It would be nice to have a place right across the street that would keep your savings completely safe and entirely liquid while paying 6% interest. Naturally, there is no such place. To get a high interest rate, you must sacrifice some other advantages, such as liquidity. To have your savings instantly available, you must be prepared to accept a lower interest rate.

It may be best, therefore, to split up your cash and put it in several places.

In making a choice, keep in the back of your mind the two different relationships possible between you and a savings institution. There is a debtor-creditor relationship, as for example when you open an account with a commercial bank. There is also an ownership relation, such as when you buy a share in a savings and loan association. The difference may sound technical, but it could be important under certain conditions. (More on this later.)

Here are the most common places where you can put your savings. Note the particular advantages and disadvantages of each.

Savings account in a commercial bank—Convenient, safe, liquid, low rate of interest.

A handy place to keep savings is in the same bank where you have your checking account. The interest rate on savings accounts is relatively low. To keep the money liquid so that it can be paid out on short notice, banks must invest it in liquid short-term notes, which earn a low rate of interest.

Technically, you could be required to give a written notice, usually 30 days, before you can withdraw your savings. This notice is not generally required. But in times of sudden depression or business panic, the bank could require you to wait the full period.

The banks reserve the right to make you give 30 days' notice because of sad experience in the big depression. In the 1920's there were many more banks than there are today. They were competing to attract money, so they paid high interest rates on both checking and savings accounts, sometimes as high as 4%. To earn these rates, the banks invested the money in longer-term securities, some of which were not of too high quality or readily convertible into cash. When the bank runs started, many banks could not get these securities and their loans converted into cash fast enough to suit depositors.

As a result, the government now prohibits any bank over which it has control from paying interest on *demand deposits,* or deposits that can be withdrawn without advance notice.

Are your savings safe in a bank? Yes, because almost all commercial banks in the country are insured by the Federal Deposit Insurance Corporation. Each insured bank contributes a small amount to the fund each year. In return the bank gets insurance up to $20,000 for each depositor. If an insured bank fails, the depositor either gets cash or else he gets another account opened in his name in a going bank. The money in this new account may be withdrawn at once without notice.

When you open a savings account in a commercial bank, you establish a debtor-creditor relationship. You are not entitled to any of the bank's profits. The stockholders get the profits. The bank merely owes you your money plus interest. If you demand your money after giving the required notice and the bank cannot or will not pay, then you, as a creditor, can get the banking authority to close the bank.

Mutual savings bank—Safe, liquid, medium rate of interest, but not locally available in most parts of the country.

Mutual savings banks were started over a hundred years ago by public-spirited men who were not seeking profit but who wished to encourage the habit of thrift among workers. At first, most of the expenses of operation were paid out of the pockets of the founders and all earnings went to the depositors. Even today the trustees of mutual savings banks receive no salaries. All earnings, after deduction of expenses and additions to surplus, go to depositors in interest dividends.

When you open an account in a mutual savings bank, you are both a creditor and, to some extent, an owner. You get the profits, just as a stockholder does in a commercial bank. But if the bank cannot pay you your money, you can also get the supervisory authority to close the bank.

There are over 500 savings banks, mostly located in the Northeast. During most times a depositor can walk into any of them and withdraw his money without giving advance notice. But all mutual savings banks have provisions on the books requiring 30, 60, or 90 days' written notice, and these regulations could be put into effect at any time.

Your money is safe in mutual savings banks. A great many of them are insured by the Federal Deposit Insurance Corporation, and most others are insured by a similar arrangement with the state in which they are located.

Savings and loan association—Good rate of dividend, safe, might not be as liquid as a bank in times of business panic.

Savings and loan associations were founded to help people save a nest egg to buy a home. Many are still called building associations or building and loan associations. In Massachusetts they are known as co-operative banks; in Louisiana as homestead associations.

When you put your money in a savings and loan association, you are buying a share. You can do it by buying $100 certificates, in which case you receive a dividend check every six months. Or you can open a savings share account of any size, in which case your dividends are added to your account. In any event, the size of your share is simply your account divided by the total of all accounts. When you want to withdraw, the association repurchases a part or all of your share. Thirty days' written notice could be required but usually is not enforced. The point is, you are a shareholder; an owner. You and the association do not have a debtor-creditor relationship.

Note the difference. A bank owes you your deposited money, and if you don't get it, you can have the bank closed. But in the case of a savings and loan association, it is recognized that home mortgages cannot be liquidated all at once. So the association has the privilege of paying off a little at a time.

If that sounds like a disadvantage, note the advantage. Eighty-five percent of savings and loan association assets are invested in first mortgages on homes. This investment pays a high rate of interest. So the associations in turn can pay high dividends.

Of the 6,200 savings and loan associations, about 2,000 are small neighborhood associations, some of which do not have regular office hours or full-time employees. Sometimes they pay higher rates of dividend than the big-city associations that are larger and more elaborately organized. Before investing in a small neighborhood association, check on its record. Many are very old and profitable. But all depend on the judgment of the directors. Most of the larger associations are insured by the Federal Savings and Loan Insurance Corporation, a government agency. The insurance covers up to $20,000 for each investor. In general, the small neighborhood associations are not insured.

If an insured savings and loan association defaults, the shareholders get new accounts in another association not in default.

Note also a movement to convert mutual savings and loan associations into stock associations. When this happens, depositors keep their deposits intact and in addition are given their prorata share of stock in the new stock association. This stock would be valuable and could be held as an investment or sold to other investors.

U.S. savings bonds—Safe, liquid, convenient, but do not pay much interest unless held several years.

Savings bonds, Series E, may be bought at almost any financial institution or post office. They are highly liquid. Once you have held a savings bond for 60 days, you can cash it at any bank.

For short periods, however, savings bonds will not pay as much interest as other types of savings. The interest rate starts out low and becomes gradually higher the longer you hold the bond. For example, in the first year it averages 4.01%. If you hold it the whole five years and ten months, of course, you receive 5½%.

Those are the four places to put your cash. There are only three if you live in a town that has no mutual savings bank. Each place has a unique combination of the qualities you want—safety, liquidity, earnings rate and convenience. If you are smart, you probably won't leave all your cash in a place where it is earning little or no interest. But neither will you put it all where it might be frozen if a recession should hit.

Measuring your reserves What if you want to count as part of your emergency fund certain other assets that can be borrowed on or converted readily into cash? These might be money in a checking account, or money invested in stocks, or the cash reserves built up in life insurance policies.

How you make up your mind on these borderline cases will depend on how conservative you want to be. Money in your checking account, strictly speaking, is working capital, which you continually turn over as you pay bills. Still, there is a residual amount below which you seldom go, say $100 or $200. If you maintain such a minimum, this could be included in an emergency fund.

When you buy stock, you buy a share of a business for better or worse and take your chances on whether or not it thrives. Most stocks are extremely liquid, so you can always get back cash. How much cash, however, is never predictable. It always seems to turn out that, when you have to sell a stock in order to obtain cash, the market is down at that particular time. Stocks, therefore, should probably not be considered as part of an emergency fund. If they are, they should never be carried at 100% of their current price. Banks will lend only 60% to 70% on stocks. So carry them, if at all, only at some percentage of their market value. This percentage might be higher for good preferreds than for speculative commons.

Cash reserves in life insurance policies are savings in one sense, since you can get them back at any time. To do so, however, you either have to borrow the money back, usually at 5% to 6% interest, or you have to cash in the policy and lose its protection.

There are other hard-to-measure assets that many families have that might be included in an emergency fund—for example, money built up in a company pension plan. This is definitely an asset under certain conditions. Perhaps the best way to measure it is to count only the amount that is vested in you; that is, the amount of money you would get if you left your job.

If you don't know exactly how much of these assets to include in your emergency fund, try making up a report on your available resources. You might arrive at two figures, the first being bona fide cash reserves readily available, the second being your ultimate resources available in extreme emergencies. Use the form below as a guide.

YOUR RESOURCES TO MEET EMERGENCIES*

Savings	$_____
MINUS	
Short-term Debts	$_____
Difference	$_____
(*amount available for emergencies*)	
PLUS	
Stocks (75% of Market Value)	$_____
Life Insurance (cash value)	$_____
Pension Fund (amount vested)	$_____
TOTAL	$_____

(*ultimate amount available for extreme emergency*)

* Copyright by *Changing Times*.

Building up an emergency fund before you start to invest will save you worry and probably save you money. With such protection you can buy good-quality growth stocks, sit back, and let them appreciate in their own good time. You won't have the haunting thought that you might have to dump them at a moment's notice.

INDEX

ABC Company, fictitious case of, 214–15, 301–2
Accumulation plans, 166, 174
Advisory services, available to investors, 128
Agriculture, and new kinds of cheap foods, 21–22
American Institution for Economic Research, 191
American Stock Exchange (AMEX), surprise yearly audit of member firms, 135; complaints to be addressed to, 138; membership in, 205; history and listing requirements of, 303, 313; dollar volume handled by, 303, 304; central computer system of, 312; mortgage trusts listed on, 341
American Stock Reports, 125
Amtrak, 22
Annuities, types of, 272–75 (*tables*), 276–81
Apartment houses, owning and operating, 325
Art objects, problems of equity in, 37
Assets, where to put, 33–41
"At the market," order to buy, 140
Auto companies, list of, 77–78

Babson, David L., 128, 196, 267
Baby "boom" or "bust," 10, 11, 12, 63
Balance sheet. *See* Financial reports
Balanced funds, 180, 198
Bank deposits, as equity, 33, 34
Banks: trust departments of, 129–30; bank loans on stocks, 148; mutual savings banks, 405–6, 407; co-operative banks, 406; homestead associations, 406. *See also* Savings and loan associations
Barron's Confidence Index, 245
Barron's *Financial Weekly,* 126
Baruch, Bernard, 226

"Bear" raids, and SEC regulations, 226
Best's life insurance rating manual, 371
Birth rate, startling change in, 11. *See also* Baby "boom" or "bust"
Biscomb, John, 169, 170
Blue Cross or Blue Shield plans, 375, 379, 382
Bond and preferred stock funds, 81
Bonds, 251–63. *See also* under specific type of bond
Borrowing against stocks, 148–49
Broad ticker of Dow Jones, 51, 54, 55, 56, 58, 139–40
Broker and brokerage house: using your broker, 127–28; choosing a broker and a brokerage house, 133–39; problems and complaints against your broker, 136–39; how to deal with your broker, 139–41; commission rates, 141 (*table*)–44
Building and home companies, list of, 78–80
Building and loan associations, 406
Building associations, 406
Business growth and development, and fields expected to benefit in the 70's, 65
Business services, list of companies, 80–83

Capital gains and losses, taxes figured on, 156–57
Capital loss on gifts, 159
Cash dividends, and taxes, 155
Cash forecast, 389–90 (*chart*)
Central Certificate Service (CCS), of N. Y. Stock Exchange, 311
Changing Times, 150 *n,* 390 *n,* 391 *n,* 409 *n*
Chartered Life Underwriter, 372
Charts and graphs, 242–46
Chemical businesses, list of, 83–86
Chicago Board of Trade, 228

Index

Climate, and weather forecasting, 22
Closed-end funds, 175–77
Closed-end investment trusts and mutual funds: various types available, 175–79; objectives, 179–83; price quotations and management fees, 183–88; the pros and cons, 188–89; making a choice, 189–92; examples of investment companies, 192–99
Coffee Exchange, and the country boy, joking financial ad about, 227, 233
Coin collection: appreciation in value of, 37–38 (*chart*); as equity investment, 41
Commission guidelines of the SEC, 178
Commission rates, uniform, of brokerage houses, 141 (*table*)–44. *See also* Markup for over-the-counter stocks
Commodity futures trading, 227–33
Common stock funds, 180
Common stocks: upward tilt in values of, 39–40 (*chart*); unique advantages of, 42; developing selectivity in choosing, 43–44; performance investing, 44; determining guidelines, 44–45; cyclical stocks, 44–45; growth stock theory, 46–47; when to buy, 47–48; P/E ratio of, 47–50; dollar cost averaging, 49; stock "rights," 214, 215
Communications of today and tomorrow, 19–20
Companies and industries to look into, examples of: autos, 77–78; building and homes, 78–80; business services, 80–83; chemicals, 83–86; consumer products, 86–92; drugs, 92–96; electrical equipment, 96–97; electronics, 97–100; environment, 100–4; financial, 104; glass, 105; health care, 106–8; insurance, 108–9; labor-saving machinery, 109–11; metals and mining, 111–12; office machines and equipment, 112–14; oils, 114–16; recreation, 116–20; research, 120; utilities, 120–22

Complaints to be addressed to stock exchanges and the SEC, 138
Computer Components, Inc., fictitious case of, 210–13
Computer system, central, of Amex, 312
Computerized quotation system. *See* NASDAG system
Computers, use of, in stock market, 294
Confirmation slips, 147–48
Connally, John, and wage and price freeze, 28
Consumer Price Index, and common stocks, 40
Consumer products, list of companies, 86–92
Consumerism, 34
Contractual plan, 270
Convertible securities, 258–60
Co-operative banks, 406
Cootner, Professor Paul, 230
Corporate bonds, 251, 254
Corporation Records, 125
"Cost-push" inflation, 26–27
Cowdin, J. Cheever, 55, 56
Curb, the. *See* American Stock Exchange
Cyclical stocks, 44–45

Demographic-economic models, and future population changes, 12
Depression, likelihood of another, 10–11
Disability income insurance, 375–77
Diversified Growth Stock Fund, 53
Dividend records, keeping of, 147–48
Dividends: cash, and taxes, 155; stock, and tax tips, 155; on mutual funds, 157–58
Dollar cost averaging: and stock shares, 49; and four points in method of investing, 161–62; how averaging works, 162 (*table*)–64; plan of your own, 164; formal plans, 164–66; mutual fund accumulation plans, 166; investment clubs, 167–72
Dow, Charles H., 245
Dow Jones Industrial Average, 34; and common stocks, 39–40

Index

(*chart*); broad ticker of, 51, 54, 55, 56, 58, 139–40; study of, by finance committee of Vassar College, 250
Dow Jones News Ticker Service, 55, 57
Dow Theory and theorists, 245–46
Drug companies, list of, 92–96
Dual-purpose funds, 182

Economy, U. S.: government controls over, 2–3; forward surge in, in the 60's, 6–7; research and development as movers of, 16
Electrical equipment companies, list of, 96–97
Electronics companies, list of, 97–100
Emergencies, resources to meet, 408–9 (*report form*)
Energy, fields of, expected to benefit in the 70's, 64
Enke, Dr. Stephen, 7–8
Environment, cleaning up the, and effect on industries, 3, 10
Environment companies, list of, 100–4
Equity (equities): definition of, 31–32; savings bonds and bank deposits as, 33, 34; assets, where to put, 33–41; common stocks as most suitable, 42–50
Equity trusts, real estate, 342–45
Equity-to-debt stock ratio, 73
Exchanges, 302–5; regional list of, their history, and issues traded, 303–5
"Ex-rights," 215, 216

Facts for Prospective Farmers, 359
Family formation, and industries expected to benefit from it in the 70's, 63–64
Farm: hankering to buy a?, 358–60; management of, 360–61; financing a, 361–62; valuation, 362–63
Farm loan associations, 362
Farmland acres, average value of, 39 (*chart*)
Federal Deposit Insurance Corporation, 405, 406
FHA: loans, 332, 333; mortgages, 326, 357

Federal Reserve Board: and inflation remedies, 2; and inflationary rise in prices, 27; and question of equities vs. savings bonds and bank deposits, 33–34; margin regulations of, 148–49, 234, 238, 399
FIFO and LIFO methods of valuing inventories, 154
Financial companies, list of, 104
Financial crisis in the stock market, 310
Financial reports, how to analyze, 149–55
Financial services, big, available to investors, 128–29
Financial Weekly, 126
Financial World, 126
500 Stock Averages, 125
Forbes Magazine, 126
Foreign securities funds, 181
"Front-end load," 166–67
Full Employment Act of 1946, 29
FundScope, 192
Futures trading in commodities, 227–33

General Electric: and studies of population changes (Tempo), 12; solid-waste disposal of, 23, 25
Geographical funds, 181
Gifts, capital loss on, 159
Gintel, Robert M., 55, 56
"Give-ups," 202, 203
Glass companies, list of, 105
Gold: forbidding of Americans to own most forms of, 35; price of, per ounce, 35–36
Gold mining stock, 36 (*chart*)
Government bonds, 253
Government controls of inflation, 67
Grain Exchange, Minneapolis, 228
Gross National Product (GNP), 6, 7, 12; growth of, despite inflation, 66
Growth stocks: investing in, 41 (*chart*); growth stock theory, 46–47; glamour growth stocks, P/E's of, 48; size of company and, 68
Guide to Mutual Fund Withdrawal Plans, A, 265–66

Hamilton, William P., 245, 246

Index

Handbook of Member Trusts, 347
Handbook of Widely Held Common Stocks, 124
Health, and American medicine, progress in, 18–19
Health care firms, list of, 106–8
Health insurance, 373–84
Hedge funds, 182–83
Hedging vs. speculation, 228
Home, and importance of the neighborhood, 352; the house itself, 352–55
Home mortgages, 326, 357
Homeowner's insurance policy, 385
Homestead associations, 406
Hospital insurance, 380–81
House, important factors in buying, 352–55
Houses: and rental income, 323–24; apartment houses, owning and operating, 325
Housing authority bonds, 256
How to Invest on a Budget, 166
Hurley, Roy T., 54

IBM stock, part ownership in, 177; and foreign operations, 181; solidity of company, 224; price growth of, 278
Income, national, personal, and median family, 6, 7, 12
Income, "real," rise of, for families in the 70's, 13–14 (*table*)
Income and safety. *See* Safety and income
Income from investments, 263–67
Income funds, 181, 198
Income protection, through insurance, 375
Income statement. *See* Financial reports
Industries, fields of: expected to benefit in the 70's, 63–65; least affected by government controls, 67
Industries and companies to look into. *See* Companies and industries to look into, examples of
Industry funds, 181
Inflation: remedies for, 2–3, 7; "cost-push" inflation, 26–27; new methods of controlling, 26–27; root causes of, and inflationary forces, 29–32; companies that can keep earnings despite government controls of, 67; size of company, and the stock market, 68
Inheritance of stock, 159
Insurance: as prerequisite to investing, 364; life insurance, 364–73; health insurance, 373–84; disability income insurance, 375–77; hospital insurance, 380–81; liability insurance, 384–85
Insurance, title, 357–58
Insurance firms, list of, 108–9
Interstate Highway System, 22–23
Inventories, valuation of, through LIFO and FIFO methods, 154
Investing, guide for, and investment clubs, 169
Investing, insurance as prerequisite to, 364
Investing in real estate, 321–30
Investment Club Selection Guide, 171
Investment clubs, 167–72
Investment Companies, 191
Investment companies, real estate, 347–48
Investment Counsel Association of America, 131
Investment counseling services, 131–32
Investment counselors, 130–31
Investment trusts, 132. *See also* Mutual funds and closed-end investment trusts
Investment trusts, closed-end. *See* Closed-end investment trusts and mutual funds
Investment trusts, real estate (REIT), 322, 340–41, 345, 346–48
Investment Trusts and Funds From the Investor's Point of View, 191
Investments, income from, 263–67
Investors, individual, role of, 317–18 (*table*), 319–20
Investors Service Bureau, 319
Issues, new. *See* New issues

Johnson, Hugh A., 6, 191
Johnson's Investment Company Charts, 6, 191

Joint or single ownership of stock, 146–47

Kansas City Board of Trade, 228
Kennedy, Joseph P., 226
Keynes, John Maynard, 225, 227
Keynes, Lord, 230
Keynesian theory of economics, 227

Laborsaving machinery firms, list of, 109–11
Land, raw, 322–23
Land values, rising trend in, 39
"Leaks," and the stock market, 56, 57
Lease-back of property, 324–25
Leave it in "street name," stock certificates and, 140, 145–46
Leverage funds, 182
Liability insurance, 384–85
Life insurance, 364–73
LIFO and FIFO methods of valuing inventories, 154
"Limit order," 140
Listed Stock Reports, 48, 70, 125
Loans: on stock, 148–49; on farms, 362; FHA loans, 332, 333
Lots (real estate), by mail, 323

Machinery, laborsaving, list of companies, 109–11
Major medical insurance policies, 377–78
Margin, buying stocks on, 233–38
Margin, pyramiding on, 235–36 (*table*)
Margin account, 140, 148
Margin calls, 234–35
Margin loan, 148–49
Margin regulations, 148–49, 234, 238, 399
Markup (commission) for over-the-counter stocks, 142–43
Martin, William McChesney, 312, 313, 315, 316
Martin Report, The, 312–13, 315, 316
Medical insurance, 381–82
Medicare, 11, 378, 380, 381, 382, 383, 384
Medicine and health in America, progress in, 18–19

Mercantile Exchanges, New York and Chicago, 228
Metal, precious. *See* Precious metal
Metals and mining firms, list of, 111–12
Microelectronics, possibilities of, 20–21
Midwest Stock Exchange, 304
Mining and metals firms, list of, 111–12
Minneapolis Grain Exchange, 228
Money management: and savings, 30–31; business methods for the family, 386–95; how to get needed funds, 395–97; programs to help you save, 397–400 (*table*), 401, 402 (*table*), 403 (*table*); rainy-day money, where to invest, 399–408
Monthly Investment Plan (MIP), of NYSE, 165, 166, 174, 189
Moody's, 128; bond ratings published by, 255
Moody's Capital Fund, Inc., 204
Moody's *Handbook of Widely Held Common Stocks*, 124
Moody's *Industrial Transportation and Public Utility Manuals*, 125
Mortgage trusts, 341, 345–46
Mortgages: second, 325–27; FHA, 326, 357; home, 326, 357
Municipal bonds, 254–56
Mutual fund accumulation plans, 166, 174
Mutual fund shares, dividends on, 157–58
Mutual funds—what's going on?: money-making functions, 200–1; protecting the shareholder, 201–2; "give-ups," 202, 203
Mutual funds and closed-end investment trusts: various types available, 175–79; objectives, 179–83; price quotations and management fees, 183–88; the pros and cons, 188–89; making a choice, 189–92; examples of investment companies, 192–99
Mutual savings banks, 405–6, 407

NASDAQ system, 142–44, 301–2, 311–12, 316, 317

Index

National Association of Investment Clubs, 167, 169, 170, 171
National Association of Real Estate Investment Funds, 347
National Association of Securities Dealers, 135; complaints to be addressed to, 138; markup guidelines of, 142–43; NASDAQ developed by, 144, 301–2, 311–12, 316, 317; policing of securities salesmen by, 219; protection of investors by, 219–20; and company prospectuses, 220–22; "pink sheets" and, 301–2; policing of over-the-counter market by, 306–7; "net-by-net" system of, 311; national clearing corporation of, 311
National Better Business Bureau, and lots-by-mail business, 323
National Clearing Corporation, of NASD, 311
National Council of Senior Citizens, 382
"National List" of stocks, 144
National Oceanic and Atmospheric Administration, 22
National Quotation Bureau, 143
National Stock Exchange, 304
Neighborhood: real estate syndicate, 333–35; real estate company, 335–38; as important factor in buying a home, 352
Net worth and cash forecast charts, 388–89, 391 (*chart*)
"Net-by-net" system of NASD, 311
New issues, 207–8; need for capital, 208–13; underwriting, 213–19; how the SEC protects investors, 219–20; should you buy?, 220–22; small-business investment companies (SBIC's), 222–24
New York Commodity Exchange, 228
New York Stock Exchange (NYSE): on disclosure of important corporate news, 56–57; and protection of customers of NYSE firms, 134–35; surprise yearly audit of member firms, 135; local branches of NYSE firms, dealing heavily in individual accounts, 136; complaints to be addressed to, 138; rules of, concerning opening of margin account, 140; commission rate, 143; quotes furnished by, 143; Monthly Investment Plan of, 165, 166, 189; closed-end shares, traded on, 176; and commissions on large trades, 204; membership in, 205; and selling of stockholders' rights and "ex-rights," 215–16; policing of securities salesmen by, 219; regulations of, wiping out "bear" raids, 226; rules of, regarding margin requirements, 234, 238; "odd-lot" transactions on, 247; historic trading day of, 299–300; listing requirements and membership qualifications of, 302–3, 313; dollar volume handled by, 303, 304; "fails" among NYSE members, 309; fund of, to pay off customers of failing firms, 310; 1970 financial crisis of, and remedies provided by, 310–11; and CCS, 311; central computer system of, 312; and the *Martin Report*, 312; projections of volume of trading by, 318–20; mortgage trusts, listed on, 341
Newspapers and magazines, stock data in, 125–26
Nicholson, George A., Jr., 169, 170
1929 stock market crash, 237–38, 309
1970 financial crisis, 310–11
Nixon, President: and wage and price freeze, 28, 299; and price of gold, 35–36
No-load mutual funds, 178–79

Oceanography, added resources through, 22
Odd-lot: orders, commission rate on, 141; statistics and transactions, 247–48, 300; prices, 300
Office machines and equipment firms, list of, 112–14
O'Hara, Thomas, 170
Oils business, list of firms in, 114–16
Open-end funds: common stock of, 166; examples of, 176

Index

Opening an account with a brokerage house, 140
Orders to buy, different types of, 140–41
Over-the-counter bids and offers, how ascertained and published, 143–44
Over-the-counter markets, 7, 305–7, 315–16
Over-the-Counter Reports, 125
Over-the-counter stocks, 142–43, 300–1

Pacific Coast Exchange, 304, 305
Paperwork crisis in the stock market, 309–19
P/E: ratio of common stocks, 47–50; of glamour growth stocks, 48
Performance funds, 44, 181–82
"Pink sheets," 142, 144, 301–2
Pollution control, 17–18, 22, 23, 25, 76
Population changes, future, and demographic-economic models, 12
Population growth, rate of, 3, 6; "baby boom" and "bust," 10, 11, 12; zero population growth, 11, 12, 13
Power sources of the future, 23
Precious metal, 35–38 (*charts*)
Preferred bond and stock funds, 81
Price and wage freeze, 28, 299
Price-to-earnings ratio of stocks (P/E), 47–50, 62
Prospectuses, company, 220–22
Public Housing Administration, 256
Puts and calls, 239–42
Pyramiding on margin, 235–36 (*table*)

"Quality of life" as new goal for Americans, 1–2, 62
Quinby, H. Dean, 166
Quotation system, computerized. See NASDAQ system
Quotes furnished by New York Stock Exchange, 143

Rand Corporation, 310
Real estate: equity value of land, 38–39; equity trusts, 342–45

Real estate investment companies, 347–48
Real estate investment trusts (REIT), 322, 340–41, 345–48
Real estate mortgage trusts, 341, 345–46
Real estate syndicates, 333–35, 348–50
Real Estate Trusts, The: America's Newest Billionaires, 347
Real estate—going it alone, 321; raw land, 322–23; rental property, 323–25; precautions when investing in real estate, 328–30
Real estate—home or farm, 351; the neighborhood, 352; the house itself, 352–55; what should you pay?, 355–56 (*table*); shopping for terms, 356; hankering to buy a farm?, 358–60; farm management, 360–61; financing a farm, 361–62; farm valuation, 362–63
Real estate—real life examples: young man starting out, 331–33; neighborhood syndicate, 333–35; neighborhood real estate company, 335–38; advice from established investor, 338–39
Records of stock certificates, confirmation slips, and dividends, how and where to keep, 147–48
Recreation companies, list of, 116–20
Recyling, machines and systems for, 23, 25
REIT's, 322, 340–41, 345, 346–48
Rental: income from houses, 323–24; property, 323–35
Research and development, as movers of the economy, 16, 24 (*chart*)
Research firms, list of, 120
Resources to meet emergencies, 408–9 (*report form*)
Responsibilities of companies to the public, 68–70
Reuter-Ultronic ticker, 51
Revenue bonds, 256
Rhea, Robert, 245
"Rights," issuance of, and common stock, 214, 215, 216
Russell, Fred C., 169, 170

Index 417

Safety and income, 249–51; bonds, 251–63; income, 263–67; withdrawal plans, 265–71 (*tables*); annuities, types of, 272–75 (*tables*), 276–81
Savings: and money management, 30–31; and programs to help you save, 397–400 (*table*), 401, 402 (*table*), 403 (*table*). *See also* Money management
Savings account in: commercial bank, 404–5; mutual savings bank, 405–6, 407
Savings and loan associations, 357, 406–7
Savings banks, 405–7
Savings bonds, as equity, 33, 34
Savings bonds, U. S., 260–63, 407
Scientific research and development, 16; money invested in, 24 (*chart*)
Seafood, harvesting of, through oceanography, 22
Second mortgages, 325–27
Securities, convertible, 258–60
Securities Act of 1933, 219
Securities and Exchange Commission (SEC): actions against brokerage firms, 53–58; procedures of, to prevent frozen accounts, 134–35; complaints to be addressed to, 138; company reports to, 154; commission guidelines of, 178, 319; "give-ups" and, 203; protection of investors by, 219–20; and company prospectuses, 220–22; regulation of, wiping out "bear" raids, 226
Securities Exchange Act of 1934, 52–53
Securities funds, foreign, 181
Securities Investors Protection Act, 310, 313
Securities markets, factors causing changes in, 4
Securities salesmen, policing of, by New York Stock Exchange, 219
Security Owner's Stock Guide, 75, 124; commission schedule of, 141
Services: advisory, available to investors, 128; big financial, available to investors, 128–29; investment counseling, 131–32

Shattuck, Mayo Adams, 369
Short selling, 226–27
Silver and gold: buying power of, 35; unpredictable values of, 36–37; gold mining stock, 36 (*chart*); silver mining stock, 37 (*chart*)
Single or joint ownership of stock, 146–47
Single round-lot, commission rate on, 141
Small Business Administration, 222
Small-business investment companies (SBIC's), 222–24
Social changes, problems causing, 4–5
Social responsibilities of companies to the public, 68–70
Society of Real Estate Counselors, 329
Soil Conservation Service, 360
Solid-waste disposal, 23, 25
Special situation funds, 181
Specialist, the, function and reasons for, 295–300
Speculating, 225; short selling, 226–27, commodity futures trading, 227–33; hedging vs. speculation, 228; buying stocks on margin, 233–38; puts and calls, 239–42; charts and graphs, 242–46
Stack's, selection of coins in a collection by, 37–38
Standard & Poor's: bond ratings of, 255 Corporation, 77, 128
Standard & Poor's publications: *American Stock Reports,* 125; *Corporation Records,* 125; *500 Stock Averages,* 125; *Listed Stock Reports,* 48, 70, 125; *Over-the-Counter Reports,* 125; *Security Owner's Stock Guide,* 75, 124, 141; *Stock Reports,* 124, 125
Stock, gold mining, 36 (*chart*)
Stock, loans on, 148–49
Stock, silver mining, 37 (*chart*)
Stock bought in blocks, 158–59
Stock broker. *See* Broker
Stock certificates: leave it in "street name," 140, 145–46; keeping records of, 147–48

Stock data in newspapers and magazines, 125–26
Stock deductions on tax return, 159–60
Stock dividends: and tax tips, 155; when sold, 158
Stock Exchanges, 302–5; regional, 303–5
Stock guides and reports, 124–27
Stock inheritance, 159
Stock market crash of 1929, 237–38, 309
Stock market "insiders," competing against, 51–60; inside information, examples of, 53–57; stock-watch program of the stock exchange, 57–59
Stock market—new style, 308; paperwork crisis, 309–10; financial crisis in, 310; remedies, 311–12; the *Martin Report*, 312–13, 315, 316; over-the-counter market, 315–16; role of individual investor, 317–18 (*table*), 319–20
Stock market—old style, 292–95; the specialist, 295–300; odd lots, 300; over-the-counter stocks, 300–1; the exchanges, 302–5; over-the-counter markets, 305–7
Stock Picture, The, 125
Stock Reports, 124, 125
Stock rights, 158
Stock splits, 158
Stockholder, how to be: leave it in "street name," 145–46; single or joint ownership, 146–47; keeping records of stock certificates, confirmation slips, and dividends, 147–48; can stockholder borrow, and how much?, 148–49; financial reports, 149–51 (*income statement* and *balance sheet*), 152–55; tax tips for, 155–60. *See also* Broker and brokerage house
Stocks, borrowing against, 148–49
Stocks, buying on margin, 233–38
Stocks, common. *See* Common stocks
Stocks, cyclical, 44–45
Stocks, factors concerning choice of: earnings growth of, 72; return on invested capital, 72; growth of sales, 72–73; operating profit, 73; equity-to-debt ratio, 73; research and development spending, 73–74; freedom from competition, 74; low labor costs, 74; price flexibility, 74; over-all quality, 74–75; formal plans for buying, 164–66
Stocks, growth. *See* Growth stocks
Stocks, "National List" of, 144
Stocks, over-the-counter, 142–43, 300–1
Stock-watch program of the stock exchange, 57–59
"Street name," leaving stocks in, 140, 145–46
Syndicates, real estate, 333–35, 348–50

Tabell, Anthony W., 60
Tabell, Edmund, 246
Tax tips for stockholders, 155–60
Taxes: and cash dividends, 155; figured on capital gains and losses, 156–57
Tax-exempt bonds, 255, 257–58 (*tables*)
Tempo, center for advanced studies of population changes, 12
Ticker. *See* Broad ticker of Dow Jones; Reuter-Ultronic ticker
Title insurance, 357–58
Traders and insiders in the stock market: competing against, 51–60; inside information, examples of, 53–57; stock-watch program of the stock exchange, 57–59
Trading day, historic, of New York Stock Exchange, 299–300
Transportation and Public Utility Manuals, 125
Transportation of the future, 22–23
Trust departments of banks, 129–30
Trust funds: definitions, 282–84; basic types of trust, 284–85; what a trust can do, 285–87; ways to use a trust, 287–89; a couple of alternatives, 289–90; common trust funds, 290–91
Trusts, equity, real estate, 342–45
Trusts, investment, 132. *See also* Mutual funds and closed-end investment trusts

Trusts, mortgage, 341, 345–46
Trusts, real estate investment (REIT), 322, 340–41, 345–48
"Turn in the Tide, A" (Hamilton), 246

Underwriter, Chartered Life, 372
Underwriting of new issues, 213–19
Unemployment: rates of, 2, 7; unemployment compensation, 11
United Business Service, 128, 192
U. S. Coast Guard, and oil spills, 22
U. S. Department of Agriculture: and land values, 39 (*chart*); study by, of small speculators, 228; books and maps on farming by, 359, 360
U. S. Department of Commerce, 13
U. S. Public Health Service, and pollution control, 17
U. S. Savings Bonds, 260–63, 407
U. S. Securities and Exchange Commission, 212, 337

Utilities companies, list of, 120–22

Vassar College, Finance Committee of, and study of Dow Jones Averages, 250
Volume discounts of New York Stock Exchange, 202–3

Wage and price freeze, 28, 299
Wall Street Journal, 183, 245, 246
Wankel automobile engine, 55
Warrants (long-lived rights), 216
Waste disposal, solid, 23, 25
Weather forecasting and climate, 22
Wharton School of Business, 7
Wisconsin Physicians Service plan, 383
Withdrawal plans, 265–71 (*tables*)

Zero population growth, 11, 12, 13